Church and Ministry
(Kirche und Amt)

Church and Ministry
(Kirche und Amt)

Witnesses of the
Evangelical Lutheran Church
on the Question of the
Church and the Ministry

by
C. F. W. Walther

Translated by J. T. Mueller

CONCORDIA PUBLISHING HOUSE · SAINT LOUIS

Originally published as *Die Stimme unserer Kirche in der Frage von Kirche und Amt*. Translated from the third edition (Erlangen: Andreas Deichert, 1875).

Printed with the permission of The Lutheran Church—Missouri Synod and the Concordia Historical Institute.

Copyright © 1987 The Lutheran Church—Missouri Synod
1333 S. Kirkwood Road, St. Louis, MO 63122-7295
Manufactured in the United States of America

Library of Congress Cataloging in Publication Data

Walther, C.F.W (Carl Ferdinand Wilhelm), 1811-1887.
      Church and ministry.

      Translation of: Die Stimme unserer Kirche in der Frage von Kirche und Amt.
      Bibliography: p.
      Includes index.
      1. Church. 2. Clergy—Office. 3. Lutheran Church—Doctrines. 4. Lutheran Church—Missouri Synod—Doctrines. I. Title. II. Title: Kirche und Amt.
BX8071. W3513 1987   262   87-6604
ISBN 0-570-04241-0

    8 9 10 11 12 13 14 15 16 17   20 19 18 17 16 15 14 13 12 11

Contents

Preface to the First Edition (1852)

The doctrines of the church and the ministry have become a question that has divided present-day Lutherans into two camps. Particularly among those who are regarded as the most faithful protagonists of the precious inheritance of our church, a striking difference has manifested itself regarding these two doctrines. It has therefore not only so appeared, but it has been actually expressed quite frequently that the doctrine of the Evangelical Lutheran Church is still not fully developed or cleared up so far as these articles are concerned. Hence, it needs not only development and completion but also clarification and correction. In the present controversy of the Lutherans on the doctrines just mentioned, it is believed that there are definite indications that now the time has arrived in which finally also these points should be clarified within our church, and that their true relation to the whole body of doctrine must and shall be pointed out.

We, the members of the German Evangelical Lutheran Synod of Missouri, Ohio, and other States, cannot share this last conviction. We are rather persuaded that present differences among the Lutherans concerning the doctrines of the church and the ministry and whatever is immediately connected with them stems from the fact that the doctrine set forth in the public confessions of our church and in the private writings of its orthodox teachers has been disregarded and abandoned. We are convinced neither that our church has failed to discuss the doctrines of the church and the ministry, nor that they now require development. Nor has our church—and this much less—obscured these doctrines in any way or assigned to them a wrong relation to the whole body of doctrine so that they must now be clarified and interpreted. We are also convinced of the fact that the great decisive battle of the Reformation, which our church fought against the papacy in the 16th century, centered in the doctrines of the church and the ministry, which have now again been called into question, and that the pure and clear teaching concerning them constitutes the precious spoils that our church gained from this warfare. We indeed do not deny that the doctrines of the church and the ministry are capable of further unfolding, as are all other doctrines of Scripture. Nevertheless, we solemnly disavow any pretended doctrinal development, which quite frequently is now demanded under the pretense of necessary development of doctrine, if it does not return to and begin with the place where our church has left off.

Now we Lutherans in the Far West, separated by the ocean from the land of science and living off the crumbs that fall from the table of the rich Mother Church, are much more convinced than anybody else can be that in our poverty we have the least call to contribute our quota to the great battle being fought in our old German fatherland on the field of theological science and to send it across the sea. But just in the very circumstances in which we find ourselves and that place on us the tragic necessity of remaining behind the onward hastening Mother Church, there lies also the blessing that we are obliged more than our brethren on the other shore, though incapable of supplying original works, all the more eagerly to sit at the feet of our ancient teachers and to seek out the treasures already gathered and gained by battling for them. If we can add little or nothing to them, we will hold and preserve them all the more faithfully.

Therefore, we believe that despite our poverty, compared with the Mother Church, we have one talent with which we can and should practice usury. And since today in our church so many raise their voice to resolve the controversy concerning the doctrines of the church and the ministry, but hardly anyone, so far as we know, has thought of letting the church of our fathers also express its opinion, and since the opinion is becoming ever more general that our church has left the doctrines in question unanswered, we therefore do not consider it superfluous if in this present book, according to the humble talent entrusted to us, we seek to make a contribution so that in the present important controverted question concerning

8

the church and the ministry also our official confessions and the private writings of its teachers may be heard and considered.

We regarded ourselves as compelled to do this especially since Pastor Grabau of Buffalo, New York, particularly in the second synodical report edited by him, has grievously slandered us before the whole church on account of our doctrines of the church and the ministry and several other teachings closely connected with them, as well as our practice based thereon. Hence, the synodical convention held in St. Louis in the fall of 1850 asked this writer to compose the present book. Its contents were presented to the synodical convention, held the next year at Milwaukee, either literally or substantially, and after they had been examined and respectively revised, it was resolved to publish the manuscript "in our name and as our unanimous confession" [that of Missouri Synod].

It was, of course, not our intention to present the doctrines of the church and the ministry in their completeness. Whoever desires this will find such a presentation in the larger dogmatic works of the teachers of our church, among others, especially in the master works of men like Chemnitz and Gerhard. It was our purpose to stress only those points concerning which there prevails a difference and to embody only so much uncontested material as is demanded by the context. We hope, therefore, that on account of this intentional incompleteness we shall not be charged with one-sidedness in our interpretation and presentation. In order to avoid misunderstanding, we declare expressly that in this monograph we are not so much concerned about how the church is to be constituted as rather about its essence and the principles according to which its manifestations [*Erscheinungen*] are to be judged and on which its polity [*Verfassung*] is to rest.

Perhaps some things in this book at first glance may appear doubtful and subject to misunderstanding and misuse. But whoever wants to be fair and go to the trouble to consider the individual matters [*das Einzelne*] in their context and according to the intention with which they have been incorporated into the whole will soon, as we hope, have his doubts disappear if he is at all favorable to our church. But whoever will not be fair but intends to remain attached to his preconceived notions of what is supposed to be truly Lutheran cannot be satisfied even with all sorts of cautions by which in our preface we might try to guard against misunderstandings.

We are willing to admit that the conditions in which we live here in America decidedly influenced us deeply to appreciate the doctrines of the church and the ministry set forth in this book so that we adhere to them as a precious jewel and confess them before the whole world. Nevertheless, we definitely repudiate the charge made against us that we twisted and patterned them to favor our conditions. Since here we do not live under inherited church conditions but must rather first lay the foundation and lay it unhindered by anything already existing, the circumstances rather compelled us most earnestly to search for the principles on which, according to God's Word and the Confessions of our church, the polity of a truly Lutheran church may rest and according to which it may be constituted.

The question facing us is not, What may we retain without sinning? but, How shall the church be constituted that is patterned after God's Word and the principles set forth and proved in our official Confession? In view of this, our need for clarity and conviction of the truth [*Glaubensgewißheit*] concerning the principles regarding the doctrines of the church, the ministry, the office of the keys, church polity, and others became all the more urgent. We did not pattern the doctrine of our church after the conditions prevailing here, but we established the church according to the doctrine of our church. Whoever doubts this, we confidently invite: "Come and see!" And whoever is astonished at the principles and doctrines of the Lutheran church presented here, which so far he may have rejected as enthusiastic, we can trustfully refer to the proofs with which we supported them, leaving him the choice either to concede to us the honor of being orthodox or to deny this honor to a whole cloud of witnesses from Luther down to Baier and Hollaz.

We chose the form of theses in order to present to our readers in brief and pithy words the chief points that are of primary importance here. Though the Scripture proof that immediately follows each thesis contains only suggestions, which are further explained in the subsequent witnesses, we nevertheless believed that these suggestions should not be missing. The witnesses of the church from the private writings of its teachers stem for the greater part from the writings of the 16th and 17th centuries. It would not have been difficult to find assenting witnesses also in later periods up to the present time, and these we might have added. But with Professor

Schmid of Erlangen we regarded it as more fitting, just as is done in his Lutheran dogmatics, to present witnesses only from the works of those teachers who are rightly recognized by all true Lutherans as absolutely faithful to the doctrine of our church, indeed as representatives of Lutheran orthodoxy.

No reader, we believe, will find it strange that we were careful to quote copiously from Luther's writings. This applies to everyone who by divine grace has recognized the fact that Luther, and no one but Luther, was the church Reformer called by God. We gladly call ourselves by his name, not because we believe in him, but because we have learned to know the doctrine that he proclaimed not as his own but as the pure Word of the everlasting God. We also hope to have proved that Luther by no means, as is so often said today, abandoned the doctrines of the church and the ministry that he taught in his earlier years after having been convinced by many experiences of something better. But this precious vessel of divine grace remained consistently true to the truth he had learned to know. However, according to the condition of those to whom he addressed himself, he more or less stressed now this aspect of the doctrine and then again another.

It may be highly annoying to some readers that we have presented in a German translation the witnesses originally written in Greek and Latin. But since, especially here in America, many who do not know the ancient languages are also greatly interested in the question treated in this book, a translation of the quotations had to be given. With regard to these translations, the venerable reader who knows the ancient languages may exercise clemency since they do not claim to have any literary merit. The translator was concerned above all to supply a faithful translation that could not be charged to depart from the original in any way to favor his own opinion. We have also added by way of an appendix as many of the writings of the teachers of the ancient church as we could find, for here we are greatly lacking especially in patristic literature. It is because of this lack also that we have presented some quotations of the Greek church fathers in Latin.

May He who regards the lowly richly bless this humble contribution from poor America to the upbuilding of our Evangelical Lutheran Zion, for usually we ask only gifts from our German Mother Church. May this book above all help somewhat to seek and exalt the treasures of wisdom and knowledge that for so many people lie buried in the dust-covered tomes of our pious and learned fathers. That would be a gain of uncountable value for our church. We, however, to whom God in His infinite mercy and by the grace of His precious Holy Spirit, as well as through the service of those faithful servants who now see what they believed, has made known the pure doctrine of His holy Word, ask Him to keep and strengthen us in His truth against all deceitful wisdom and trickery of men as we thank, praise, laud, and honor Him through Jesus Christ, our Lord and Savior. Amen.

Preface to the Second Edition (1865)

This second edition differs from the first by the careful correction of errata found in the former edition, by the deletion of some repetitions found in the former, and by a number of new quotations, as well as by an added index of the Christian authors quoted and an alphabetical subject index.

May God for Jesus' sake bless this humble contribution also in its new form toward the spread of the truth.

Preface to the Third Edition (1875)

This third edition differs from the second revised and enlarged edition only by the deletion of errata that were overlooked as well as by the addition of some Greek originals in places where in the former editions the patristic quotations could be given only in Latin.

We humbly commend to the continued blessing of the invisible Head of His church also this newly reprinted anthology of witnesses of orthodox teachers concerning two so important teachings of Christian doctrine as the church and the ministry.

St. Louis, Missouri, 29 September 1874.

Translator's Preface

The undersigned herewith presents to the public Dr. C. F. W. Walther's third monumental work on the church and the ministry in an English translation based on the third edition, published in 1875.

As the reader peruses this unique anthology of witnesses to the Scriptural doctrines of the church and the ministry, he is moved to admire both the learning and industry that Dr. Walther devoted to his project of presenting what the Scriptures, the Lutheran Confessions, and the outstanding ancient and later Christian writers have to say on these teachings that have always been controverted not only in Roman Catholic and enthusiastic but also in Lutheran theological arenas. There is no doubt that the church Dr. Walther founded in America was within the framework of Scripture and sound theology.

The book is not without faults so far as accidental matters are concerned. Dr. Walther often quoted his sources inaccurately and sometimes even incorrectly, and it was not always possible for the translator to make the necessary adjustments. But following the advice of his counselor, Dr. Lewis Spitz, he tried to reproduce Dr. Walther as precisely as possible. For the sake of comparison, he used the German edition of the Lutheran Confessions in the *Concordia Triglotta* and Luther's works in the St. Louis edition (Walch 2d ed.). Where ancient and later church teachers were quoted, he gave careful attention to the Greek or Latin originals.

The translator began his work on May 29, 1962, and worked during the following months without a vacation until on December 31, 1962, he could add this brief preface. He acknowledges his indebtedness to his counselor, Dr. Lewis Spitz; to Prof. Lorenz Wunderlich of the Missouri Synod's Commission on Church Literature; to Rev. August Suelflow for historical research; and to Miss Rosemary

Lipka and her assistant, Carole House, for the typing of the manuscript.

May God's rich blessings rest on this English translation of a great and good book by a great and good teacher of American Lutheranism, whose sole purpose it was in all his preaching, teaching, and writing to glorify Jesus Christ, the divine-human Savior of the world by confessing His divine Word.

Soli Deo Gloria.

St. Louis, Missouri   John Theodore Mueller
New Year's Eve, 1962

The Theses

Part One

Concerning the Church

Thesis I

The church in the proper sense of the term is the congregation [*Gemeinde*] of saints, that is, the aggregate of all those who, called out of the lost and condemned human race by the Holy Spirit through the Word, truly believe in Christ and by faith are sanctified and incorporated in Christ.

Thesis II

To the church in the proper sense of the term belongs no wicked person, no hypocrite, no unregenerate, no heretic.

Thesis III

The church in the proper sense of the word is invisible.

Thesis IV

It is to this true church of believers and saints that Christ gave the keys of the kingdom of heaven, and it is the proper and only possessor and bearer of the spiritual, divine, and heavenly gifts, rights, powers, offices, and the like that Christ has procured and are found in His church.

THESIS V

Though the true church in the proper sense of the term is essentially [according to its true nature] invisible, its existence can nevertheless be definitely recognized, namely, by the marks of the pure preaching of God's Word and the administration of the sacraments according to Christ's institution.

THESIS VI

In an improper sense Scripture also calls the visible aggregate of all the called, that is, of all who confess and adhere to the proclaimed Word and use the holy sacraments, which consists of good and evil [persons], "church" (the universal [catholic] church); so also it calls its several divisions, that is, the congregations that are found here and there, in which the Word of God is preached and the holy sacraments are administered, "churches" (*Partikularkirchen* [particular or individual churches]). This it does especially because in this visible assembly the invisible, true, and properly so-called church of believers, saints, and children of God is hidden; outside this assembly of the called no elect are to be looked for [anywhere].

THESIS VII

As visible congregations that still have the Word and the sacraments essentially according to God's Word bear the name "church" because of the true invisible church of sincere believers that is found in them, so also they possess the power [authority] that Christ has given to His whole church, on account of the true invisible church hidden in them, even if there were only two or three [believers].

THESIS VIII

Although God gathers for Himself a holy church of elect also where His Word is not taught in its perfect purity and the sacraments are not administered altogether according to the institution of Jesus

Christ, if only God's Word and the sacraments are not denied entirely but both remain in their essential parts, nevertheless, every believer must, at the peril of losing his salvation, flee all false teachers, avoid all heterodox congregations or sects, and acknowledge and adhere to orthodox congregations and their orthodox pastors wherever such may be found.

A. Also in heterodox and heretical churches there are children of God, and also there the true church is made manifest by the pure Word and the sacraments that still remain.

B. Every believer for the sake of his salvation must flee all false teachers and avoid all heterodox congregations or sects.

C. Every Christian for the sake of his salvation is in duty bound to acknowledge and adhere to orthodox congregations and orthodox pastors, wherever he can find such.

Thesis IX

To obtain salvation, only fellowship in the invisible church, to which alone all the glorious promises regarding the church were originally given, is absolutely necessary.

Part Two

Concerning the Holy Ministry or the Pastoral Office

Thesis I

The holy ministry or pastoral office is an office distinct from the priesthood of all believers.

Thesis II

The ministry of the Word or the pastoral office is not a human institution but an office that God Himself has established.

Thesis III

The ministry is not an arbitrary office but one whose establishment has been commanded to the church and to which the church is ordinarily bound till the end of time.

Thesis IV

The ministry is not a special or, in opposition to that of ordinary Christians, a more holy state, as was the Levitical priesthood, but it is a ministry of service.

Thesis V

The public ministry [*Predigtamt*] has the power to preach the Gospel and administer the holy sacraments as well as the power of spiritual judgment.

Thesis VI

A. The ministry of the Word [*Predigtamt*] is conferred by God through the congregation as the possessor of all ecclesiastical power, or the power of the keys, by means of its call, which God Himself has prescribed.

B. The ordination of the called [persons] with the laying on of hands is not a divine institution but merely an ecclesiastical rite [*Ordnung*] established by the apostles; it is no more than a solemn public confirmation of the call.

Thesis VII

The holy ministry [*Predigtamt*] is the power, conferred by God through the congregation as the possessor of the priesthood and all church power, to exercise the rights of the spiritual priesthood in public office in the name of the congregation.

Thesis VIII

The pastoral ministry [*Predigtamt*] is the highest office in the church, and from it stem all other offices in the church.

Thesis IX

A. To the ministry there is due respect as well as unconditional obedience when the pastor uses God's Word.

B. The minister must not tyrannize the church. He has no authority to introduce new laws or arbitrarily to establish adiaphora or ceremonies.

C. The minister has no right to inflict and carry out excommunication without his having first informed the whole congregation.

Thesis X

To the ministry of the Word, according to divine right, belongs also the duty [*Amt*] to judge doctrine, but laymen also possess this right. Therefore, in the ecclesiastical courts (consistories) and councils they are accorded both a seat and vote together with the clergy.

PART ONE

Concerning the Church

Thesis I

The church in the proper sense of the term is the congregation [Gemeinde] *of saints, that is, the aggregate of all those who, called out of the lost and condemned human race by the Holy Spirit through the Word, truly believe in Christ and by faith are sanctified and incorporated in Christ.*

1. Scripture Proof

Thus writes the holy apostle Paul (Eph. 1:22–23): "[God] put all things under His feet, and gave Him to be head over all things to the church, which is His body, the fullness of Him who fills all in all." If, according to these words, Christ is the Head of the congregation or church, and this is His body, then the true church in its proper sense is the sum total of all those who are joined to Christ, just as the members of the body are joined to their head.

The same apostle further writes (Eph. 5:23–27): "The husband is head of the wife, as also Christ is head of the church; and He is the Savior of the body. Therefore, just as the church is subject to Christ, so let the wives be to their own husbands in everything. Husbands, love your wives, just as Christ also loved the church and gave Himself for it, that He might sanctify and cleanse it with the washing of water by the word, that He might present it to Himself a glorious church, not having spot or wrinkle or any such thing, but that it should be holy and without blemish."

The same apostle writes further (1 Cor. 3:16–17): "Do you not know that you are the temple of God and that the Spirit of God dwells in you? If anyone defiles the temple of God, God will destroy him. For the temple of God is holy, which temple you are." For this reason the same apostle calls the church "the general assembly and church of the firstborn who are registered in heaven" (Heb. 12:23).

27

The Lord Himself says of His church (Matt. 16:18): "On this rock I will build My church, and the gates of Hades shall not prevail against it." Accordingly, the church in its proper sense, that is, its members, is built on the Rock of Christ and His Word. But on this only he is built who is built on it by a living faith.

Finally, the evangelist St. John writes in John 11:51–52: "Jesus would die for the nation, and not for that nation only, but also that he would gather together in one the children of God who were scattered abroad." The church, for whose institution and gathering Christ came into the world and died, therefore, is the sum total of God's children.

2. Witnesses of the Church in Its Official Confessions[1]

1. *Apostles' Creed:* "I believe in the Holy Ghost; the holy Christian church, the communion of saints" (*Triglot,* p. 31). The addition of "communion of saints" does not indicate a new article of faith, as the Romanists teach, but it explains the word "church." The Large Catechism [of Luther] explains it thus:

> The word *Kirche* (*church*) means really nothing else than a common assembly, and is not German by idiom, but Greek (as is also the word *ecclesia*); for in their own language they call it *kyria,* as in Latin it is called *curia.* Therefore in genuine German, in our mother-tongue, it ought to be called a Christian congregation or assembly (*eine christliche Gemeinde oder Sammlung*), or, best of all and most clearly, a holy Christendom (*eine heilige Christenheit*).
>
> So also the word *communio,* which is added, ought not to be rendered communion (*Gemeinschaft*), but congregation (*Gemeinde*). And it is nothing else than an interpretation or explanation by which someone meant to explain what the Christian church is.... But to speak correct German, it ought to be *eine Gemeinde der Heiligen* (a congregation of saints), that is, a congregation made up purely of saints, or, to speak yet more plainly, *eine heilige Gemeinde,* a holy congregation. ...
>
> But this is the meaning and substance of the addition: I believe that there is upon earth a little holy group and congregation of pure saints, under one head, even Christ, called together by the Holy Ghost. (Art. III, par. 48–51; *Triglot,* p. 691)

28

2. *Augsburg Confession,* Art. VIII, "What the Church Is": "Although the Church properly is the congregation of saints and true believers," etc. (*Triglot,* p. 47). While the Augsburg Confession in Art. VII desires not so much to describe the church according to its essence, but merely wishes to state that at all times there is and must remain a holy Christian church, where it is and by what marks it can be recognized, Art. VIII tells us what the church is, and indeed, what it is properly. This must be well observed when defining the concept that our church has set forth in its Symbols regarding the church.

3. *Apology:* "But it certainly remains a fact that the true church is the assembly and the people who here and there in the world, from the rising to the setting of the sun, truly believe in Christ. . . .

"Although therefore hypocrites and wicked men associate with the true church in outward rites, titles, and offices, nevertheless, when we would properly define what the church is, we must say that it is the church that is called the body of Christ and has fellowship not merely in outward signs but has the [divine] gifts in the heart, [namely,] the Holy Spirit and faith. . . . For we must well understand by what we become members of Christ and what makes us living members of the church. If we would say that the church is merely an outward polity, as are other governments, in which there are evil and good persons and the like, then no one would know or understand that Christ's kingdom is spiritual, as indeed it is, and that in it Christ inwardly rules, strengthens, and comforts the hearts and imparts the Holy Ghost and various spiritual gifts, but people would think that it is merely the outward observance of certain forms of worship and rites. Again, what difference would there be between the people of [under] the Law and the church if the church would be merely an outward polity? But Paul distinguishes the church from the Jews in that he says the church is a spiritual people, that is to say, one that distinguishes itself from the heathen not merely by its polity and civil affairs but by being the true people of God, enlightened in heart and born again by the Holy Ghost" (Art. VII, VIII, par. 11–14; German expanded text, *Triglot,* pp. 228, 230). "That is properly the Christian church that has the Holy Spirit" (ibid., par. 22; *Triglot,* p. 234).

Apology: "And yet . . . God still preserved His church, i.e., some saints, under the papacy so that the Christian church did not perish altogether" (Art. XXIV [XII], par. 98; *Triglot,* pp. 416, 418).

4. *Smalcald Articles:* "Thank God, [today] a child seven years old knows what the Church is, namely, the holy believers and lambs who hear the voice of their Shepherd. For the children pray thus: 'I believe in one holy Christian church' " (Art. XII; *Triglot,* p. 499).

3. Witnesses of the Church in the Private Writings of Its Teachers

Thus *Luther* writes: "Christians are a special, called people and are denominated not merely *ecclesia,* church or assembly, but *sancta, catholica, Christiana,* that is, a Christian holy people that believes in Christ, for which reason it is named a Christian people and has the Holy Spirit who sanctifies it daily, not only through the forgiveness of sins (as the Antinomians[2] foolishly assert), but also through the putting away, purging, and destroying of sins, wherefore it is called a holy people. Hence the 'holy Christian church' means as much as the people that is Christian and holy, or, as it is commonly said, the holy Christendom, or the whole Christendom. In the Old Testament it was called God's people (Is. 1:24; 12:3, etc.). If in the children's confession such words would have been used as 'I believe that there is a Christian holy people,' then all confusion would easily have been avoided that was caused by the dark and obscure word 'church.' The expression 'a Christian holy people' would clearly and convincingly have shown both the meaning and scope of what the church is and what it is not. Whoever would have heard the expression 'a Christian holy people' would at once have argued that the pope is no people, much less a holy Christian people. So also the bishops, priests, and monks are not a holy Christian people, for they do not believe in Christ, nor do they lead a holy life, but they are the devil's wicked and perverse people. Whoever does not truly believe in Christ is neither Christian nor a Christian, and he who does not have the Holy Spirit against sin is not holy. Therefore they [the papists] cannot be a Christian holy people, that is, *sancta et catholica ecclesia,* which means the holy and universal church" ("Concerning Councils and Churches," St. Louis edition, 16:2269–70).

John Gerhard: "We define the church as the communion of saints in order that no one may think that the church is merely a certain outward polity of good and bad persons, since it is, to speak properly and accurately, the holy assembly of those who are united by the bond of the Holy Spirit in true faith and true love. But we by no means use the expression 'of saints' in the sense of the Anabaptists or Pelagians. Nor do we fictitiously teach that the true members of the church in this sinful life are perfectly or altogether sinless. Nor do we change the church into a Platonic concept and a vain visionary idea that exists only in one's imagination, but we distinguish between sins of weakness with which faith, repentance, and zeal for sanctification may coexist, and sins against conscience by which the regenerate cease to be true and living members of the church" (*Loci theologici,* "De ecclesia," par. 51).

The same: "Of a genuine member of the true church there is required not only the outward confession of faith and the outward use of the sacraments but also the inward renewal by the Holy Spirit, because the church is not only a body but also a soul, that is, a living and animated body. Hence in order that anyone may truly belong to Christ's body, he must be ruled, led, and, as it were, animated by the Holy Spirit" (ibid., par. 53).

The same: "We declare that catechumens, as also all others who are endowed with the true inward faith, are in the church, even if they have not yet actually received Baptism" (ibid., par. 54).

Quenstedt: "Properly and principally the church is the assembly of saints and true believers" (*Theologia didactico-polemica,* part IV, 15.2). "We prove our judgment that the church properly is the assembly of saints by the nature and peculiarity of the church; for in Holy Scripture the church is called 1. Christ's mystical body. . . . 2. The church is the mother not of the [spiritually] dead, but of the living, or the true believers. . . . 3. The church is Christ's fold and the true members of the church are Christ's sheep. . . . 4. The prophets and the apostles often bestow on the church such expressions of praise as cannot be referred to the whole assembly of the called, comprising both the good and the evil. . . . Therefore, we must assume a church, properly and primarily so called, to which principally and immediately these expressions of praise and these ascribed properties belong; for here and there in the Old Testament and in the New it is called 'Christ's spouse or bride' (Song of Sol. 4:8–10; Is. 61:10; Hos. 2:19–20; John 3:29; 2 Cor. 11:2; Rev. 21:9); 'Christ's fair and spotless love' (Song of Sol. 4:7); 'a chaste virgin of Christ'

31

(2 Cor. 11:2); 'one flesh with Christ' as are husband and wife (Eph. 5:30). None of these epithets applies to the wicked. [Moreover the church is called] 'the house of the living God' (1 Tim. 3:15); 'a spiritual house' (1 Peter 2:5); 'a peculiar people, zealous of good works' (Titus 2:14) etc., to which none belong but those who are 'living stones, built on the chief cornerstone, Jesus Christ' (Eph. 2:20; 1 Peter 2:5)" (ibid.).

Quenstedt: "Those who have been excommunicated truly are members of the church if they have faith and love" (ibid.).

J. W. Baier: "The church militant is used in a twofold sense: first, properly and accurately defined, for the assembly of the true believers and saints who by faith have been implanted into Christ the Head, and with Him as living members constitute one mystical body" (*Compendium theologiae positivae,* part III, 13.2).

This truth the church has taught from the beginning. Thus, among other things, *Ignatius* writes: "In order that He [Christ] by His resurrection might establish forever a sign for His saints and believers, whether Jews or Gentiles, in [the] one body of His church," etc. (*Ep. ad Smyrnaeos* 1).

The same: "Ignatius to the holy church, beloved of God, which is at Tralles in Asia, the elect and worthy of God" (*Ep. ad Trall. ineunt.*).

Cyprian: "Peter, replying in the name of the church, says: 'Lord, to whom shall we go? You have the words of eternal life. Also we have come to believe and know that You are the Christ, the Son of the living God' (John 6:68–69). He wanted to show and prove that those who have separated themselves from Christ are lost by their own fault, but that the church, which believes in Christ and firmly holds to what it has once learned to know, does not depart from Him, and that [therefore] those are the church who remain in the house of God. But we see that those who have not been planted by the Father do not remain firm as a fruit but are sifted by the wind of the enemy. Of these John says in his letter: 'They went out from us, but they were not of us; for if they had been of us, they would have continued with us' [1 John 2:19]" (*Epp. l.* 1.3).

Chrysostom comments on 2 Tim. 2:20: "But in a great house there are not only vessels of gold and of silver," etc., as follows: "He (the apostle) speaks this (parable) not of the church but of the whole world. Therefore, do not refer it to the church, for there are in it

32

no vessels of earth or wood, but all are of silver and of gold; for here is the body of Christ, the chaste virgin that has neither spot nor wrinkle" ("Hom. VI in 2 ep. ad Tim.," *J. Chrysostomi opera,* ed. Bern. de Montfaucon [Paris, 1734], 11:692).

The same: "When you flee to the church, do not flee to a place, but flee to it with your heart; for the essence of the church does not consist in wall and masonry but in faith and virtue. . . . It is called a mountain because of its firmness; a virgin because of its sanctity; a queen because of its glory; a king's daughter because of its relation with God; a mother, having given birth, because of the great number of her children whom it conceived after it had been childless for a long time, not to speak of uncountable other names that Holy Scripture gives to it in addition" ("Second Sermon on the Fall of Eutropius," trans. Cramer, 7:22, 36; "Hom. 2. de capto Eutropio," *J. Chrysostomi opera* [Paris, 1721], 3:386, 391).

Jerome: "The church is the congregation of all saints" (on Job 20).

The same: "The church of Christ is none other than the soul of all those who believe in Christ" (on Ps. 87).

Augustine: "The body of this Head is the church, not the one which is [merely] in this place, but the one which is here and in the whole world; nor the one which is [merely] at the present time, but the one from Abel to all who will be born till the end of the world and who believe in Christ, the whole assembly of saints, belonging to one city, which city is the body of Christ, whose Head is Christ" (on Ps. 92).

Isidore of Pelusium: "The fact that the church is the assembly of saints having the true faith and leading a godly life is known to all who have tasted the truth even only a little" (*Isid. Pelusiotae de interpretatione div. script.,* book 5 [Paris: Morelli, 1638], folio 236, lib. 2, ep. 246. [The most complete but unfortunately very defective edition of Isidore of Pelusium; cf. Herzog, *Realencyklopädie,* 7:89]).

Thesis II

To the church in the proper sense of the term belongs no wicked person, no hypocrite, no unregenerate, no heretic.

1. Scripture Proof

Thus writes St. Paul (Rom. 8:9): "If anyone does not have the Spirit of Christ, he is not His." Whoever does not belong to Christ is not a member of the true church, which is His spiritual body.

So also writes John in 1 John 2:19 of the hypocrites who finally also left the fellowship of the church outwardly: "They went out from us, but they were not of us; for if they had been of us, they would have continued with us; but they went out that they might be made manifest, that none of them were of us."

Again our Lord says (John 15:6): "If anyone does not abide in Me, he is cast out as a branch and is withered."

2. Witnesses of the Church in Its Official Confessions

Apology of the Augsburg Confession: "Those in whom Christ does not work anything through His Spirit are not members of Christ. . . . So also we confess in our holy creed and faith: 'I believe in a holy Christian church.' There we say that the church is holy, but the wicked and ungodly cannot be the holy church. . . . If the church, which is truly the kingdom of Christ and God, is distinguished from the kingdom of the devil, the wicked, who are in the devil's kingdom, cannot be the church. Hence the wicked in this life are not the kingdom of Christ, because it has not yet been revealed. . . . The wolves and wicked teachers, though they rage and do injury in the church, yet are not the church. . . . And since the true church in Scripture is called Christ's body, it is impossible to speak of it in

34

any other way than we have spoken of it. For it is certain that the hypocrites and wicked are not Christ's body but belong to the kingdom of the devil, who holds them captive and moves them to whatever he desires" (Art. VII, VIII [IV], par. 6, 8, 17, 22, 29; German expanded text, *Triglot,* pp. 228–36).

3. Witnesses of the Church in the Private Writings of Its Teachers

Luther: "Concerning the church they (the papists) will contend that 'church' designates also the wicked multitude that holds office; this they contend because they refer the promise to themselves" ("Considerations of the Protestant Theologians for the Smalcald Convention," 1540, St. Louis edition, 17:322).

The same: "Whoever does not believe rightly nor is holy and justified, does not belong to the holy Christian church. . . . And this is the article that was condemned by the honorable Council of Constance together with this statement and all of Holy Scripture. For John Huss confessed at that time that there is a holy Christian church. [But] if the pope would not be pious and holy, he could not be a member, much less the head, of the holy church, though in it he would occupy the office. For that reason he [Huss] had to be burned and anathematized. They counter and say: Though the pope, bishops, and they all alike would sin very grievously, they nevertheless are not of the devil nor of his synagogue, but they are of Christ and of God, members and heads of holy Christendom. Indeed, they are members of the church just as spittle, snot, pus, sweat, excrements, urine, stench, scab, smallpox, glandular swellings, sexual diseases, and all other sicknesses are members of the body. These also are in and on the body, and the body must bear them with great peril, trouble, and disgust" ("Exposition of Psalm 118," 1530, Halle edition, 5:1792–94).

The same: "The pope says he is the Christian church. This we deny, though there are some under the papacy who belong to the Christian church, just as among the Turks, in England, and in France there are many who belong to the Christian church. They were baptized, believe the Gospel, use the sacraments rightly, and are true Christians. But the fact that they [the papists] condemn us and declare that our doctrine is not the right one, asserting their innocence over against it, and justify themselves with their laws, fables, brotherhoods, and good works and say that whoever keeps these is a true Christian and the true Christian church—this too we deny. We admit and readily concede that they are in the church, but they are not true members of the church, though they have the pulpit, Baptism, the pastoral ministry, and Sacrament. So they are in the church but are not righteous. Just so among our followers there are many who are baptized, partake of the Sacrament, pretend to be Christians, yet under the skin they are rascals and are not righteous. Therefore, we say that among the large numbers of Christians many have the name, appearance, and semblance of Christians, but they are not Christians. . . . Such are in the Christian church as mouse-dung is in the pepper or the cockle in the corn; they merely help to fill the bushel. So also in the human body there are fine, clean, sound, and proper members, which a person may use as he needs them. But there is in the body also perspiration and other filth. . . . So the heretics, false teachers, or wicked, while being in the church, are not real or right members but the filth that the body gives forth" ("Exposition of John 6–8," St. Louis edition, 8:99–100).

Gerhard: "We believe that the hypocrites, the wicked, and the hidden unbelievers and in general all reprobates, as long as they are and remain such, are not true members of the true church, though outwardly they confess the same faith as the saints and use the same sacraments" (*Loci theologici,* "De ecclesia," par. 51).

The same: "As Christ says of His disciples, John 17:14, that they are in the world but not of the world, so we say contrariwise that the wicked are in the church, but not of the church" (ibid., par. 64).

Abraham Calov: "Though the hypocrites are in the assembly in which the church is, they are not properly the assembly that is the church. . . . We do not make a twofold church: one of the saints and another that is mixed. But we say that we make this distinction only insofar as the word 'church' is taken homonymically (that is, that two altogether different things have one and the same name) now for the assembly of believers and then again for the assembly in which hypocrites are mingled with the believers" (*Systema locorum theologicorum,* loc. 8, pp. 253ff.).

Quenstedt: "The evil fluids are not members of the body, and the wicked are like the evil fluids. They are not members of the body, namely, that of Christ, but they are attached to the church like boils to the body from which they may be separated without any injury to the body, indeed, to its great advantage" (*Theologia didactico-polemica,* part IV, 15.2, folio 1634).

The same: "The wicked and hypocrites may be called parts of the true church but not members in the proper sense of the term" (ibid., folio 1637).

This truth the church has taught at all times.

Thus writes *Augustine:* "The church is uncorrupt, chaste, and pure, and therefore the avaricious, robbers, usurers do not belong to it, not only those who are without but also those who are within it" (*De baptismo* 4.2).

The same: "We must not think that the heretics are in the body of Christ because they are in the church, personally partake of His sacraments, and so forth. They are not in the union of Christ that in the members of Christ grows to the growth of God by its connection and contact; for the church rests on a rock, as the Lord says: 'On this rock I will build My church' [Matt. 16:18]. But they are built on sand as the Lord also says: 'Everyone who hears these sayings of Mine, and does not do them, will be like a foolish man who built his house on the sand' [Matt 7:26]" (*Contra lit. Petiliani* 2.118).

Jerome: "Whoever is a sinner and is besmirched with any blemish cannot be named from the church of Christ, nor can it be said of him that he is subject to Christ" (on Ephesians 5).

Thesis III

The church in the proper sense of the word is invisible.

1. Scripture Proof

Thus says the Lord (Luke 17:20–21): "The kingdom of God does not come with observation; nor will they say, 'See here!' or 'See there!' For indeed, the kingdom of God is within you." (The *Glossa ordinaria* comments on the words, "The kingdom of God does not come with observation": "It cannot be observed, because My kingdom is not temporal but spiritual and now begins by faith.")

Again, St. Peter writes (1 Peter 2:5): "You also as living stones are built up a spiritual house, a holy priesthood, to offer up spiritual sacrifices acceptable to God through Jesus Christ." According to these words the true church is a spiritual building and therefore not visible.

The apostle St. Paul moreover writes (2 Tim. 2:19): "Nevertheless the solid foundation of God stands, having this seal: 'The Lord knows those who are His,' and, 'Let every one who names the name of Christ depart from iniquity.' " According to these words only the Lord knows those who are His. But only those who are the Lord's are the true church. Hence no man can see the church.

Compare also the Scripture proof under Thesis I.

2. Witnesses of the Church in Its Official Confessions

In the first place we read in the oldest Confession of the church, the *Apostles' Creed:* "I believe . . . a holy Christian church, the communion of saints." If, according to these words, the church is something that must be believed, it cannot be visible, for "faith is the substance of things hoped for, the evidence of things not seen"

38

(Heb. 11:1). For this reason Augustine writes: "This is faith, to believe what you do not see" (Tract. 10 on John); and in another place: "You fool, what you see is not faith."

The *Apology of the Augsburg Confession:* "If we would say that the church is merely an outward polity as are other governments, in which there are wicked and good [persons], etc., no one would know or understand from this that Christ's kingdom is spiritual, as indeed it is, in which Christ inwardly rules, strengthens, and comforts the hearts and imparts the Holy Spirit and various spiritual gifts, but people would think that it is merely the outward observance of certain forms of worship and rites. Likewise, what difference would there be between the people of [under] the Law and the church, if the church were merely an outward polity? But Paul distinguishes the church from the Jews thus that the church is a spiritual people, that is, a people that is distinguished from the heathen not merely by polity and civil affairs, but that it is the true people of God, regenerated in heart and born again by the Holy Ghost. Again, among the Jewish people all those who were by nature Jews, stemming from the seed of Abraham, had besides the promise of the spiritual gifts in Christ also many promises concerning temporal blessings, such as those of government and the like, and because of the divine promise also the wicked among them were called God's people. For God had separated the bodily seed of Abraham and all who were born Jews from other heathen by these very temporal promises. Yet despite these [promises] the ungodly and wicked were not the true people of God, nor did they please God.

"But the Gospel that is preached in the church brings not merely the shadow of the eternal gifts, but every true Christian partakes [even] here on earth of the eternal gifts themselves. . . . Therefore, according to the Gospel, only those are God's people who receive the spiritual gifts [and] the Holy Ghost, and this church is the kingdom of Christ, distinguished from the kingdom of the devil.

"If (then) the church, which surely is the kingdom of Christ and God, is distinguished from the devil's kingdom, the wicked, who are in the devil's kingdom, cannot be the church, although in this life, since the kingdom of Christ is not yet made manifest, they are among the true Christians and in the church, in which they also have the ministry of teaching and other offices. Yet the wicked in this life are not a part of Christ's kingdom for the reason that it has not yet been made manifest. For the true kingdom of Christ, true assembly of Christ, is and remains forever only those whom the Spirit of God enlightens, strengthens, and rules, though it is not yet revealed to the world, but is hidden under the cross. . . .

"And with this clearly agree the parables of Christ, who says (Matt. 13:38) that the good seed are the children of the kingdom, but the tares are the children of the devil, and that the acre is the world, not the church. . . . And when Christ says (Matt. 13:47): 'The kingdom of heaven is like a dragnet,' and likewise, like ten virgins, He does not want the wicked to be the church but shows how the church appears in this world. Therefore, He says that it is 'like,' and so forth; that is to say, as in a catch of fish the good and bad lie all mixed up, so the church here is hidden in the crowd and multitude of the wicked, and He does not want the pious to be offended [by this fact]. . . . And since the true church is called in Scripture the body of Christ, it is not at all possible to speak of it in any other way than we have spoken of it. For it is certain that the hypocrites and wicked cannot be the body of Christ" (VII, VIII [IV], par. 13–29; German expanded text, *Triglot,* pp. 230–236).

Again the *Apology* declares: "Because of that [the large number of the wicked] the true doctrine and church often are so utterly suppressed and crushed, as this happened under the papacy, [that it seems] as though there were no longer any church, and it often appears that the church has completely perished. Against this, in order that we may be sure and not doubt but believe firmly and fully that there will be and remain on earth properly a Christian church till the end of the world, . . . which is the bride of Christ, though the crowd of the wicked is more and larger, also that the Lord Christ here on earth daily works in the assembly, which is called 'church,' . . . , therefore, this comforting article has been placed in the Creed: 'I believe a catholic, universal Christian church,' so that no one might think that the church, like any other outward polity, is bound to this or that land, kingdom, or state, as the pope at Rome would have it" (ibid., par. 9–11; *Triglot,* p. 228).

3. Witnesses of the Church in the Private Writings of Its Teachers

Luther: "Since a person consists of two natures, body and soul, he is not classified as a member of Christendom according to the body

40

but according to the soul, indeed, according to his faith. . . . Hence it is manifest that Christendom is a spiritual communion that cannot be classified among the secular communities, as little as souls may be [classified] among bodies, or faith among secular gifts. . . . If Christendom were a bodily [visible] assembly, everyone could judge from the body whether anyone is a Christian, a Turk, or a Jew, just as I can judge from the body whether anyone is a man, a woman, or a child [or whether he is] black or white. Likewise, in a secular community I can judge whether anyone is gathered with others at Wittenberg or Leipzig, here or there, but not at all whether he believes or not. Therefore, let him who does not want to err hold fast that Christendom is a spiritual assembly of souls [united] in one faith" ("Concerning the Papacy at Rome, Against the Illustrious Romanists at Leipzig," 1520, St. Louis edition, 18:1016–17).

The same: "Therefore we rightly confess in the Creed and say: 'I believe a holy Christian church.' For it is invisible and lives in the Spirit at a place to which no one can come. Hence, it is impossible to see its holiness. For God often covers and veils it so much with weakness, sin, and error and with many tribulations and offenses that we can find it nowhere with our senses" (Comment on Galatians 5:19, Halle edition, 8:2745).

The same: "This part, 'I believe a holy Christian church,' is as much an article of faith as are the others. Therefore, reason cannot perceive it, though it would put on all glasses [spectacles]. The devil can so cover it with offenses and factions that it might offend you. So also God can hide it with weaknesses and all kinds of failings that you make a fool out of yourself as you judge it wrongly. The church does not want to be seen but to be believed. However, you believe what you do not see (Heb. 11:1)" ("Preface to the Revelation of St. John," Halle edition, 14:161).

The same: "The church is a high and deeply hidden thing so that no one can recognize or know it, but you must apprehend and believe it solely by [its] Baptism, the Lord's Supper, and the [divine] Word" (Luther's writing "Against Johnny Sausage [Hans Wurst]," Halle edition, 17:1678).

The same: "It no longer concerns us that we run to Jerusalem or to any other special place, . . . but [for] now He has built another temple or church, whose wall encircles the whole world, as St. Paul says in Col. 1:23, and as we read in Ps. 19:5" (Comment on Ps. 65:4, Halle edition, 5:937–38).

The same: "When I called the Christian church a spiritual assembly, you made fun of me, as though I wanted to build a church as Plato built a city, [namely, one] that exists nowhere. And you are greatly pleased with your whim as though you had hit the nail on the head. You say: 'That indeed would be a fine city that would have spiritual walls, spiritual towers, spiritual guns, spiritual cavalry, and everything in it would be spiritual.' And it is your final judgment that the Christian church could not exist without a tangible city, space, and goods. My dear Murnar, let me tell you: Should I, because of reason, deny Scripture and place you above God? Why do you not answer the passages I have quoted as, for example: 'There is no partiality with Him' (Eph. 6:9) or 'The kingdom of God does not come with observation; nor will they say, "See here!" or "See there!" For indeed, the kingdom of God is within you' (Luke 17:20)? . . .

"Therefore, I conclude that the Christian church is not bound to any place, person, or time, and although the ignorant crowd—the pope with his cardinals, bishops, priests, and monks—do not understand this, yet there sides with me Mr. Omnes (that is, Mr. All, namely, the common Christian people), even the children in the street, and the whole assembly of Christians throughout the world. They all take my side against the obscure, fictitious church of the pope and his papists.

"Now, if you ask me how that could be, I answer briefly: All Christians throughout the world confess: 'I believe in the Holy Spirit; the holy Christian church, the communion of saints.' If that article is true, it follows that no one can see or feel the holy Christian church, nor can you say, 'Behold, here it is or there.' For whatever anyone believes, he does not see or feel, as St. Paul teaches (Heb. 11:1).

"Again, what anyone sees or feels, he does not believe. Is not that sufficiently clear, my dear Murnar and Emser? Let me hear what you will reply to that. Are not at this point the children and peasants more learned than the pope, cardinals, bishops, priests, and monks? Who are you, my dear sirs, who assume to expound Scripture and explain the Creed? Do you mean to cry out that the common man does not understand anything in it? The very reverse is true, for the pope and his bishops, with their whole following, do not understand as much [of it] as do the unlearned peasants and children. So they place in opposition to the holy church of Christ the absurd church of the pope. The holy church of Christ says: 'I believe a holy Christian church.' The former says: 'The church is neither here nor there'; the latter: 'The church is here and there' " ("Reply to the Book of Emser at Leipzig with an Appendix to Murnar," Halle edition, 18:1652–55).

Chemnitz: "Eck indeed ridicules this meaning of the term [invisible church] and says that this is a mathematical church and a Platonic idea. But let him laugh as much as he cares to. What to us is an 'idea' and cannot be seen is for that reason not hidden to God (Col. 3:3): 'Your life is hidden with Christ in God.' But on that account our [Christian] life is not a Platonic idea, that is, an enthusiastic illusion; for we know that when Christ, our Life, will appear, then we also shall appear with him in glory (v. 4). Luther, however, never approved the absurdities of the Anabaptists, who, because the church is invisible, under this pretense kept in hiding and crept into the houses in order to establish a hidden church. Against them Luther in 1532 directed an earnest warning under the title 'Against the Sneak Prophets' [*Wider die Winkelprediger*]. The true and holy church of the elect nevertheless remains invisible, especially when it is described not as an assembly of one people, as the Jewish or Israelite [church] was in the Old Testament, but as the universal communion that is gathered together at all places, in every nation, tongue, and time, accepts the Gospel of Christ with a firm faith, administers the sacraments, and under the cross constantly fights for Christ to life everlasting" (*Loci theologici,* part 3, p. 117).

John Gerhard: "When we say: 'I believe one holy Christian church,' the word 'believe' shows clearly that we speak of the invisible church, which is proved also by the added adjective 'holy' " (*Loci theologici,* "De ecclesia," par. 151).

The same: "We do not say that the church is invisible for the reason that we mean to show that the church has been preserved under the papacy; we say that the true, holy, and universal church is always invisible, even now when the newly kindled light of the Gospel shines most brightly in many kingdoms and provinces" (ibid., par. 69).

The same: " 'But the hour is coming, and now is, when the true worshipers will worship the Father in spirit and truth' (John 4:23).

According to these words the church of the New Testament does not consist in outward signs and is not bound locally to any place or any ceremonies. The true church, properly so called, consists of true worshipers. But human eyes cannot see who the true worshipers are because they worship in spirit and in truth. The eye cannot decide who does this because the hypocrites according to outward appearance do the same. Therefore, the true church, properly so called, cannot be seen. . . . It indeed has an outward worship and outward ceremonies, but these are not the real worship. Therefore, no one can judge from the outward worship and the outward ceremonies, which are seen, who really is a citizen of the Christian church and its true member. But the judgment must rest on the inward and spiritual worship, which is not subject to human eyes. So those who engage in spiritual and inward worship cannot be seen" (ibid., par. 73).

The same: "Whatever is spiritual is invisible. The church is the spiritual Zion and spiritual city (Heb. 12:18). Therefore it is invisible" (ibid., par. 74).

The same: "We admit that those persons [the members of the true church] can be seen, but because they who belong to the building of the church (1 Peter 2:5) are seen as bodily persons and not as spiritual, it still remains true that the church as a spiritual house, which is built of spiritual people, is invisible" (ibid., par. 74).

The same: "Because the apostle declares (Rom. 2:29) that only he is a true Jew who is one inwardly and in the hiddenness of his heart, we in the same way can declare that not what outwardly pretends to be the church and glitters in the eyes of men is to be recognized as the true church, but that those who are Christians inwardly in hiddenness are the true Christians and the true church. Hence the church in its first [proper] meaning is invisible" (ibid., par. 75).

The same: "Every mystical (spiritual) body is invisible. The church is Christ's mystical body. Therefore, it is invisible. The Head of the universal church in this life is invisible. Therefore, also the church itself [as His body] is invisible" (ibid., par. 77).

The same: "(Bellarmine objects) that in Is. 2:2; Dan. 2:35; and Micah 4:1 the church is compared to a great and conspicuous mountain that can in no wise be hidden, as Jerome explains these passages. I reply that Isaiah and Micah describe the greatness and clarity of the church that was to be in the days of the Messiah through the universal preaching of the Gospel. The fulfillment corresponded to this prophecy, but what objection can be raised from this against our statement? . . . At the same time, when the clarity of the particular [local] churches was greatest, the universal church of the saints remained invisible. . . . (Bellarmine further quotes) Matt. 5:14: 'A city that is set on a hill cannot be hidden.' I reply that in this passage Christ addresses the apostles and witnesses that their life and doctrine will be open to the view of all" (ibid., par. 80).

Balthasar Meisner: "The church is called invisible in a fourfold respect: (1) inasmuch as we speak of it as the universal church, the assembly of all Christians, those in the militant church as well as in the triumphant, who, as we live in this world, certainly are invisible to us; (2) inasmuch as we speak of the universal church in a special sense, [namely,] inasmuch as it is the assembly of only the militant church, yet [at the same time] that of all Christians who are scattered throughout the world, for also in this sense it is invisible; we indeed see the particular churches but never at one time the catholic or universal [church]; (3) inasmuch as we speak of particular churches or with respect to the faithful and elect [in them]; for since we cannot look into the hearts of men and know for sure whether their faith is living, or dead and hypocritical, therefore, the church with regard to the saints [in it] is rightly called unobservable and invisible; (4) inasmuch as we speak of the church with respect to the ministry of the Word and the public observance of pure worship. And here is the acme of the controversy between us and the papists who contend that the church can never be without the public observance of pure worship, but that there always has been and will be a large assembly in which the Word of God is preached purely and the sacraments are rightly administered. However, since before Luther there was no other communion of believers than their synagogue, they conclude that the true church is found only with them" (*Philosophia sobria,* part 2, 1.1.9, pp. 129–30).

This last comment of the learned and pious theologian Meisner shows how important the doctrine is that the true church properly is invisible. This doctrine is of great comfort especially in those times in which a believing Christian cannot see or find an orthodox congregation. It also prevents false teachers from disturbing, confusing, and terrifying such Christians as either are separated or have been excommunicated unjustly with their boast that they are the true church and that outside their communion no one can be saved.

Balthasar Mentzer: "The (Augsburg) Confession describes (the church) thus: 'The church is the congregation of saints and true believers.' This church Luther called invisible, because of its faith and election, which human eyes cannot see (1 Kings 8:39; 19:18; Rom. 2:28–29; Ps. 45:14[13?]; 1 Peter 3:4; Col. 3:3; 2 Tim. 2:19). This church Cyprian in the second book of his letters calls 'the assembly of believers in Christ' with whom by faith they are betrothed and united. So also Chrysostom in the tenth sermon on Eph. 4 [calls it] 'a house built out of our souls.' Ambrose in his second book on Luke, chap. 3, [calls it] 'the mother of the living' that 'God has built on the supreme cornerstone, Jesus Christ.' Clement of Alexandria in the seventh book of his *Stromata* [calls it] 'the assembly of the elect.' Lactantius in chap. 13 of his fourth book concerning true wisdom [calls it] 'the true temple of God,' which consists not of walls but in the heart and faith of people who believe in Him and are called believers.

"If now the papists cry out that this is a metaphysical and mathematical church, that is, a vain and worthless fabrication, they shamefully contradict the clear witnesses of Scripture, godly antiquity, and the truth itself.... As said before, the church is called invisible because inward faith and election are not manifest to the human eye, just as Elijah said (1 Kings 19:14): 'I alone am left,' to which the Lord replied: 'I have reserved seven thousand in Israel, all whose knees have not bowed to Baal, and every mouth that has not kissed him' [v. 18]. This most important passage St. Paul repeats in Rom. 11:3–4 and applies it to the argument concerning the rejection of the Jews because of their contempt for the Gospel. From this [passage] we draw the unanswerable conclusion: Those seven thousand persons were the church of God, yet not the visible one, for Elijah did not see it, but the invisible" (*Exegesis Confessionis Augustanae,* ed. 6, pp. 291–94).

Hülsemann: "What gives the church its essential nature, that is, the inward union with its Head, Christ, and its other members, is not visible except by spiritual sight according to the Creed: 'I believe a holy Christian church.' But the object of faith is invisible according to the apostle's statement in Heb. 11:1 and the well-known saying of Augustine: 'You fool, what you see is not faith.' Since then the

46

naming must be done according to its [the church's] principal part, and what gives the church its essential nature is as its principal part in itself invisible, it follows that the church according to its essence not only can be called invisible but also is rightly so called and that the invectives of the papists, which they hurl against our church as [being] utopian, are absurd, that is, existing nowhere except in our imagination" (*Praelect. in lib. Concordiae,* p. 821).

Dannhauer: "An invisible church, which is the object of faith, must be recognized, and we must say of it with certainty and effect: 'I believe a church.' The church is one in spirit, holy according to its inward holiness, the treasure, crown, bride, and daughter of God. But of the visible church according to all its members all these and similar titles [of honor] cannot be predicated. In this visible assembly there exists something that is invisible and is the proper crown and heart of the mass of Christians. To this [the crown and heart] alone belong whatever glorious things are said of the church" (*Hodosophiae phaen.* 2, p. 58).

Calov: "The multitude in which the church exists can indeed be seen, distinguished, and pointed out with the finger, for in it the Word is taught and the sacraments are administered according to Christ's command. But the assembly that properly is the church, that is, the communion of believers and saints, is invisible and cannot be pointed out" (*Systema locorum theologicorum,* 8:264).

Quenstedt: "The church is described as a mystical body and a spiritual kingdom, whose Head is the Lord Christ. Since, according to 1 Peter 1:8, He is invisible, He must have members that are uniform to Him" [that is, who are invisible] (*Theologia didactico-polemica,* part IV, 15.2).

The same: "Bellarmine objects: 'Not one passage can be quoted in which the name church is applied to an invisible communion, but wherever the name church is recorded, there always is indicated a visible congregation.' To this I reply: 'Wherever the name church occurs in its proper sense and is applied to the universal church, there it, always denotes the invisible assembly of saints and true believers, for the true members of the universal church are none other than the true members of the invisible church" (ibid.).

The same: "The multitude of people that constitute the church we do see, but whether those persons are the church, that we do not see; that is, the people that belong to the church we see and notice, but whether these persons are true and living members of the church, that is not manifest to us" (ibid.).

The fact that also the ancient [Christian] church has always taught the same as we do is quite evident especially from the Apostles' Creed, in which the church is designated as an object of faith. In addition to the witnesses of the ancient fathers quoted by our teachers above, the following may be mentioned: In the first place *Chrysostom* calls the church "a house built out of our souls" (Sermon 10, on Eph. 4). Then *St. Augustine* writes: "When I consider everything, I believe I am able to say with excellent reason that some are in the house of God, of which it is said that it is built on a rock, that it is called a dove, a beautiful bride without spot or wrinkle, a closed garden, a sealed fountain, a source of living water, a paradise with its fruits. But others obviously are in the house in such a way that they do not belong to the cohesion of the house and the communion of the fruitful and peaceful righteousness, but they are, as it is said, the chaff among the wheat" (*De bapt.* 7.51).

Thesis IV

It is to this true church of believers and saints that Christ gave the keys of the kingdom of heaven, and it is the proper and only possessor and bearer of the spiritual, divine, and heavenly gifts, rights, powers, offices, and the like that Christ has procured and are found in His church.

1. Scripture Proof

Thus it is written (Matt. 16:15–19): "He said to them, 'But who do you say that I am?' And Simon Peter answered and said, 'You are the Christ, the Son of the living God.' Jesus answered and said to him, 'Blessed are you, Simon Bar-Jonah, for flesh and blood has not revealed this to you, but My Father who is in heaven. And I also say to you that you are Peter, and on this rock will I build My church, and the gates of Hades shall not prevail against it. And I will give you the keys of the kingdom of heaven, and whatever you bind on earth will be bound in heaven, and whatever you loose on earth will be loosed in heaven.' " Here Christ attests what power those have who with Peter are built on this rock, namely, those who believe on Him and confess this faith of their heart with their mouth, or briefly expressed, His true church, His holy, believing congregation, which is His body, the fullness of Him who fills all in all.

So also we read (Matt. 18:18): "Assuredly, I say to you, whatever you bind on earth will be bound in heaven, and whatever you loose on earth will be loosed in heaven." Here Jesus declares that what shortly before He had said to Peter pertained to all His disciples.

Again we read in John 20:22–23: "When He had said this, He breathed on them, and said to them, 'Receive the Holy Spirit. If you forgive the sins of any, they are forgiven them; if you retain the sins of any, they are retained.' " Here Christ witnesses that only the

49

communion of those who have the Holy Spirit, that is, the holy Christian church, can open and close heaven.

Furthermore, the Lord says (Matt. 28:20) as He was about to leave the world: "Lo, I am with you always, even to the end of the age." If Christ is with His own, they possess with Him all things.

So said John the Baptist [of Christ] (John 3:28–29): "You yourselves bear me witness, that I said, 'I am not the Christ,' but, 'I have been sent before Him.' He who has the bride is the bridegroom." If, according to these words, the communion of believers is the bride of Christ, then this communion is also the true possessor of all the goods of Christ, the bridegroom. Compare 2 Cor. 11:2: "I have betrothed you to one husband, that I may present you as a chaste virgin to Christ." (For this reason the high priest, as a prototype, was permitted to marry only a virgin, Lev. 21:13–14.) Eph. 5:32: "This is a great mystery, but I speak concerning Christ and the church." According to these words Christ is espoused to His church; therefore, it is the wife and matron in Christ's house. Of this already David prophesied (Ps. 68:13[12]): "The matron of the house divides the spoils" [Luther's translation], that is, as the Weimar Bible explains it, "the blessings that Christ has secured by His war and victory."

Thus writes St. Paul (1 Cor. 3:21–23): "Therefore let no one glory in men. For all things are yours: whether Paul or Apollos or Cephas, or the world or life or death, or things present or things to come—all are yours. And you are Christ's, and Christ is God's." From this [passage] we learn that all things that even Paul and Peter had were only treasures from the jewel room of the believing Christians or the church.

Again, the same apostle writes (Gal. 4:26) of the church of the New Testament: "The Jerusalem above is free, which is the mother of us all." Hence everything by which children of God are born is the church.

Finally, St. Peter writes to the believing Christians (1 Peter 2:9): "You are a chosen generation, a royal priesthood, a holy nation, His own special people, that you may proclaim the praises of Him who called you out of darkness into His marvelous light."

2[a]. Witnesses of the Church in Its Official Confessions

Augsburg Confession: "Since then the power of the church or bishops grants eternal gifts, and these are exercised and executed only through the ministry of the Word, therefore, . . . " (Art. XXVIII, par. 10; German text, *Triglot,* p. 84).

Smalcald Articles: "The keys are an office and power given by Christ to the church" (Part III, Art. VII; *Triglot,* p. 493).

Smalcald Articles: "In 1 Cor. 3 Paul makes all ministers equal and teaches that the church is more than the ministers. . . . He says: 'All things are yours: whether Paul or Apollos or Cephas,' which means that neither Peter nor any other minister dare assume for himself lordship or superiority over the church" ("Of the Power and Primacy of the Pope," part I, par. V; German text, *Triglot,* p. 506).

The same: "Here several passages are quoted against us, for example, Matt. 16: 'You are Peter, and on this rock I will build My church.' Also: 'I will give you the keys.' Also [John 21:15]: 'Feed my sheep,' and many more. But because this whole matter has been treated diligently and sufficiently by our theologians before, we here refer to these writings and now [merely] reply briefly how the quoted passages are rightly to be understood.

"In all these passages Peter appears as an ordinary person and does not speak only for himself but for all apostles. This fact is clearly proved by the text, for Christ did not ask only Peter but said: 'Who do *you* [plural] say that I am?' And what Christ here said only to Peter, namely: 'I will give you the keys of the kingdom of heaven,' or, 'Whatever you bind,' etc., in other passages He addresses to the whole assembly: 'Whatever *you* [plural] bind on earth will be bound in heaven,' or, 'If you forgive the sins of any,' etc.

"These passages attest that the keys were given to all in common, and that they [the apostles] were all alike sent forth to preach the Gospel. In addition, we must acknowledge that the keys do not belong and were not given merely to one person but to the whole church as this can sufficiently be proved by clear and convincing evidence. For as the promise of the Gospel belongs to the whole church primarily and immediately, so also the keys belong to the whole church immediately (Latin text: *principaliter et immediate*); for the keys are nothing else than the ministry of the Word by which that promise is communicated to all who desire it, just as it is manifest that the church has the power to ordain ministers of the Word. Christ expressly states [this] when saying: 'Whatever you bind,' etc., indicating to whom the keys are given, namely, to the church: 'Where

51

two or three are gathered together in My name, I am there in the midst of them.' Again, Christ gives to the church the supreme and final jurisdiction [Gericht] when He says: 'Tell it to the church.' " (ibid., part XI, par. 22ff.; German text, *Triglot*, p. 510).

From this we learn that the doctrine of our church is that of the Word of God, [namely,] that Christ has given the ministry and all gifts and powers procured by Him, just as the Gospel, immediately to the church as their original and primary possessor, so that the church possesses the ministry, etc., not mediately, that is, Christ having granted it to certain persons who should continue and administer it for the benefit of the church. The reverse is true: The church does not have the ministry mediately through official persons, but the official persons have the ministry [mediately] through the church, which as the communion of believers and saints possesses this and all [other] prerogatives.

Smalcald Articles: "Wherever the church is, there is also the command to preach the Gospel. Therefore, the churches must retain the power to call, elect, and ordain ministers of the Word; this power is a gift, granted to the church properly by God, and it cannot be wrested from it by any human force. This [fact] St. Paul attests (Eph. 4:8): 'He ascended . . . and gave gifts to men.' Among the gifts that properly belong to the church, he enumerates pastors and teachers and adds that such are given for the edifying of the body of Christ. . . . Here belong [also] the passages of Christ that declare that the keys have been given to the whole church and not to some special persons, as the text affirms: 'Where two or three are gathered together in My name, I am there in the midst of them.' Finally, this [truth] is also confirmed by the statement of Peter: 'You are a royal priesthood.' These words properly pertain only to the true church, since, because it alone has the priesthood, it must also have the power to call and ordain ministers of the Word" ("Of the Power and Jurisdiction of Bishops," part II, par. 67–69).

From all this it is evident: Our church teaches according to God's Word, [namely,] that God has commanded the whole, true, holy, Christian church to preach His precious Gospel and to make it known. Wherever, therefore, [even only] a small congregation of believing Christians, that is, a true church, is found, there also such a congregation has the command to preach the Gospel. But if it has this command, then thereby it naturally also has the power, even the duty, to ordain ministers of the Gospel. From where these ministers are to be taken the church cannot be in doubt, since pastors and teachers are gifts that properly belong to the church. It consists not only of true spiritual priests, but the Lord gives to it also without fail men who are especially equipped with the necessary gifts for the administration of the ministry, and so He offers them to the church for [its] service.

2b. Witnesses of the Church in Other Writings Having an Official Character

Thus sings the church:

> Das ist der heil'gen Schlüssel Kraft
> Sie bind't und wieder ledig macht;
> Die Kirch' trägt sie an ihrer Seit,
> Die Hausmutter der Christenheit.

> Such is the power of holy keys:
> They bind and loose, the Lord to please;
> The church e'er bear them at its side
> As matron and all Christians' guide.

> That is the power of holy keys:
> They bind and again loose;
> The church bears them at its side,
> As the matron of [all] Christendom. [Literal translation]

The Dresden Catechism, written in 1683 and published in 1688 by order of the Elector, says: "The office of the keys is the peculiar church power that Christ has given to His church on earth."

Again, the Erfurt Catechism, published in 1678, declares: "The absolution or forgiveness of sins is the special official power that Christ has given to His church on earth, so that it should have authority, through its ordained pastors, to forgive in God's place all penitent and believing sinners their transgressions, both generally [to all] and to each individually, and thereby to open heaven to them."

3. Witnesses of the Church in the Private Writings of Its Teachers

Luther: "The keys do not belong to the pope (as he lies), but to the church, that is, to the people of Christ, the people of God, or the holy, Christian people, as far as the world extends, or wherever there are Christians. For they cannot all be at Rome, unless first the whole world would be at Rome, which will not happen for a long time. Just as Baptism, the Lord's Supper, and God's Word do not belong to the pope but to Christ's people and are also called *claves ecclesiae,* not *claves papae,* that is, the keys of the church, not the keys of the pope" ("Concerning Councils and Churches," St. Louis edition, 16:2279).

The same: "Therefore the word *you* ('I will give *you* the keys of the kingdom of heaven') is rightly understood of no person, no bishop, but alone of the church that endures and has the office of the ministry that continues forever" ("Comment on the Evangelist Matthew," Halle edition, 7:439).

The same enumerates among the "articles and errors of the canonical rights and papal books that should be burned and avoided" the thirteenth [article], which reads: "The keys are given alone to St. Peter." [He adds:] "But in Matt. 18:18–20 and John 20:23 Christ gives them to the whole church" (Halle edition, 15:1933).

The same writes in his church postil: "It is true that the keys were given to St. Peter, yet not to him personally, but by him [lit., "in person"] to the Christian church, and thus they are given to me and you to comfort our consciences. St. Peter or a priest is a servant of the keys; the church is the matron and bride whom he is to serve by the power of the keys" (Halle edition, 11:3079).

The same: "Only the Christian church has the keys and no one else, though the bishop and pope may use them as those to whom they have been entrusted by the church" (Halle edition, 11:3070).

The same: "But note what it means that Christ, before commanding [the apostles] to forgive and bind sins, breathed on them and said: 'Receive the Holy Spirit. If you forgive the sins of any, they are forgiven them'; etc. (John 20:22–23). Here it is determined that no one can forgive sins unless he has the Holy Spirit, for the words are very clear and cannot be disputed. It does not help [the papists] to bluster that this is the doctrine of John Huss or of Wycliffe, which

54

was condemned at Constance. It is not enough to condemn; they must refute [it]. Nor is it enough to point out that in Matt. 23:3 it says: 'Therefore whatever they tell you to observe, that observe and do, but do not do according to their works.' That was said of the ministry of the Word, to which Christ commissioned the apostles. Then He did not breathe on them, nor did He give them the Holy Spirit, as He did here [John 20:22–23]. What then about the keys of the pope? I judge that they must slip out of his hand much against his will, and that it must become known that he most offensively has them only in his coat of arms; for here it says very clearly that no one has the keys unless he has the Holy Spirit. Therefore, someone ought to paint in his coat of arms (I certainly know what) and tear out the keys. The coat of arms belongs to someone else and not to the pope. But on the other hand, were I not to receive remission of sins unless my pastor would have the Holy Spirit (and no one can be sure whether another person has Him), how, then, could I be sure of my absolution and obtain a quiet conscience? It would then be just as it was before [absolution].

"To this I reply: I mentioned this in order that we may have a firm foundation in this matter. There is no doubt that no one can bind or forgive sins unless he has the Holy Spirit so surely that you and I know it, as the words of Christ here persuasively declare. But that is none other than the Christian church, that is, the communion of all believers in Christ. This church alone has these keys; about that you must not be in doubt. Whoever appropriates the keys to himself besides that [the church] is a truly inveterate *sacrilegus* (sacrilegious person) whether he is the pope or anyone else. Concerning the church, everyone is sure that it has the Holy Spirit, as Paul, following Christ and all Scripture, proves this most convincingly, and as this is briefly set forth in the Creed, in which we say: 'I believe that there is a holy Christian church.' It is holy because of the Holy Spirit whom it surely has. Therefore, no one shall receive absolution from the pope or a bishop as though it were they [by their own right] who absolve. May God keep us from the absolution of the pope and bishops, which now fills the world, [for] that is the absolution of the devil.

"But you should do as Christ says in Matt. 10:41: 'He who receives a prophet in the name of a prophet shall receive a prophet's reward. And he who receives a righteous man in the name of a righteous man shall receive a righteous man's reward.' Hence if a stone or a piece of wood could absolve me in the name of the Christian church, I would receive it. Again if the pope in the name of his [own] power would be seated in the highest choir of the angels, I would shut both my ears [to his claim] and regard him as the greatest blasphemer. He is a servant of the keys as are all other priests; the keys belong only to the church. An owner may permit his servant to bear his coat of arms if he does not presume [to say] that it is his own above all other servants and anyone else. So the Christian church gives the keys to the pope and commands him to administer and use them in its name. But for that reason it does not suffer them to be his own.

"Our Creed, therefore, is so arranged that the phrase 'forgiveness of sins' must stand behind 'a holy Christian church' and after 'I believe in the Holy Spirit,' so that people may know that without the Holy Spirit there is no holy church, and without the holy church, no forgiveness of sins. In short, it is not true that the pope has the keys. The church alone has them, and not he. It alone binds and absolves, and in it he and all priests serve. From this it follows that the pope in his office should be a servant of servants, as he claims to be, though he does not act accordingly. A [baptized] child in the cradle has a greater claim to the keys than he, together with all those who have the Holy Spirit" ("Tract Concerning Confession," Halle edition, 19:1051–54).

The same: "At this point I do not worry about these maskers and their masquerade who, regarding Matt. 18:15–18, make this distinction: 'It is quite another thing to have the right or power of the keys than to use them.' This [distinction] stems from their own arrogance and not from Scripture. They should prove this from a sound source [*Anfang*] and reason; that they do as they are accustomed to do all things. They should first show and prove that they have another power [of the keys] than the common power of the church. But they make the assertion as though they had already shown and proved it and so bluster with their fabricated distinction and falsehood: 'The church indeed has the right and power of the keys, but their use belongs to the bishops.' That is frivolous talk that of itself falls by the wayside. Christ gives to every Christian the power and use of the keys when He says: 'Let him be to you like a heathen.' Who is meant by 'you'? Whom does Christ address with the little pronoun 'you'? Perhaps the pope? No, He speaks to every Christian in particular.

"But when He says 'to you,' He not only grants [to every Christian] the right and power [of the keys], but He orders and commands also their use and administration. For what does it mean, 'Let him be to you like a heathen,' that is, you should regard him as such? Does that not mean as much as 'You should not associate with him nor have any communion with him'? That, however, does not mean anything else than to excommunicate such a one, to bind him and shut him out of heaven. This is confirmed by the following statement: 'Whatever you bind on earth will be bound in heaven' (v. 18). Whom does He address here? Does He not mean all Christians? Is it not the Christian church? If they say that here only the power or right of the keys is given to the church, we answer that [then], according to Matt. 16:19, He gave the use of the keys to no one, not even to St. Peter. For the words of Christ are the same everywhere by which He confers this office. And if they mean that the power has been conferred at one place or on one person, they everywhere else mean the same thing. Again, if they mean that the use [of the keys] has been given at one place, they [the words] everywhere mean that the same use has been conferred. It is not proper that anyone should interpret the same divine words in one place in one way and in another passage in another. But this these maskers do and so make mockery of the mystery of God by their fabrications, which are nothing else than human lies.

"The keys belong to the whole communion of Christians and to everyone who is a member of that communion, and this pertains not only to their possession but also to their use and whatever else there may be. We must not distort the words of Christ, who speaks directly and generally to all [Christians]: 'Let him be to you,' etc. Again: 'Whatever you bind,' etc. I might also adduce for confirmation the passage that Christ addressed to St. Peter alone: 'I will give you the keys of the kingdom of heaven' (Matt. 16:19). Again: 'If two of you agree on earth,' etc. (Matt. 18:19); and: 'Where two or three are gathered together in My name, I am there in the midst of them' (v. 20). In these passages the supreme right and use are granted and confirmed [to all] in the most emphatic way that they might bind and loose, unless we would want to deny Christ Himself the right and use of the keys, were He to be in the midst of two" ("Letter

57

to the Council and Congregation in the City of Prague," Halle edition, 10:1845–47).

Chemnitz: "Against these tyrannical principles Luther taught, according to God's Word, that Christ gave and entrusted the keys, that is, the ministry of the Word and the sacraments, to the whole church" (*Examen concilii Tridentini,* p. 223. a).

The same: "What means, then, would God ordinarily use to call and commission ministers? He does not want to do this through angels but through His church or congregation, that is, the royal priesthood (1 Peter 5:9). For to it, as to His beloved bride, He has entrusted the keys (Matt. 18:18), His Word and sacraments (Rom. 3:2). In short: The ministry with all its servants belongs to the church (1 Cor. 3:21; Eph. 4:11)" (Georg Dedekennus, *Thesaurus consiliorum et decisionum,* vol. 1, part 2, p. 418).

Polycarp Leyser (in the gospel harmony of Martin Chemnitz): "Above all, we must inquire what is to be understood by the keys of the kingdom of heaven that Christ here [Matt. 18:18] has promised. We recall that Christ in His conversation with His apostles compared the church either to a city or to a house that He Himself builds. The church of Christ is truly His city, into which He gathers the citizens and subjects of His kingdom. It is also His house, in which He has deposited all His goods and treasures as, for example, divine grace, forgiveness of sins, righteousness, salvation, eternal life, and similar blessings. But all these gifts together with the house are closed to us by nature; for as soon as our first parents, who were not content with the dignity that had been graciously granted them, looked for keys by which they might ascend to the supreme majesty and become equal to God, they immediately lost all the glory that they possessed by virtue of the divine image in which they had been created. They were cast out of paradise, and in order that they might not return to it, the door was closed, and cherubim with a flaming sword were placed there to keep them from the way to the tree of life (Gen. 3:24).

"This closed door to the kingdom of heaven no man could unlock and open. . . . But what the Law could not do in that it was weak through the flesh, God did by sending His Son (Rom. 8:3). He, being delivered for our offenses and raised again for our justification, has again opened [to us] the gates of heaven. . . . Moreover, though the gates of heaven have been opened to all men through

Jesus Christ, . . . [nevertheless,] since everyone by his sins, especially by his impenitence, closes them [to himself], and Christ still desires to save the whole world, He has committed to us the Word of reconciliation, having reconciled us to Himself, not imputing our trespasses to us (2 Cor. 5:19). Hence, as Christ has the keys of David, that is, the complete, supreme, and absolute power in the kingdom of His Father, so here the apostles and all others who administer their office, receive a part of the administration in this kingdom. . . . The conferring of the keys has for ages been the symbol of a certain entrusted and imparted authority, so that he who has the keys has access to everything [in the house].

"When, for example, a husband hands over to his wife the keys, he [thereby] testifies that he recognizes her as his mate and entrusts her with the care of the home. Similarly, the keys are conferred by masters on their stewards and managers; by these at the same time they are given authority over all rooms, cellars, chests, and whatever is kept in them. So also the princes, whenever they are admitted into a city, are given the keys by the citizens to indicate that they are willing to subject themselves to their rule, acknowledging at the same time that they [the princes] have the authority either to admit anyone to the city or to exclude him.

"This idea Christ here applies to the church, whose keys He promises to Peter and his fellow ministers. By that He teaches that He appoints them as His stewards and managers so that they might open His treasures to the worthy, allowing them to have and use them, while to the unworthy and unrighteous they close them and thus thrust them out of the kingdom of God (1 Cor. 4:1). The expression 'keys of the kingdom' therefore embraces every official transaction, power, and authority by which all things are done that are necessary for the kingdom of Christ and the rule of His church. That cannot be explained better than by the symbol of the keys. For as it is the duty of anyone who has received from a king the keys of a city, if indeed he desires to be faithful to his ruler, to receive the true citizens into the city, to submit to the subjects not his own but the king's commandments, to provide for the food and clothing of the subjects, to cast those out of the city who do not want to live according to the rule of the realm, and, if he alone is unable to administer all duties himself, to appoint others who together with him govern the city properly; so also the office of the keys of the kingdom of heaven is essentially just that.

"For it is the duty of ministers of the Word, first to receive into the church by Baptism, the sacrament of initiation, children as well as adults, as many as offer themselves to receive Jesus as their Lord, King, and Redeemer. Again, it is their duty to teach those who have been received not human fancies nor the principles of philosophy nor the decrees of church councils but the doctrine of Christ, according to Matt. 28:20: 'Teaching them to observe all things that I have commanded you.' Third, it must be their concern that the believers are nourished and refreshed by the use of the Lord's Supper, the living food of the new man, and that they [the believers], clothed by faith with a wedding garment, adorn themselves at the same time with good works. Fourth, whenever some disturb the peace of the church or by their wicked life give offense to others and refuse to be admonished, they are to exclude these from the communion of saints and put them out of the church; however, when they penitently return and by asking pardon put away the offense, they should again receive them into fellowship. Finally, since one minister does not suffice for a large congregation or an entire city, it is the duty of the church administrators to ordain and appoint others as deacons, pastors, or fellow ministers. Among these there should be a certain order or rank in order that, for the furtherance of the salvation of the believers and the strengthening of the kingdom of Christ, all things shall be done decently and in order. . . .

"We must consider also to whom the keys of the kingdom of heaven have been entrusted; for since Christ says to Peter, 'I will give *you*,' etc., the papists may try to prove from this [word] the superiority that Peter might have received over all [other ministers] and even over the apostles, later basing on this superiority that of all those who are his [Peter's] successors on the papal throne. Here, however, in order that we might have the certain, true, and indisputable meaning, we must consider the whole matter in its context. Christ indeed asked *all* apostles who they said He was. Peter replied in the name of all and made a confession of their common faith. Hence, Christ's reply to him must be applied to all apostles. Indeed, He shortly afterwards applies (Matt. 18:18) what He here has said not only to the apostles but to the whole church. In addition, He clearly shows in the actual exposition of what He promises in Matt. 16:19 who the one is whom He wishes to have regarded as having been given the keys by breathing on all apostles (John 20:22) and conferring this power on them all. And the fact that this is the true and universal understanding of this passage is attested by the oldest Christian writers. . . .

"St. Augustine thus writes in his first book 'Concerning Christian Doctrine' (ch. 18): 'These keys He conferred on His church so that what it should loose on earth should be loosed in heaven and what it should bind on earth should be bound in heaven.' Similarly, he writes in his last tract on the Gospel According to John: 'When He tells him [Peter], "I will give you the keys of the kingdom of heaven," He designated the whole church.' So also writes Origen in his first homily on the Gospel According to Matthew: 'It is indeed said to Peter, "You are Peter, and on this rock I will build My church, and the gates of Hades shall not prevail against it." Nevertheless this seems to have been said to all apostles and to all and every true believer, because all are Peters and rocks, and on them all the church of Christ is built, and the gates of hell shall prevail against none of those who are such. Therefore [herewith] you hear the universal [Christian] exposition of this passage.'

"For this reason it is rightly stated in the Smalcald Articles not only that in ancient times no distinction was made between elders and bishops, but also that the congregations have the right to elect, call, and hear (ordain?), namely, when bishops either are heretics or when such as are qualified refuse to ordain. For Christ has left the keys of the kingdom of heaven to the church (Matt. 18:18)" (*Harmonia quatuor evangelistarum,* c. 85, p. 1626; [cf. Smalcald Articles, "Of the Power and Jurisdiction of Bishops," par. 60–72; German text, *Triglot,* pp. 520–24]).

Heshusius: "Whoever, then, is a believing Christian and a living member of Christ has his part and right in the holy ministry of the Word as well as in everything that belongs to the ministry of the church. Christ gives power to the whole church, according to God's Word and promise, to forgive the penitent their sins. And if called pastors exercise this power, they do it not by their own authority but by the power and command of the church, which has entrusted this prerogative, received from Christ, to the pastors for administration. But if the pastors do not administer their office as they

61

should, or if there are no pastors, then the office goes back to the churches, which have the privilege to confer it" (cf. the tract of Heshusius, "Who Has the Power, Authority, and Right to Call Ministers?").

Balthasar Mentzer: "Christ has entrusted the keys of the kingdom of heaven (Matt. 18:17–18) and the Word and the sacraments (Rom. 3:2; 9:4) to the church as to His bride. Therefore, the whole office belongs to the church (Eph. 4:12; 1 Cor. 3:21), and the pastors are called ministers of the church (1 Cor. 3:5)" (*Exegesis Confessionis Augustanae,* p. 643).

Balduin: "The church is Christ's bride (John 3:29) and queen (Ps. 45:9; [Luther's translation of v. 10 is here quoted: *Gemahl,* wife]) and the matron of the house (Ps. 68:13; [Luther's translation]). As, therefore, the master of the house gives to his bride the keys, so Christ, the Lord of the house, namely, of the church, has given the keys to the church, His bride, who entrusts them to her servants, who are called stewards or managers of the mysteries of God" (*Tractatus de casibus conscientiae,* p. 1104).

John Gerhard: "In Matt. 16:19 the keys of the kingdom of heaven were promised to all apostles, indeed, to the whole church, personally by Peter, and they should be used [by it] for loosing and binding, that is, for forgiving and retaining sins; for so this promise is explained in Matt. 18:18. But here (John 20:23) the keys of the church are actually conferred on the apostles by granting them the power to forgive and retain sins. This we are to consider thus: The church is the house of God (1 Tim. 3:15; Heb. 3:6). The Lord of the house is Christ, the Son of God (Heb. 3:6). He also is its chief cornerstone (Ps. 118:22; Matt. 21:42; Mark 12:10), 'in whom the whole building, being joined together, grows into a holy temple in the Lord' (Eph. 2:21). The family members in this house are all believers who have been 'built on the foundation of the apostles and prophets' (v. 20).

"In this house there are stored up all treasures and gifts that Christ has merited by His precious suffering and death, as, for example, divine grace, forgiveness of sins, righteousness, the gift of the Holy Spirit, and eternal life. Hence Irenaeus calls the church in the third book 'Against the Heretics,' ch. 4, 'the right jewel-room of all gracious gifts' [*dives depositarium omnium gratiarum et charismatum*]. The matron of this house is also the church, Christ's beloved bride (Ps. 68:13): 'The matron divides the spoils' [Luther's translation], namely, those that Christ the Victor has wrested from His enemies.

"Nor dare we regard it as a contradiction that the church is called the house of God and at the same time the matron of the house, for this is done in a twofold relation. The church is the house because of the divine indwelling; it is the matron of the house because of its administration [of the keys] and of God's love. For as a matron receives the keys, by which she as a diligent and faithful manager should open and close the [stores of] good and other family necessities, so Christ has given His church the keys as His bride, who is to use them for remitting and retaining sins, indeed, to open and close the kingdom of heaven. The stewards or managers who are called by the heavenly Lord of the house to administer the keys in the name of the church or matron of the house are the ministers of the church (1 Cor. 4:1)" (*Harmonia hist. evang.,* last part, c. VIII, p. 426. 6).

The same: "Bellarmine, in his first book 'Concerning the Clergy,' (ch. 7) objects first: 'Peter received the keys in the person of the church, because he received them for the benefit and use of the whole church, and since he could not himself use them alone, he was to leave them to his successors and all bishops and priests.' To this I reply: We admit that Peter received the keys for the benefit and use of the church and to have them in common with other bishops and presbyters. But we deny that this is to be understood exclusively, as though the keys were given only to Peter and the bishops and not to the whole church. For as Peter confessed Christ in the person of the church not only because his confession redounded to the benefit of the whole church but also because in the confession of Peter the church itself confessed, so the keys of the kingdom of heaven were given to Peter in the person of the church not only because they were given to him for the benefit and use of the whole church but also because the church received them in the person of Peter, in order that it should administer them itself as in other matters designated by the term 'office of the keys,' so also in electing and calling capable ministers of the Word.

"John Ferus writes in his exposition of Matt. 16:19: 'The church has the keys as a matron and bride, but Peter has them as a servant, not as a master.' Thus our interpretation is clearly proved by the circumstances of the text and from Matt. 18:18. To this Bellarmine objects in the second place: 'To the church the power is promised to loose and bind, but this is done by the prelates, not by the remaining multitude. It is indeed said truthfully that the church binds and looses because its prelates bind and loose, just as it is said of a man that he speaks and sees, though it is only the tongue that speaks and the eye that sees.' ... We reverse the figure of Bellarmine thus: As a man speaks with the tongue and sees with the eye as by the natural means that are moved by the soul, for which reason speech and vision are ascribed to a man as the principal cause or the 'principle which' but to the tongue and the eye as the instrumental causes or the 'principle by which,' so the church elects and appoints the ministers by the elders, who do not act according to their own will and private authority but do all things in the name of the church, so that the church acts principally, while the elders act instrumentally; hence the called ministers are denominated servants not of the elders but of the church" (*Loci theologici,* "De ministerio ecclesiae," p. 87).

Dannhauer: "The church is a holy communion (2) through the immediate and habitual [inherent in its essence] possession of the ecclesiastical rights and offices. For the church is first the bride of Christ that divides the spoils (Ps. 68:13) and the matron that bears the keys, to whom through Peter the keys are given in order that [with them] he might not only faithfully provide for the welfare of the church but also act in place of the church, into whose hand after the death of Peter the keys are again returned. In it that power is rooted and ceaselessly perpetuated when pastors die or turn into wolves or when the sons of Levi defile themselves" (*Hodosophiae phaen.* 1, p. 79).

The same: "Though in one man the gifts of the church might be preserved, nevertheless, one man cannot constitute the church, although two or three suffice to make a congregation" (ibid., 2, p. 61).

Quenstedt: "To whom the keys of the kingdom of heaven have been given by Christ Himself, he has the right to call ministers of the church; for by the keys that church power is meant of which the right of calling and appointing ministers of the church is a part. Now, however, the keys of the kingdom of heaven have been conferred by Christ on the whole church according to the passages quoted. Therefore the church has the right to appoint the ministers of the church. . . . The church is called the royal priesthood (1 Peter 2:9) to which the Savior has entrusted, as to His bride and matron (John 3:29), the treasure of His Word and the sacraments, and on which He has conferred also the keys of the kingdom of heaven (Matt. 16:19; 18:18)." (*Theologia didactico-polemica,* part IV, 12. 2, pp. 402–03).

John Meisner: "Though that power to bind and loose has been granted in one place by way of promise only to Peter (Matt. 16:19), in another to all apostles at the same time (John 20:23), nevertheless, the exercise of this power, in view of the fact that it is said of the one [excommunicated] that he is to be regarded as a heathen man (we call this the greater ban), is granted especially to the congregation (Matt. 18), inasmuch as it is placed in opposition to one or more ministers of the church on account of its more reliable verdict, which indeed in its totality has the rights of its bridegroom basically [*radicaliter*] but exercises them through the ministry" (*Exercitationes theol. in ev. Matth. Viteb.,* 1664; on chap. 18).

The witness of the ancient church regarding this doctrine is found already in the testimonies of our church teachers, but the following may be quoted in addition.

Ignatius: "It behooves you as a church of God to elect a deacon by vote in order that he may there administer the ambassadorship of God" (*Ep. ad Philadelphenses,* 15).

Irenaeus: "Where the church is, there also is the Spirit; and where the Spirit of God is, there also is the church and all grace" (*Adversus haereses* 1.5).

Tertullian: "We err if we think that what is not permitted to the priests is permitted to the laity. Are not also we laymen priests? It is written: 'He has made us kings and priests before God.' The church has authoritatively established the distinction between rank [clergy] and congregation, and by the assembly of ranking persons the rank itself gained higher honor. Hence, wherever there is no assembly of members of the ecclesiastical rank, you administer the Lord's Supper and baptize and are to yourself alone a priest. Wherever there are three, there is the church, though they are only laymen; for everyone lives to himself, and God is not a respecter of persons" (*Exhort. ad castit.* 5).

Firmilianus: "Therefore the power to forgive sins is granted to the apostles and the churches that those founded who were sent by Christ" (*Ep.* 75).

Augustine: "When He said to him (Peter): 'I will give you the keys of the kingdom of heaven,' etc., He designated the whole church. . . . The church, founded by Peter, received of Him through Peter the keys of the kingdom of heaven, for what the church is properly on Christ, that Peter is figuratively on the rock; by rock Christ is symbolized, by Peter the church" (*De doctrina Christiana* 1.18).

The same: "Not one man but the whole church has received the keys. Therefore also the preferring [excellentia] of Peter is praised because he symbolizes the universal and one church" (*De diversis,* par. 108).

Thesis V

Though the true church in the proper sense of the term is essentially [according to its true nature] invisible, its existence can nevertheless be definitely recognized, namely, by the marks of the pure preaching of God's Word and the administration of the sacraments according to Christ's institution.

1. Scripture Proof

Holy Scripture tells us: "The kingdom of God (that is, the church) is as if a man should scatter seed on the ground, and should sleep by night and rise by day, and the seed should sprout and grow, he himself does not know how" (Mark 4:26–27). Scripture also tells us what the seed is, when it says: "The sower sows the Word" (v. 14). Hence, according to Scripture it is the Word of God from which the members of the church or, as Scripture puts it, "the sons of the kingdom" (Matt. 13:38) grow forth and are begotten. At the same time God in Scripture gives us the precious promise: "For as the rain comes down, and the snow from heaven, and do not return there, but water the earth, and make it bring forth and bud, that it may give seed to the sower and bread to the eater, so shall My Word be that goes forth from My mouth; it shall not return to Me void, but it shall accomplish what I please, and it shall prosper in the thing for which I sent it" (Is. 55:10–11).

From this we learn that the Word is not only the seed out of which alone the members of the church are born, but also that out of which at all times most surely, wherever this heavenly seed is sown, some "sons of the kingdom" grow forth, "he himself does not know how," according to the divine, unfailing, and infallible promise. Hence, wherever this seed is sown, we indeed do not see the church, but there we have an infallible mark that here is the church, a little flock of true believers and saints in Christ Jesus, a little congregation of children of God.

According to Scripture the sacred sacraments, in addition to the divine Word, are the means by which the church, the holy congregation of God, is to be established, gathered, preserved, and spread; for according to Matt. 28:18–20 and Mark 16:15–16 the Lord gave to His chosen apostles the command and promise: "All authority has been given to Me in heaven and on earth. Go therefore and make disciples of all nations, baptizing them in the name of the Father and of the Son and of the Holy Spirit, teaching them to observe all things that I have commanded you." And: "Go into all the world and preach the Gospel to every creature. He who believes and is baptized will be saved; but he who does not believe will be condemned." And: "Lo, I am with you always, even to the end of the age."

Hence, wherever, along with the divine Word, the sacrament of Holy Baptism is administered, there the invisible gates of the church are opened; there people will be found who believe and are saved; there the Lord is graciously present; there we have an infallible mark of the church's existence; there we must joyously exclaim: "Surely the Lord is in this place, and I did not know it. How sacred [Luther's translation] is this place! This is none other than the house of God, and this is the gate of heaven!" (Gen. 28:16–17). Scripture tells us the same also of the Lord's Supper, for so we read (1 Cor. 10:17): "We being many are one bread and one body, for we are all partakers of that one bread." Again (1 Cor. 12:13): "By one Spirit we were all baptized into one body . . . and have all been made to drink [Luther: *getränket,* that is, communed] into one Spirit" [one spiritual communion; Luther's translation]. Wherever, therefore, the Word of God is preached and Holy Baptism and the Sacrament of the body and blood of Christ are administered, there are members of the body of Christ. There we must assume: Here is a holy Christian church.

2. Witnesses of the Church in Its Official Confessions

Augsburg Confession: "They also teach that there must be and remain at all times one holy Christian church, which is the congregation of all believers, among whom the Gospel is purely taught and the sacraments are administered according to the Gospel" (Art. VII; German text). The Confession here obviously speaks of the marks of the true church, properly so called, for it says expressly: "which is the congregation of all believers." Of this, among other things, also J. Benedict Carpzov reminds us in his introduction to the Symbolical Books of the Evangelical Lutheran Church, where he writes: "The church is considered in a twofold relation, either as it exists principally and properly according to its intrinsic nature and its fellowship of true faith and pure love, or as it exists according to its outward assembly, namely, as a group of good and evil [persons] who are gathered together. In Article VII [of the Augsburg Confession] the church is considered according to the first mode, as this is further explained in the Apology" (Art. VII, VIII, par. 1–22; German text, *Triglot,* pp. 226–34. J. Benedict Carpzov, *Isagoge in libros ecclesiarum luth. symbolicos* [Leipzig, 1675, 1699], p. 300).

Apology: "The Christian church consists not only in the fellowship of outward signs but above all in the inward fellowship of eternal gifts in the heart as the Holy Spirit, faith, [and] the fear and love of God. Nevertheless this church has also its outward marks by which it can be recognized, namely, where God's Word is found pure and where the sacraments are administered according to it; there surely is the church; there are Christians, and this church alone is called in Scripture the body of Christ" (Art. VII, VIII, par. 5; German text). "So also Paul explains in Eph. 5:25ff. what the church is, and he adds also the outward marks, namely, the Gospel and the sacraments; for he writes: 'Christ also loved the church and gave Himself for it, that He might sanctify and cleanse it with the washing of water by the Word, that He might present it to Himself a glorious church,' etc." (ibid., par. 7).

The same: "And we do not speak of a fictitious church that can nowhere be found, but we say and know for sure that this church, in which saints live, is and remains truly on earth, namely, that some children of God are here and there in the whole world, in all kinds of kingdoms, islands, lands, cities, from the rising to the setting of the sun, who have rightly learned to know Christ and His Gospel, and we say that this church has these outward marks: the ministry of the Word, or the Gospel and the sacraments" (ibid., par. 20; German text, *Triglot,* p. 232).

The same: "Because the bishops do not want to tolerate us unless we surrender this doctrine that we have confessed, and since we owe it to God to confess and preserve this doctrine, we must renounce the bishops and rather obey God. We know that the Christian church is there where the Word of God is rightly taught" (Art. XIV, par. 25; German text, *Triglot,* p. 314).

The same: "To the right outward adornment of the church belong also the right preaching, the right use of the Sacrament, and the thorough training of the people to gather diligently and properly, to learn and to pray" (Art. XXIV [XII], par. 50–51; German text, *Triglot,* p. 400).

3. Witnesses of the Church in the Private Writings of Its Teachers

Luther: "You might say: If now the church is altogether in the Spirit and something altogether spiritual, then no one will be able to know where anywhere in the world a part of it may be found; that [indeed] would be a strange and unheard of thing. . . . And what about Christ's teaching that we should feed His lambs (John 21:16–17) and that of Paul that we should take heed to the church of God (Acts 20:28) and that of Peter that we should feed the flock of Christ (1 Peter 5:2) if the church can nowhere in the world be found in certain places? For who could preach to spirits? Or what spirit could preach to us? . . . So you ask: By what mark may I recognize the church? There must be a visible mark by which we are gathered as a congregation to hear God's Word. To this I reply that such marks are indeed necessary, and these we certainly have, namely, Baptism, the Bread [the Lord's Supper], and above all, the Gospel. These three are the signs and marks of Christians. Wherever you see that these exist, namely, Baptism, the Bread, and the Gospel, there, do not doubt, is the church, no matter where or among whom it may be.

"Christ desired that on these three signs all [Christians] agree, as St. Paul writes: 'One Lord, one faith, one baptism' (Eph. 4:5). Truly the Gospel is the one most sure and noble mark of the church, much surer than Baptism and the Bread [the Lord's Supper], because it [the church] is conceived, made, nurtured, borne, trained, fed, clothed, adorned, armed, and preserved only through the Gospel. In short, the church's whole life and being consists in the Word of God as Christ says: Man shall live 'by every word that proceeds from the mouth of God' (Matt. 4:4). These marks, and especially the Gospel, were, in my opinion, in olden times prefigured by Solomon when the ends of the staves by which the ark was borne were seen in the holy place before the oracle and were not seen from outside (1 Kings 8:8). By that the Holy Spirit meant to signify that only through the clear and public preaching of the Gospel may we know where the church and the mystery of the kingdom of heaven are to be found. For just as through the protruding ends of the staves, as through certain marks, it was known that the ark was in the holy of holies, though it was kept hidden, so also no one sees the church, but we must believe solely by the mark of the Word that it exists. This Word can nowhere be heard than alone in the church by the Holy Spirit" (From Luther's writing, "Revelation of the Antichrist," taken from Dan. 8 and directed against Ambrosius Catharinus in 1521, Halle edition, 18:1792, 1795, 1796).

The same: "Therefore all are called Christians and all have the Gospel, but only the fourth part of the seed turns out good and bears fruit. Such Christian people I have never seen on earth. . . . I cannot count the persons [the true Christians], but this I can say: Wherever the Gospel is, there also are Christians" (Exposition of Ex. 16:24, Halle edition, 3:1432).

The same: "We may learn that the church and congregation of God exists wherever the Word is heard and taught, be it in the midst of Turkey or the papacy or even in hell. For it is God's Word that creates the church; that is the master everywhere. Wherever that is heard, you must certainly believe, conclude, and declare: Surely here is God's house; here heaven stands open" (Exposition of Gen. 28:16, Halle edition, 2:626).

The same: "The Creed teaches us that there is and must remain a Christian holy people on earth till the end of the world; for that is an article of faith that can never cease until what it [the church] believes appears. So Christ has promised: 'I am with you always, even to the end of the age' (Matt. 28:20). But from what can and will a poor, fallible person know where such a Christian holy people exists in the world? . . .

"In the first place, this Christian holy people is to be recognized from the place where there is the holy Word of God. That, however, is not found everywhere in the same way, as St. Paul teaches in 1 Cor. 3:12–13. Some have it pure; others have it not so pure. Those who have it pure are such as build gold, silver, and precious stones on the foundation. Those who do not have it pure are such as build hay, straw, and stubble on the foundation, though they will be saved, yet as by fire. . . . But we [here] speak of the external Word, proclaimed by men orally, as by you and me; for Christ has left this [Word] here on earth as an outward sign by which we should recognize His church or His holy Christian people in the world. We also speak of the oral Word that is earnestly believed and publicly confessed before the world, as He says in Matt. 10:32–33 and Luke 12:8 [the original wrongly has Mark 8:9]: 'Whoever confesses me before men, him will I confess also before my Father and His angels' [Luther here quotes the passages freely].

"For there are many who know it [the Word] secretly, but do not want to confess it. Many have it, but they do not believe it or do according to it. There are a few who believe and keep it. So we read of the mystery of the seed in Matt. 13:3–9 that indeed three parts of the field receive and have it, but only the fourth part, the good, fertile ground, brings forth fruit abundantly. Wherever, then, you hear or see that the Word is preached, believed, confessed, and lived, there, do not doubt, certainly exists a true *ecclesia sancta catholica,* that is, a holy Christian people (1 Peter 2:9), even if there are only a few. For God's Word does not return to Him void (Is. 55:11) but must claim at least one-fourth of the ground. Even if there were no other mark than this, that would suffice to show that here must be a Christian holy people. For God's Word can never be without God's people, nor can God's people ever be without God's Word.

"For who otherwise would preach or hear the preaching if there were no people of God? And what would or could God's people believe if the Word of God would not be there? . . . We know how this chief part, this holy of holies, fosters, preserves, nourishes, strengthens, and protects the church. So also St. Augustine says: *Ecclesia verbo Dei generatur, alitur, nutritur, roboratur* (The church is begotten, fed, nourished, and made strong by the Word of God).

"Second, God's people or the Christian holy people is recognized by the holy sacrament of Baptism where it is rightly taught, believed, and used according to Christ's institution. For this also is a public mark and a precious, sacred means by which the people of God are sanctified. For it is the sanctifying washing of the new birth by the Holy Spirit (Titus 3:5), in which we are cleansed and washed by the Holy Spirit from sin and death as in the pure, holy blood of the Lamb of God. Where you see this mark, there, be assured, must certainly be the church or the Christian holy people.

"Third, God's people, or the Christian holy people, are recognized by the holy Sacrament of the Altar wherever it is administered, believed, and received according to Christ's institution. This also is a precious, holy means left by Christ on earth by which His people can be known and by which also it might exercise itself and publicly confess that it is Christian, just as it does this by the Word and Baptism.... For what was said above of the [divine] Word, namely, that wherever there is God's Word, there also is the church, must be said also of Baptism and the Sacrament [the Lord's Supper], namely, that there must be God's people, and vice versa. For such holy things no one has, gives, exercises, or confesses than only God's people, although some false, unbelieving persons dwell among them in secret. The church, or God's people, does not tolerate the manifest [sinners] in its midst, but it reproves and corrects them, or if they harden themselves, it casts them out of the sanctuary by excommunication and regards them as heathen (Matt. 18:17).

"Fourth, God's people or the holy Christian [church] is recognized by the keys, which it uses publicly, that is, as Christ commands (Matt. 18:15–16), [namely], that if a Christian sins, he should be reproved, and if he refuses to make amends, he should be bound and excommunicated; but if he repents, he should be absolved. Such are the keys.... If, then, you see that sin is forgiven or punished [by excommunication] in some cases, be it publicly or privately, there, be assured, is God's people. For wherever God's people is not, there also are not the keys; and where the keys are not, there also God's people is not. For Christ has left them here on earth that they should be a public mark and sacred means by which the Holy Spirit (procured by Christ's death) again sanctifies the fallen sinners, and the Christians confess that under Christ they are a holy people in this world. But those who refuse to repent and be sanctified should be cast out from this holy people, that is, they should be bound and banned by the keys, as this will be done with the impenitent Antinomians [who taught that the Law should not be preached to Christians]....

"Fifth, the church is outwardly recognized by the fact that it calls and ordains ministers of the Word, or that it has offices that it should fill.... If, then, you see that, you should be sure that there is God's church and a Christian holy people....

"Sixth, God's people is outwardly recognized by public prayer to God as well as by praise and thanksgiving. Where, then, you hear that a congregation prays the Lord's Prayer and teaches [its children] to pray and sing psalms and spiritual songs according to God's Word and the true [Christian] faith, and that it inculcates the Creed, the Ten Commandments, and the [whole] Catechism publicly, there, be assured, is the holy Christian people of God....

"Seventh, the holy Christian people is outwardly recognized by the chastening affliction of the holy cross" (Luther's tract on councils and churches of 1535, Halle edition, 16:2784ff.).

The same: "But the fact that they [the papists] say: 'Everything that is ordained and instituted by the church is ordained and instituted by God, whose Spirit the church has; hence the priests cannot be of the devil'—that is spoken without cause or reason. Who will show us this church, since it is hidden in the Spirit and can only be believed? For so we confess: 'I believe a holy Christian church. ...' A true Christian knows that the church does not ordain or institute anything apart from the Word of God, and whatever church does this is no church, except in name only, as Jesus says (John 10:27): 'My sheep hear My voice.' 'They will by no means follow a stranger' [v. 5]. It is not the Word of God just because the church says so, but because the Word of God is preached, by that the church comes into existence. The church does not make the Word, but it is created by the Word.

"God's Word is a reliable mark by which we can recognize where the church is, as Paul writes (1 Cor. 14:24–25): 'If all prophesy, and an unbeliever or an uninformed person comes in, he is convinced by all, he is judged by all. And thus the secrets of his heart are revealed; and so, falling down on his face, he will worship God and report that God is truly among you.' This the unbeliever does because he hears them [the Christians] prophesy. Not the church but the Word of God moves him; by it he is overcome and convicted.... For he (Paul) does not say that the unbeliever falls down on his face because he hears them prophesy but because God is truly with them. But how could he know that? So also with us, how can we know where the church is, unless we hear its prophecies and the witness of the Holy Spirit? It is certain that the church, [namely,] those in whom God truly dwells, prophesies [that is, preaches God's Word], but it is uncertain where the church is that can prophesy unless it does prophesy" ("Concerning the Abuse of the Mass," 1522, St. Louis edition, 19:1080–81).

We here quote several witnesses who show that also the ancient church regarded the Word and sacraments as the marks by which the true church can be recognized.

Tertullian thus writes: "Those are the true churches that firmly hold what they received of the apostles and what the apostles received of Christ and what Christ received of God. But other churches that were not founded by the apostles, if they agree to the same faith, are nevertheless to be regarded as no less apostolic because of their agreement in the doctrine" (*Lib. de praescript. adversus haeres.* 24).

Jerome: "The church does not consist of walls but in the truth of its teachings. The church is there, where there is the true faith" (on Ps. 133).

Chrysostom: "When you perceive an impious heresy, which is an army of Antichrist, standing in the holy place of the church, then let him who is in Judea flee into the mountains; that is to say, let him who is in Christendom turn to Holy Scripture. For the true Judea is Christendom, but the mountains are the Scriptures of the prophets and apostles. But why does the Lord command that then all Christians should turn to Scripture? ... Knowing full well that in the last days there will be great confusion, the Lord commands the Christians, who are true Christians and desire to obtain the firmness of the true faith, to seek refuge nowhere else than in Scripture. Otherwise, if they look to something else, they will be offended and be lost, for they will not recognize which is the church, and so they will succumb to the abomination of desolation that stands in the holy place" (*Homil. 49* [?] *operis imperf. in Matt.*).

Ambrose: "There is the church of God in which God reveals Himself and speaks with His servants" (*Lib. 2 de Jacob. et vita beata* 7).

The same: "Those do not have the heritage of Peter who do not have his faith" (*Lib. 1 de poenit.* 6).

Augustine: "There is a controversy between us and the Donatists concerning the place where the church exists. What, then, are we going to do? Shall we seek it in the words of Donatus or in the words of their Head, our Lord Jesus Christ? I judge that we should seek it in the words of Him who is the Truth and who knows His body best; for He knows who are His own" (*Lib. de unitate ecclesiae* 2).

The same: "Let us not hear it said: 'This I say' and 'That is what you say.' But let us hear it said: 'Thus says the Lord.' We have divine books about whose authority there is no controversy between us. Let us both [both parties] believe them; let us both [both parties] submit to them. Here let us look for the church; here let us resolve our controversy" (ibid., chap. 3).

The same: "When you seek Him who first sought you, and when you have become His sheep, and you hear the voice of your Shepherd and follow Him, then consider what He reveals to you about Himself and what He reveals to you about His (spiritual) body, in order that you may not fall into error regarding Him nor regarding His church, so that no one may tell you: 'That is Christ,' who is not Christ, or 'That is the church,' which is not the church. Listen only to the voice of the Shepherd, [for] He reveals Himself to you; follow His voice. He will reveal to you also the church, in order that no one may deceive you by the name of the church" (on Ps. 69).

Thesis VI

In an improper sense Scripture also calls the visible aggregate of all the called, that is, of all who confess and adhere to the proclaimed Word and use the holy sacraments, which consists of good and evil [persons], "church" (the universal [catholic] church); so also it calls its several divisions, that is, the congregations that are found here and there, in which the Word of God is preached and the holy sacraments are administered, "churches" (Partikularkirchen [particular or individual churches]). This it does especially because in this visible assembly the invisible, true, and properly so-called church of believers, saints, and children of God is hidden; outside this assembly of the called no elect are to be looked for [anywhere].

1. Scripture Proof

When the Lord says: "The kingdom of heaven is like a dragnet that was cast into a sea and gathered some of every kind, which, when it was full, they drew to shore; and they sat down and gathered the good into vessels, but threw the bad away" (Matt. 13:47–48); again: "The kingdom of heaven shall be likened to ten virgins who took their lamps and went out to meet the bridegroom. Now five of them were wise, and five were foolish" (Matt. 25:1–2); again: "The kingdom of heaven is like a certain king who arranged a marriage for his son. . . . But when the king came in to see the guests, he saw a man there who did not have on a wedding garment" (Matt. 22:2, 11), He clearly shows by the little word "like" that the kingdom of heaven or the church in its proper sense does not indeed consist of good and evil or of true believers and hypocrites but rather that the church in this world appears like a net full of good and bad fish or an assembly of wise and foolish virgins or a wedding hall full of guests with fine wedding garments and without them. Hence the visible church, which embraces both good and evil, true and hypocritical Christians, genuine believers and such as err in the faith, is given and deserves the name "church" only in an improper, synecdochic sense, namely, inasmuch as the totality bears the honorable name [church] only because of a part, which alone properly deserves this name. Therefore, the whole visible aggregate of all the called bears the name "universal church," and the individual divisions of this visible aggregate bear the name "churches" or "particular churches" only because of the true members of the true church who are found in this assembly, even if it were only the baptized infants.

But that the name "church" is also applied to the entire visible assembly that has the Word and the sacraments, not by mistake but rightly, indeed, that it should bear this name, Holy Scripture too shows us; for though it clearly teaches that only true believers are true members of the church, nevertheless it applies the name "church" also to the mixed, visible assembly. Thus Scripture commands: "Tell it to the church" (Matt. 18:17), where evidently it speaks of a visible particular [individual] congregation. So also the holy apostle Paul calls those who were called in Galatia and in Corinth "congregations" [Luther's translation] or churches. In fact, in the latter case he calls them "the church of God, them that are sanctified in Christ Jesus, the called saints" [Luther's translation]. Despite this, the holy apostle attests that most of the Galatians [church members] had lost Christ and that the church at Corinth had many members who had fallen into grievous sins and had besmirched themselves in both doctrine and life.

2. Witnesses of the Church in Its Official Confessions

Augsburg Confession: "Although the Christian church properly is nothing else than the assembly of all believers and saints, nevertheless, since in this life many false Christians and hypocrites are [in it and] even manifest sinners remain among the pious, nevertheless," etc. (Art. VIII). Since our Confession here declares that the church in its proper sense is only the congregation of saints, it attests at the same time that a communion that embraces good and evil [persons] bears the name "church" only in an improper sense.

Apology: "Even the decree of Gratian clearly explains the gloss that the word 'church' is to be taken large [in its wide sense] and embraces both evil and good; likewise, that the wicked are in the church only in name, not in fact; but the good are in it both in name and in fact.... Although, then, the wicked and the ungodly hypocrites have fellowship with the true church in outward rites, titles, and offices, nevertheless, when we wish to declare what the church is properly, we must say that the church is called the body of Christ and not only has fellowship in outward signs but has the gifts [of Christ] in the heart, [namely,] the Holy Ghost and faith" (Art. VII, VIII [IV], par. 11ff.; German text, *Triglot,* pp. 228ff.).

The same: "And when Christ says: 'The kingdom of heaven is like a dragnet' [Matt. 13:47], likewise like 'ten virgins' [Matt. 25:1], He does not desire that there should be wicked [persons] in the church, but He teaches how the church appears in this world. Therefore, He says that it [the church] is like this, etc. That is to say, as in a catch of fish the good and evil lie together pell-mell, so here on earth the [true] church is hidden among the large multitude or assembly of the wicked" (ibid., par. 19; German text, *Triglot,* p. 232).[3]

The same: "And we also confess that, as long as this life endures on earth, there are many hypocrites and wicked [persons] in the church among the true Christians, who also are members of the church according to the outward signs" (ibid., par. 28; German text, *Triglot,* p. 236).

Formula of Concord: Here there is rejected as an erroneous doctrine of the Anabaptists [the teaching] that "there is no Christian congregation [church] in which sinners are still found" (Epitome, Art. XII, par. 7; *Triglot,* p. 838; Thorough Declaration, XII, par. 5; *Triglot,* p. 1099).

3. Witnesses of the Church in the Private Writings of Its Teachers

Luther: "This passage (Joel 3:17 [the original has 3:22]) embraces an article of our Christian faith in which we confess and say: 'I believe [in] a holy Christian church, the communion of saints'; for he says that 'then Jerusalem shall be holy, and no aliens shall ever pass through her again.' This article the papists have obscured altogether; indeed, they interred and buried it just as that of the Gospel and the forgiveness of sins. For how can they teach what the holy Christian church is, since they say that a person must doubt whether or not he is in divine grace? . . .

"But in order that this article [concerning the church] might be understood better and more clearly, the reader must remember that Scripture speaks of the church in a twofold way. For in the first place it in a general way calls [those] church who publicly confess the same doctrine and administer the same sacraments, though there are mingled with them many hypocrites and wicked [persons], as Christ says: 'For many are called, but few chosen' (Matt. 20:16); again: 'He who believes and is baptized will be saved; but he who does not believe will be condemned' (Mark 16:16). The last part of this sentence shows that some are baptized and yet do not believe. For this reason they are condemned, as the parable of the wedding feast also teaches (Matt. 22:11–14). For all the guests were indeed called, but not all had on a wedding garment; hence they were cast out into outer darkness.

"But also the parables of the net of fish and of the good seed and the tares (Matt. 13:24–30, 47–50) depict and present to us such a church in which there are good and evil [persons], and there always are more evil than good persons as the passage attests: 'For many are called, but few are chosen' (Matt. 22:14). Nevertheless in this mixed multitude there are always some elect, that is, such as receive and hold God's Word in true faith and [so] receive the Holy Spirit, for the ministry of the Word is never without benefit and fruit. This true, pure little flock Scripture calls 'the church'; it also properly deserves the epithet 'holy' " ("Exposition of the Prophet Joel," 3:17, 1545, St. Louis edition, 6:1628–29).

The same: "Jerome here raises an important question: 'Why does St. Paul classify the Galatians as a Christian congregation or church since they were no longer a Christian congregation or church?' For St. Paul (as Jerome says) writes to the Galatians that they had fallen from Christ and grace and had again turned to Moses and the Law. To this I reply that St. Paul here speaks according to the figure of speech called synecdoche,[4] which in Scripture is used quite commonly. Thus he writes to the Corinthians that he rejoices with them over the grace of God given to them by Jesus Christ, [namely,] that by Him they were enriched "in all utterance and all knowledge" (1 Cor. 1:4–5). Yet many of them were misled by false teachers and no longer believed that there is a resurrection of the dead. Just so we today call the Roman church and all bishoprics 'holy,' though they also have been misled and their ministers have become godless. For our Lord God rules in the midst of His enemies (Ps. 110:2) and the Antichrist sits in the temple of God (2 Thess. 2:4); indeed, Satan is found in the midst of the children of God (Job 1:6).

"Therefore, though the church or Christendom is in the midst of a crooked and perverse generation, as St. Paul says (Phil. 2:15), and though it is in the midst of wolves and murderers, that is, in the midst of its spiritual enemies and tyrants, it nevertheless is and remains a holy Christendom, a congregation and church of Christ. Although Rome is worse than Sodom and Gomorrah, there are and remain in this city Holy Baptism, the Sacrament [the Lord's Supper], the Word and text of the Gospel, Holy Scripture, the office and name of Christ and of God. He who has it, possesses it; but he who does not have it, is not excused; for the treasure is present there. . . .

"Hence, though the Galatians were misled, they nevertheless retained Baptism, God's Word, and the name of Christ so that there were among them some believers who did not apostatize from the doctrine of St. Paul. These purely retained and rightly used the Word and the sacraments so that they were not defiled and desecrated by the others who had become apostates. . . .

"Therefore, the church is everywhere holy, even in places where it is ruled by enthusiasts [*Schwärmer:* visionaries departing from God's Word] and factious spirits [*Rottengeister:* false teachers causing schisms in the church], as long as they do not deny the Word and the sacraments altogether; for those who reject these things altogether are no longer a church. But where the Word and sacraments remain essentially, there also remains a holy church. That is true even if Antichrist rules there, for he sits not in a synagogue of Satan nor in a pigsty nor among crass infidels but in the most noble and holy place, namely, in the temple of God (2 Thess. 2:4). This shows definitely and clearly that the temple of God must be and remain even if it is ruled by spiritual tyrants who have the upper hand and are raging in it. Everywhere, even among such tyrants, there are found such as rightly believe.

"Hence, the answer to the question [of Jerome] is readily given: The church is found everywhere in the whole world wherever the Gospel and the sacraments are preserved. But the Jews, Turks, enthusiasts, factious spirits, and heretics are not the church; they rather deny and destroy these things" [the Gospel and the sacraments] ("Exposition of St. Paul's Letter to the Galatians," 1:2, 1535, Halle edition, 8:1588).

The same: "When we speak of its outward fellowship, the church on earth is the assembly that hears, believes, and confesses the true doctrine of the Gospel of Christ and has the Holy Spirit, who sanctifies it and works in it by the Word and the sacraments. In it there are nevertheless some false Christians and hypocrites, who still unanimously hold the same doctrine and enjoy the same fellowship of the sacraments and other official offices of the church" (*Church Postil: Gospel Portion,* "On the 20th Sunday After Trinity," St. Louis edition, 11:1759).

Aegidius Hunnius: "The papists now say: The heretics[5] are cut off from the church; how then can they be in it? The fact that they are in the visible church is clear from the fact that the seat of Antichrist has been placed by the apostle (2 Thess. 2:4) in the temple of the church. Again we are told: 'There must also be factions among you' (1 Cor. 11:19). Therefore, the heretics are in the church but not of the church (1 John 2:19), just as Christ says that His elect are in the world but not of the world (John 17:11, 14, 16). The situation of the Jews, Mohammedans, and others who absolutely refuse to confess the Christian religion is quite different. Though these may live among Christians, they are not in the church.

"The reason for this difference lies in the sacrament of initiation, Holy Baptism, and the confession connected with it. Baptism effects that the heretics are still in the visible assembly of the called. But others like the heathen who have not been baptized are by no means in the church but outside of it because they have never been admitted into it by the sacrament of initiation nor have they confessed Christ. Finally, since God, according to Is. 1:3 and Jer. 2:11–12, calls His wicked and idolatrous people His people just the same, let the papists consider and take heed whether they rightly and theologically [in harmony with Scripture] put the heretics outside the visible church and whether they thereby do not accuse the Lord in the quoted prophetic witnesses of falsehood" (*Proposition. de praecip. christ. rel. capp.,* pp. 358ff.).

The same: "The church is the assembly of people who in the name of the Holy Trinity have been baptized into Christ's death, who accept the doctrine of Christ and the prophets and apostles,

82

and who use the sacraments instituted by Christ. It is considered either according to its election or its call. Considered according to its election, and so called invisible, it is the assembly of all those who apprehend Christ with one and the same true faith, rooted in the divine Word, and who obtain the end of their faith, even life everlasting. Considered according to its call, the church is visible and is divided into such as are pure and such as are corrupt. Those are pure that have the pure proclamation of the Word and the right use of the sacraments; those are corrupt in which these are lacking. In each of the two there is the universal Christian church. Wherever, therefore, the one or the other exists and is recognized, there exists also and must be recognized the true Christian church" (ibid., p. 371).

Gerhard: "We also say the same thing, namely, that according to the figure of speech known as synecdoche, there is ascribed to the whole [visible] church what properly belongs only to a part. . . . Scripture speaks of the church in various ways, first, in general and synecdochically, designating by this name [church] the whole multitude of the called; second, in a strict, proper, and primary sense, designating only the elect or saints in this assembly" (*Loci theologici,* "De ecclesia," par. 65).

The same: "Of the church of the Ephesians and of every particular [individual] church it can be said that it is a house of God, [namely,] on account of the true believers and elect who are in it and in whom God dwells with His grace. In that case there is ascribed to the whole particular church or the whole assembly of the called by way of a synecdoche what properly belongs only to some in it" (ibid., par. 79).

The same: "The church is called catholic or universal primarily and above all in view of the elect and saints, inasmuch as it embraces all true believers in Christ, the whole mystic spiritual body whose head is Christ. And this is the genuine and proper meaning of this word [church]. . . . But since the elect and true believers are not outside the assembly of the called but in the assembly of the called, with whom hypocrites are mingled, therefore, in a secondary sense also the visible church of the called is denominated the catholic or universal [church]" (ibid., par. 151).

The same: "In this treatise we use the term 'church,' in its proper and strict sense, of the assembly of saints and true believers as the

Augsburg Confession defines it in Art. VII. . . . Nevertheless, because there are joined to the saints and true believers in the church such as are not saints, [namely, those] who lack the inward [spiritual] new birth and regeneration yet are united with the communion of saints in this life according to the outward fellowship (which consists in the confession of faith and the use of the sacraments), therefore, it happens that at times the [term] church is used in a more general sense for the whole multitude of the called. To this [multitude] those honorable titles that Scripture ascribes to the church [proper] belong only by way of the figure of speech known as synecdoche, which Scripture uses because of the elect who are in this assembly. This is just as though someone would ascribe to a city extraordinary praise on account of the upright and well-mannered citizens, with whom however also wicked and perverse [citizens] are mingled" (ibid., par. 15).

Zeämann: "The universal visible church is the whole assembly of called Christians. . . . But since the true catholic church now in the New Testament is spread throughout the world in all particular churches, found here and there, and it is not to be looked for outside the assembly of the called, therefore, at times by the [term] 'catholic church' there is designated in a wider sense the whole assembly of Christians, called by the Word and baptized, throughout the world, and so all Christendom or the entire church of the New Testament. By the expression 'catholic' it is distinguished not only from the church of the Old Testament (which ordinarily was the assembly of only the Jewish people) but also from all particular churches of which the catholic church is composed. . . . However, when there is designated by the [expression] 'catholic church' the whole visible assembly of called Christians and so the whole building, composed of particular churches, this is done synecdochically because of its nobler members, namely, the orthodox, elect Christians who are in the visible church" (*Eröffnung des unkatholischen Pabsttums,* p. 230).

Dannhauer: "They (the hypocrites) indeed are not members of the invisible church nor of the true visible church, but they do belong to the visible church inasmuch as they with the other members constitute a unit [*ein Ganzes*]. The tares as such are not a part of the field of wheat, yet they are a part of the field inasmuch as they constitute one field consisting of wheat and tares" (*Hodoso-phiae phaen.* 2, p. 61).

The same: "Either the bishop presiding over the congregation excommunicates all these (churches) or a stranger who is separated from this particular church. The presiding bishop dare not eradicate the tares with the wheat, for there is no visible particular church in which there is not hidden also the invisible. The stranger dare not do this because ordinarily he has no jurisdiction over the congregation that does not belong to him. None of them dare attempt what is physically impossible, namely, to cast a communion out of its very communion" (*Christeid.,* p. 97).

J. B. Carpzov: "The Augsburg Confession does not use the term 'church' in the wider sense in which it embraces both the chaff and the grain; it does not designate by the term 'church' all those who are baptized and are opposed to all heathen and nonbaptized [persons]. But it uses the term in its strict, proper, and original sense to designate the multitude of those who on earth are united with Christ as their Head and with one another by true faith and sincere love.... And this meaning is not impaired by the nonsaints and hypocrites in doctrine and morals who are mingled with the church. For an assembly consisting of hypocrites and true and sincere believers is something different from an assembly with which hypocrites are mingled.

"The church properly so called is not an assembly consisting of hypocrites and nonsaints, but it is an assembly with which hypocrites and nonsaints are mingled. This fact the Augsburg Confession carefully explains in the beginning of Art. VIII.... Hence, when an assembly composed of hypocrites and saints is called a church, this designation is merely synecdochic or figurative and denotes the saints who are found in the assembly. So also a pile of grain is called wheat even if most of it is chaff" (*Isagoge in libros eccl. luther. symbolicos,* pp. 305–06).

J. W. Baier: "Also the militant church is taken in a twofold sense; first, in a proper and narrow sense, for the communion of true believers and saints who by faith are implanted into Christ their Head, just as they, as living members, constitute with Him one spiritual body. In the second place, it is used improperly and by way of a synecdoche for the whole assembly of true believers and saints with which are mingled hypocrites and wicked [persons].... On account of the true believers this mixed assembly possesses what is called church" (*Compendium theologiae positivae* 3.13.2).

Here we append also some witnesses of the teachers of the ancient [Christian] church.

Augustine: "It is the way of Scripture to speak of a part as of the whole. Thus the apostle praises the Corinthians in the first parts of his epistle as though all were such as deserve praise, as were some. Afterwards in some places of the same letter he reproves them as though all were culpable, though only some were such. He who diligently considers this way of Scripture, which is frequently found in the whole Bible, will explain many things that are seemingly contradictory" (*Ep. 59 ad Paulin.*).

The same: "We confess that in the catholic [universal] church there are good as well as evil [persons], but as chaff and wheat" (*Tract.* 6 on John).

Fulgentius (of Ruspe, North Africa): "You must firmly hold and not doubt that the catholic [universal] church is God's threshing floor, which contains till the end of the world the chaff mixed together with the grain. This means that with the good there are mingled through participation in the sacraments also the evil" (*De fide ad Pet.* 43).

Gregory: "Now we are together, both good and evil, in the net of faith, just as different kinds of fish are together. But the shore will make manifest what the net of the church has drawn out [of the water].... The church now embraces both good and evil, nor does it select those that it wants to draw out, because it does not know whom to select" (*Hom. 11 et 24 in Evang.*).

Nicholas of Lyra: "The church does not consist of persons inasmuch as they have ecclesiastical or secular power and dignity, for many princes and priests, high and low, have proved themselves apostates. The church rather consists of persons in whom there is true knowledge and a right confession of the faith and the truth" (Commentary on Matt. 16:10).

Thesis VII

As visible congregations that still have the Word and the sacraments essentially according to God's Word bear the name "church" because of the true invisible church of sincere believers that is found in them, so also they possess the power [authority] that Christ has given to His whole church, on account of the true invisible church hidden in them, even if there were only two or three [believers].

1. Scripture Proof

Thus says the Lord: "Tell it to the church. But if he refuses even to hear the church, let him be to you like a heathen and a tax collector" (Matt. 18:17). It requires no proof that the Lord here speaks of a visible, particular church. But when the Lord immediately after these words continues: "Assuredly, I say to you, whatever you bind on earth will be bound in heaven, and whatever you loose on earth will be loosed in heaven" (v. 18), He thereby ascribes the keys of the kingdom of heaven or the church power [*Kirchengewalt*], which in Matt. 16:19 He had given by Peter to His whole holy church, also to every visible particular church [individual congregation]. But in order that no one might think that this great power was given only to large and populous congregations, He adds in vv. 19–20: "Again I say to you that if two of you agree on earth concerning anything that they ask, it will be done for them by My Father in heaven. For where two or three are gathered together in My name, I am there in the midst of them." Hence, if there were in any particular congregation even only two or three true believers, true children of God, true members of the spiritual body of Christ, then because of them that congregation would be a congregation of God and the rightful possessor of all rights and powers that Christ has procured for and given to His church.

87

2. Witnesses of the Church in Its Official Confessions

The *Apology* thus says: "That also we may not doubt that a Christian church, which is Christ's bride, is alive and exists on earth, though the horde of the wicked is more and larger, and that our Lord Christ here on earth daily works in the assembly that is called the church, forgiving sins, daily hearing prayers, daily comforting His own in their trials by His rich and strong consolation and always restoring them, there is placed in the consoling article of the Creed [the confession]: 'I believe [in] a catholic, universal Christian church' " (Art. VII, VIII, par. 9; German text, *Triglot*, p. 228). According to these words the Apology confesses that we can be sure that God works in the assembly, called the "church," though this assembly contains also many who are not saints, because we may and should believe that in this assemblage there is hidden a holy Christian church and that this church in its midst possesses Christ and His gifts.

Again the *Apology* declares: "And we also confess that as long as this life on earth endures, many hypocrites and wicked [persons] will be in the church among the true Christians, and that these also are members of the church so far as the outward signs are concerned. For they hold office in the church, preach, administer the sacraments, and bear the title and name of Christians. And the Sacrament [Lord's Supper], Baptism, etc., are not without efficacy or power because they are administered by unworthy or wicked [persons], for these are not there because of their own person but because of their call and because of Christ,[6] as He attests: 'He who hears you hears Me' (Luke 10:16)" (ibid., par. 28; German text, *Triglot,* p. 236). Whatever therefore those do in the church (whether they preach, administer the sacraments, elect and ordain ministers of the Word, etc.) who refuse to believe and so are not members of the [true] church and therefore have no right to administer the office of the keys, yet they do this as ministers or delegates of the church, that is, of the true believers.

Smalcald Articles: "And Christ says when speaking the words: 'Whatever you bind,' etc. (Matt. 18:18), in order to indicate to whom the keys have been given, namely, to the church: 'Where two or three are gathered together in My name,' etc. (Matt. 18:20)" (Of the

Power and Primacy of the Pope, par. 24; German text, *Triglot*, p. 510).

The same: "For wherever the church is, there also is the command to preach the Gospel; hence the churches must retain the power to call, elect, and ordain, and this power is a gift that the church has properly received from God and that cannot be wrested from it by any human tyranny, as St. Paul attests: 'When He ascended on high, He ... gave gifts to men' (Eph. 4:8). Here also belong the declarations of Christ that declare that the keys were given to the whole church and not [merely] to some persons as, for example: 'Where two or three are gathered together,' etc. Finally, this [truth] is confirmed also by the passage of Peter: 'You are ... a royal priesthood' (1 Peter 2:9). These words pertain properly to the true church, which, because it alone has the priesthood, must also have the power [right] to elect and ordain ministers of the church" (ibid., par. 67–69; German text, *Triglot*, p. 522).

3. Witnesses of the Church in the Private Writings of Its Teachers

Luther: "In Matt. 18:19–20 we read that even two or three, gathered in Christ's name, have the same power over all things as St. Peter and all [other] apostles. For the Lord Himself is there present, just as He says: 'If anyone loves Me, he will keep My Word; and My Father will love him, and We will come to him and make Our home with him' (John 14:23). Therefore it has happened that often one man who believed in Christ withstood a whole group, as did Paphnutius at the Nicene Council or as the prophets opposed the kings of Israel, priests, and all the people. In short, God does not want to be bound to a multitude, greatness, height, power, and whatever else is personable among people, but He wants to be only with those who love and keep His Word, even if they were mere stableboys. What does He care for the high, great, and mighty lords? He alone is the greatest, highest, and mightiest. . . .

"Here we have the Lord Himself, [ruling] over all angels and [other] creatures, who says that they should all have the same power, keys, and office, even two humble Christians gathered in His name. Of this Lord the pope and all devils shall not make a fool, liar, or drunkard, but we shall tread the pope under our feet and declare

89

that he is a horrible liar, blasphemer, and idolatrous demon, who under the name of St. Peter has appropriated the keys to himself alone, though Christ gave them to all alike and in common" ("Against the Papacy at Rome Instituted by the Devil," 1545, St. Louis edition, 17:1074–75).

The same: "That is and must remain our foundation and firm rock: Wherever the Gospel is preached, there must be a holy Christian church, and whoever doubts this might just as well doubt that the Gospel is the Word of God. But wherever there is a holy Christian church, there must be all sacraments, Christ Himself, and His Holy Spirit. If then we are to be a holy Christian church and are to possess the greatest and most necessary gifts [*Stücke*] as God's Word, Christ, the Spirit, faith, prayer, Baptism, the Sacrament [Lord's Supper], the office of the keys, and so forth, and are not to possess the least gift [*Stueck*], namely, the power and right to call some to the office [of the ministry] who are to serve us and give us the Word, Baptism, the Sacrament, forgiveness of sins (all of which are already present), what kind of church would that be? What would become of the Word of Christ, which says: 'Where two or three are gathered together in My name, I am there in the midst of them' (Matt. 18:20)? Or in v. 19: 'If two of you agree on earth concerning anything that they ask, it will be done for them by My Father in heaven'? If two or three have such power, how much more a whole church?" (Monograph against the private mass and holy orders, 1533, St. Louis edition, 19:1283).

The same: "We confess that under the papacy there are many Christian gifts [*Gutes*], indeed, every Christian gift that from there has come to us, for we confess that the papacy has the true Holy Bible, the true Baptism, the true Sacrament of the Altar, the true keys for the forgiveness of sins, the true ministry, the true Catechism as the Ten Commandments, the Creed, and the Lord's Prayer, just as the pope also confesses (though he condemns us as heretics) that we and all [other] heretics have the Holy Scriptures, Baptism, the office of the keys, the Catechism, etc. 'Oh, [Luther,] what a hypocrite you are now!' But why am I a hypocrite? I speak of what the pope and we have in common. In the same way he also acts the hypocrite with us and all [other] heretics in a gross way by saying what we have in common with him. I could act the hypocrite still more and yet it would not help me.[7]

90

"I say that the papacy has the true Christendom [the true Christian church, *Christenheit*], indeed, the true pick of Christendom and many great and pious saints. Should I stop acting the hypocrite? Listen to what St. Paul says in 2 Thess. 2:4: 'Antichrist sits as God in the temple of God.' If then the pope (as I truly believe) is the very Antichrist, he will not sit or rule in the stable of the devil but in the temple of God. No, indeed, he will not sit where there are only devils and infidels or where there is no Christ or Christendom, for since he is the Antichrist, he must sit in the midst of Christians. And if he should sit and rule there, he must have under himself Christians, for it says 'temple of God,' not a stone pile but holy Christendom (1 Cor. 3:7); there shall he rule. If therefore the papacy has Christendom [the Christian church, *die Christenheit*], then truly it [Christendom] must be Christ's body and member. But if it is His body, then it has the right Spirit, the Gospel, faith, the Sacrament [the Lord's Supper], the keys, the ministry, prayer, Holy Scripture, and all things that Christendom [*die Christenheit*] has. We too are still under the papacy and have these Christian gifts from it. But [Luther: for] he [the pope] persecutes us, curses us, excommunicates us, outlaws and burns us, kills us, and deals with us poor Christians as the real Antichrist is to treat Christians [*Christenheit*].

"But such Christians must be rightly baptized and be sincere members of Christ; otherwise they could not obtain the victory over Antichrist by martyrdom. We do not rave, as do the enthusiasts [*Rottengeister*], that we reject every gift that the pope possesses; for then we would reject also the Christian church [*die Christenheit*], the 'temple of God,' together with all blessings that it has obtained from Christ. But against this we contend that the pope does not want to remain with the gifts of Christendom [Christenheit] that he has received from the apostles, but he adds to them his own devilish additions and much more and does not use the gifts for the upbuilding of the temple of God but for its destruction, since he demands that his command and order should be regarded higher than the command of Christ. Nevertheless, despite this destruction Christ preserves His Christendom [*Christenheit*], just as He preserved Lot in Sodom and as St. Peter writes of this in 2 Peter 2:6–7.

"So then both must remain: By the working of the devil (2 Thess. 2:4, 9) Antichrist must sit in the temple of God; nevertheless, the temple of God must be and remain God's temple through Christ's [gracious] preservation. If the pope can tolerate and accept this my 'hypocrisy,' then certainly I will be his obedient son and a pious papist; that I gladly would be, and I would take back everything by which I have hurt his feelings. Therefore, the Anabaptists and enthusiasts err when they say that whatever the pope has is wrong, or because this and that happens under the papacy, we are bound to change it. It is just as though they want to prove themselves eager enemies of Antichrist, but they do not see that they greatly strengthen[8] him, while they greatly weaken Christendom [*Christenheit*] and deceive themselves. They ought to help us reject the abuse and additions [of the pope], but by that they would not obtain any special glory, since they see that they are not the first in this matter. Therefore they attack what no one else has attacked in order that they might be the first in doing it and claim the honor for it.

"But this honor must be turned into shame, for they attack the temple of God and miss the Antichrist who sits in it; they are like the blind people who search for water but put their hand into the fire.[9] Indeed, they do as one brother did to another in the Thuringian Forest. They walked together through the woods when suddenly a bear attacked them and threw one of them under his body. The other wanted to help his brother, stabbed at the bear, but missed him and wretchedly pierced the brother who was under the bear.

"Just so the enthusiasts do. They should help the poor Christians [*Christenheit*] whom the pope still has in his power and tortures and who bitterly oppose the pope, but in this they fail and murder the poor Christians [*Christenheit*] under the pope all the more miserably. For if they would leave intact Baptism and the Sacrament [the Lord's Supper], the souls of the Christians under the pope might yet escape and be saved, as it happened in the past. But since now the sacraments are taken from them, they undoubtedly will be lost, since also Christ Himself is taken away with them [the sacraments]. My dear friend, that is not the way to attack the pope, because Christ's saints are under him. It requires a careful, modest spirit to let stand God's temple and to oppose the additions by which he [the pope] destroys God's temple" ("Letter to Two Ministers Concerning Anabaptism," 1528, St. Louis edition, 17:2190–93).

The same: "Here no doubt they might ask us: 'Why do you describe us as so very atrocious, [that is,] as a new and apostate church despite the fact that we retain Baptism, the Sacrament, the keys, the Creed, and the Gospel just as did the ancient church from which we stem, especially since before this you admitted that we, as well as you, stem from the ancient church?' To this I reply: It is true, and I do confess that the church in which you are stems from the ancient church, just as do we, and that it [your church] has Baptism, the same Sacrament, the keys, and the same text of the Bible and the Gospel. Indeed, I will accord you still higher praise and confess that we have received from the ancient church, together with you (not from you), all these good things [alles]. What more do you want? Are we not pious enough for you? Will you not now declare that we are no heretics?

"We do not regard you as Turks or Jews (as stated before), who are outside the church. But we do say that you do not remain with it [the church], but you become a straying, apostate, whorish church (as the prophets used to say), which does not stay with the church from which it was born and by which it was brought up. You run away from the [ancient] church and from the right husband or bridegroom (as Hosea says of the people of Israel, Hos. 1:2) to the devil Baal, Moloch, Ashtaroth. Do you not understand this?

"Let me explain it to you: You were surely baptized with the Baptism of the ancient church, just as we, especially in your infancy, and whoever lives and dies till the seventh or eighth year in that Baptism, before he understands the whorish church of the pope, he certainly is blessed [selig] and will be saved. That we do not doubt. But when he grows up and hears, believes, and follows your false teachings concerning your satanic innovations, he becomes the devil's harlot together with you and falls away from his Baptism and Bridegroom, as it happens to others, builds on and trusts in its own works. . . . Of such harlots Hosea speaks, and much more coarsely— indeed, even almost too coarsely—the prophet Ezekiel (23:3ff.). Read that in order that you may know what kind of harlot your church is. . . .

"Also St. Peter speaks of this [harlotry] when he says of your new prophets and churches: ' "A dog returns to his own vomit," and "a sow, having washed, to her wallowing in the mire" ' (2 Peter 2:22). Such you are, just as we have been such. Here your new, apostate, straying church is graphically described and clearly depicted before your eyes. We confess not only that you (papists) came with us out of the true church and that with us you were bathed and washed in Holy Baptism through the blood of our Lord and Savior Jesus Christ, as St. Peter here says (2 Peter 2:20–21), but we say also that you are and remain in the church, indeed, that you sit and rule in it as St. Paul predicts (2 Thess. 2:4) that the accursed Antichrist will sit in the temple of God (not in a cow shed). But you are no longer in that church, nor are you members of it, but in the holy temple of God you establish your new apostate church, which is the devil's house of prostitution, and with it unspeakable harlotry, idolatry, and innovations. By this you mislead, together with yourselves, the baptized and redeemed souls and cause them to be swallowed up by the abyss of hell through its infernal jaws, together with uncounted others, to the unspeakable sorrow and heartache of all those who see and recognize this with their spiritual eyes.

"But it is God, who by His wonderful almighty power, despite the great abomination and the harlotry of the devil, preserves among you through Baptism some infants and a few older persons, only alas, too few who, when dying, hold to Christ, of whom I have known many. Therefore, the true ancient church with its Baptism and God's Word remains with you, and your idol, the devil, cannot altogether destroy it [the true church] despite so much new idolatry and all your satanic harlotry. It is just as it was in the days of Elijah (1 Kings 19:18), when everybody was dedicated only to Baal, idolatry, and harlotry in the land (though all were called God's people and the holy church and gloried in the God who had led them out of Egypt). Then there was preserved not one altar to God [the true God], and yet of all the many thousands, among whom were the greatest and best that went to the devil, God kept for Himself 7,000" ("Against Johnny Sausage" [Hans Wurst], 1541, St. Louis edition, 17:1334–38).

The same: "But if such doubts should assail and trouble you that you think you were not a church or God's people, let me tell you: You cannot recognize the church by its outward conduct. You can recognize it only by God's Word, which says: 'If all prophesy, and an unbeliever or an uninformed person comes in, he is convinced by all, he is judged of all. And thus the secrets of his heart are revealed; and so, falling down on his face, he will worship God and report that God is truly among you' (1 Cor. 14:24–25). But it is surely true of you that in many of you there is God's Word and the knowledge of Christ. But be it wherever it may, wherever the Word of God is, together with the knowledge of Christ, it is never without fruit, no matter how weak it may appear by the outward conduct of those who heed it. For the church, though it is weak because of sin [of its members] is never unchristian but always Christian by the Word. It [its members] indeed sins, but it confesses and knows the Word and does not deny it. Therefore, we must not cast out those who praise and confess the Word even though they do not shine or glitter by any outstanding holiness as long as they do not live in manifest sins or lead a perverse life.

"Therefore, do not doubt that the church is with you, even though there were only ten or six who thus keep the Word. For regarding whatever these do in this matter [calling and ordaining pastors], also with the approbation of the others who do not keep the Word, you should surely believe that Christ does it, if only they administer the matter in humility and with prayer, as said before" ("How One Should Choose and Ordain Pastors," letter to the council and congregation of the city of Prague, 1523, St. Louis edition, 10:1599–1600).

The same: "He (Dr. Eck) says that it is manifestly false and contrary to the custom of the whole church that every priest should absolve a penitent person from the punishment and guilt [of sin]. Otherwise every village pastor would be a bishop, archbishop, and pope. To this let me make a twofold reply: In the first place, I do not see, really and to this day, how this restraint of jurisdiction could accomplish the purpose for which it is pretended. . . . Since according to Acts 20 a bishop is the same as an elder, and since according to Titus 1 every city should have its own bishop [minister] according to divine right, it would be best to reprove sin if every pastor in his parish would bind or loose his members [*den Büßenden*]. St. Paul shows this by his own example in 1 Corinthians 5. . . .

"In the second place, let me say that the church would certainly not go under if a village pastor would be at the same time bishop, archbishop, and pope (that is, if he would have no higher cleric over him), but it [the church] would cohere, as Cyprian says, only by concord, as it was the custom in the first church" (Leipzig Disputation of 1519, St. Louis edition, 15:1095–96).

John Wigand: "Every congregation in every place, that is, the whole assembly, laymen, as we call them now, together with their pastor, has the power to elect, call, and ordain able ministers of the Word and to remove from office and avoid false teachers or such as by their wicked life hinder the upbuilding of the church. This is clear from the passages pertaining to the office of the keys, for the keys have been given to the whole church" (*Centuriae Magdeburgenses* 1.2.4; p. 803. Basil edition, I. b; p. 392). From the way Wigand here reasons, it is obvious that when he ascribes the office of the keys to the whole church, he ascribes them at the same time also to every part of the church [to every local congregation].

Matthias Flacius: "It is obvious that the keys have been given not only to Peter nor only to the apostles but to the whole church of God. This is manifest partly from the very words of the Lord Himself and partly also from the writings of the fathers and ancient interpreters of the words: 'I will give you the keys of the kingdom of heaven' (Matt. 16:19), who clearly understood and interpreted these words as pertaining to the whole church and not merely to Peter.... While then these miserable people [the papists] do not recognize in *Petro* the *petra* (the rock) and do not want to believe that the keys of the kingdom of heaven were given to the church, they themselves have lost them [the keys] out of their hands. Indeed, the Lord Himself soon afterwards applies His saying concerning the keys to the whole church and all believers [Fromme] and not alone to the pope and the clergy, for He says: 'If your brother sins against you, ... tell it to the church.' But the keys embrace all rightful power and authority of church government [*ecclesiastici regiminis*], either to do or to omit something. This cannot be denied, nor is it commonly denied" (*Demonstr., quod electio praesulum et episc. non ad ecclesiasticos solum, sed et ad laicos pertineat,* pp. 55–56).

Chemnitz: "Canon X [of the Council of Trent]: 'If anyone says that all Christians have power to administer the Word and all the sacraments, let him be anathema.' Examination: The words which they [the papists] condemn in this canon they have culled from Luther's booklet *De captivitate Babylonica.* But they have both mutilated the words and corrupted the meaning, in order that they may make Luther's doctrine hateful to the inexperienced, as if it [Luther's doctrine] were a disturber of all divine and human order in the church. But Luther never meant that any Christian whatever either could or should indiscriminately, without a legitimate call, arrogate to himself or usurp the ministry of the Word and the administration of the sacraments in the church.... Against these tyrannical opinions (of the papists) Luther taught from the Word of God that

Christ gave and committed the keys, that is, the ministry of the Word and of the sacraments, to the whole church ... so that the highest power of the Word and of the sacraments is with God; then, that the ministry belongs to the church, so that God calls, chooses, and sends ministers through it. Thirdly, then, it [the ministry] is with those who are legitimately chosen and called by God through the church, therefore with the ministers to whom the use or administration of the ministry of the Word and the sacraments has been committed.

"With this distinction, which is true and plain, Luther meant to restrain the arrogance of the priests who were puffed up by the opinion that they alone possessed all power with respect to the Word and sacraments, so that the sacraments were valid on account of the imprinting on them of some kind of character from ordination. And lest the rest of the church should dare to say by so much as a silent sigh, 'What are you doing?' they pretended that the rest of the church had no power whatever in matters of the Word and the sacraments. That Luther touched this sore spot and applied the knife from the Word of God, that is truly what gives the papalists a burning pain even today, after so many years, and it sits badly" (*Examination of the Council of Trent,* trans. Fred Kramer [St. Louis: Concordia Publishing House, 1978], 2:96–97).

John Gerhard: "Wherever there is gathered and preserved for God a congregation, there ordination, which is administered with the laying on of hands by the ministers and by the public prayers of the church, is to be regarded as valid, though the ministers of that congregation may not be sound in all points [of doctrine] and free from all errors; for ordination is administered not in the private names of the ministers but in the name of the whole congregation. However, there is gathered and preserved a church [even] where the pastors (the possessors of the ministry of the Word) are not absolutely sound [in doctrine] if only Baptism, the Ten Commandments, the Apostles' Creed, the sacred Passion narrative, and other essential fundamentals of the Christian faith are retained. Therefore, also in such places in which the ministers are not altogether doctrinally sound and free from error, ordination can be administered in the name of the congregation, and it is to be regarded as valid if it has been administered" (*Loci theologici,* "De min. eccl.," par. 156).

The same: "Christ has given to His church, as to His bride, the keys of the kingdom of heaven (Matt. 16:18; 18:17). To His church He has promised that where two would agree as touching anything that they would ask, it should be done for them by His Father, who is in heaven (Matt. 18:19). To His church He has entrusted the Word and the sacraments, as the apostle says that to the Israelite church were committed the oracles of God (Rom. 3:2) and that to it (Rom. 9:4) pertained the adoption, the glory, the covenant, the giving of the Law, the service of God, and the promises [Gerhard: the sacraments]. The church is the house of God (1 Tim. 3:15), in which the ministers are appointed stewards (1 Cor. 4:1). To the church, therefore, belongs the ministry, as we read: 'All things are yours: whether Paul or Apollos or Cephas' (1 Cor. 3:21–22). To the church, therefore, also belongs the delegated right, as it is called, to appoint able ministers of the Word, and God desires to use the work of the church by the mediate calling of pious teachers" (ibid., "De min.," par. 85).

The same: "Christ says: 'Where two or three are gathered together in My name, I am there in the midst of them' (Matt 18:20). But where thus Christ is, there, according to His promise, is the church. The apostle Paul calls the Christian family of a house a 'church' (Rom. 16:5; 1 Cor. 16:19; Col. 4:15; Philemon 2). Since, however, two persons, namely, man and wife, constitute a family, they also constitute a church" (ibid., "De eccl.," par. 87).

Calov: "We must distinguish between what remains of the catholic in the Roman religion and what is papistic or stems from the pope. For it [the Roman religion] retains some fundamentals of the true and universal Christian faith, namely, the Holy Trinity, the incarnation of the Son of God, the atonement [satisfactio] of Christ, and others. It retains also the sacrament of initiation, by which children are implanted into the church, and it permits the Word of God, which is a means of salvation, to be read on Sundays and festival days.

"Hence we readily admit that the Roman Catholic religion of the Roman empire, in the things just named and in [other] similar matters, has the right [of a church]. Nor do we object to the fact that to the church of the Romanists on that account [because of its right] there is given the name 'Catholic,' namely, inasmuch as, together with other true believers that are everywhere, it teaches some fundamentals of the faith and in part administers the sacraments. But we do not admit that it is catholic in the sense that it has the uncorrupt faith that agrees with Holy Scripture in all things. It is papistic inasmuch as it cherishes papistic doctrines and sacraments that crept into it without and against Holy Scripture. These certainly do not entitle it to any right, neither in the Roman empire nor anywhere else in the world, though [this is claimed] through the deception and arrogated tyranny of the pope" (*Tract. de natura pacis relig. Aug. Quaest.* XXX).

Balthasar Mentzer: "Passing over other matters, let the papists themselves say who in a large ecclesiastical assembly are the true believers and elect. If they cannot do this, and surely they cannot since they cannot look into the hearts, let them confess that the church of the saints and elect is invisible. For since many are called but few are chosen, we certainly can know the called, but we cannot know those who among them are the elect. And yet we must confess that all the glorious things that are said of the church are said of it because of the elect. Of this synecdoche St. Augustine speaks in the 59th letter to Paulinus. . . .

"This is done just as someone would give to an acre laudable names because of the wheat, though with it there are mixed many tares, or to a city on account of its excellent citizens, though among them there are many wicked and perverse [persons], or to a university, on account of its excellent and learned students, though there are many ignorant and indolent fools among them" (*Exegesis Confessionis Augustanae*, pp. 291–96).

Frederick Balduin: "It is our opinion that the right of ordination belongs to the whole church, for it calls and ordains the ministers; but it executes this its right through the ministers. . . . Has every ministerium in every place the power to ordain its ministers of the Word? If we would speak of the right of the church in a narrow sense, we would not deny this, since every particular church [individual congregation] has the right to ordain. . . . Wherever a church retains Baptism uncorrupt in its essential parts, a part of God's Word as the Gospels and Epistles for the various Sundays, the Passion narrative, and the Apostles' Creed, there also can be a true ordination to the ministry, though it [the church] may be corrupt so far as outward ceremonies [nonessentials] are concerned. But if it remains uncorrupt in the essentials, then [by the ordination] there is committed to the ordained by the prayers of the church the right to teach the Word. We cannot deny that this is also true of the papistic church, though there the ministry is quite corrupt. We motivate this our statement ... by the fact that ordination is not an act of the corrupt clergy but of the whole church, which also corrupt clergymen can perform" (*Tract. de cas. consc.*, pp. 1037, 1039–40).

J. W. Baier: "The right or power to ordain ministers belongs also to the particular churches [individual congregations] that have been separated from others by unjust excommunication. For what has been granted to the universal church for the common purpose, namely, for edification, that the individual congregations rightly claim for themselves inasmuch as they belong to the universal Christian church. The unjust excommunication that they suffer does not make them cease being true churches; hence they do not lose the rights that belong to all true churches of Christ" (*Compendium theologiae positivae* 3.11.4; p. 150).

Tertullian: "In this one as in the other is the church, but the church is Christ. Hence when you bow down at the feet of brethren, you take hold of Christ and supplicate Christ" (*De poenit.* 10).

The same: "Keep in mind that the Lord has left the keys of the kingdom of heaven to Peter and through him to the church; every one (of the disciples) henceforth bears them with him, since every one of them was asked and every one of them confessed" (*Scorpiace.* 10).

Thesis VIII

Although God gathers for Himself a holy church of elect also there where His Word is not taught in its perfect purity and the sacraments are not administered altogether according to the institution of Jesus Christ, if only God's Word and the sacraments are not denied entirely but both remain in their essential parts, nevertheless, every believer must, at the peril of losing his salvation, flee all false teachers, avoid all heterodox congregations or sects, and acknowledge and adhere to orthodox congregations and their orthodox pastors wherever such may be found.

A. Also in heterodox and heretical churches there are children of God, and also there the true church is made manifest by the pure Word and the sacraments that still remain.

1. Scripture Proof

When the holy apostle denominates the called Galatians "congregations" or "churches" (Gal. 1:2: "To the churches of Galatia") this proves conclusively that also in such communions as have been misled by false teachers into error and have largely departed from Christ there remains the hidden seed of the church of true believers.

From 1 Kings 19:14, 18 we learn that God had preserved for Himself, where the priests of Baal had the ascendancy, seven thousand elect whom even Elijah did not know. These are such as inwardly cling to Christ by a living faith, though outwardly they follow the false prophets, because they "have not known the depths of Satan" (Rev. 2:24). They are like the two hundred men who followed rebellious Absalom and his mutinous mob but "went along innocently and did not know anything" (2 Sam. 15:11).

101

2. Witnesses of the Church in Its Official Confessions

Preface to the Book of Concord: "As to the condemnations, censures, and rejections of godless doctrines, and especially of that which has arisen concerning the Lord's Supper, . . . it is in no way our design and purpose to condemn those men who err from a certain simplicity of mind, but are not blasphemers against the truth of the heavenly doctrine, much less, indeed, entire churches; . . . rather has it been our intention and disposition in this manner openly to censure and condemn only the fanatical opinions and their obstinate and blasphemous teachers. . . . For we have no doubt whatever that even in those churches which have hitherto not agreed with us in all things many godly and by no means wicked men are found who follow their own simplicity, and do not understand aright the matter itself, but in no way approve the blasphemies which are cast forth against the Holy Supper as it is administered in our churches, according to Christ's institution, and, with the unanimous approval of all good men, is taught in accordance with the words of the testament itself. We are also in great hope that, if they would be taught aright concerning all these things, the Spirit of the Lord abiding in them, they would agree with us, and with our churches and schools, to the infallible truth of God's Word" (par. 19 [unmarked]; *Triglot,* p. 19).

Apology: "The wolves and false teachers, though they are in the church and do great harm, yet are not the church and the kingdom of Christ" (par. 22; German text, *Triglot,* p. 234). Here our church confesses that the heretics are not outside the church, but that they sow their pernicious seed within the church, so that therefore also in the multitude that the heretics gather around themselves, the true church is hidden. Hence the Apology also says: "The multitude of the wicked is much greater, indeed, almost uncountable, who despise the Word, bitterly hate it, and persecute it most vehemently, as this is done by the Turks, Mohammedans, and other tyrants and heretics. Therefore, the true doctrine and church are at times almost entirely suppressed and lost as this has happened under the papacy, just as though there were no longer any church" (Art. VII, VIII, par. 9; German text, *Triglot,* p. 228). Here our church declares that because of the raging of the heretics it often seems as though there were no longer any church, though Christ rules in the midst of his enemies (Ps. 110:2).

The same: "We do not speak of all [condemning all monks], for there may be some in the monasteries who know the holy Gospel of Christ and do not build their holiness [their righteousness] on their traditions" (Art. XXVII [XIII], par. 8; German text, *Triglot,* p. 420).

3. Witnesses of the Church in the Private Writings of Its Teachers

Luther: "There have always been some under the papacy who have believed, and of these there are still many today whom we do not know; these God preserves [in the faith] by His Word and sacraments despite the devil and the pope" ("Exposition of Ps. 45," 1533, St. Louis edition, 5:468).

The same: "The Christian church [*Christenheit*] is not only in the Roman communion or under the pope but throughout the world. So the prophets predicted that Christ's Gospel should go into all the world (Ps. 2:8). Therefore, the Christian church [*Christenheit*] is dispersed everywhere according to its outward appearance [*leiblich*]: under pope, Turks, Persians, and Tartars; but they are gathered spiritually [as a spiritual body] by one Gospel and one faith under one Head, Jesus Christ" ("Confession Concerning the Lord's Supper," 1528, St. Louis edition, 20:1101).

The same: "St. Augustine directs this passage (Ps. 19:6) against the Donatists, who confined the church to a little corner in [North] Africa. But the passage must rather be directed against our modern Donatists, who deny that there are believers in India, Persia, and Asia. Wherever there is the preaching and Word of the Spirit of Christ, there beyond doubt is always the true church of Christ, for Christ's Spirit never speaks anywhere except in His church. Therefore, since the text here clearly says that the words of the apostles are gone out to the end of the world (Ps. 19:4), and there is no passage in which this truth is retracted, we must take heed that we do not, with the wicked Donatists, either these or those, either the old or the new, glory in ourselves as though we were the only believers, since today we hear neither the Word nor the proclamation of the apostles anywhere" ("Ps. 19," 1521, St. Louis edition, 4:1136).

The same: "Therefore, the church is holy everywhere, even in those places where the enthusiasts and factious spirits [*Rottengeister*] are ruling, provided they do not utterly deny and reject the Word and the sacraments. For those who repudiate these things altogether are no longer a church. But where the Word and the sacraments remain in their essential parts, there also remains a holy church; and it does not matter even if Antichrist were to rule there; for he does not sit in a stable of the devil nor in a pigsty nor among infidels but in the most exalted and sacred place, namely, in the temple of God (2 Thess. 2:4). Therefore, it is manifest and certain that the temple of God must be and remain even under the spiritual tyrants who rule and rage in it. Everywhere, even under such tyrants, we find some who rightly believe. Hence the question can briefly and easily be answered, namely, that the Jews, Turks, enthusiasts, factious spirits, or heretics are not the church, for they deny and destroy these things [the Gospel and sacraments]" ("Detailed Interpretation of the Epistle to the Galatians," 1535, St. Louis edition, 9:44).

The same: "We must confess that the enthusiasts have Scripture and God's Word in other articles, and whoever hears it of them and believes it will be saved, though they are unholy heretics and blasphemers of Christ" ("Letter to Two Pastors Concerning Anabaptism," 1528, St. Louis edition, 17:2212).

The same: "No Christian can or should pray for the enthusiasts [Schwärmer] nor take up their cause. They are hardened and commit mortal sin (as St. John says [1 John 5:16]). I am speaking of their teachers. May our dear Lord Jesus Christ help the poor people that are under them against these murderers of souls. They have been admonished earnestly and often enough, but they do not want [to listen to] me" ("Brief Confession of the Holy Sacrament Against the Enthusiasts," 1544, St. Louis edition, 20:1771).

Nikolaus Selnecker: "During the persecutions in France, the Netherlands, and elsewhere, no doubt many innocent people were tortured to death on account of their religion, and there were many martyrs also among the Sacramentarians [*Sacramentirer:* Protestants who followed Zwingli in denying the Real Presence in the Lord's Supper], on whom even those who have hearts of stone must have compassion. But, dear Lord, these were not killed because of their [erroneous] doctrine of the Lord's Supper but because they refused to acknowledge the papistic abomination, and so were murdered as *Lutherans*. Therefore, God also graciously stood by them and took them to Himself, having granted them joy and comfort and having covered and patiently borne with their weakness and their error [*Nebenwahn*], which they harbored and into which they had been misled concerning the Lord's Supper. Thus our merciful Lord always condones the errors and weaknesses of His believing children that they do not defend willfully, purposely, or maliciously" (*Brev. resp. ad crim. Danaei*).

Jacob Heilbrunner, after having shown that "we do not owe it to the Calvinists to acknowledge them as our brethren," continues: "This is not said of the common Christians [*Zuhörer*] who err from simplicity or from lack of better instruction, who perhaps believe much better and more sincerely than do their teachers, and who, because they have turned away from the papacy, must suffer persecution. With these we deeply sympathize and intercede for them before God. These also we gladly acknowledge as our dear brethren, for they do not err maliciously, and we have the comforting hope that God will not charge against them their errors. For it is not the erring that makes anyone a heretic but the stubborn adherence to error against one or more articles of the Christian faith despite thorough instruction, warning, and admonition" (*Synopsis doctr. Calvin.: Summarischer Begriff und gegründ. Widerl. der Zwingl. und Calv. Lehre,* p. 140a).

John Gerhard: "The true Church is placed in contrast to the false, either exclusively, that is, as a nonchurch or one that subverts the essence of Baptism and the entire [Christian] religion, or privately in the sense that it is not an orthodox church. In the latter sense of the term, a church that is guilty of partial apostasy is not the true church on account of its perversion of [the Christian] religion, but it is a false, that is, a corrupt and impure church. With regard to the first contrast, we admit that [in] such a church there is the true one, and this appears (1) from the true sacrament of initiation that it retains, for which reason those who were baptized by the Arians were not again baptized by the ancients [the Christian church] (cf. Augustine's 103d letter); (2) from the communication of the Word by means of the public reading of the Biblical texts that also is a proclamation in a certain sense according to Acts 15:21"[10] (cf. *Conf. catho,* fol. 728).

The same: "It is to be noted that there are certain grades of such purity, because the Word of God is preached in the church sometimes more purely and at times less purely. But it does not at once cease to be a church even if in some fundamentals of religion it does not teach purely. The more purely and scripturally the Word of God is proclaimed in a church, the more closely the proclamation and teaching approaches the norm of the Word, the more pure and scriptural the church will be. But the farther it departs from the norm of the Word, the more impure and corrupt the condition of the church will be. Still it does not cease to be a church because of every perversion [of doctrine], since, as we have shown above, God will produce and preserve for Himself a holy seed and spiritual children even if in a visible church the Word is corrupted.

"Therefore the visible church is considered according to its outward form or, what is the same, according to its ministry of the Word as being either in a pure and uncorrupt condition or in one that is impure and partially corrupt. If we call the pure proclamation of the Word and the legitimate administration of the Sacrament [according to Christ's institution] marks of the church, then we consider the church in the condition mentioned first and in contrast not only to secular communions but also to corrupt and impure churches. That this is rightly so done is obvious from the fact that definitions, rules, and canons must be deduced from the ideal, so that corrupt churches must be reformed, renewed, and purified according to the form and norm of the more pure and scriptural doctrine.

"It is to be noted finally that churches must be judged not only according to their pastors or a few of their members. Whole churches, therefore, must not be condemned at once if either their pastors or some of their members deviate from the purity and soundness of the doctrine, since often the ears of the hearers are purer than the lips of the teachers. For this reason, many [members], despite the corrupt condition of the church, retain the fundamental doctrines and either do not assent to the errors that the false teachers spread or adhere to them without pertinacity or free themselves from them before the end of their life" (*Loci theologici,* "De eccl.," par. 126).

The same: "When the pure preaching of the Word is called the mark of the true church, then the term 'preaching' is generally taken for the confession of the doctrine that all members of a church, both pastors and hearers, have in common and for the reading of the Biblical texts, which also is a preaching in a certain sense according to Acts 15:21. Preaching in a narrow sense is more properly a function of the pastor rather than of the whole congregation and not absolutely and unconditionally necessary. The extremely trying periods of persecution show that a church can be preserved by the mere reading of Scripture without the public preaching of the pure doctrine" (*Conf. cathol.,* fol. 728–29).

The same: "Baptism is a special gift of the church. Wherever, therefore, Baptism is administered in its true and unmutilated form, there God gathers a church. Baptism is the sacrament of initiation, which secures entrance into the church. Hence, where infants are baptized, there is the gate and door to the kingdom of heaven. Wherever Baptism is administered in its true and unmutilated form, there it is the washing of regeneration and renewing of the Holy Spirit, as the apostle describes it (Titus 3:5); there salvation is offered to those who are baptized, as God tells us that He saves us by Baptism (1 Peter 3:21). But outside the church there is no regeneration and no salvation. Hence, wherever Baptism is administered, there is a church of Christ" (*Loci theologici,* "De eccl.," par. 128).

The same: "It must be repeated here from what was said above, [namely,] that a church, as regards purity of the Word, has various grades, so that at times it is more and then again less sound and pure. Hence, as the preaching of the Word and the administration of the sacraments are the marks of the church when we speak of it unconditionally and absolutely, the pure teaching of the Word and the legitimate administration of the sacraments are the marks of the pure and uncorrupt church. As by the preaching of the Word and the administration of the sacraments the church distinguishes itself from secular communions, which are outside the church, so it distinguishes itself from heretical communions within the church by the pure preaching of the Word and the legitimate administration of the sacraments" (ibid., par. 131).

The same: "If Baptism and some fundamental doctrines are retained in their unmutilated form, then God gathers for Himself in the corrupt visible church, indeed, in a congregation of heretics, by the means just mentioned, the invisible church of the elect" (ibid., par. 141).

The same: "To the objection that also in a congregation of heretics Baptism is administered, so that it [Baptism] cannot be a mark of the true church, I reply: When we speak unconditionally, the Word and the sacraments are the marks of the church; for only there a church exists where the Word is proclaimed and the sacraments are administered. But since in the churches there are not the same grades of purity and soundness, we say that the pure teaching of the Word and the legitimate administration of the sacraments are the marks of the church by which the pure and sound church distinguishes itself from those that are corrupt and impure.

"We must also carefully distinguish in a congregation of heretics what is valuable from what is valueless; that is, what properly belongs to the church must be distinguished from the additions of human reason. Baptism that is administered in its unmutilated form by heretics and the fundamental doctrines that they still retain pure and unmutilated are the proper gifts of the church, but the added falsifications and errors are a leaven that does not belong to it. Therefore, even if Baptism is administered in a congregation of heretics, it does not cease to be a proper gift of the church, and so also it is its unmistakable mark" (ibid., par. 128).

Jerome Kromayer: "It may happen that the ears of the hearers may take from what is presented to them something that is better and more consonant with the truth than was intended by the teachers. Thus, for example, in the papacy, despite the rubbish of human traditions, Christ nevertheless was apprehended and retained by [some] devout hearers, and again among the hearers that recently left the papacy [Calvinists], who did not recognize the depths of Satan despite the subtle discussions of the absolute [divine] decree, some had the doctrine of the justification of a sinner by faith in Christ's merits deeply engraved on their hearts. Therefore, we by no means absolutely condemn those who toward the end of the preceding century were put to death by the command of Duke Alva in Belgium [in 1567]. Most of them did not recognize the depths of Satan, and far from trusting in their good works, they desired to be justified and saved solely by faith in Christ. The [practical] use of this doctrine in the area of teaching is that we must carefully distinguish between the teachers and the hearers and not ascribe the errors to the whole church [to all members]. In controversies this doctrine is to be used against those severe judges who often condemn whole churches, often such as are innocent, if there arises religious persecution" (*Theologia positivo-polemica,* part 2, pp. 512–13).

John Benedict Carpzov [the Elder]: "In Article VII of the Augsburg Confession the church is described not as it often happens to be but as it should be as such and in its natural [proper] condition, namely, when it is not oppressed by persecutors or troubled by heretics. Therefore, it can easily happen, as indeed it has happened, that the church was hidden under tyrants or existed under a corrupt ministry. Nevertheless, it does not cease to be a church, as the Apology of the Augsburg Confession explains very nicely on page 145" [Rechenberg Edition] (*Isagoge in libros ecclesiarum luth. symbolicos,* p. 306).

The same: "In the Smalcald Articles Luther says, 'We do not admit that they [the papists] are the church.' Here he speaks not of the Roman church as such but of the papists or what adheres to the Roman church as a blemish or cancer cleaves to the body. For the Roman church is something else than is the papacy in the Roman church. Regarding the Roman church, we do not deny that it is a church, inasmuch as it retains the 'matrimonial documents,' as Augustine calls them, that is, the Word with its seals [sacraments], and inasmuch as it teaches some fundamentals of the faith that also all other true believers profess, no matter where they may be. But what is attached to the modern Roman church, namely, the papistic doctrine, the [papistic] worship, and the [papistic] hierarchy, and what renders it impure and contagious so far as the ministry and the unadulterated faith are concerned is not the church but an evil that is attached to the church just as a cancer or any other disease adheres to the human body; that does not change the body into a nonbody, but merely makes it an impure and diseased body.

"Hence it happens that also in the diseased Roman church there have remained and still remain true believers [*Fromme*]. These are partly hidden, as are the infants who by the impure ministry are brought to the new birth through Baptism and the simple adults who do not recognize the depths of Satan (Rev 2:24), for the Word that is still proclaimed in it does not return void (Is. 55:10). But these are also partly manifest, [namely,] those who abhor the abominations and accept what is better. . . .

"Luther therefore did not have in mind the Roman church as such or inasmuch as it is still a church or inasmuch as it is the Roman church, but he had in mind the papists or the papistic crowd that perverted the Roman church or the Roman church inasmuch as it is papistic and teaches and professes the papistic doctrine, worship, and hierarchy. Of this [papistic crowd] he says that it is no church, just as a cancer is not the body but only something that is in and corrupts the body. Here we must consider also the distinction between the Roman church and the Roman hierarchy [*Stuhl*] to which the evangelical [Lutheran] states referred at the Diet of Augsburg" (ibid., pp. 874–75).

The same: "We have not separated ourselves from the Roman church by the Reformation, but we have only abrogated the evil adhering to it, namely, the papacy. We admit that our church is a particular church, but we do not say that it is the only true church. For though, so far as visible churches are concerned, there may be none that are purer and more exempt from blemishes than is the Lutheran, yet we do not deny that there may be some other particular church, known only to God so far as the sincere members are concerned, who are hidden in such another visible assembly, even in one that is corrupt; for of them the true church properly consists. . . .

"It is shown (in the Smalcald Articles, III, 12) that the true church is none other than what is holy, that is, adheres to God's Word in true faith. And even if otherwise 'true church' and 'pure church' are not synonymous since the one embraces more than the other (as a body may be a true body and yet not one that is pure) yet in this passage, as also in the Augsburg Confession, both [terms] are taken as synonymous, since essentially the church consists of the members who adhere to God's Word and to Christ in true faith, or since the church, inasmuch as it is corrupt, is no church, though the true and pure church is in it so far as there are [in it] hidden members [of the true church] who are known only to God" (ibid., pp. 876–77).

From this it is obvious that our venerable teachers use the term "Lutheran church" in a twofold sense. Sometimes they use the expression in the general sense of the church that Luther and all Lutherans acknowledged as their spiritual mother and that has one

Spirit, one faith, one doctrine and is spread all over the earth. This church existed even before Luther, indeed from the beginning of the world. Of the Lutheran church in this sense, therefore, our teachers certainly confess according to God's Word that it is the only true church outside of which there is no life and salvation. For in that case, they mean to designate no other church than the one holy Christian universal invisible church of the saints and elect. This church, however, our venerable teachers designated the Lutheran church not because they thought that the proper kingdom and inheritance of Christ is the sum total of all those who rightly call themselves Lutherans, but because the enemies called the holy doctrine that the Lutherans profess, which is the doctrine of the whole true Christian church, "Lutheran," just as they called all churches that accepted this doctrine "Lutheran churches."

Again, the teachers of our Lutheran church designated [by that term] also the visible communion of all those who bear the name "Lutheran" and expressly profess the official Confessions that those Christians drafted who in the 16th century left the papacy and were derided by the papists as "Lutherans." Of the Lutheran church in this sense our teachers of course admit that it is not the only true church but merely a particular church. This distinction is of the greatest importance. The failure to understand it has caused the greatest confusion, as it is evident.

J. Conrad Göbel: "In this article (Article VII of the Augsburg Confession) the church, so far as pure doctrine and pure worship are concerned, is described not as it always is but as it always should be, so also in what condition it was when it flourished and was in its greatest glory as, for example, in the days of our Lord Jesus Christ and those of His holy and beloved apostles and as by God's grace it is found today in the evangelical [Lutheran] churches. But though the church here on earth is not always found in the same condition and the same fortunate state of well-being, so that it does not always flourish, just as the moon at times waxes and then again wanes, so at one time the Gospel is proclaimed more purely than at another. Such changes are noticed even at the time of the apostles in the very congregations that they themselves had founded. Nevertheless, just as at the time of a lunar eclipse the sky does not disappear, so God preserves His church in the midst of darkness, [that is,] when

111

the divine Word and the sacraments are corrupted and obscured by false teachers....

"Though, therefore, the holy Gospel is not always kept equally pure and the sacraments are not always administered according to the Gospel, but often great eclipses and obscurations darken the church, the church does not lose its name [of church]. From Rev. 2 and 3 we learn that the churches in Ephesus, Pergamum, Thyatira, Sardis, Laodicea, and other cities suffered from severe blemishes [*naevos*] and corruptions, yet they retained their names and were called churches of God; this is true also of the church at Corinth, as we are told in the salutation (1 Cor. 1:2). Hence, though a church may be corrupt, and its condition could be much better, we must not at once throw out the child with the bath water and turn over such a church to the evil foe with cordial New Year's greetings, but we must distinguish the good from the evil, just as experienced goldsmiths separate the gold from copper, and the silver from the dross. The prophet Malachi uses these examples in Mal. 3:3" (Sermons preached by J. C. Göbel, pastor at Augsburg, in 1654 on the Augsburg Confession, fol. 524, 532).

Augustine: "Do not flatter yourselves (you Donatists) because we do not reject your Baptism. It is not your Baptism but that of the universal Christian church that we possess. Therefore, when you separated yourselves [from the Christian church], you took it along, not for your salvation but for your harm. For the sacred vessels of the Lord remained holy even among the heathen, for which reason the king [of Babylon], who dared desecrate them, was punished by the angry God. Nor did the ark of covenant lose its characteristic [*virtutem*] of holiness even when it was captured by its enemies. If then those sacred vessels in no wise lost the characteristic of holiness when they were with the heathen and no longer with their proper owners [the Israelites], how much more do not the Christian sacraments retain their holiness when they pass over to the heretics in such a way that they remain also with us!" (*Contra gaudentium* 3.14).

The same: "In consequence of the darkness of the flesh, even some good [members] erred in that faction for a long time, though the fury of the evil [heretics] against the church of God without doubt had become manifest" (*De unit. eccl.* 20).

The same: "Those who separate themselves from the communion of the rest [the Christian church] violate Christian love, destroy the bond of unity, and are separate themselves in all things if they fail to do what they received in that communion [the church]. Hence, if anyone who has joined their communion [that of the heretics] desires to return to the church, he must first receive what he did not receive [in the heretical communion]. But if they [the heretics] in some things do the same [as the Christian church], they have not separated themselves in these things, and so far as their adherence is concerned, they remain in the structures of the whole [the Christian church]. In the rest they are cut off. If then they [the heretical churches] receive someone [who strayed away] into their fellowship, he will remain connected with the church in those parts in which they [the heretics] are not separated. Hence, when such a one [who has left the church] wishes to return to it, he will be healed in those parts in which he erred and was miserably mauled. But where he was received [by the heretics] as a believer, there he will not be healed [if he return to the church], but he will be acknowledged, so that we may not rather wound him when we desire to heal that which is sound in him" (*De pabt.* 1.8).

Hilary: "The ears of the people are holier than the hearts of the priests.... Hence Christ's people will not perish under the priests of Antichrist, since they believe that they [the priests] mean what they hear of them. They [the people] thus hear of them that Christ is God; so they believe that it is so as they say. They are told of the Son of God; so they believe that God, who became incarnate, is and remains true God. They hear (about Christ) that He was before time; so they believe that this 'before time' means 'forever' " (*Lib. adv. Auxentium* 215). Here Hilary shows that even under the Arian ministers, who denied Christ's deity, since they retained the orthodox terminology, God's church of true believers could be preserved.

Chrysostom: "It is not he who departs from the church bodily that leaves it but he who in his mind forsakes the fundamentals of the truth confessed by the church" (Homily 46 on Matthew [?]).

B. Every believer for the sake of his salvation must flee all false teachers and avoid all heterodox congregations or sects.

1. Scripture Proof

Many, on hearing that the church exists wherever the Word and the sacraments are still found essentially, infer from this fact that it is a matter of indifference whether they belong to an orthodox [*rechtgläubige*] or to an unorthodox [*falschgläubige*] church, since after all they are in the church and so can be saved. But they are mistaken. True, it is not necessary to leave a heterodox communion in order to be in the church, and many indeed are saved who, for lack of knowledge, outwardly belong to sects and nevertheless continue in the [true] faith. But what does it profit anyone to be in the church if he is not of the church and [so] does not belong to it? Whoever has learned to know the false doctrine of the sects and their teachers and despite this fact continues to belong to them is indeed still in the church but not of the [true] church. Such a person does not belong to the divine seed that is hidden in the sects. His communion with the sects is not a sin of weakness, with which the state of grace can exist, for such a person acts willfully and contrary to the will of God, who in His holy Word commands us to flee and avoid false teachers and their false worship.

As little, therefore, as the doctrine that true [*begnadigte*] Christians still commit sins of weakness justifies those who think that for that reason they knowingly and willfully may continue in sin, indeed, as surely as those who thus sin against [divine] grace are children of perdition, so little also does the doctrine that in the sects there are children of God justify those who contrary to God's Word knowingly desire to continue in them; indeed, so surely also such willful partakers of the perversion of the Word of truth are children of perdition; for thus it is written:

Deut. 13:1–3: "If there arises among you a prophet or a dreamer of dreams, and he gives you a sign or a wonder, and the sign or the wonder of which he spoke to you comes to pass, saying, 'Let us go after other gods which you have not known, and let us serve them,' you shall not listen to the words of that prophet or that dreamer of dreams, for the Lord your God is testing you to know whether you love the Lord your God with all your heart and with all your soul."

Matt. 7:15: "Beware of false prophets, who come to you in sheep's clothing, but inwardly they are ravenous wolves."

Matt. 24:23–24: "If anyone says to you, 'Look, here is the Christ!' or 'There!' do not believe it. For false christs and false prophets will arise and show great signs and wonders, so as to deceive, if possible, even the elect."

Acts 20:30–31: "Also from among yourselves men will rise up, speaking perverse things, to draw away the disciples after themselves. Therefore watch, and remember that for three years I did not cease to warn everyone night and day with tears."

Rom. 16:17–18: "I urge you, brethren, note those who cause divisions and offenses, contrary to the doctrine which you learned, and avoid them. For those who are such do not serve our Lord Jesus Christ, but their own belly, and by smooth words and flattering speech deceive the hearts of the simple."

1 Cor. 10:18, 21: "Observe Israel after the flesh: Are not those who eat of the sacrifices partakers of the altar? . . . You cannot drink the cup of the Lord and the cup of demons; you cannot partake of the Lord's table and of the table of demons."

1 Cor. 11:19: "There must also be factions [Luther: *Rotten*] among you, that they which are approved may be recognized among you."

2 Cor. 6:14–18: "Do not be unequally yoked together with unbelievers. For what fellowship has righteousness with lawlessness? And what communion has light with darkness? And what accord has Christ with Belial? Or what part has a believer with an unbeliever? And what agreement has the temple of God with idols? For you are the temple of the living God. As God has said: 'I will dwell in them and walk among them. I will be their God, and they shall be My people.' 'Come out from among them and be separate, says the Lord. Do not touch what is unclean. And I will receive you.' 'I will be a Father to you, and you shall be My sons and daughters, says the Lord Almighty.' "

Gal. 5:9: "A little leaven leavens the whole lump."

Titus 3:10–11: "Reject a divisive man after the first and second admonition, knowing that such a person is warped and sinning, being self-condemned."

2 John 10–11: "If anyone comes to you and does not bring this doctrine, do not receive him into your house nor greet him; for he who greets him shares in his evil deeds."

Rev. 18:4: "Come out of her, my people, lest you share in her sins, and lest you receive of her plagues."

115

2. Witnesses of the Church in Its Official Confessions

Apology: "Nevertheless, we should not receive or listen to false teachers, for they no longer stand in Christ's place but are antichrists. And Christ commands us regarding them: 'Beware of false prophets' (Matt. 7:15). And Paul [writes] to the Galatians: 'If anyone preaches any other gospel to you, . . . let him be accursed' (Gal. 1:9)" (Art. VII, VIII [IV], par. 48; German text, *Triglot,* pp. 242–43).

Smalcald Articles, Appendix: "In the third place we must know also that though the pope had the primacy and superiority by divine right, we do not owe obedience to such popes as propose false worship, idolatry, and false doctrine contrary to the Gospel. Indeed we should regard such popes and such rule as anathema and an accursed matter, as Paul clearly teaches in Gal. 1:8 and as it is written in Acts 5:29" (Of the Power and Primacy of the Pope, par. 38; German text, *Triglot,* p. 515).

The same: "This being the case, all Christians should beware most diligently that they do not make themselves partakers of such godless doctrine, blasphemy, and unjust tyranny, but they should flee from and curse the pope and all his members or adherents, as Christ has commanded: 'Beware of false prophets' (Matt. 7:15). And Paul commands that we should avoid false teachers and execrate them as an abomination. He says: 'Do not be unequally yoked together with unbelievers. For what . . . communion has light with darkness?' (2 Cor. 6:14). It is indeed difficult for us to separate ourselves from so many lands and people and teach a different doctrine. But here is God's command that everyone should take care and not consent to those who teach false doctrine or intend to uphold it by tyranny" (ibid., par. 41; German text, *Triglot,* p. 517).

The same: "For so Paul commands that all bishops who either teach false doctrine or defend false doctrine and false worship should be regarded as criminal people" [Latin text: *tamquam anathemate*] (ibid., par. 72; German text, *Triglot,* p. 524).

Formula of Concord, Thorough Declaration: "In like manner, too, such ceremonies should not be reckoned among the genuine free adiaphora, or matters of indifference, as make a show or feign the appearance, as though our religion and that of the papists were not far apart, thus to avoid persecution, or as though the latter were not at least highly offensive to us; or when such ceremonies are designed for the purpose, and required and received in this sense, as though by and through them both contrary religions were reconciled and became one body; or when a reentering into the papacy and a departure from the pure doctrine of the Gospel and true religion should occur or gradually follow therefrom. For in this case what Paul writes (2 Cor. 6:14, 17) shall and must obtain: 'Do not be unequally yoked together with unbelievers. For . . . what communion has light with darkness? . . . Therefore "come out from among them and be separate, says the Lord" ' " (Art. X, par. 5, 6; *Triglot,* pp. 1053, 1055).

3. Witnesses of the Church in the Private Writings of Its Teachers

Luther: "Whoever knows that his preacher teaches Zwinglian [Reformed] doctrine, he should avoid him and rather go without the sacrament as long as he lives than receive it of him; indeed, he should rather die and suffer all things because of it. . . . In fine, while I am treating this subject, I hear with great horror that in the same church and at the same altar both parties [Lutherans and Reformed] receive and obtain the same sacrament, one party believing that they receive mere bread and wine and the other that they receive the true body and blood of Christ. Often I hesitate to believe that a preacher or minister can be so hardened and malicious as silently to let both parties go [to the Sacrament], each in the illusion that they receive the same Sacrament according to their belief. If such a minister should exist, he must have a heart that is harder than stone, steel, or diamond can be. Truly, the Turks and Jews are much better, for they deny our Sacrament and confess this publicly; so we remain undeceived by them and do not fall prey to idolatry. But these guys [*Gesellen*] must be the really high-ranking archdevils, for they give me mere bread and wine and yet let me believe that I receive Christ's body and blood, and so they cheat me atrociously. Such [fraud] is too hot and hard; God will punish that before long. Therefore, whoever has such preachers or may expect that [fraud] from them should be warned of them as of the very devil himself" ("Warning Addressed to the Christians at Frankfurt to Guard Against Zwinglian Doctrine and Teachers," St. Louis edition, 17:2011, 2016).

117

The same: "Whoever regards his doctrine, faith, and confession as true and certain cannot stand in one stall with others who teach false doctrine or are agreeable to it, nor can he continue to speak sweet words to the devil and his followers. A teacher who is silent over against error and nevertheless pretends to be a true teacher is worse than an outspoken enthusiast [*ein öffentlicher Schwärmer*] and by his hypocrisy does greater harm than a heretic, so that no one should put confidence in him. He is a wolf and a fox, a hireling and a belly server; he despises and rejects the doctrine, the Word, the faith, the Sacrament, the church and school. He either secretly lies with the enemies [of the truth] under one cover, or he is a cynic and a windbag who wants to see how things will turn out, whether Christ will win the victory or the devil, or he is altogether uncertain in his mind and not worthy to be called a pupil, let alone a teacher. He does not desire to offend anyone; he wants neither to confess Christ nor to hurt the feelings of the devil and the world" ("Conversation with Dr. George Major," St. Louis edition, 17:1180).

The same: " 'A little leaven leavens the whole lump' (Gal. 5:9). St. Paul regarded that warning very highly, and we should too, especially in our time. For the factions [*Rotten*] that declare that Christ's body and blood are not present in the Lord's Supper slander and defame us as though we were contentious, stubborn, and unfriendly because on account of this one article concerning the Sacrament we violate Christian love and destroy the unity of the church. They think that we should not regard this article, which is not too important anyhow and of which we cannot be sure since the apostles did not explain it as much as is necessary, so highly and greatly that on account of it we let the whole Christian doctrine and the general unity of so many Christian congregations go to pieces, [especially] because they certainly agree with us in other doctrines of the Christian faith, which [they say] are more necessary and also more important.

"With this argument, which makes a favorable impression on and sounds well in the ears of the common people, they effect not only that those who adhere to them become extremely inimical to us, but they also induce many pious people to become angry with us and imagine that we do not want to fellowship with them because of sheer stubbornness or some special grudge. But all that is clever trickery and craftiness of the devil, by which he endeavors nothing else than to pervert and overthrow not only this article [concerning the Holy Supper] but also the whole Christian doctrine.

"Therefore, we reply to their pretext with St. Paul: 'A little leaven leavens the whole lump.' Just as in philosophy a little mistake in the beginning (in principle) will end in a very great and enormous error, so also in theology a little error will pervert and corrupt the whole Christian doctrine. Therefore, we must distinguish carefully between doctrine and life. The doctrine is not ours but God's, who has called us merely to be its servants and ministers. Therefore, we neither shall nor can yield or surrender even the least tittle or letter of it. But the life is ours, and therefore the sacramentarians may demand of us nothing that we would and should not gladly do, suffer, forgive, etc., yet in such a way that we do not surrender anything of the doctrine and faith. For we always maintain with St. Paul: 'A little leaven leavens the whole lump.'

"Therefore, in this article we cannot yield a single hair's breadth, for the doctrine is so carefully gauged and measured off that you cannot add to it or subtract from it without great and serious harm. But the life is such that you can easily assume or also give up something, do or suffer something, as necessity demands.

"If a little speck of dust gets into the eye, you cannot endure it; so you let someone take it out, or otherwise it will harm the eye. Therefore, we Germans are accustomed to say of the treatment of the eye: 'Nothing is good in the eye.' And Christ says: 'The lamp of the body is the eye. If therefore your eye is good, your whole body will be full of light' (Matt. 6:22; Luke 11:34), and again in Luke 11:36: If then your whole body is full of light, having no part dark, the whole body will be full of light.' By this allegory or parable Christ indicates that the eye, that is, the doctrine, must be absolutely pure and uncorrupt, clear and bright, so that not a particle of darkness, not even a little cloud, can be noticed in it.

"So also St. James in his epistle says very nicely and aptly, not indeed of his own spirit but as he heard it of the apostles: 'Whoever shall keep the whole Law, and yet stumble in one point, he is guilty of all' (James 2:10). Therefore, the doctrine must be like a precious and pure golden ring that has no rent or flaw; for as soon as such a ring suffers a flaw or rent, it is no longer perfect. What would it benefit the Jews if they believe that there is one God and Creator of all things; indeed, if they were to believe all articles [of the Christian faith] and accept the whole Bible, but deny Christ? Therefore, the saying of St. James is true: 'Whoever stumbles in one point is guilty of all.'

"Therefore, we must carefully consider this passage against the argument of the sacramentarians, who charge us with the lie that we tear asunder Christian love and unity to the great harm and detriment of the holy church. We certainly are ready and willing to keep peace with them and show them love, but only as long as they allow our doctrine to remain inviolate and pure. If we cannot obtain that from them, it is in vain for them to praise Christian love so highly. May that love be cursed to the depth of hell that is maintained to the harm and detriment of the doctrine of faith, to which whatever there may be must be subject: love, apostle, angel from heaven, and everything else.

"Hence, by the fact that they regard this matter so lightly and of such little importance, they clearly show what they think of the majesty and glory of the divine Word. If they would seriously and heartily believe that they were dealing with God's Word, they would not jest and joke so frivolously with it, but they would hold it in highest esteem and would believe without any doubt or disputation what it tells and prescribes to them. They would also recognize that one Word of God is all, and again that all words of God are one. They would recognize that all articles of our Christian faith are one, and again that one is all, so that if they surrender one, they in the course of time will gradually surrender all, one after the other; for they all cleave together and belong together.

"Therefore, we will let them exalt Christian love as much as they may. But we will glory in the majesty and glory of the Word and faith. Regarding love, you may yield somewhat without any harm or danger. But that cannot be done with the Word and faith. Love should suffer all things and yield to everyone. But faith can and should not suffer anything and should yield to absolutely no one. Love, which gladly yields, believes all things, puts the best construction on all things, forgives, and suffers, is often deceived. But nevertheless all deceptions cannot harm it with a real harm rightly so called, for it never denies Christ even if it is deceived. Therefore, love does not permit itself to be disturbed but always continues helping and benefiting everyone, even those who are ungrateful and unworthy. On the other hand, when the matter concerns salvation, and the enthusiasts teach their falsehood and error under the pretense of the truth so as to deceive and mislead many people, we certainly must show no love and must not approve and justify their error; for then we lose not [merely] a gift granted to an ingrate, but we lose the Word, faith, Christ Himself, and eternal life.

"Therefore, do not doubt that if you deny God in one article, you deny Him most surely in all. For He does not permit Himself to be divided piecemeal into many articles, but He is altogether one God in every article and in all. Hence, when the sacramentarians accuse us at great length and in many words that we do not consider love, as we justly should, we answer them with the one passage of St. Paul: 'A little leaven leavens the whole lump.' Again: It is an evil thing to jest with honor, faith, and the eyes.

"All this I have said in so many words in order to confirm our adherents and to teach others who might be offended by our stead-fastness [*Beständigkeit*], as they think that we are so very obstinate and stubborn, and that without valid reason. Therefore, it does not trouble us if they greatly boast how eager they are to preserve love and unity between us and them and how sorry the separation makes them. Whoever does not love and honor God and His Word is not benefited, even if he loves whomever he wills.

"For this reason St. Paul in this passage admonishes both teachers and hearers not to think that the doctrine of faith is so unimportant and frivolous a matter that they might jest and amuse themselves with it as they please. It is rather a glory light of the sun, coming directly down from heaven to illuminate, warm, and rule us. As the world with all its wisdom and power cannot change the glory light of the sun, which comes down directly from heaven, so also we can neither subtract from nor add anything to the doctrine of faith, unless we want to destroy it altogether. . . .

" 'He who troubles you shall bear his judgment, whoever he is' (Gal. 5:10). With these words St. Paul condemns the false apostles most vehemently, as though he were pronouncing this verdict on them from the judgment seat of Christ. He ascribes to them the very offensive term 'deceivers of the Galatians,' though the unsophisticated Galatians regarded them as the most holy people and as far greater teachers than even St. Paul himself.

"With this dreadful verdict, by which he so vehemently condemns the false apostles, he at the same time wanted to persuade

121

the Galatians to guard and take care of themselves against them, as though they were the most dangerous poison. He meant to tell them: Why do you listen to these harmful and venomous liars who teach you nothing [good] but only lead you astray? With their teaching they accomplish nothing else than merely to confuse your consciences. Therefore, they will bear their judgment no matter how great or exalted they might be.

"From the words 'whoever he is,' we may conclude that according to their outward appearance the false apostles must have been very pious and holy people. It may be that among them there was an especially great and famous man who perhaps had been a disciple of the true apostles and therefore was held in highest esteem; for certainly St. Paul had just cause to use such hard, condemning words. In the same way he speaks above: 'Even if we, or an angel from heaven, preach any other gospel to you than what we have preached to you, let him be accursed' (Gal. 1:8). No doubt many were greatly offended at these hefty and hasty words, and they may have thought: How can St. Paul act so hastily contrary to [Christian] love? Why should he be so stern and stubborn in a matter so unimportant and insignificant? Why does he hand over to the devil and everlasting perdition those who are Christ's servants just as much as he is? But for all that he does not care an iota, nor does it matter to him that they [the false teachers] were regarded as pious, holy, and learned men and so were highly esteemed. But because they pervert the doctrine of faith he curses and condemns them most vehemently, nor does he doubt by a hair's breadth that his way of treating them is right.

"So also today we regard all as cursed and condemned who say that the article concerning the Sacrament of the body and blood of our Lord Jesus Christ is unclear, or who distort the words of Christ in the Holy Supper. For we desire to retain all articles of the Christian doctrine absolutely pure and sure, whether they be great or small (though not one is small or insignificant), and we do not want to surrender one tittle of it. And that is as it should be; for the doctrine is our only light that lights and guides us and shows us the way to heaven. If we let it be made weak and dim in one particle, then we may be sure that it will become altogether powerless. If we fail here, love will do us no good. We certainly can be saved without the love and unity of the sacramentarians, but we cannot be saved without the pure doctrine and faith. Hence, we gladly keep peace and unity with those who with us treat and believe all articles of the Christian faith in a Christian and right way. Indeed, we are willing as much as possible to keep peace even with our enemies; we will pray for those who in ignorance slander and persecute our doctrine but never for those who knowingly and contrary to their conscience attack one or more articles of the Christian faith.

"And if we are so stern and stubborn, we are taught that by the very example of St. Paul, who publicly and vehemently condemns the false apostles in a matter that they and their adherents regarded not only as insignificant and secondary but even as highly unfair (for they believed both, [namely,] that they [the teachers] taught rightly according to God's Word and that they [the hearers] believed rightly and according to God's Word); for he says: 'He who troubles you shall bear his judgment, whoever he is.' Therefore, as I often and in many words have admonished to do, we must diligently distinguish between doctrine and life. Doctrine is heaven; life is earth. In life there is sin, error, discord, labor, and sorrow. There love must not listen but overlook; it must suffer and always forgive sins, that is, if sin and error are not defended. But doctrine is a far different matter, for it is holy, pure, undefiled, heavenly, divine. Whoever desires to pervert that, to him must be shown neither love nor mercy. [Pure] doctrine requires no remission of sins.

"Therefore, it is not at all proper to try to compare doctrine with life; for a single letter, indeed a single tittle of Scripture is of more and greater importance than heaven and earth. Hence, we will not have anyone pervert it in the least. We can well excuse and overlook weaknesses and faults in life, for we too are weak human beings who daily fail and sin; indeed, all dear saints confess most earnestly in the Lord's Prayer that they are sinners and that they believe in the forgiveness of sins. But by the grace of God our doctrine is pure. There is not a single article of our faith that is not well and firmly grounded in Scripture. But these [articles] the devil would like to besmirch and pervert. Therefore, he also attacks us so insidiously with the argument, accusing us through the factious spirits that we do not keep the peace but are quarrelsome and destroy the unity and love in the church or Christendom.

"Here, then, we learn how St. Paul regards a little error in doctrine that might appear as very insignificant, if not even as the truth.

He regards it as so great and dangerous that he dares curse the false apostles, though these seemed to be great persons. Therefore, we dare not regard the leaven of false doctrine as insignificant. No matter how small it may appear, its result is that the truth and salvation will be suppressed and crushed and God will be denied unless we guard against it. For if the Word is blasphemed and God is denied and blasphemed (and this must follow of necessity), then there is no longer any hope for salvation. But though we are slandered, cursed, and killed, we shall not be overpowered; for He who is never destroyed can again raise us up and deliver us from the curse, death, and hell.

"Therefore, we should learn to regard the majesty and glory of the Word greatly and highly; for it is not so insignificant and trifling as the enthusiasts of our time think, but a single tittle [of it] is greater than heaven and earth. So here we do not care anything for Christian unity and love, but we directly make use of the judgment seat, that is, we curse and condemn all those who pervert and corrupt the majesty of the Word even in the least; for a little leaven leavens the whole lump. But if they will let us have the Word wholly and unmutilated, then we will not only keep love and peace with them, but we offer ourselves gladly to be their servants and to do all they ask of us. If, however, they do not let us retain the Word, then may God grant that before they and all the world, and we with them, perish and be cast into the abyss of hell, He may remain true in His Word. If He remains, then there remains life and salvation. Then also those who believe His Word will truly remain and be preserved, even if they were in the abyss of hell" ("Detailed Interpretation of the Epistle to the Galatians" [Gal. 5:9–12], 1535, St. Louis edition, 9:642ff.).

The same: "We will begin with the fact that they (the Zwinglians) write whole books and admonish us that we should not on account of these causes [differences regarding the Lord's Supper] destroy Christian unity, love, and peace; for, they say, it is an insignificant matter and an unimportant controversy because of which Christian love should not be violated. So they reprove us for adhering so sternly and firmly to it [the doctrine of the Lord's Supper] and causing divisions.... But may such love and unity be cursed into the depth of hell, because such a unity not only tears apart the Christian

124

church [*die Christenheit*], but it also mocks and ridicules its great distress. . . .

"No, my dear sirs, I will have nothing to do with such peace and love! If I would kill someone's father and mother, wife and child, and purpose to destroy also him, and then would say: 'Keep the peace, my friend; we want to love each other, for the matter is not of such importance that we quarrel about it,' what [do you think] he would tell me? Oh, how he would love me! So then the enthusiasts destroy my Christ, my Lord, and God my Father, in addition also my mother, the Christian church [*die Christenheit*], together with my brethren, as well as me, and [yet] they want to cultivate my friendship [*Liebe*]. . . . Nor does it benefit them to say that otherwise they esteem the Word of God and the whole Gospel most dearly and highly except only this doctrine. My dear friend, God's Word is *God's* Word and does not bear any criticism. Whoever accuses God of lying in His Word and [so] blasphemes Him, or whoever says that it is a small matter in which He is being blasphemed and called a liar, he blasphemes the whole God and regards as insignificant all blasphemy of God. God is one and cannot be divided. He cannot be praised in one place and reproved in another, nor can He be honored in one place and despised in another. . . .

"But we poor sinners [we Lutherans who oppose the sacramentarians], who are 'altogether without the Spirit,' answer these pious Christians [the sacramentarians] from the holy Gospel: 'He who loves father and mother, wife and child, house and home, as well as his own soul more than Me, is not worthy of me' (Matt. 10:37 [Luther's paraphrase, largely based on Luke 14:26]); and again: 'I did not come to bring peace but a sword' (v. 34). So also Paul says: 'What accord has Christ with Belial?' (2 Cor. 6:15). If then we are to live in Christian unity and preserve Christian love with them, we must also love their doctrine and practice and assent to it or at least condone it. Whoever cares to do this, let him do it, but not I! Christian unity, according to Eph. 6:4, is in the Spirit and means that we are of one faith, one mind, and one judgment [*eines Mutes*]. We gladly will be united with them in secular matters; that is, we are willing to keep bodily or temporal peace with them. But in spiritual matters we will avoid, condemn, and reprove them as long as they live as idolaters, perverters of God's Word, blasphemers, and liars. In addition we are willing to suffer persecution and separation from them as from enemies if and so long as God permits this. We also want to ask and admonish them to desist [from their error]. But to yield to their blasphemies, ignore and approve them, that we neither can nor want to do. . . .

"Therefore, we shall say to these enthusiasts and visionaries who offer us peace what Christ said to Judas, the betrayer, in the garden: 'Judas, are you betraying the Son of Man with a kiss?' (Luke 22:48). Most certainly it would be a Pharisaic [*jüdischer*] peace and a kiss of betrayal if they ask us to be their friends and keep silence as we watch their burning and murdering by which they lead so many souls eternally into hell. And yet they insist that this [their teaching] should be regarded as insignificant and of no importance" ("That the Words of Christ, 'This Is My Body,' Still Stand Firmly Against the Enthusiasts," 1527, St. Louis edition, 20:772ff.)

The same: "Because so many and great warnings and admonitions of God have been addressed to them (the sacramentarians), . . . I must let them go and avoid them as self-condemned (*autokatakritos;* Titus 3:11), for knowingly and maliciously they want to be condemned. Nor will I have fellowship with any of them, whether he be Stenkefeld [Schwenkfeld], Zwingli, or whoever he may be, neither by letters, writings, words, nor deeds, as the Lord commands (Matt. 18:17). I regard them all as one ilk [*Kuchen*], for they refuse to believe that the Lord's bread in the Holy Supper is His true or real body, which the wicked and Judas receive orally as well as St. Peter and all [other] saints. Whoever refuses to believe this (I declare), let him not molest me with letters, writings, or words. Let him not expect me to have fellowship with him, since that will never happen" ("Brief Confession of the Holy Sacrament Against the Enthusiasts," 1544, St. Louis edition, 20:1778).

The same: "Some unreasonable persons [*Geister*], deceived by the devil, say regarding the Sacrament and other errors that we should not contend so sternly about one article and because of it destroy Christian love or deliver each other to the devil. But though they err in a minor matter, we must yield and concede a little and preserve brotherly and Christian peace since they agree in other articles. No, dear friend, I will not have peace and unity if that means to deny God's Word, for this means to lose eternal life and all things [all spiritual blessings]. It is not proper here to yield or concede anything to please you and a few [other] people. But to the Word all things must yield, whether he is foe or friend. For that was given us solely for eternal life and not for outward or temporal unity and peace. The Word and doctrine must bring about Christian unity and fellowship. Where people are agreed and united in that, all other things [such as Christian fellowship] will follow, but where that is not the case, no unity will remain.

"Therefore, do not speak to me of love and friendship if the Word and doctrine are to be destroyed; for it is not love but the Word that brings eternal life, divine grace, and all heavenly gifts. We will be glad to be friends with them in outward things as we must be with everyone else in this world, even with our worst enemies. Let that be done in this life and secular affairs about which we do not contend. But in the matter of doctrine and Christian fellowship we will have nothing to do with them nor regard them as brethren but rather as enemies because they knowingly continue in their error, and we will contend against them in our spiritual warfare. It is only a satanic, deceitful, and crafty attack by which they declare and demand that we should somewhat yield to them and condone their error for the sake of unity. By that [attack] he [Satan] insidiously tries to lead us away from the [divine] Word. If we would concede to this and agree on this point, he already has gained ground, and if we would yield to him the breadth of a finger, he soon would have the whole hand. Then in a short time he would have us altogether in his power.

"It may not appear that there is much danger and harm [*Macht*] connected with this matter, but St. Paul represents it as very great; in fact, there is at stake the loss of God and eternal life, not merely money or goods, the love and favor of men, earthly peace and quietness, or whatever else flesh and blood may give or do or whatever else the world may give or take. Let these things [these earthly gifts] remain or perish, whatever may remain or perish; by that he [Satan] has not yet gained anything. But if you permit him to take from you this one thing—the Word—you have lost all things and nothing can counsel or help you; for then the chief thing is lost without which there is no good [blessed] life. Whatever you can do will neither avail nor stand before God, and yet with such fine show and pretense the devil seeks and endeavors to rob you of this [eternal life]; for it is his intention to deprive you of it. Therefore we dare not jest on this point nor be secure" ("Sermon on the Christian's Armor and Weapons," 1532, St. Louis edition, 9:831–32).

Chemnitz: "It is true that doctrine is the chief part of the ministry, and that if true doctrine is perverted and perverse opinions are established, then the very ministry is changed. But the ministry of those who pervert doctrine must be avoided, as it is written: 'Beware of false prophets' [Matt. 7:15]; and again: 'They will by no means follow a stranger, but will flee from him, for they do not know the voice of strangers' [John 10:5]" (*Examen concilii Tridentini,* p. 237, a).

Gerhard: "We concede that in a certain good sense we are schismatics, namely, inasmuch as we have separated ourselves from the Roman church and its head, the Roman pope. But we have not separated ourselves from the unity of the catholic [the universal Christian] church and its Head, Christ Jesus. What a blessed schism [this is] by which we were united with Christ and the true catholic church! Such a schism it was in ancient times when the Christian church severed its connection with the Jewish synagogue, and that by the divine command: 'Be saved from this perverse generation' (Acts 2:40), and again: 'Come out of her, my people' (Rev. 18:4).

"Such a schism also the fathers command. Ignatius thus writes in his letter to the Philadelphians (chap. 6): 'If anyone follows him who has deviated from the truth, he will not inherit the kingdom of God, and he who refuses to avoid a false prophet will be condemned to hell.' Ambrosius in his commentary on Luke remarks (chap. 6): 'If any church rejects the faith, it must be forsaken.' Chrysostom, in his 46th sermon on Matthew, says: 'He does not leave the church who leaves it physically, but he who in spirit leaves the foundation of the Christian truth. We indeed leave them (the Arians) in a physical way, but they [leave the church] by their faith' [their error of denying the deity of Christ]. Admonished by these commands and examples, we have separated ourselves from the idolatrous Roman church but not from Zion; we [merely] fled out of Babylon. We have not divided the church, but we have separated the disciples, following the example of Paul in the church at Ephesus (Acts 19:9). We have not erected an altar against an altar, following the examples of Jeroboam and the Donatists, but we cast the altar of Damascus out of the house of the Lord and restored true worship (2 Kings 16)" (*Loci theologici,* "De ecclesia," par. 156).

Balduin: "The admonition of Paul is most serious: 'Do not be unequally yoked together with unbelievers. For what fellowship has righteousness with unrighteousness?' (2 Cor. 6:14); and again: 'Have no fellowship with the unfruitful works of darkness' (Eph. 5:11); or: 'Flee from idolatry' (1 Cor. 10:14). This [admonition] separates all believers [*Fromme*] from fellowship with the wicked and severs the adherents of various religions from one another in their religious exercises [worship]. It is the duty of every pious and steadfast confessor to guard the treasure of sound doctrine, of whose truth he is convinced in his conscience, in order that it may not be defiled, diminished, or lost altogether, which can easily happen through indiscreet association with opponents of the true religion. Therefore, we are in duty bound, as much as possible, to keep away from their worship [that of the heterodox] in order that we may not burden our consciences nor offend the weak by appearing to fellowship with the opponents. Against the admonition of St. Paul some here sin in a twofold way. In the first place, they of their own accord and without any outside command take part in such sacrilegious worship either because they are epicureans, to whom religion is of no concern so that they regard it as immaterial to what communion they belong, or because they seek some advantage that they could not obtain if they would refrain from fellowshiping with others. Such, however, sin most grievously since there is only one faith, and of this everyone must be sure in his heart; for according to Rom. 14:23, whatever is done with a doubting conscience is sin, and in matters of religion sinful gain must be avoided altogether. Such people halt between two opinions, and if they are not inveterate epicureans, they at least are lax in religion and must face the Lord's severe judgment.

"In the second place, there are those who allege that they are compelled by the government to attend such [heterodox] worship. But since the government has no authority over conscience and religion, it is right to refuse it obedience in this matter, for we must obey God rather than men (Acts 5:29). So also we must render to Caesar the things that are Caesar's and to God the things that are God's (Matt. 22:21). . . . Augustine, in his sixth sermon on the words of the Lord in the Gospel According to St. Matthew, says: 'When the emperor commands one thing but God another, what do you judge? God's power is the greater; that of the government is the lesser. Give to the government your taxes, but render obedience to God.

Be complaisant: the government threatens you with prison, God with hell.'

"Nevertheless there are cases in which someone may attend the worship of unbelievers or heretics. In the first place, in order to observe it, attending it only that one may bear better and surer witness against the ungodly nature of the unbelievers or heretics. Thus tourists attend the synagogues of the Jews or the papistic mass and view their processions in order to be eyewitnesses of what they saw when they tell others about it, to whom it might seem hardly credible. But here great care is needed in order not to make it appear as though we agreed with the opponents. Therefore, we must refrain from the opponents' acts of worship [*Geberden*]; we must not bow our knees or beat our breast as the papists do at the mass. But we must rather make it publicly known by some signs that we do not agree with them, though we should not show our attitude toward the worship of the opponents by laughter or any other sign of contempt.

"Where it is impossible publicly to show that we do not agree with them, it is better to remain away from such worship in order that we may not burden our conscience or expose ourselves to any peril from the opponents. Here is no place for hypocritical dissimulation, for this offends both God and man. 'No one can serve two masters; for either he will hate the one and love the other, or else he will be loyal to the one and despise the other' (Matt. 6:24). Thus Paul at Athens entered the temple of the idol; yet he did not approve idolatry, but he rather made use of the occasion better to inform the idolaters (Acts 17:22–23). It is necessary, however, that anyone who, without endangering his conscience, desires to attend the worship of the heretics merely as an observer should above all be sure that what he sees and hears there is contrary to true worship. . . . Then he who in his heart is firmly convinced of this [the error] will, because of his own greater illumination through the Gospel, feel sorry for these blind persons and intercede before God for those so miserably deceived that He may not impute to them their sin but rather lead them to the knowledge of the truth.

"In the second place, it is permitted to attend the worship of heretics if that is demanded by the government. If, for example, someone accompanies his papistic prince or master to the mass or the papistic processions, he is free to do so, but he must in no way approve the idolatry of his superior or deny any part of his religion to please him, nor dare he hypocritically take part in the papistic superstition, bow his knees before papistic objects of worship, beat his breast, invoke the saints, offer gifts to the priests reading mass, or show respect for or interest in it in any other way. But he must attend merely as an observer, not on account of the worship but merely for the sake of his master whom he must accompany in his secular service. Thus Elisha permitted Naaman the Syrian to accompany his king to the temple of Rimmon, where the king indeed worshiped his idol, but Naaman did not, for he merely served him by conducting him there (2 Kings 5:18).

"But here also care must be taken in a twofold way. In the first place, this political service must not give offense to the weak, for if such conduct of an evangelical [Lutheran] servant in a papistic temple would offend the weak, who perhaps might think that he harbors doubts about the evangelical faith [*Religion*] and approves the papistic idolatry, then he should rather desist from such service. For even things not forbidden must be left undone if they cannot be performed without giving offense, as Paul writes concerning the eating of meat: 'If food makes my brother stumble, I will never again eat meat, lest I make my brother stumble' (1 Cor. 8:13). In such a case either the weak is to be instructed and shown the true cause of such conduct, or the papistic master should be asked to spare him such service by which a weak brother is offended.

"In the second place, it may happen that such a service is required of evangelical [Lutheran] servants to tempt them, namely, whether they will collude with their superiors or whether by their presence they will approve or confirm the wicked worship. In such cases it is not permitted to attend false worship. For if our liberty is tried and our consent is forced from us against our will by fraud, then according to Paul's example (Gal. 2:5) we must in no way yield to the enemies of the truth. Thus the Protestant electors and princes at the famous Diet of Augsburg in 1530 declined to accompany emperor Charles V to the masses and Corpus Christi processions because they perceived that this service was purposely asked of them at the instigation of the monks, not merely to do the emperor a political service but to confirm by their presence the papistic abomination. This they knew well because that Diet was convened largely because the Confession might be heard that opposed the papistic abomination. Hence, they did not wish to act contrary to this [Confession] by this dangerous action" (*Tractatus de casibus conscientiae* 2.6.6).

The same: "We have the command of the apostle: 'Do not be unequally yoked together with unbelievers' (2 Cor. 6:14); and: 'Flee from idolatry' (1 Cor. 10:14). Those who knowingly and willingly take part in the idolatrous worship of the papists and the heterodox worship of the Calvinists are unequally yoked together with unbelievers by publicly participating in strange [heterodox] worship, even though they do not approve of it in their hearts. Those who have learned to know the truth must flee all lies and errors. Second, we here have the example of the primitive church, when the Christians would have nothing to do with the Jews in the public exercise of their religion. Though they agreed in many chief parts of religion, every party practiced its religion in its own communion in order that they might not seem to mingle religions [commit synecretism], which God had forbidden in the Law (Deut. 22:9; Lev. 19:19).

"In the third place, we must not confirm heretics in their errors, which would be done if we would take part in their worship. For by that we would lead them to believe that in the course of time we would join them also in other matters. Indeed, they would mock us as though we would thereby signify that we had separated ourselves from them without [just] cause since now we approve their worship by our conduct.

"In the fourth place, we would make ourselves partakers of the many blasphemies and abominations of which the sect is guilty, and this we must avoid with the greatest earnestness. For we are commanded to come out from them in order that we may not be partakers of their sins and may not receive their plagues (Rev. 18:4). If this coming out cannot be done with the body, it should be done in spirit by avoiding their worship.

"In the fifth place, we would greatly offend the weak as though we were not sufficiently firm in our faith and had done wrong by contradicting the adversaries so long and consistently. For why should we participate in the worship of those whose religion we know to be false? 'Woe to that man by whom the offense comes!' (Matt. 18:7).

"In the sixth place, the sacraments are also marks of the church and its confession. Hence, whoever knows that the papistic or Calvinistic churches are not the true church must refrain from the sacraments of these churches; otherwise he silently approves the faith of such a church. Indeed, the use of the sacraments is a special act of confessing. Hence, if we intensely loathe the [false] doctrine of a [heterodox] church, we must shun its sacraments in order not to commit hypocrisy; for nothing is more dangerous in matters of religion than this pest. Indeed, what kind of faith or religion would that be of which by our action we attest the very opposite. For His service God demands the whole person (Deut. 6:5; Matt. 22:37). In general, even a protest made by this outward action to show disapproval of the religion of the opponents cannot avert the danger of hypocrisy, for such a protest would be contrary to our action [fellowshiping with the heterodox], which supports or confirms the papists and similar opponents in their errors and silently admits that they are right.

"Here finally we must add the example of the believers [*Fromme*] in the primitive church, who refused to fellowship with false teachers. As Irenaeus reports, the apostle John declined to sit next to Cerinthus [a gnostic heretic]. Polycarp, a student of John, spurned the greeting of the heretic Marcion so that the latter exclaimed: 'Do you not know me?' Polycarp answered him: 'I know you as the firstborn of Satan.' So also Cyprian of old prescribed (book 1, chap. 4): 'A faithful and compliant people must separate itself from a public sinner and may not take part in the worship of a godless priest.' When Arsacius, after the banishment of Chrysostom, became his successor in the congregation at Constantinople, not one of the believers honored him by addressing or hearing him, as Theodoret, Sozomen, and Nicephorus attest. Indeed, many preferred to be exiled rather than attend the worship of this hireling. Of Lucius the Arian, as Socrates reports, someone said: 'God forbid that your hand should ordain me.'

"Thus the [ancient] believers abhorred the worship of the heretics as long as they could still find a purer ministry elsewhere. In the same way we must avoid the worship of those whose religion we know for sure is false and contrary to God's Word. If the government should compel us to attend such worship, we must disobey it, since this is contrary to conscience, which no one dare domineer. . . . But this matter [fellowshiping with the heterodox] must be observed still more with regard to the Sacrament of the Holy Supper, which is not as necessary as is Baptism. That should be received neither from the papists nor the Calvinists, who do not have the true Lord's Supper, because they pervert the essence of this Sacrament. . . . Here the saying of Augustine holds: 'Believe and you have eaten.' As I said before: To receive the Sacrament is a mark of confession and doctrine. Whoever, therefore, does not regard as true the doctrine of the church in which he intends to attend the Sacrament cannot partake of the Sacrament in that church with a clear conscience" (ibid., 2.6.7).

Here we may add a few more testimonies from the writings of the teachers of the ancient church:

Ignatius: "I admonish you, not I but the love of Christ, that you use only Christian food and abstain from the fodder of the heretics. They mix into their poison Jesus Christ by teaching what is unworthy of belief and are like those who put deadly poison into honey-sweet wine. Whoever does not know this receives it gladly to die in evil joy. Therefore, beware of those. In this you will succeed if you do not become puffed up but adhere to God, Jesus Christ, the bishop, and the commands of the apostles" (*Ep. ad Trullian.* 6.7).

The same: "Some are accustomed to carry about with wicked deceit the name (Christ) but do things that are unworthy of God. Such you must avoid as wild beasts, for they are mad dogs that bite secretly [unexpectedly]. Of these you must beware as of persons who suffer from a [contagious] disease that is hard to heal" (*Ep. ad Ephes.* 7).

The same: "As many as are of God and Jesus Christ remain with the bishop, and as many as penitently come to the unity of the church will also be of God henceforth to live to Jesus Christ. Be not deceived, my brethren; if anyone causes divisions, he will not inherit the kingdom of God. If anyone follows strange [heterodox] doctrine, he will not consent to the suffering (of the Lord)" (*Ep. ad Philadel.* C).

The same: "I arm you as against beasts in human form. Do not receive them; indeed, if possible, do not even meet them, but pray for them that they may repent. . . . They remain away from the Holy Supper and the (common) prayers because they do not confess that the Holy Supper is the body of our Lord Jesus Christ, who suffered for our sins and was raised again by the loving-kindness of the Father. Those who oppose this divine gift of grace will perish in their attacks. It would serve them better to love in order that they might also be raised. It behooves us to keep away from them and speak of them neither privately nor publicly. We should rather pay attention to the prophets and above all to the Gospel, in which the suffering (of Christ) is set forth to us in graphic description and His resurrection in perfect presentation. But flee divisions as the beginning of all evils" (*Ep. ad Smyrn.* 4, 7).

Irenaeus: "The apostles as well as their disciples exercised such great caution not even to converse with any of those who deceitfully tried to pervert the truth by their own fabrications" (*Lib. adv. haer.* 3.3).

Cyprian: "We must remain separate from the heretics as far as they themselves have separated themselves from the church" (*Ep. I, 3 ad Cornel.*).

Ambrose: "When a church spurns the faith and does not possess the foundation of the apostolic preaching, we must desert it in order that we may not besmirch ourselves with the stain of perfidy. That is what the apostle clearly demands when he says: 'Reject a divisive man after the first and second admonition' " [Titus 3:10].

Augustine: "All who leave the church and are cut off from the unity of the church are antichrists. This [truth] no one should doubt, for he (the apostle) himself designates them thus: 'They went out from us, but they were not of us; for if they had been of us, they would have continued with us; but they went out that they might be made manifest, that none of them were of us' (1 John 2:19). All therefore who do not remain with us but go out from us make it manifest that they are antichrists. . . . Either we are antichrists or they are antichrists. They call us antichrists and say that we went out from them; we say the same thing of them. But this epistle (of St. John) describes the antichrists. Everyone who denies that Jesus is the Christ is an antichrist. Let us therefore consider those who deny this, and let us not take notice of what they say but of what they do. For if they are asked, they all with one accord profess that Jesus is the Christ. Let the tongue be silent for a while, and let us look at the life. If we find this [the life], as Scripture itself tells us that the denial is done not merely with the tongue but by deed, then we certainly shall find many antichrists who indeed profess Christ with their mouth but depart from Christ by their conduct [*moribus*].

"Where do we find this in Scripture? Listen to the apostle Paul.

When he spoke of such [heretics], he said: 'They profess to know God, but in works they deny Him' (Titus 1:16). Here we learn who is an antichrist; whoever denies Christ in works is an antichrist. I do not listen to what is said; I consider what is lived. If the works speak, do we demand words? For what evil [person] does not wish to speak what is good? But what does the Lord say of such? 'Brood of vipers! How can you, being evil, speak good things?' (Matt. 12:34). You bring to my ears your words, but I regard your thoughts. There I behold an evil will, and you bring forth evil fruits.

"He is a doubly lying antichrist who confesses with his mouth that Jesus is the Christ but denies it with his works. He is a liar because he speaks one way and acts in another. Therefore, my brethren, if works are to be questioned, we find not only that many antichrists have gone out from us, but that many are not yet so manifest as to have gone out from us. For as many perjurers, deceivers, evildoers, and the like as are in the church, and whatever else there is that we cannot enumerate, all that is opposed to the doctrine of Christ and the Word of God. But the Word of God is Christ. Hence, everything that is opposed to the Word of God is antichristian [*in Antichristo*]. For antichrist is opposed to Christ. And do you want to know who manifestly opposes Christ? When it happens that they do evil and we begin to reprove them, they will blaspheme—because they do not dare blaspheme Christ—His servants by whom they are reproved. And when you show them that you tell them not your own words but those of Christ, they will try, as long as they can, to prove to you that you speak your own words and not those of Christ. But when it becomes clear that you have spoken the words of Christ, they will oppose also Christ and will begin to criticize also Him" (*Expos. in ep. I. Joh.* 3).

C. Every Christian for the sake of his salvation is in duty bound to acknowledge and adhere to orthodox congregations and orthodox pastors, wherever he can find such.

1. Scripture Proof

Our Lord says: "Whoever confesses Me before men, him I will also confess before My Father who is in heaven. But whoever denies Me before men, him I will also deny before My Father who is in heaven" (Matt. 10:32–33). Again: "Whoever is ashamed of Me and My words, of him the Son of Man will be ashamed when He comes in His own glory, and in His Father's, and of the holy angels" (Luke 9:26). Finally, His holy apostle writes: "If you confess with your mouth the Lord Jesus and believe in your heart that God has raised Him from the dead, you will be saved. For with the heart one believes to righteousness, and with the mouth confession is made to salvation" (Rom. 10:9–10).

According to these words, a person who has faith in Christ and His truth in his heart but refuses to confess it with his mouth cannot be saved. Hence, every Christian is in duty bound, at the peril of losing his salvation, publicly to renounce those who, as he knows, pervert Christ's Word and publicly to acknowledge and adhere to those who, he knows, publicly witness to Christ and His truth. Hence our Lord says: "He who hears you hears Me, he who rejects you rejects Me" (Luke 10:16). And again: "Whoever will not receive you nor hear your words, when you depart from that house or city, shake off the dust from your feet. Assuredly, I say to you, it will be more tolerable for the land of Sodom and Gomorrah in the day of judgment than for that city! . . . He who receives you receives Me, and he who receives Me receives Him who sent Me. He who receives a prophet in the name of a prophet shall receive a prophet's reward. And he who receives a righteous man in the name of a righteous man shall receive a righteous man's reward" (Matt. 10:14–15, 40–41). So also St. Paul writes to Timothy: "Therefore do not be ashamed of the testimony of our Lord, nor of me His prisoner, but share with me in the suffering for the Gospel according to the power of God" (2 Tim. 1:8).

God's Word also declares very emphatically that a Christian should have fellowship with those who confess the true faith and beware of causing divisions and schisms, be it by word or deed. For thus it is written: "I plead with you, brethren, by the name of our Lord Jesus Christ, that you all speak the same thing, and that there be no divisions among you, but that you be perfectly joined together in the same mind and in the same judgment. For it has been declared to me concerning you, my brethren, by those of Chloe's household, that there are contentions among you. Now I say this, that each of you says, 'I am of Paul,' or 'I am of Apollos,' or 'I am of Cephas,' or 'I am of Christ.' Is Christ divided? Was Paul crucified for you? Or were you baptized in the name of Paul?" (1 Cor. 1:10–13). Again: " . . . endeavoring to keep the unity of the Spirit in the bond of peace. There is one body and one Spirit, just as you were called in one hope of your calling; one Lord, one faith, one baptism; one God and Father of all, who is above all, and through all, and in you all" (Eph. 4:3–6). Finally: "They went out from us, but they were not of us; for if they had been of us, they would have continued with us; but they went out that they might be made manifest, that none of them were of us" (1 John 2:19). All these are grounds on which the apostle bases his admonition: " . . . not forsaking the assembling of ourselves together, as is the manner of some" (Heb. 10:25), and Christ His command: "If he refuses even to hear the church, let him be to you like a heathen and a tax collector" (Matt. 18:17).

Accordingly, we are told of the first Christians not only that "they continued steadfastly in the apostles' doctrine" but also in "fellowship, in the breaking of bread, and in prayers." So also that "all who believed were together. . . . So continuing daily with one accord in the temple, and breaking bread from house to house, they ate their food with gladness and simplicity of heart, praising God and having favor with all the people. And the Lord added to the church daily those who were being saved" (Acts 2:42, 44, 46–47).

2. Witnesses of the Church in Its Official Confessions

Formula of Concord: "And because directly after the times of the apostles, and even while they were still living, false teachers and heretics arose, and symbols, i.e., brief, succinct confessions were composed against them in the early church, which were regarded as the unanimous, universal Christian faith and confession of the orthodox and true church, namely, the Apostles' Creed, the Nicene Creed, and the Athanasian Creed, we pledge ourselves to them, and hereby reject all heresies and dogmas which, contrary to them, have been introduced into the church of God" ("Of the Summary Content, Rule, and Standard," Epitome, par. 3; *Triglot,* p. 777).

The same: "In the third place, since in these last times God, out of special grace, has brought the truth of His Word to light again from the darkness of the papacy through the faithful service of the precious man of God, Dr. Luther, and since this doctrine has been collected from, and according to, God's Word into articles and chapters of the Augsburg Confession against the corruptions of the papacy and also of other sects, we confess also the First, Unaltered Augsburg Confession as our symbol for this time, not because it was composed by our theologians, but because it has been taken from God's Word and is founded firmly and well therein, precisely in the form in which it was committed to writing in the year 1530, and presented to the emperor Charles V at Augsburg by some Christian electors, princes, and estates of the Roman Empire as a common confession of the reformed[11] churches, whereby our reformed churches are distinguished from the papists and other repudiated and condemned sects and heresies, after the custom and usage of the early church, whereby succeeding councils, Christian bishops and teachers appealed to the Nicene Creed, and confessed it" ("Comprehensive Summary," Thorough Declaration, par. 5; *Triglot,* pp. 851, 853).

From this we see very clearly that our church was not at all separating itself from the true, orthodox Christian church by separating itself from the papacy. By that [separation] it rather wanted to be faithful to the true church of the past. Indeed, it was so far removed from separating itself from it that in its Augsburg Confession it referred to its agreement not only with Scripture but also with the church, and not merely with the church in general but especially also with the true Roman [Catholic] church as it declares: "Since then this [doctrine] is clearly rooted in Scripture and also is not contrary to or against the universal Christian, indeed also Roman, church, so far as we can judge from the writings of the fathers, we hold that our opponents cannot disagree with us regarding the articles mentioned above" (Augsburg Confession, Conclusion of Art. XXI, par. 1ff.; German text, *Triglot,* p. 58).

But as the whole later church should always acknowledge the early church, so every Christian should always acknowledge and adhere to the orthodox church.

3. Witnesses of the Church in the Private Writings of Its Teachers

Luther: "I see that it is very necessary to admonish those whom Satan is now beginning to persecute. Among them are some who think that they, when attacked, might escape danger if they say: 'I do not adhere to Luther nor to anyone else but cleave to the holy Gospel and the holy or Roman church; for then we shall remain unmolested.' And yet they retain my doctrine in their heart as evangelical and hold to it. Truly, such a subterfuge will not help them, and it means as much as denying Christ. Therefore, I beseech them earnestly to beware.

"It is true that you by no means should say: 'I am a Lutheran or a papist,' for none died for you nor is your Master than Christ alone, and you should regard yourself as a Christian. But if you believe that Luther's doctrine is evangelical and the pope's unevangelical, you must not cast Luther aside; otherwise you will cast aside his doctrine, which you regard as that of Christ. So you must say: 'Luther may be a scoundrel or a saint, for that I do not care; yet the doctrine is not his but that of Christ Himself.' For you see that the tyrants have in mind not [merely] to kill Luther but to destroy his doctrine. It is on account of his doctrine that they attack you and ask you whether you are a Lutheran. Here surely you must not reply evasively, but you must frankly confess Christ, whether He be preached by Luther, Claus, or George. The person you may ignore, but the doctrine you must confess.

"For thus St. Paul writes to Timothy: 'Therefore do not be ashamed of the testimony of our Lord, nor of me His prisoner' (2 Tim. 1:8). If it would have sufficed for Timothy [merely] to confess the Gospel, Paul would not have commanded him not to be ashamed of himself, yet not of the person of Paul, but of Paul as a prisoner on account of the Gospel. If then Timothy would have said: 'I hold neither to Paul nor to Peter but to Christ,' though he knew that Peter and Paul taught Christ, he thereby would have denied Christ Himself. For Christ says of those who preach Him: 'He who receives you receives Me,' and 'he who rejects you rejects Me' (Matt. 10:40; Luke 10:16). Therefore, since they thus treat His messengers (who preach His Word), it is as if they treated Christ Himself and His Word in the same way" ("Opinion on Receiving the Sacrament in Both Kinds," 1522, St. Louis edition, 20:90–92).

The same: "In addition, this article (concerning the real presence of Christ's body and blood in the Holy Supper) is not an article or teaching fabricated by men apart from Scripture, but it is clearly established and rooted in the Gospel by clear, pure, unmistakable

140

words of Christ and has been believed and taught with one accord from the beginning of the Christian church in the whole world until this very hour. This is proved by the books and writings of the dear fathers, both in the Greek and the Latin language, as well as by the experience of its daily use and work [*Werk*] until this very hour. The testimony of the whole holy Christian church (if we would have nothing more) should alone suffice us to remain true to this article and to hear or to tolerate no factious spirit [*Rottengeist*]. For it is dangerous and atrocious to hear and believe anything against the unanimous testimony, belief, and teaching of the whole holy Christian church that from its beginning now for more than fifteen hundred years has been taught with one accord all over the world.

"If it would be a new article and would not have been taught so unanimously by the entire Christian church [*Christenheit*] in the whole world ever since its beginning, it would not be so dangerous or atrocious to doubt it or to dispute about whether it is right. But since it has been taught with one accord from the beginning by the whole Christian church [*Christenheit*], whoever will doubt it does as much as though he refuses to believe that there is a Christian church. And thereby he not only condemns the whole holy Christian church as a damnable heretic but Christ Himself with all the apostles and prophets, who established and mightily attested this article in which we confess: 'I believe a holy Christian church,' namely, by the words of Christ: 'Lo, I am with you always, even to the end of the age' (Matt. 28:20), and by those of St. Paul: ' . . . the house of God, which is the church of the living God, the pillar and ground of the truth' (1 Tim. 3:15).

"Let Your Honorable Princely Grace consider that if you let such factious spirits come in and tolerate them—since you may hinder and prevent them—you would greatly burden your conscience and perhaps never again let it be at rest, not only on account of the souls that by them might be misled and go to perdition, whom Your Grace might have saved, but also on account of the whole holy Christian church against whose faith, inherited of old and taught everywhere, and against whose witness to let anything be taught, if you could hinder it, would be an intolerable burden for [your] conscience. I would rather let not only all factious spirits testify against me but also all emperors, kings, princes, wisdom, and right than let one iota or tittle of the whole holy Christian church witness or stand against me. For you dare not jest with any article of faith that has been taught from the beginning in the whole church with one accord, just as little as one may jest with papal or imperial rights or other human traditions of the fathers or councils" ("Letter Against Some Factious Spirits [*Rottengeister*] to Margrave Albrecht of Brandenburg," 1532, St. Louis edition, 20:1684–86).

Melanchthon: "We should know that there must be a public ministry of the Gospel and public assemblies, as we are taught in Eph. 4:10–12. And this assembly we must join; of this visible assembly we must be citizens and members, as the psalmist commands us: 'Lord, I have loved the habitation of Your house, and the place where Your glory dwells' (Ps. 26:8); and again: 'How lovely is Your tabernacle, O Lord of hosts!' (Ps. 84:1). These and similar passages do not speak of a Platonic idea but of the visible church, in which the voice of the Gospel resounds and where there is witnessed the ministry of the Gospel; by this God has revealed Himself and is efficacious. And we should not praise those vagabonds who roam about and join no congregation because they cannot find an ideal [church] in which there is not something lacking in morals and discipline. We should rather seek the church in which the articles of faith are taught purely and no idolatry is defended. That church we should join and hear and love its doctrine as we unite our intercession and confession with their prayers and confession. . . . We should also learn to support it in order that it may not be devastated. For where there are no assemblies, there the voice of the Gospel becomes silent. So the Mohammedan tyrants in many places destroyed all churches and did not permit even their own people to assemble. We should recognize that such satanic devastations and dispersions are a dreadful and very great evil. Therefore, we should ask God that He may preserve His congregations, and we ourselves should support them with all our resources" (*Loci theologici,* [Leipzig, 1552], pp. 420–22).

Gerhard: "Since outside the church there is no salvation, and he does not have God in heaven for his Father who does not have the church on earth for his mother, we must be sure which assembly deserves the name and definition of a church in order that we may join that church and keep away from the gatherings of the wicked. The necessity of knowing this doctrine [of the church] the papists by their disputations force on us, for on this article they place their chief hope of victory, since they appropriate the name catholic church exclusively to themselves. . . .

"There are also other errors of visionary persons concerning the church. Some, despising the ministry of the Word and the sacraments, boast of their [new] inspirations and revelations and extol themselves as being the true church of Christ. Others, when thinking of a church, look for the greatest assembly or for what the mighty and learned are inclined to regard as the church. Still others ascribe salvation also to the heathen who are outside the church and without the saving knowledge of Christ. Others again falsely imagine that the church is the aggregate of all sects, if only they bear the name of Christ. Some do not join any congregation and do not concern themselves about any church, especially if they indulge in their own special opinions and nevertheless hope to be saved. Some, finally, on account of the wicked persons who in this life mingle with the congregations, separate themselves from the church. On account of this and other perversions, the doctrine of the church must be diligently explained from the passages of Scripture" (*Loci theologici,* "De ecclesia," par. 2).

Kromayer: "It is necessary for us to look for the true church. This is denied by the Remonstrants [a Dutch Arminian group], who follow in the footsteps of Socinus. He regarded the question of which is the [true] church and where it is to be found as unnecessary, indeed as useless. This he did to hide himself and his followers all the better and more securely and to spread his [heterodox] articles of faith. But we are commanded not only to seek the pure doctrine and to distinguish it from the false but also to join the true church and have fellowship with it. This we prove from (1) Matt. 7:13–14: 'Enter by the narrow gate,' etc.; (2) Rom. 16:17: 'Now I urge you, brethren, note those who cause divisions and offenses, contrary to the doctrine which you learned, and avoid them'; (3) 1 John 4:1: 'Beloved, do not believe every spirit,' etc.; (4) 2 Cor. 6:14–15: 'Do not be unequally yoked together with unbelievers,' etc.; (5) Eph. 4:3ff.: ' . . . endeavoring to keep the unity of the Spirit in the bond of peace,' etc. . . . We therefore must not only confess the [divine] truth, but we also must practice fellowship with those who confess it, according to Eph. 4:3 and 1 Cor. 12:12ff.: 'For as the body is one and has many members, but all the members of that one body, being many, are one body, so also is Christ. For by one Spirit we were all baptized into one body,' etc.; and Heb. 10:25: ' ... not forsaking the assembling of ourselves together,' etc." (*Theologia positivo-polemica,* [Leipzig, 1677], pp. 1028–29).

Calov: "Must we seek the true church in order to join it? Socinus, in the first chapter of his tract on the church and sending out ministers, judges that the question of which the church is and with whom it is to be found is not necessary, indeed almost useless. Then he tries to prove that the church cannot of necessity be known by its marks, because it is not in itself necessary to seek and recognize the true church. This last point he again tries to prove from the fact that it is sufficient for salvation to keep Christ's commandments, and Christ has nowhere commanded us to seek the true church.

"If then he is faced with the objection that everyone must be in the true church of Christ, and that from this it follows of necessity that everyone must seek and recognize the true Christian church, he denies this conclusion. He rather says that as soon as anyone has the doctrine of Christ, he is actually in the true church, and to be in it, he need not inquire which is the true church of Christ since he already knows it, and he knows also the others who have the same saving doctrine of Christ.

"Now though we indeed admit that it is not directly and absolutely necessary for anyone to know which is the true church and with whom it is to be found (so that a person could not be saved unless he knows it and has joined a visible church as a member), if only he belongs to the invisible church, which [truth] in other places we prove against the papists, nevertheless, we cannot agree with the Socinians, who judge too carelessly and indifferently concerning the necessity and benefit of seeking the true church, as though it were in no way necessary to recognize and join the true church, since it is not only not commanded but really not necessary to seek it.

"The statement of Socinus is no doubt made in order that he may have for himself and others a subterfuge; for this sect neither would nor could join a church, as that does not matter to it. And no wonder, for they regard the sacraments, which are only administered in the church, as amounting to nothing or at least to very little, and they do not at all consider them to be means of salvation [grace]. Against Socinus we briefly quote:

"In the first place, the names of the church, for it is called the 'body of Christ' (Eph. 1:23; 4:12); the 'kingdom of heaven' (Matt. 3:2); the 'city of God' (Rev. 3:12; 11:2); and the 'house of God' (1 Tim. 3:15). The members, therefore, dare not be separated from the body; the sons of the kingdom should, as much as possible, be in the kingdom; the spiritual citizens must be in the city of God; and the God's family members must be in His house. They must never be away from the body, the kingdom, the city, and the house of God. This they must join, as much as possible, also according to the outward communion.

"In the second place, the type of the ark of Noah, which no doubt prefigured the true church. Since only those were saved who were in the ark of Noah, while the others, who were outside the ark, perished in the flood, so there is no salvation outside the church, but only in it are we preserved from the deluge of God's wrath (1 Peter 3:18). Similar is the pattern of the homes of the Israelites in Egypt, which the angel of death did not touch, while outside them he killed all the firstborn (Ex. 12:13). Such also is the house of Rahab, in which all were saved who were received into it, while those who were outside were destroyed (Joshua 2:9; 6:21. Cf. the letters of Cyprian).

"In the third place, the parables. In John 10:1ff. the church is compared to a sheepfold. Now, as the sheep that roam about outside the sheepfold fall prey to the wolves or thieves, so also we shall perish unless we join the church. The church is compared to Jerusalem (Gal. 4:26; Heb. 12:22; Rev. 3:12). But just as those who desired to worship God and bring an offering to Him had to come to Jerusalem (Ps. 87:2), where God had His fire and hearth (Jer. 31:9), so we must join the church to worship God. The church is called our mother (Gal. 4:26), and so all her children must be gathered to her in order that they might be nurtured by her to life everlasting (cf. Irenaeus).

"In the fourth place, the command of Christ: 'Tell it to the church' (Matt. 18:17). If we are to tell anything to the church, we must of necessity know where and which the true church is. So we must inquire which is the true church and by no means regard this as something useless.

"In the fifth place, the command of the apostle: ' . . . not forsaking the assembling of ourselves together' (Heb. 10:25). If we are not to forsake the assembling of ourselves together, we must join the holy assembly or church, and therefore it is necessary for us to find out where it is.

"In the sixth place, the generally accepted principle: 'Outside the church there is no salvation,' which can be proved from Eph. 2:12ff.; 4:16; 5:8; 1 Peter 2:9–10; Rev. 22:15. If ordinarily there is no salvation outside the church, we must seek the church in order to have a part in salvation. If we cannot be joined with it in deed, we should be joined with it at least in our longing for it, and if possible, we should rejoice also in having outward fellowship with it. Hence, we dare not omit the search for it.

"In the seventh place, the blessings entrusted to the church. If God has entrusted to the church His spiritual and heavenly blessings, in order that they might ordinarily be imparted there, then we must not regard it as useless and unnecessary to seek it. To the church God has entrusted the Word, the sacraments, the keys of the kingdom of heaven, the power to bind and to loose, in order that these spiritual gifts may be imparted [to man]. Therefore also regeneration, renewal, illumination, remission of sins, sanctification, and the gift of the Holy Spirit are gifts that properly belong to the church. And as they are found in the church, we must certainly seek to find the church in order that we may enjoy these blessings.

"In the eighth place, the promise given to the communion of saints; for to it Christ has promised His special presence: 'Where two or three are gathered together in My name, I am there in the midst of them' (Matt. 18:20). It is therefore necessary that we are among those who are gathered together in Christ's name; so we must seek them and cleave to them in order that we may take part in this special promise.

"In the ninth place, the cordial desire of believers, who, far from regarding fellowship with the church as not at all necessary or even as useless, heartily and ardently yearn for it (Ps. 26:8; 27:4; 42:3; 84:4). The psalmist says: 'Blessed are those who dwell in Your house; they will be still praising You. Selah' (Ps. 84:4).

"In the tenth place, the consensus of the ancient fathers. Irenaeus thus says: 'Those will not partake of the work of the Holy Spirit who do not adhere to the church; for where the church is, there is also the Spirit, and where the Spirit of the Lord is, there is also the church and all grace' (11.3.40; cf. also Cyprian on the unity of the church). Augustine writes: 'He who does not have God for his Father,

146

does not have the church for his mother' (*De Symbol. ad catech.* 4.10; et serm., c. IX, De temp.). Again: 'Whoever has separated himself from the church may think he were living ever so praiseworthy; yet for this one sin, that he has separated himself from the communion of Christ, he will not inherit life, but the wrath of God will abide on him' (Ep. CLII)" (*Socinismus profligatus,* pp. 888–91).

Quenstedt: "Outside the visible church no invisible church is to be looked for, for the invisible church is included in the visible" (*Theologia didactico-polemica,* part IV, 15; fol. 1639).

This [truth] is attested also by the ancient church [fathers]:

Ignatius: "Let no one deceive himself. Wherever anyone is not within the altar, he loses his part in the bread of the Lord. If the prayer of the one or the other has so great power, how much more has what the bishop and the whole church offer up. Whoever, therefore, does not come to the assembly, he already has exalted and judged himself. For it is written: God resists the proud. We should therefore take care that we may not resist the bishop in order to be subject to God" (*Ep. ad Eph.* 5).

The same: "Just as the Lord did nothing without the Father, since He was one with Him, neither in His own person nor by His apostles, so you should do nothing without the bishop or presbyter [minister]. So also do not try to decide what is fitting according to your own private opinion, but in fellowship [let there be] one prayer, one supplication, one mind, one hope in love and in holy joy. Jesus Christ is one, and there is nothing higher than He. So then let all come together in one temple of God, as to one altar and to one Jesus Christ, who has come from one Father and is with one [Father], to whom He has ascended. Be not misled by false opinions nor by old fables, which are things that do not profit" (*Ep. ad Magnes.* 7–8).

Clement of Rome: "You, therefore, who have laid the foundation of the uprising, be obedient to the elders and receive their punishment as your penance while you bow your knees. Learn to subject yourselves and put away the boastful and proud arrogance of your tongue, for it is better to be found small and of good reputation in the flock of Christ than to lose that hope by esteeming yourselves above measure" (*Ep. ad Cor.* 57).

Irenaeus: "In the church God has established the apostles, prophets, teachers, and all the other operations of the Holy Spirit.

In all this those do not participate who do not come to church but cheat themselves out of [eternal] life by their wicked opinions and their very wicked works" (Book 3, 40).

Thesis IX

To obtain salvation, only fellowship in the invisible church, to which alone all the glorious promises regarding the church were originally given, is absolutely necessary.

1. Scripture Proof

God's Word says: "Therefore we conclude that a man is justified by faith apart from the deeds of the law" (Rom. 3:28); again: "Nor is there salvation in any other, for there is no other name under heaven given among men by which we must be saved" (Acts 4:12). According to these passages fellowship with Christ by faith absolutely and alone is necessary for salvation. The principle: "Outside the church there is no salvation" or "Who does not have the church for a mother, does not have God for his Father," therefore, is true only in the sense that outside the invisible church there is no salvation and no divine sonship of grace. The principle means no more than that outside of Christ there is no salvation. Whoever has no spiritual [*innerliche*] fellowship with the believers and saints also has no fellowship with Christ. On the other hand, whoever by faith has fellowship with Christ, has fellowship also with all those in whom Christ dwells, that is, with the invisible church.

Whoever, therefore, binds salvation to any visible church subverts the article of the justification of a poor sinner before God alone by faith in Jesus Christ. It is indeed true that also outside the visible church there is no salvation, if by visible church we mean not a particular church [*Partikularkirche*] but the assembly of all the called. For outside the assembly of the called there are no elect. This means that without the Word of God, which is proclaimed only in the assembly of the called, there is no faith and so also no Christ and salvation. " 'Whoever calls upon the name of the Lord shall be

149

saved.' How then shall they call on Him in whom they have not believed? And how shall they believe in Him of whom they have not heard? And how shall they hear without a preacher? . . . So then faith comes by hearing, and hearing by the Word of God" (Rom. 10:13–14, 17).

2. Witnesses of the Church in Its Official Confessions

Apology: "Because of this [the persecution of the church by its enemies] the true doctrine and church are often so entirely suppressed and lost, as this happened under the papacy, as though there were no longer any church, and it frequently appears as though it had perished altogether" (Art. VII, VIII [IV], par. 9; German text, *Triglot*, p. 228).

Large Catechism: "Thus the Holy Spirit effects sanctification by the following means [*Stücke*], that is, through the communion of saints, the forgiveness of sins, the resurrection of the body, and the life everlasting. That is to say: He first leads us into His holy communion and places us into the bosom of the church, in which He preaches to us and brings us to Christ. . . .

"Therefore, learn from this Article [the third of the Apostles' Creed] to understand this very clearly. If someone asks: 'What do you believe by saying: I believe in the Holy Spirit?' you should answer: 'I believe that the Holy Spirit makes me holy as His name implies.' 'But by what means does He do this? What is His way or method?' Then reply: 'He does this through the Christian church, the forgiveness of sins, the resurrection of the body, and the life everlasting. For in the first place He has a special communion in the world, which is the mother that brings forth and bears every Christian by the Word of God. . . .

"For where He does not let it be preached and awaken the hearts so that we believe it, there it is lost as it happened under the papacy, where faith was put entirely under the bench, and no one recognized Christ as his Savior. . . .

"But what then was lacking? This, that the Holy Spirit was not there to have it [the Gospel] revealed and preached, but there were men and evil spirits who taught us to be saved and obtain grace by our works. Therefore, it is also no Christian church; for where Christ is not preached, there is no Holy Spirit, who creates, calls, and gathers the Christian church, outside of which no one can come to Christ the Lord. . . .

"Outside the Christian church [*Christenheit*], where there is no Gospel, there is no forgiveness, and there also can be no holiness [sanctification]. . . .

"For whoever is outside the Christian church, whether heathen, Turks, Jews, false Christians, and hypocrites,[12] though they believe in and worship only one God, yet they cannot know His mind toward them, and [so] they cannot expect any love or blessing from Him. Therefore they remain in eternal wrath and damnation" (*Triglot,* pp. 686–96, par. 37, 40–45, 56, 66).

Smalcald Articles: "And in these things that concern the spoken outward Word we must firmly hold that God grants His Spirit or grace to no one except through or with the preceding outward Word. . . . Therefore, we ought and must constantly maintain that God does not desire to deal with us men otherwise than through His spoken [*äusserlich*] Word and the sacraments. But everything that is extolled [as coming] from the Spirit without the Word and sacraments is [of] the devil" (Part III, Art. VIII, par. 3, 10; *Triglot,* pp. 494, 496).

3. Witnesses of the Church in the Private Writings of Its Teachers

Luther: "These are called the offenses [*scandala*] and objections against the precious Gospel, just as today it is said in the papacy that no doctor should be created anywhere except in Christendom [*Christenheit*] and the church. On this they stand and rest as a he-goat relies on his horns. And it is indeed true that there is no preacher except in the Christian church; that is impossible. It has been determined that God will not create any Christians unless they are baptized and called by the Gospel. He desires that all who are called Christians should be separated from the world by the Gospel and Baptism. Therefore, there is no true preacher or prophet outside the church. That is taught by the Scripture, and no one can deny it, just as here the Jews say: 'Will the Christ come out of Galilee?' (John 7:41).

"This is a powerful argument that concerns many who know that our doctrine is true and cannot gainsay it; nevertheless, they stand there as a steady horse and only say that the holy Christian church has not yet decided and approved it. With the term 'Christian church' they capture both the simple and the learned guys [*Hansen*], just as this text destroys all. In the Athanasian Symbol we read: *Credo unam ecclesiam christianam* (I believe [in] one Christian church). Again: *Credo etiam in Spiritum Sanctum* (I believe also in the Holy Spirit). Now, outside this Christian church there is neither salvation nor the Holy Spirit, for the Confession says: I believe in the Holy Spirit, the holy Christian church. The Holy Spirit sanctifies the Christian church through His holiness, just as also Christ sanctifies the church. And here we must neither waver nor give way; for that is true, just as true as that Christ came from Bethlehem and Judah. . . .

"Now, we do not deny that Christ was to come out of Bethlehem, but we do not say for that reason that He was not to come out of Galilee. That also is true! Whoever is not in the Christian church and whose doctrine is not determined by it, he is a truly false and unlawful preacher. It is otherwise taught sufficiently that God made man out of a clod of clay; then the devil took clay and made of it a toad or a monk. It is likewise said: Where God builds a church, there the devil places a chapel next to it. The Christian church [according to the papist's opinion] is twofold. They call that the Christian church that is not it, and what is the true church, they refuse to call it such. The question is not whether we should believe the church or whether there is a church, but this is the question: Which is the true church? For we agree with the pope that there is a church. We certainly believe that there is a Christian church, just as also the pope believes this. There must be a Christian church on earth—that we believe as firmly and strongly as they [the papists]. But here is the point, and there we disagree: Which is the Christian church? The devil changes, perverts, and corrupts all names, just as does the pope. . . .

"Now the pope says that he is the Christian church. That we deny, though there are some under the papacy that belong to the Christian church. . . . When they [those who vacillate] now say that they will wait until the church has determined [the doctrine], let the devil wait that long. I certainly will not wait so long; for the Christian church has already decided all things [doctrines]. The members of the body are to be one body and dare not wait until the excrement declares and determines whether it is healthy or not. . . . Therefore it is [rightly] said: The Christian church has so determined it [the doctrine]; for everywhere it is being taught, and all Christians who are baptized believe what this doctrine declares. This determination [of the doctrine] does not occur in a public convention, but it is a spiritual council [that decides the doctrine] and does not require a convention. . . .

"To determine whether the Christian doctrine is right, no convention is necessary. But I declare: I hold to Baptism and believe the Gospel, that it is true and holy, and I believe and adhere to the Sacrament of the Lord's Supper. If they tell me, 'But you do not believe rightly,' then the controversy begins; then there is required a spiritual council [to show] that, as I believe and preach, my brother also believes, indeed so all Christians believe, wherever they are; for they all agree. That is called a Christian church that believes in Christ and desires to be saved by Him, not by works or merits. And what the Holy Spirit tells us, He tells all Christians, wherever they may be. That is [our] Bethlehem and the [our] tribe of Judah from which Christ stems. So also it is true that outside the church there is no prophet, no Christian [*Christe*] or teacher and preacher; for it [the church] is one body and soul, cleaving together as the members cleave to the body since they are members of the body.

"An amputated fist is dead and does not live, nor does it adhere to the body. So also a heretic is cut off from the Christian church by his false teaching and unbelief, and he is dead; for those who are outside the Christian church are dead. The Christian church is not called an assembly of bishops and cardinals. It indeed may be called a council, or it may become a council, but it is not a Christian church. For it [the Christian church] cannot be brought together into one [visible] communion, but it is scattered throughout the world. It believes as I believe, and I believe as it believes. We have no disagreement or inequality regarding the faith: we all believe [in] one Christian church. Outside this church there is nothing" ("Exposition of John 6–8," St. Louis edition, 8:97ff. [So much has been omitted here from Luther's exposition that at times the words quoted lack in clarity—Tr.]).

The same: "I would gladly interpret the spiritual sacrifice (Dan. 12:11) in a figurative sense, namely, that it prefigures the holy Gospel, which must remain till the end of the world, together with faith and the church. But it may happen that the world will become so utterly epicurean that in all the earth there will be no ministry, but only epicurean abominations will be proclaimed, and the Gospel will be preserved only in the homes by the fathers. And this may be the time between Christ's Words on the cross, *'Consummatum est'* (it is finished) and *'Pater in manus tuas commendo spiritum meum'* (Father, into Your hands I commend My spirit). For as Christ lived for a little while after this *Consummatum,* so the church may remain for a little while after it has ceased to be heard publicly. And as the daily sacrifice of the Jews was abrogated in the seventh week through the council of the apostles, yet after that it remained till the destruction of Jerusalem and was observed even by the apostles wherever they wished (though not of necessity), so also the Gospel may be publicly suppressed and silenced as regards the public ministry, and yet it may be preserved by believing Christians in their homes. This distress shall not endure longer that 1,290 days or about four and a half years; for without public preaching faith cannot continue, especially since at this time the world will become more and more wicked even in a year" ("Exposition of Daniel," chap. 12, St. Louis edition, 6:938–39).

Chemnitz: "Also this must be observed, that even in the true church wood, hay, and stubble are built on the foundation [of Christ] (1 Cor. 3:12). While the other, the false assembly prevails and predominates, the true church at times is, as it were, so greatly hidden that Elijah says: 'I alone am left' (1 Kings 19:4). 'When the Son of Man comes, will He really find faith on the earth?' (Luke 18:8). If then at the time of Elijah someone would have judged the truth of the doctrine according to the consensus of the visible assembly, he certainly would have erred" (*Exam. de epist. Apostolorum,* p. 43).

Gerhard: "Although at times corruptions overtake the whole visible church and its public ministry in all particular churches at all places, so that nowhere there remains an unadulterated and pure ministry, nevertheless the entire church never errs in such a way that there will not be persons who, following the simple guidance of the Word, are so sanctified by the control and efficacious operation of the Holy Spirit that they retain the foundation of salvation, remain unspotted from the pernicious errors, and through God's power by faith are preserved to salvation. At times these may be only a few, and because of the general raging of persecutions and corruptions they may be so hidden that they will not be recognized publicly before the world" (*Loci theologici,* "De ecclesia," par. 104).

The same: "If such a time occurs that the outward splendor of the visible church will be lost, then it is not absolutely necessary for salvation that anyone should join a visible or particular church, but it suffices that anyone by true faith is a member of the catholic church, for it is properly to be understood that outside the church there is no salvation" (ibid., par. 101).

The same: "As the moon at times shines in its full light and at times disappears and becomes invisible and in general has various phases, wanes and waxes, decreases and increases, so the church of Christ sometimes shines by its public and free exercise of its pure, divine worship, while at other times it is darkened by severe persecutions and increasing heresies. But finally it again rises out of darkness and gloriously triumphs over the heresies. . . . We by no means deny that the promises concerning the perpetuity of the church are the sure and unchangeable truth, but we add that they are not fulfilled, as the papists imagine, as though the outward splendor of the church would remain uninterrupted and the ministry would always be free from corruptions. These promises are fulfilled, if not in the visible church, that is, in a flourishing and visible assembly of the called, then in the invisible church, that is, in the hidden flock of the elect. Christ gathers and preserves for Himself a church at all times, if not in populous cities and areas, then at least in barren deserts; if not by public pulpits, at least in hidden caverns of the earth" (ibid., par. 86).

The same: "Bellarmine objects: 'We all are held, at the peril of everlasting death, to join the true church and to remain in it. But this cannot happen if the church is invisible.' I reply:

"1. This is not to be understood of the catholic church if we are united by true faith with Christ, its Head. This faith manifests itself in love, and by this we are united with the other members of this mystic body.

"2. Although neither Christ, the Head of the catholic church, nor His true and genuine members are visible to us, yet it is sufficient for our salvation that we are united with them by the inward bond of the Spirit.

"3. It is indeed necessary for us to join also the visible church according to its outward communion, in which the heavenly doctrine is purely proclaimed and the sacraments are legitimately administered. But this union with the outward communion of the visible church is not absolutely and unconditionally necessary.

"4. There may be a time when a particular church that is generally known and esteemed because of the purity of its doctrine and the legitimate administration of the sacraments cannot be found, but the outward ministry is corrupted, as this will be known in the following from examples of the Israelite church in the Old and the Christian church in the New Testament.

"5. Then also a distinction must be made between a twofold access to the church. The first is a local and manifest access to a particular church by outward profession of the faith; the other is a spiritual and hidden access to the universal church by inward assent of the heart. If the former does not take place at times of persecution and increasing perversions [of doctrine], the latter nevertheless always takes place in the church.

"6. Bellarmine cannot deny, when considering the example of Zechariah, Simeon, Hannah, and others who believed before the coming of the Messiah, that they could nowhere find a particular church that was free from corruptions and had a pure ministry. Therefore, they united themselves with the catholic church by faith and the inward assent of the heart, while at the same time they continued fellowship with the outward assembly of the corrupt church.

"7. It may happen that someone may be led into Turkish captivity and there lie hidden in prison. Such a one certainly cannot enjoy external communion with any particular church, but for him the inward union of the catholic church is sufficient for salvation.

"8. Bellarmine admits that someone who is excommunicated unjustly may be saved, since according to his soul and his longing [for the church] he is still in the church, though not according to his body and the outward communion (cf. chap. 6, response to no. 1). Hence, the necessity of union with the church neither can nor should be understood of the outward union with the visible church, but [it must be understood] of the inward and spiritual union with the catholic church. A person unjustly excommunicated is deprived of outward communion and union with the visible church, but he is not deprived of inward communion and union with the catholic or invisible church; hence, he is not deprived of his salvation" (ibid., par. 84).

156

Quenstedt: "Bellarmine objects: 'We all are held, at the peril of everlasting death, to join the true church and to remain in it. But this cannot happen if the church is invisible.' I reply:

"1. Union with the external communion of the visible church is not absolutely and unconditionally necessary. Hence, for a Christian, imprisoned by the Turks or barbarians and so unable to join a particular church, inward union with the catholic church is sufficient for salvation.

"2. And what shall we say of the seven thousand who did not bow their knees to Baal and so did not adhere to the church that at that time was most corrupt?

"3. However we do not deny that every believer or Christian should join a particular church, if one is known to him and he may find it.

"4. We must distinguish between a twofold access to the church. The first is local and visible access to a particular church by profession of faith. The second is the spiritual and hidden access to the universal church by inward assent of the heart. If the former does not take place at times of persecution or of increasing corruptions, the latter always takes place in the church" (*Theologia didactico-polemica,* part IV, 15).

Baier: "After one or the other assembly of the called has defiled itself with heresy or has separated itself from the others by schism, the others no longer regard such a church as the one catholic church, outside of which there are no true believers or saints, and outside of which there is no salvation. For outside of it there may be and are the Word of God and Baptism, by which faith and salvation are imparted to men. . . . It may happen—and it has been predicted by God that it would happen—that the church for a time will be visible in none of its parts or that the visible church will altogether perish. . . . Nevertheless, we do not believe that the whole church has perished or that it will perish, because we recognize that there always have remained and that there always will remain some true believers and saints, free from pernicious error and the fellowship of wickedness, though they are hidden" (*Compendium theologiae positivae,* part III, c. 13, par. 26, 29).

Hollaz: "We confess that it is not by all means and absolutely necessary to know which and where the true visible church is. For against the papists we ourselves teach that this is only ordinarily and not unconditionally necessary and that a person can be saved if only he is a member of the invisible church. It may indeed happen that someone may die blessedly, even as an adult, who does not know what the church is" (*Examen theologicum acroamaticum,* part IV, 1.35, p. 1306).

The fact that also the ancient church held this doctrine is evident from the statements of its trustworthy teachers, who admit that there are children of God also in the assemblies gathered by heretics and separated from the visible, orthodox church and that the visible church at times may disappear altogether. We shall here mention only a few witnesses.

Augustine: "Let him be who he may, and let him be constituted as he would be, if he is not in the church of Christ, he is not a Christian" ("Serm. 1. in vigil. Pentec.").

The same: "He will not have God for a Father who does not have the church for his mother" (Book 4, "De symbolo").

Gregory: "If you desire to live of the Spirit of Christ, then be in the body of Christ" (*In Psalm. 5 poenitentialem*).

It is evident that the fathers with such statements did not wish to attach salvation so much to the visible church and its outward communion as rather to the invisible Christian church of God's children and to communion with them by one faith, worked by the Word and the sacraments.

PART TWO

Concerning
the Holy Ministry or
the Pastoral Office

Thesis I

The holy ministry or pastoral office is an office distinct from the priesthood of all believers.

1. Scripture Proof

Although Holy Scripture attests that all believing Christians are priests (1 Peter 2:9; Rev. 1:6; 5:10), it at the same time teaches very expressly that in the church there is an office to teach, feed, and rule, which Christians by virtue of their general calling as Christians do not possess. For thus it is written: "Are all apostles? Are all prophets? Are all teachers?" (1 Cor. 12:29). Again: "How shall they preach unless they are sent?" (Rom. 10:15). Or: "My brethren, let not many of you become teachers, knowing that we shall receive a stricter judgment" (James 3:1).

2. Witnesses of the Church in Its Official Confessions

Augsburg Confession: "Concerning church government it is taught that no one should publicly teach or preach in the church or administer the sacraments without a proper call" (Art. XIV; German text, *Triglot,* p. 48).

3. Witnesses of the Church in the Private Writings of Its Teachers

Luther: "But all these things we have said only of the common rights and powers of all Christians. For since all Christians have all [spiritual] things in common, as we have always taught, it does not behoove anyone of his own accord to put himself forward and appropriate to himself what belongs to us all. Claim this right and use it, if there is no one else who has received this right. But it is demanded by the [common] right of the congregation that one, or as many as please the congregation, shall be chosen and received who, in the place and in the name of all those who have the same right, publicly administer these offices so that no destructive disorder might arise among God's people and the church may not be changed into a Babylon, but in it all things should be done decently and in order, as the apostle teaches in 1 Cor. 14:40. There is a difference between administering a common right by the command of a congregation and using that right in an emergency. In a congregation in which everyone has the right, none should use that right without the will and appointment of the congregation. But in an emergency anyone may use it who so desires" ("How One Should Choose and Ordain Pastors," letter to the council and congregation of the city of Prague, 1523, St. Louis edition, 10:1589).

The same: "You also lie so greatly [in saying] that I have made all laymen to be bishops, priests, and pastors so that they may administer the office [the holy ministry] without a call. But since you are so pious, you do not state that I added at once: 'Let no one take on himself that [office] for which he is not called except in an extreme emergency' " ("Reply to the Superchristian . . . Book of the Goat Emser," 1521, St. Louis edition, 18:1303).

The same: "Therefore also the Holy Spirit in the New Testament diligently prevented the name *sacerdos,* priest, or cleric [*Pfaffe*] from being given to any apostle or to any other office, but this is the name only of the baptized or of Christians as a congenital or inherited name from Baptism. For none of us becomes an apostle, preacher, teacher, or pastor by Baptism, but we all are born only priests and kings [Luther has *Pfaffen*]. Then you take from such born priests and call or choose them for such offices to execute that office [ministry] in the name of all of us" (Monograph against the private mass and holy orders, 1533, St. Louis edition, 19:1260).

The same: "And thus it happens also in the Christian church [*Christenheit*], where one must first be a Christian or a priest by [his spiritual] birth before he can become a priest or bishop; no one, neither the pope nor anyone else, can make him a priest. But when by Baptism he has been born a priest, then later there follows the office [of the ministry], which distinguishes him from other Christians. For from the whole assembly of Christians some must be taken

162

who shall rule the others, [namely,] to whom God has given special gifts and skills so that they are competent to administer the office. Thus St. Paul says: 'And He Himself gave some to be apostles, some prophets, some evangelists, and some pastors and teachers, for the equipping of the saints (that is, those who already have become Christians and baptized priests) for the work of the ministry, for the edifying of the body of Christ' (that is, the Christian congregation or church). For though we all are priests, we cannot for that reason all preach, teach, or rule. So we must set apart and select some from the whole assembly to whom the office is entrusted" ("Second Exposition of Ps. 110," 1539, St. Louis edition, 5:1037).

The same: "No one can deny that every Christian has God's Word and is taught and anointed of God to be a priest, as Christ says: 'They shall be all taught by God' (John 6:45); and again: 'God, Your God, has anointed You with the oil of gladness more than Your companions' (Ps. 45:7). These companions are Christians, Christ's brothers, who have been anointed with Him to be priests, as also Peter writes: 'You are a chosen generation, a royal priesthood, a holy nation, His own special people, that you may proclaim the praises of Him who called you out of darkness into His marvelous light' (1 Peter 2:9). But if it is true that they have the Word of God and are anointed by Him, they also are in duty bound to confess, teach, and spread [the truth], as Paul says: 'Since we have the same spirit of faith, . . . we also believe and therefore speak' (2 Cor. 4:13); and the prophet: 'I believed; therefore I spoke' (Ps. 116:10). In Ps. 51:13 he [David] says of all Christians: 'Then I will teach transgressors Your ways, and sinners shall be converted to You.'

"Here then we are again assured that a Christian does not only have the right and authority to teach the Word of God, but also that he is in duty bound to do so at the peril of losing his soul and God's grace. You may say: 'But how? If he has not been called to do so, as you yourself have often taught, he dare not preach.' To this I reply: Here you must place a Christian in two places. First, if he is where there are no Christians, he needs no other call than that he is a Christian, inwardly called by God and anointed. There he owes it to the erring heathen or non-Christian to preach and teach them the Gospel, moved by Christian love, even though no Christian has called him to do so. Thus St. Stephen did, as we are told in Acts 7:1–53; though the apostles had not entrusted him with the office

163

of preaching, yet he preached and performed great miracles among the people (Acts 6:8). So also did Philip, the deacon, Stephen's partner (Acts 8:5), though also to him the ministry had not been entrusted. So also did Apollos (Acts 18:25–26). In such cases a Christian out of Christian love has compassion on the distress of the poor, perverted souls and does not wait until he receives a command or letter from a prince or bishop, for necessity ignores all laws and recognizes no law. Hence Christian love makes it one's duty to help, where otherwise there is no one who helps or should help.

"In the second place, if he [the Christian] is where there are other Christians who have the same power and right as he, he should not put himself forward but let others call and put him forth so that he might preach and teach in the place and at the command of the others" ("Reason and Proof from Scripture that a Christian Assembly or Congregation Has the Right and Power to Judge Doctrine and to Call, Install, and Dismiss Teachers," 1523, St. Louis edition, 10:1543–44).

The same: "But the apostles were commanded first to go into the houses of strangers and there to preach, since for this [purpose] they were called and sent that they should preach everywhere, as Christ commanded them: 'Go into all the world and preach the Gospel to every creature' (Mark 16:15). But after them no one has such a general apostolic command, but every bishop or pastor has his special parish, which therefore St. Peter in 1 Pet. 5:3 calls his *kleros,* that is, his part, so that to everyone there is entrusted his part of the people, as also St. Paul writes to Titus. In this [parish] no one else should dare teach his parishioners without his knowledge and consent, neither secretly nor publicly, and no one should by any means listen to him, but they should tell and announce this to his pastor or to the government.

"And this you must also firmly maintain that no minister, no matter how pious or righteous he may be, dare preach or teach secretly the people of a papistic or a heretical pastor without the knowledge or consent of that pastor, for he is not commanded to do. But what we have not been commanded to do, we must leave undone, for we have enough to do to perform what we have been commanded. Nor does it help them [the enthusiasts] that they declare that all Christians are priests. It is true: All Christians *are* priests, but they are not all pastors, for they must not only be Christians

164

and priests but also be in charge of the office [ministry] and a parish. It is the call and command that makes pastors and ministers. Just as a citizen or layman may be ever so learned, yet for that reason he is not a doctor [professor], so that he may publicly teach in the schools, nor may he appropriate that office to himself; he must be called to it.

"This I had to say of the sneaky, treacherous preachers, of whom there now are many, to alert the pastors and governments diligently to warn the people and to command them to take care of such intruders and vagabonds and to guard against them as the devil's own sure messengers. They must show their credentials and proofs that they are sent by God for such work in the parish; otherwise they are not to be admitted and heard, even though they wanted to teach the pure Gospel, indeed even if they were angels and Gabriel himself come down from heaven. For God does not want to have anything done by our own choice or devotion but everything only by [His] command or call, especially in the holy ministry. Thus St. Peter says: 'Knowing this first, that no prophecy of Scripture is of any private interpretation, ... but holy men of God spoke as they were moved by the Holy Spirit' (2 Peter 1:20–21). Therefore Christ also did not permit the devils to speak, though they declared Him to be the Son of God and proclaimed the truth (Luke 4:34–35; Mark 1:24–25). He did not want to permit such an example to preach without a call" ("Exposition of Ps. 82," 1530, St. Louis edition, 5:721–22).

The same: "And first you may well and easily convict them (the sneak preachers) if you ask them regarding their call, [namely,] who has commanded them to sneak in and come to preach secretly [*im Winkel*]; that they cannot answer nor show their command. And I indeed declare that if such sneaks would have no other faults and would be true saints, nevertheless this one act [*Stück*], that they sneaked in without a command or request, must convincingly prove them to be the devil's messengers and teachers. For the Holy Spirit does not sneak but comes publicly from heaven. Snakes sneak, but doves fly. Hence such sneaking is the real way of the devil, and that never fails.

"I heard it said that the sneaks go to the laborers in the harvest to preach to them as they work. So also they go to the colliers and individual workers in the woods, and everywhere they sow their seed and spread their poison and so turn the people away from their parish churches. Here you see how the devil really walks and acts, how he avoids the light and pilfers [mauset] in the dark. Who could be so stupid as not to notice that here are the devil's true messengers? If they would be of God and upright, they would first go to the pastor and speak to him, showing their call and telling him what they believed, [asking him also] whether he would permit them to preach publicly. If the pastor would not permit them, they would be excused before God and could shake the dust from their feet. For the pastor has charge of the pulpit, Baptism, the Sacrament, and the whole care of souls that is entrusted to him. But as it is, they intend secretly to oust the pastor together with all that is commanded him. So they are real thieves and murderers of souls, blasphemers of Christ and of His church.

"Here then nothing else remains to be done than that both governments [Ämter], the spiritual and the secular, cooperate with all diligence. The spiritual office must truly instruct the people constantly and diligently, inculcating in them what has been said above, [namely,] that they are not to admit any sneak but to regard them truly as messengers of Satan and learn to ask them: 'Where do you come from? Who has sent you? Who has commanded you to preach? Where are your credentials and letters [showing] that you have been sent by men? Where are your miracles [showing] that God sent you? Why do you not go to our pastor? Why do you come to me in such a sneaky way and remain in hiding? Why do you not preach publicly? If you are a child of the light, why do you fear the light?' With such questions, I think, you can easily hinder them, for they cannot prove their call. If we could bring the people to such a knowledge of the call, we could easily stop the sneaks. Again, we must constantly instruct and admonish them to tell the pastor of such sneaks, for this they are bound to do if they want to be Christians and desire to be saved. For if they refuse to do this, they help the messengers of Satan and sneaks to steal secretly from the pastor (indeed, from God Himself) his ministry, his Baptism, his Sacrament, his care of souls, as well as his parishioners, and so [they help them] devastate and destroy the parish that God has established.

"If they [the parishioners] will hear and understand this meaning of the call, some upright persons will surely inform the pastor of such sneaky, treacherous preachers; for, as said before, we can easily scare the devil with the call if we insist on it. A pastor may indeed glory publicly and rightly that he has charge of the ministry, Baptism, the Sacrament, and the care of souls, and that these are commanded him, but in that these strange, sneaky, treacherous preachers cannot glory. They must confess that they have sneaked in as strangers and that they attack and invade an office that is not theirs. But that cannot be [of] the Holy Spirit but must be [of] the accursed devil.

"The secular government [*Amt*] must also see to it . . . and like the spiritual government must insist on the call, asking the sneak or his host: 'Where do you come from? Who has sent you?' and so forth, as stated above. In addition it must ask the host: 'Who commanded you to shelter the sneak and to listen to his sneaky preaching? How do you know that the sneak has been commanded to teach you or that you are to learn of him? Why did you not inform the pastor or the government? Why do you forsake your church in which you were baptized, instructed, confirmed, and to which, according to God's order, you belong, hiding yourself in a corner? Who has given you power to split the parish and to create factions among us? Who has taught you to despise your pastor, to judge him, and behind his back to condemn him before he had a hearing or was accused? Why have you become such a judge of your pastor, indeed, your own judge?'

"All such wrongs, and many more, everyone commits who cleaves to the sneaks, and therefore he should justly be charged with them. I have good hopes that if the [secular] government would be diligent in this matter, it would be of great help, and many pious persons would help to make known such vagabonds, if they would know what great danger is connected with the sneaks and that the call or command matters so much. If we would not insist firmly on the call or command, there would at last remain no more church. For as the sneaks now come to us, desiring to split up and destroy our churches, so later other sneaks would invade, split up, and destroy their churches, and there never will be an end to the sneaking and splitting up, one after the other, and soon nothing will be left of the church on earth. That is just what the devil wants and tries to do by these factious spirits and sneaks.

"Therefore, you either prove your call and command, or you keep silence and quit preaching. For it is called an office and indeed an office of preaching. But no one can have an office except and without a command or call. Therefore, Christ also says in the parable, Matt. 25:14–30, that the man traveling into a far country did not give his servants the talents with which they were to trade until he had called them and given them the command to trade. 'Vocatis servis' (the text says) 'et negotiemini,' etc. He called his servants and commanded them to trade with his talents. Such a *vocatus* (vocation) and command also the sneaks should show, or else they should leave the master's goods in peace; otherwise, they will be convicted as robbers or rascals. So also, as recorded in Matt. 20:1–16, the laborers did not go into the vineyard of the householder until they were hired and commanded to go; they rather were idle the whole day without the command and call. Jeremiah speaks of such sneaks: 'I have not sent these prophets, yet they ran; I have not spoken to them, yet they prophesied' (Jer. 23:21).

"It takes much care and labor that those who have a definite call and command from God Himself or from men in God's place preach rightly and adhere to the true doctrine. But what shall come of it if men preach without God's command, indeed, against His command and prohibition, merely at the instigation and incitation of the devil? In that case there can be no other preaching than what is inspired by the evil foe, and it [surely] must be altogether the teaching of the devil, no matter how good it may appear. Who had a greater and better call than Aaron, the first high priest? Yet he became guilty of idolatry and permitted the Israelites to make the golden calf (Ex. 32:4). Afterward, the Levitical priesthood for the greater part fell into idolatry and in addition persecuted God's Word and all true prophets. So also King Solomon was called and established in great glory; yet in his old age he fell away and instituted idolatrous worship (1 Kings 11:4–13). Do not the bishops and popes have a glorious call and command? Are they not seated in the chairs of the apostles and in Christ's place? Yet they are all the greatest enemies of the Gospel unless they teach rightly and preserve the true worship.

"If then the devil can so deceive the teachers whom God Himself has called, established, and anointed, how will he not, rather than teaching anything good, teach his own downright satanic lies through those teachers whom he himself has anointed and moves without, indeed against, God's command? I have often said, and still say, that I would not take all the goods of the world for my doctorate.

168

For I certainly would have to despair at last over the great and difficult matters that rest on me, had I started them as a sneak without a call and command. But now God and the whole world must attest that I have started them publicly in my office as doctor [of Holy Scripture] and pastor, and by God's grace and help I have continued them until now. There are some who say that St. Paul in 1 Cor. 14:30 gives everyone liberty to preach in a congregation and even to bark against the regular minister when he says: 'If anything is revealed to another who sits by, let the first keep silent.' From these words some sneaks judge that when they come into a church, they have the power and right to judge the pastor and to preach another doctrine. But they are greatly mistaken. The sneaks do not consider the text rightly; in fact, they argue from it, or rather argue into it, whatever they desire, for here the apostle speaks of the prophets who are to teach and not of the people who are to listen. Prophets, however, are teachers who in the church are entrusted with the ministry. Why otherwise should they be called prophets? So then let a sneak prove from the start that he is a prophet or teacher in the church into which he has entered and who has entrusted him with this office; then indeed, according to St. Paul's teaching, he could be heard. If he does not prove that, let him go to the devil, who has sent him with the command to appropriate to himself an office that does not belong to him in a church to which he does not belong, especially not as a prophet and teacher.

"What a fine pattern that would be if a pastor would be preaching and everybody would have the right to interrupt and correct him! Then another might interrupt the two and tell them to keep quiet. After that a drunkard might come in and interrupt the three, commanding also the third to shut up. Finally also the women might claim the right, as those sitting by, to tell the man to hush up, and at last one woman would command the other. Oh, what a wonderful church turmoil, billingsgate, and racket that would be! In what pigsty would it not be more orderly than in such a church? But the blinded sneaks do not consider this. They believe that they are the only ones sitting by and do not see that all the others have the same right and could bid them be silent. They do not know what it means to sit by or to speak, to be a prophet or layman according to this passage of St. Paul.

"Let anyone read the whole chapter and then he will clearly

understand that St. Paul here speaks of prophesying, teaching, and preaching in the congregation or church. He does not command the congregation to preach but deals with the ministers who preach in the assembly or congregation; otherwise he would not have to forbid the women to preach, who also belong to the congregation. As the text indicates, it may have been that in the church the prophets sat among the people as the lawful pastors and preachers, and one or two sang or read the pericope, as even today two used to chant the Gospel together in some churches. One of the prophets whose turn it was explained and interpreted such a text, just as it was done with the homilies in the Roman churches. If the first had finished, then another added something to it, confirming and further explaining it. So also St. James did, according to Acts 15:13, with the speech of St. Peter, confirming and interpreting it. St. Paul acted similarly in the synagogues, especially at Antioch in Pisidia. Luke tells us that after the reading of the Law, the elders of the synagogue permitted him to speak. Then Paul arose and spoke on what the elders had asked him to speak, but as a commissioned apostle, not as the sneaks. So it seems well taken that the 'sitting by' refers only to the called prophets or ministers. Whoever of those was to speak arose or sat by, depending on the importance of the matter. It is just as when a prince deliberates on a problem with his counselors or when a mayor [deliberates] with his counselors. Then one arises and speaks, then another, and finally with one accord all follow the one who has given the best advice. Thus one helps the other in counseling, and all things are done decently.

"Should we then allow a strange vagabond to sneak in or a citizen intrude into the council to reprove or command the mayor? Of that nothing good would come. Such a one should be taken by the crew and delivered to the executioner; he certainly would teach him where to sit and would decide his right to speak. Much less may it be tolerated that a strange sneak or an undesirable layman imposes himself on a spiritual council, that is, on the [holy] ministry or the office of a prophet. The prophets have and must retain the right [of teaching]. They should attend to the teaching one after the other and should faithfully help one another in such a way that all things are done decently and in order, as St. Paul says in 1 Cor. 14:40. But how can all things be done decently and in order if everyone becomes a busybody in another's business, which is not commanded to him, and every layman would arise in the church and begin to preach?

"But I am surprised that they [the sneaks] do not also quote the example of the women who likewise prophesied and so ruled the men, the country, and its people. Thus did Deborah, as we read in Judg. 4:4ff., who slew King Jabin and Sisera and ruled Israel; so also did the prophetess at Abel, who lived at the time of David, as we read in 2 Sam. 20:16ff. There was also Huldah at the time of King Josiah, of whom we are told in 2 Kings 22:14ff. But long before that, there was Sarah, who told her lord and master Abraham that he should cast out Ishmael and his mother Hagar, and God commanded him to obey her, as we read in Gen. 21:9ff. Many more examples might be given, like that of Anna, of whom we read in Luke 2:36ff., and the virgin Mary, of whom Luke 1:26ff. tells us, and many more. Here they [the sneaks] might glory and grant the right to preach in the churches also to women. But how much more can the men, following the [given] examples, preach when and where they desire [as the sneaks judge].

"We shall not discuss here what right these women in the Old Testament had to teach and rule. They certainly did not do it as the sneaks without a call or of their own devotion and desire; otherwise God would not have confirmed their office and work with miracles and marvelous deeds. But in the New Testament the Holy Spirit has ordered through St. Paul that the women should keep silence in the congregation or church, and he [Paul] says that it is the commandment of the Lord (1 Cor. 14:37). He certainly knew that the prophet Joel predicted how God [in the New Testament] would pour out His Spirit also on the handmaids (Joel 2:28–29) as well as how the daughters of Philip prophesied (Acts 21:9). Yet in the ministry of the congregation or church they should keep silence and not preach. Otherwise they may join in singing, praying, praising, and saying Amen. They may also read [the Bible] at home and teach, admonish, and comfort one another, interpreting the Scriptures as well as they can. In short, St. Paul does not tolerate the outrage and offense that one becomes a busybody in another man's business, but everyone should consider his own command and call and take care of that, in order that he may leave the call of another unhindered and in peace. Otherwise he may show his skill by teaching, singing, reading, and interpreting, for which he has the right and authority until he has enough and is tired of it. If God desires to do something beyond His order of the office and call, He will prove it by signs and wonders, as He commanded the donkey to speak and rebuke Balaam, its master (Num. 22:28). If He does not want to do that, we should respect and remain with the ordered office and call. If people do not teach rightly, what business is that of yours? Of that you need not give an account.

"Therefore, St. Paul often uses the word 'congregation' in this chapter (1 Cor. 14) to show the difference between the prophets and the people. The prophets speak, but the congregation listens. For so he says: 'He who prophesies edifies the church' (1 Cor. 14:4); and again: 'Let it be for the edification of the church that you seek to excel' (v. 12). But who are those who are to edify the church? Are they not the prophets or, as he calls them, those speaking with tongues, that is, those who read or chant the text while the congregation listens, as well as the prophets who interpret the text? It is certainly clear that he here commands the congregation to hear and be edified but not to teach or preach. Afterward he makes the difference still clearer by calling the congregation 'laymen,' saying: 'Otherwise, if you bless with the spirit, how will he who occupies the place of the uninformed say "Amen" at your giving of thanks, since he does not understand what you say? For you indeed give thanks well, but the other is not edified' (1 Cor. 14:16–17). Here again a distinction is made between ministers and laymen.

"But why should I continue to speak on this point? The text is clear, and also reason suggests that no one should be a busybody in other men's matters. For St. Paul says: 'Let two or three prophets speak, and let the others judge' (v. 29). This is said only of the prophets, of whom two or three should speak while the others judge. But who are the 'others'? Are they the people? By no means. But he means the other prophets or interpreters [*Weissager*], who should assist in the church by teaching and edifying the congregation; these should judge and help by seeing to it that in the church the preaching is right. And if it should happen that one of the prophets or preachers should teach best, then the others should stand corrected and say: You are right. I have not understood it so well. So also it happens at the table that one yields to the other (even in secular matters). But especially in this [spiritual] matter one should yield to the other.

172

"From this you can see how carefully the sneaks have studied the words of St. Paul, by which they think they can prove to be 'sitting by' in all churches, that is, attack, judge, and slander all pastors in the whole Christian church [*Christenheit*] and impose themselves and become judges of a ministry that is not their own. So they are real thieves and murderers, who wickedly and tyrannically become busybodies in other men's matters. Against this St. Peter says: 'Let none of you suffer as ... an evildoer, or as a busybody in other people's matters' (1 Peter 4:15)" ("Letter to Eberhard von der Tannen Concerning the Sneaks and Secret Preachers" [Winkelpredigern], 1531, St. Louis edition, 20:1665ff.).

The same: "Grace and peace in Christ. Reverend and beloved pastor: This is my reply to the question that your good friend at Linz, Sigmund Hangreuter, has submitted to you in writing with the request that it may be sent to me. Kindly tell your dear sir and friend that he is not in duty bound to go ahead in this matter and give Holy Communion to himself and his household. Nor is this necessary since he is neither called nor commanded to do this. And if the tyrannical ministers will not administer it to him and his family, though they should do it, yet he can be saved by his faith through the Word. It would also give great offense to administer the Sacrament here and there in the homes, and in the end no good would come of it, for there will be factions and sects, as now the people are strange and the devil is raging.

"The first Christians, mentioned in Acts, did not administer the Sacrament individually [*insonderheit*] in the houses, but they came together. And though they might have done it, such an example is no longer to be followed today, just as it cannot be permitted that today Christians have all things in common as was the case with the first Christians. For now the Gospel is spread throughout the world [*öffentlich*], as are the sacraments also. But if a father wishes to teach the Word of God to his family, that is right and should be done, for it is God's command that we should teach and bring up our children and household; that is commanded to everyone. But the Sacrament is a public confession and should be administered by public ministers, because, as Christ says, we should do it in remembrance of Him; that is, as St. Paul explains it, we should show forth or preach the Lord's death till He comes. And here he [Paul] also says that we should come together, and he severely rebukes those who, each in his own way, use the Lord's Supper individually. On the other hand, it is not forbidden but rather commanded that everyone individually should instruct his household in God's Word as well as himself, though he should not baptize. For there is a great difference between the public office [the ministry] in the church and [the care of] a father in his household. Hence the two must neither be mingled into each other nor be separated from each other. Since there is neither any necessity nor a call here, we must do nothing out of our own devotion without God's definite command, for no good will come from it" ("Concerning House Communion," letter to Wolfgang Brauer, 1536, St. Louis edition, 10:2225).

Chemnitz: "All Christians are indeed priests (1 Peter 2:9; Rev. 1:6) because they offer spiritual sacrifices to God. Everyone can and should teach the Word of God in his home (Deut. 6:7; 1 Cor. 14:26). But not every Christian may take on and arrogate to himself the public ministry of the Word and the sacraments. For not all are apostles; not all are teachers (1 Cor. 12:29), but only those who by a special and legitimate call have been set apart for the ministry (Acts 13:2–3; Jer. 23:4; Rom. 10:15). This is done either mediately [by the congregation or its representative] or immediately [by God's direct call and appointment]" (*Examen concilii Tridentini* 2.1).

Gerhard: "Bellarmine castigates Luther because he supposedly said that every baptized person has the authority and right to administer the sacraments. But Bellarmine knows that we do not tolerate disorder in the church and that we accord to no one the authority to administer the Holy Supper, not even in an emergency situation, except to those who are legitimately called into the office, although the circumstances are different with Baptism and with the Holy Supper. Luther does not accord to all baptized persons the authority to administer the Holy Supper absolutely and unconditionally but [merely] speaks of a certain general aptitude that Christians have for the sacraments in opposition to unbelievers; for by Baptism they have been received into God's covenant and so are qualified and apt for this office, that is, if they are legitimately called. This general aptitude Luther opposes to the sacerdotal character about which the scholastics and papists dispute, [saying] that through the sacrament of ordination there is created in the soul of the recipient [of ordination] a certain spiritual power by which a priest is enabled to effect the Sacrament of the Altar, so that without that

174

(power) it can in no wise be effected; they say that as a sign of this power the soul is impressed with a special character" (*Loci theologici,* "De sacr.," par. 29).

The same: "As from the fact that the believers are called kings it cannot be concluded that without a call everyone may administer the office of the government, since the apostles speak of a spiritual kingdom, so also from the fact that believers are called priests it cannot be concluded that everyone without a call may take over the ministry in the church, since this is likewise said of spiritual priests. They [the believers] are called spiritual priests not in view of the ministry in the church ... but in view of the spiritual sacrifices that they are to offer to God, as Peter himself explains this (1 Peter 5:2) and also in view of prayer (Ps. 141:2; Rev. 5:8; 8:4), thanksgiving (Heb. 13:15), beneficence toward the poor (Phil. 4:18; Heb. 13:16), the crucifixion of the old Adam (Rom. 12:1), and martyrdom that they endure for Christ's sake (Phil. 2:17; 2 Tim. 4:6). Such sacrifices can be offered by all believers as spiritual priests.

"Augustine comments on Ps. 94: 'If we are God's temple, then our soul is God's altar. But what is the sacrifice of God? We place the sacrifice on the altar by praising God.' He also writes in *The City of God* (book 20, chap. 10): 'We are called priests because we are members of one Priest.' Although the preaching of the Gospel belongs to the spiritual sacrifice (Mal. 1:11; Rom. 15:16), it cannot be proved from the expression 'spiritual priests,' which is given to all believers, that this [special] sacrifice concerns all, namely, the proclamation of the Gospel that is heard in the public assembly of the church, since the meaning of the expression is taken from the other spiritual sacrifices, which all can offer up, and not from the sacrifice that not all have in common. This is inferred very clearly from the words of the apostle: 'Are all prophets? Are all teachers?' (1 Cor. 12:29). All believers are spiritual priests; yet not all are at the same time teachers or prophets, since they are not all equipped with the gift of prophecy, nor have they been called into the ministry. 'He Himself gave some to be apostles, some prophets, some evangelists, and some pastors and teachers' (Eph. 4:11).

"Another invalid objection is based on the apostle's words that believers are a royal priesthood to show forth the praises of Him who has called them out of darkness into His marvelous light (1 Peter 2:9). For a distinction is to be made between the general command and call that all believers receive as they become dedicated Christians [by Baptism] and by which they are demanded to offer to God the due praises for which they are called into the fellowship of the church, to confess Him by word and deed (Deut. 6:20), to let the words of Christ dwell richly in them in all wisdom, teaching and admonishing one another in psalms and hymns and spiritual songs, singing with grace in their hearts to the Lord (Eph. 5:19; Col. 3:16), as well as to comfort one another with the Word of God (1 Thess. 4:18), and the special call by which the administration of the Word and the sacraments at the public assemblies of the church is entrusted to certain competent persons by the public consent of the church. But the fact that this call does not belong to all Christians is clear from 1 Cor. 12:29; Eph. 4:11; James 3:1" (*Loci theologici,* "De min. eccl.," par. 67).

Deyling: "The right to preach and administer the sacraments belongs basically to the whole church, but its public exercise [belongs] only to its legitimately called ministers. Nevertheless, every member of the church, as well as the whole church [together], has with equal right the keys and authority to teach, yet only for private application and not for public and solemn use, so that there may be no disorder by which the church would miserably be torn to pieces. When the congregation gathers publicly, then the keys are to be administered only by those on whom the whole congregation has conferred their exercise and use through the public call" (*Institutiones prudentiae pastoralis* 3.4.7).

Regarding the witness of the ancient church on this point we find, among others, the following:

Tertullian: "So much more is it the duty of laymen to keep themselves within the boundaries of respectful modesty, as this is to be shown to elderly persons, so that they do not arrogate to themselves the office of a bishop. Envy is the mother of factions. All things are allowed, says the apostle, but not all things edify" (1 Cor. 6:12).

Again, the 98th canon of the Fourth Council of Carthage in A.D. 398 declares: "In the presence of bishops, a layman should not presume to teach, unless he is asked to do so."

Thesis II

The ministry of the Word or the pastoral office is not a human institution but an office that God Himself has established.

1. Scripture Proof

The fact that the ministry of the Word or the ministry [*Amt*] of the New Testament is not a human institution or an ecclesiastical contrivance but a work of divine wisdom and an office established by God Himself is evident from the following:

In the first place, from the predictions of the prophets that God Himself would give to the church of the New Testament pastors or teachers: "The Lord gave the Word; great was the company of those who proclaimed it" (Ps. 68:11). "I will give you shepherds according to My heart, who will feed you with knowledge and understanding" (Jer. 3:15). "Be glad then, you children of Zion, and rejoice in the Lord your God, for He has given you the teacher of righteousness" (Joel 2:23; alternate reading).

In the second place, the divine institution of the holy ministry is evident from the call of the holy apostles into the ministry of the Word by the Son of God according to Matt. 10; 28:18–20; Luke 9:1–10; Mark 16:15; John 20:21–23; 21:15–17 ("Feed My sheep"), as well as from the call of the 70 disciples in Luke 10:1–22.

In the third place, the divine character of the ministry of the Gospel is evident from all passages in which those called mediately are represented as having been called by God Himself: "Therefore take heed to yourselves and to all the flock, among which the Holy Spirit has made you overseers, to shepherd the church of God which He purchased with His own blood" (Acts 20:28). "God has appointed these in the church: first apostles, second prophets, third teachers, after that miracles, then gifts of healings, helps, administrations, varieties of tongues. Are all apostles? Are all prophets? Are all teachers? Are all workers of miracles?" (1 Cor. 12:28–29). "He Himself (Christ) gave some to be apostles, some prophets, some evangelists, and some pastors and teachers" (Eph. 4:11).

In the fourth place, the divine institution of the holy ministry is evident from the fact that the holy apostles place themselves on an equal footing with the servants of the church who were called mediately as their co-laborers in the ministry: "The elders who are among you I exhort, I who am a fellow elder" (1 Peter 5:1). Compare also 2 John 1; 3 John 1, where John calls himself presbyter or elder; also Col. 4:7, where Paul calls Tychicus his fellow servant; also Phil. 2:25, where Paul calls Epaphroditus his fellow worker and fellow soldier, as well as the apostle of the Philippians ["your messenger"]; finally 1 Cor. 4:1; 1:1, where Paul calls himself and Sosthenes servants of Christ and stewards of the mysteries of God.

2. Witnesses of the Church in Its Official Confessions

Augsburg Confession: "That we may obtain this faith, the ministry of teaching the Gospel and administering the sacraments was instituted" (Art. V; *Triglot,* p. 45).

This statement, of course, does not speak of the ministry of the Word *in concreto* or of the pastoral office but only of the ministry of the Word *in abstracto,* of which Ludwig Hartmann, among others, rightly reminds us in his pastoral theology: "The ministry of the Word may be treated in two ways: first, in an abstract way when the state or the office itself is being considered, as Art. V of the Augsburg Confession treats it; second, in a concrete way, when the persons are considered who minister in this holy office, as Art. XIV of the Augsburg Confession treats it" (*Pastorale evangelicum* [Nuremberg, 1697], 4:25).

The same truth appears also in Luther's *Schwabach Articles,* from which Art. V of the Augsburg Confession is taken. This reads: "In order that we may obtain such faith or to grant it to us men, God has instituted the ministry or the oral Word, namely, the Gospel, through which He causes such faith with its power, benefit, and fruit to be proclaimed, and through it, as through His means, He also grants faith together with His Holy Spirit how and where He wills. Otherwise there is no method or means, no way or path to

178

obtain faith. For all thoughts, outside and before the oral proclamation, are nothing but lies and falsehoods, no matter how holy or
good they seem to be" (David Chytraeus, *Historia Augustanae Confessionis* [Frankfurt, 1580], p. 25).

Therefore also the *Formula of Concord* says: "Ministerium ec-
clesiasticum, hoc est, verbum Dei praedicatum et auditum" (the
ministry of the church, that is, the Word, preached and heard; Thorough Declaration, Art. XII, par. 30; *Triglot,* p. 1100). Again: "Verbum
enim illud, quo vocamur, ministerium Spiritus est" (the Word,
whereby we are called, is a ministration of the Spirit; Thorough
Declaration, Art. II, par. 29; *Triglot,* p. 1072).

It is important to understand this because of those who desire
to make the pastoral office a means of grace and coordinate it with
the Word and sacraments, as they assert that it is absolutely necessary
for anyone to obtain salvation, so that no one without the service
of an ordained minister can either come to faith or obtain absolution
of his sins. But our church teaches this [necessity] only of the oral
or outward Word in opposition to the alleged inner word and every
[other] form of enthusiasm. Nevertheless, the Augsburg Confession
in Art. V no doubt intends to attest also the divine institution of the
pastoral office, even if only indirectly, as all commentaries of our
orthodox theologians in their comments on this article clearly show.
(Cf. Mylius, Carpzov, Menzer, Frank, and others)

Smalcald Articles: "According to John 20:21 Christ sends forth
His disciples on an equality, without any distinction, so that no one
of them was to have more or less power than any other.... Since
Paul, then, clearly testifies that he did not even wish to ask Peter to
let him preach, even when he came to him for the last time, we
have [here] a clear teaching that the ministry stems from the common call of the apostles" (Of the Power and Primacy of the Pope,
par. 9, 10; German text, *Triglot,* pp. 504–06).

3. Witnesses of the Church in the Private Writings of Its Teachers

Luther: "In the first place, there are some preachers [*Apostel*] who
were elected not by men nor through men but by Jesus Christ and
God the Father, as were the prophets and all the apostles. In the
second place, there are some who were elected by God but through

men, such as the disciples of the apostles (apostolic fathers) as well as all those who till the end of the world will lawfully enter the ministry in place of the apostles as bishops and priests. And these cannot be without the first from whom they have their beginning" (*Church Postil: Gospel Portion,* "On St. Andrew's Day," St. Louis edition, 2:1914).

The same: "With these words ('As the Father has sent Me, I also send you' [John 20:21]) the apostles and their successors [in the ministry] are made teachers [*Herren*] till the end of the world, and to them, according to their office, there has been given such great power and authority as Christ the Son of God, Himself had, . . . and yet this [office] neither can nor shall reach any farther than beyond what before God is called sin" (*Church Postil: Gospel Portion,* "On the First Sunday After Easter," St. Louis edition, 11:757).

The same: "I hope that all believers and those who desire to be called Christians well know that the spiritual state [the ministry] has been established and instituted by God not with gold or silver but with the precious blood and bitter death of His only Son, our Lord Jesus Christ. For out of His wounds truly flow (as it was formerly represented on pictures) the sacraments, which He certainly earned dearly enough, so that we have in the whole world the office to preach, baptize, loose, bind, administer the sacraments, comfort, warn, admonish with God's Word, and whatever else belongs to the office of a pastor. . . . But I do not mean the present spiritual state in cloisters and convents. . . . I mean the state that has the office of preaching and the ministry of the Word and sacraments. This imparts the Spirit and salvation, which no chanting or pomp can secure, such as that of pastors, teachers, readers, priests (as we call the chaplains), sacristans, school teachers, and whoever else belongs to such offices and personnel. This state Scripture indeed praises and extols very highly.

"But if it is true and certain that God Himself has established and instituted this spiritual state with His own blood and death, it is evident that He wants it to be honored highly and that He will not let it perish or cease, but He will preserve it until Judgment Day. For the Gospel and the Christian church [*Christenheit*] must remain till the last day, as Christ says: 'Lo, I am with you always, even to the end of the age' " ("A Sermon on Keeping Children in School," 1530, St. Louis edition, 10:423–24).

The same: "Therefore the laying on of hands is not a human ordinance, but God creates and ordains the ministers, and it is not the pastor who absolves you, but it is the mouth and hand of God" (Exposition of Gen. 28:17, St. Louis edition, 2:435). Here Luther seems to declare that the laying on of hands at the ordination of ministers has been instituted by God, but it only seems so. In other places Luther explains the ceremonies at the ordination consistently as ceremonies introduced by the church. Luther's expression quoted above is explained by such statements of his as: "If then the sacrament of ordination is anything, it certainly is nothing more than a common ceremony [*Gebrauch*] to call anyone into the service of the church" ("On the Babylonian Captivity of the Church," St. Louis edition, 3:117). Luther's way of speaking obviously is synecdochical. When Luther says that the laying on of hands is not a human ordinance, he merely means to defend the divine institution of the mediate call into the ministry, which is commonly attested by the laying on of hands.

The same: "The holy orders and true institutions established by God are these three: the ministry, marriage, and civil government" ("Confession Concerning the Lord's Supper," St. Louis edition, 20:1098).

The same: "This witness (concerning Christ) has been ordained by Christ Himself so that it must always remain and prevail in the church. For this purpose He sent His Holy Spirit and Himself has called and given the apostles and their successors—pastors, ministers, teachers, as St. Paul witnesses in Eph. 4:11–13—who should be active and let it [the Gospel] resound throughout the world so that it will reach the children's children and their descendants" (*Church Postil: Epistle Portion,* "On the First Sunday After Easter," St. Louis edition, 12:535).

The same: "I myself know some who think that we need no ministers or pastors and that we [merely] tolerate the preachers [*Pfaffen*] because of custom and ancient usage. We might use their annual salaries and expenses in other and better ways, as though they [the ministers] were, as someone has said, a *necessarium malum* (necessary evil). Especially some of the nobility and some smart alecks [*Klüglinge*] say, 'We have books from which we can learn what we hear the preachers [*Pfaffen*] say in the church. You will read the devil on your head who has taken possession of you!'

181

If our Lord and God knew that the ministry would not be necessary, He would have been so wise and prudent as not to let Moses preach, and according to your wicked, satanic, and foolish thoughts and comments, it would not have been necessary for Him to ordain the Levitical priesthood and always send out prophets, as He Himself says in Matt. 23:34. Then also today He certainly would command the ministers and pastors to stay at home" ("Exposition of Deuteronomy," chap. 6, St. Louis edition, 3:1736).

The same: "Paul tells his disciple: 'For this reason I left you in Crete, that you should set in order the things that are lacking, and appoint elders in every city as I commanded you—if a man is blameless, the husband of one wife, having faithful children not accused of dissipation or insubordination. For a bishop must be blameless, as a steward of God' (Titus 1:5–7). Whoever believes that here the Spirit of God speaks and commands by Paul knows well that it is a divine institution and order that in every city there should be many bishops, at least one" ("On the Abuse of the Mass," St. Louis edition, 19:1093).

The same: "You are not lords over the pastors and the ministry, for you have not instituted it, but God's Son alone [has]. Nor have you added anything to it, so you have a lesser claim to it than the devil has to the kingdom of heaven. Therefore, you must neither criticize nor instruct, neither hinder nor rebuke it [the ministry]. For it is God's [business] to punish and not man's. He wants to be unhampered and have His command recognized. Therefore, take care of your office, and do not interfere with God's rule before you force Him to teach you [a lesson]. None of you would tolerate it if a stranger would grant his servant, whom he cannot spare, a furlough or drive him away. No shepherd's lad is so humble as to suffer an unkind word from a stranger. But God's servant must be everybody's scapegoat and suffer all things from everybody. But on the other hand, no one wants or can suffer anything from him, not even God's own Word" ("That One Cannot Remove Pastors from Office Because They Sharply Rebuked Public Vices," 1543, St. Louis edition, 10:1627).

Chemnitz: "The fact that the Son of God has instituted the ministry of the Word and sacraments also in the New Testament cannot be doubted. The church has been commanded to call and appoint ministers, and to this has been added, in the first place, the promise

182

that God approves the ministry of those who have been called by voice of the church and have been set apart for this office. Thus Paul declares in Acts 20:28 that those who were called mediately were made overseers by the Holy Spirit to feed the church of God. In Eph. 4:11 we are told that God grants as His gifts not only the apostles but also the pastors and teachers who are called mediately.

"In the second place, there is added the promise that God will grant His grace and gifts in order that those who are called legitimately may by these (gifts) rightly, faithfully, and successfully perform and execute everything pertaining to their office. 'Receive the Holy Spirit' (John 20:22). 'He opened their understanding that they might comprehend the Scriptures' (Luke 24:45). 'Lo, I am with you always, even to the end of the age' (Matt. 28:20). 'Do not neglect the gift that is in you, which was given to you by prophecy with the laying on of the hands of the presbytery' (1 Tim. 4:14). 'Stir up the gift of God which is in you through the laying on of my hands' (2 Tim. 1:6). 'I will give you a mouth and wisdom' (Luke 21:15). 'It will be given to you in that hour what you should speak; for it is not you who speak, but the Spirit of your Father who speaks in you' (Matt. 10:19–20).

"In the third place, there is added also the promise that God will be present with the ministry and that through His blessing the planting and watering shall have growth, as well as that through the ministry He will be truly efficacious, calling, illuminating, converting, and working repentance, faith, the new birth, regeneration: in short, that He will through the ministry carry out the whole matter of salvation. 'Receive the Holy Spirit. If you forgive the sins of any, they are forgiven them'; etc. (John 20:22–23). 'I will give you the keys of the kingdom of heaven, and whatever you bind on earth will be bound in heaven' (Matt. 16:19). 'Who also made us sufficient as ministers of the new covenant, not of the letter but of the Spirit' (2 Cor. 3:6). By this He makes alive, removes the veil from the heart, converts, and frees [us] so that 'we all, with unveiled face, beholding as in a mirror the glory of the Lord, are being transformed into the same image from glory to glory, just as by the Spirit of the Lord' (v. 18). 'God ... has committed to us the word of reconciliation. Therefore we are ambassadors for Christ, as though God were pleading through us' (2 Cor. 5:19–20). 'Since you seek a proof of Christ speaking in me, who is not weak toward you, but mighty in you'

(2 Cor. 13:3). 'He ... gave gifts to men. ... He Himself gave some to be apostles, some prophets, some evangelists, and some pastors, and teachers, for the equipping of the saints for the work of ministry, for the edifying of the body of Christ, till we all come to the unity of the faith and the knowledge of the Son of God, to a perfect man, ... that we should no longer be children, tossed to and fro and carried about with every wind of doctrine' (Eph. 4:8–14). 'God ... gives the increase' (1 Cor. 3:7). 'Your labor is not in vain in the Lord' (1 Cor. 15:58). 'Through whom we have received grace and apostleship for obedience to the faith. ... That I may impart to you some spiritual gift. ... [The Gospel] is the power of God to salvation for everyone who believes' (Rom. 1:5, 11, 16). 'Take heed to yourself and to the doctrine. Continue in them, for in doing this you will save both yourself and those who hear you' (1 Tim. 4:16). 'In Christ Jesus I have begotten you through the gospel' (1 Cor. 4:15).

"These most gracious and comforting promises concerning the ministry we must, as it were, publicly exhibit in the church in order that the dignity of the office might be glorified against the enthusiasts, that those entrusted with the ministry may with all the greater alacrity take on themselves its hardships and endure its difficulties, and that men might learn to regard the ministry with reverence" (*Examen Concilii Tridentini*, "De sacr. ordin.," fol. 579).

Gerhard: "The principal efficient cause of the ministry is the one and only true God, Father, Son, and Holy Spirit. This is proved (1) by express passages of Scripture as Ps. 68:11; 1 Cor. 12:28; 2 Cor. 5:18: 'God ... has given us (the apostles and other teachers of the church) the ministry of reconciliation.' (2) By God's generous promises that He would grant to His church pastors and that He would preserve the ministry. Jer. 3:15; 23:4: 'I will set up shepherds over them who will feed them' Joel 2:23 [cf. Luther's translation]. (3) By God's special titles of honor, which show that the care and preservation of the ministry greatly concern Him. Thus in Matt. 9:38 He is called the Lord of the harvest, who sends laborers into His harvest; in Matt. 20:1 the householder who hires laborers for His vineyard; in Matt. 21:33 the householder who plants a vineyard and sends His servants to the husbandmen in order that they might receive its fruits; in Luke 13:8 the gardener who has a fig tree planted in his vineyard and digs about it and fertilizes it that it may bear fruit (cf. John 15:1); in 1 Cor. 3:9 the husbandman who in his spiritual field has fellow workers. (4) By the exhortations to ask God for pastors. In Matt. 9:38 Christ admonishes us to pray to the Lord of the harvest to send laborers into His harvest. In Acts we read that the church supplicated God whenever pastors were to be elected. But if God is to be asked for pastors, then certainly it is He who grants to His church competent ministers. Here it may be pertinent to remark that one of the apostles was called Matthias, that is, a gift of God. (5) By the testimonies that accrue from experience. For God not only attended to the ministry in His own person when in the state of innocence He issued the command not to eat of the fruit of the forbidden tree and then after the Fall announced the promise concerning the blessed Seed of the woman, revealing it out of the deepest depths of His divine decree, but He also transmitted the ministry to men by placing Adam and the other patriarchs at the head of the church, which then was limited almost entirely to their families. Afterward He sent Moses and other prophets and established the Levitical priesthood. In this way God in the Old Testament instituted and preserved the holy ministry.

"In the New Testament the Son of God Himself in His assumed human nature administered this office. He also chose His apostles, whom He adequately equipped with the necessary gifts for the preaching of the Gospel and then sent them out into the whole world. After His session at the right hand of God, He still grants to His church pastors and teachers in order that His saints may be perfected for the work of the ministry, by which His mystical body [the church] is edified (Eph. 4:11–12). Although the institution and preservation of the ministry is an outward work, as we are accustomed to say, and so is common to the whole Trinity, yet as in other similar works, the Triune God acts also here, preserving the distinction and order of the persons. As the Father is the fountainhead of the Trinity, He is also the source of the benefactions that are granted to the church, to which also the institution and preservation of the ministry belongs. God the Father in the Old Testament called the patriarchs, Moses, and the prophets. He chose the Levites to be the priests, and in the fulness of the time He sent His Son in order that in His assumed flesh He might not only carry out the work of redemption but also execute on earth the ministry of teaching. 'God, who at various times and in different ways spoke in time past to the fathers by the prophets, has in these last days spoken to us by His Son' (Heb. 1:1–2).

"For this reason Christ so often appeals to His Father as the One who sent Him (Matt. 10:40; Luke 4:18; John 5:23, and others). In this sense and respect the Father is called the Lord of the harvest, the Lord of the vineyard, the Householder, the Husbandman, etc., namely, not only because He sent His servants, the prophets, but also at last His only and beloved Son (Matt. 21:37; Mark 12:6; Luke 20:13, etc.) into the vineyard of the church (2 Cor. 5:18; Gal. 1:16).

"The Son speaks to the fathers from the beginning, for which reason He also is called the Word. . . . He is the angel who, sent by the Father, went before the Israelites as they left Egypt, guided them through the wilderness, and after the destruction of the Canaanites led them into the Promised Land (Ex. 23:33; 33:2; Is. 63:9). It was He who spoke to Moses and the Israelites on Mount Sinai (Ex. 19:19; Acts 7:38) and from the cherubim on the ark of covenant (Ex. 25:22). It was He who in the fulness of the time assumed human nature and came as a teacher sent of God (John 3:2), spreading the heavenly seed of the Word in Judea, Galilee, and Samaria. He is the Wisdom of God (Prov. 9:1–12; Luke 11:49; 1 Cor. 1:24), saying in Matt. 23:34: 'Therefore, indeed, I send you prophets and wise men.' He joined to Himself apostles, whom He instructed for three years, then placed them into the ministry, and sent them out into the whole world to preach the Gospel (Matt. 10:1; Luke 9:1; John 20:21; Matt. 28:19; Mark 16:15). Exalted to the right hand of the Father, He gave some to be apostles, some to be prophets, etc. (Eph. 4:11–12; 1 Cor. 12:28). In a marvelous way He called Saul into the apostleship (Acts 9:15), who therefore says: 'Christ sent me to preach the Gospel' (1 Cor. 1:17). As the Son in the house of God, namely, the church, He ordains the householders, to whom He gives the keys to loose and bind (Heb. 3:6; 1 Tim. 3:15; 1 Cor. 4:1; Matt. 16:19), wherefore He calls Himself the Master of the house (Matt. 10:25).

"The Holy Spirit once spoke through the prophets inspired by God and through teachers of the church. 'The Spirit of the Lord spoke by me, and His Word was on my tongue' (2 Sam. 23:2; Acts 28:25; 1 Peter 1:11; 2 Peter 1:21). He it is who anointed Christ in the flesh above His fellows and sent Him forth to preach (Ps. 45:8; Is. 42:1; 61:1; Luke 4:18). He was poured out on the apostles visibly so that they, furnished with power from on high, preached the

Gospel to all nations (Acts. 1:8; Luke 24:49). He commanded the apostles, as they worshipped the Lord and fasted, to separate Barnabas and Saul for the work to which He had called them (Acts 13:2). They, therefore, are said to have been sent by the Holy Spirit (v. 4); that is said also of the elders of the church at Ephesus (Acts 20:28). He still supplies the ministers of the Word with the gifts they need for the right and salutary administration of their office (1 Cor. 12:4–11). Therefore, the ministry of the Gospel is also called the ministry of the Spirit (2 Cor. 3:6), not only because the Holy Spirit is given by the preaching of the Gospel (Gal. 3:2), but also because the Holy Spirit has instituted and still preserves the ministry, for He supplies the ministers with the needed gifts. Therefore, when Christ desired to entrust His apostles with the ministry, He first gave them the Holy Spirit by breathing on them (John 20:22) so that whatever they rightly and salutarily did in their capacity as ministers of the church is justly ascribed to the Holy Spirit, who mightily operated in and through them. 'It is not you who speak, but the Spirit of your Father who speaks in you' (Matt. 10:20)" (*Loci theologici,* "De ministerio ecclesiastico," par. 49ff.)

Mentzer: "We must hold above all things that Christ Himself instituted the ministry of the Gospel, and from this [fact] its authority and dignity are to be estimated. This institution is described in Matt. 10:1; 28:18–20; Mark 3:14; 16:15; Luke 6:13; 24:47; John 20:21; Acts 1:8; 2:3, and often elsewhere. Therefore, the apostles and all faithful teachers are called ministers of Christ who serve as ambassadors in His stead (2 Cor. 5:20) and also God's co-workers (1 Cor. 3:9). The ministry is also called a ministry of the Spirit (2 Cor. 3:6, 8), not only because the Holy Spirit, together with the Father and the Son, has instituted it, but in particular also because the Holy Spirit, as the Sanctifier, is active in this office with His special grace, working through it with might. In this office the Holy Spirit is offered, presented, and imparted to us to work faith in us.

"The power and efficacy of the ministry is to be estimated according to all this, for it is altogether ascribed to the Holy Spirit, working in it, however, not immediately but [mediately] through the Word and sacraments. . . . From all this is obvious (1) the dignity of the evangelical ministry, which is to be judged as of God, who has instituted it; (2) the fact that the Holy Spirit is present in it and mightily works through it; (3) the fact that the power, dignity, and efficacy, which are ascribed to the ministry, come not from any [good] quality of creatures or men but are truly divine, and that therefore they must be ascribed to God Himself, in whose name and by whose authority everything is done that belongs to the ministry" (*Exeges. Aug. Conf.,* pp. 229–30).

Heshusius: "God's Word earnestly forbids us to enter an office or ministry without a call and an express divine command. Speaking of uncalled prophets, God says: 'I have not sent these prophets, yet they ran' (Jer. 23:21). And He threatens them with destruction. Again: 'Let none of you suffer as a murderer, a thief, an evildoer, or as a busybody in other people's matters' (1 Peter 4:15). Or: 'We urge you, brethren, that you increase more and more; that you also aspire to lead a quiet life, to mind your own business . . . as we commanded you' (1 Thess. 4:10–11).

"In all these passages the Spirit of God shows us that God has no pleasure in the arrogance of those who take on themselves offices in the church without a legitimate call, for He desires that in His church all things should be done decently and in order. Therefore He appointed some apostles, some prophets, some pastors, some rulers, and some hearers and subjects. By His Spirit God distributes His several gifts and desires that no one should hinder the other in his calling or ministry. Therefore, if these are true ministers or pastors who teach the pure and sound doctrine and profess membership in the true Christian church and are appointed by the church for the ministry, let no private [uncalled] person dare administer the sacraments, even if some fault is to be found with the life of the pastors; for the sacraments are not to be avoided because of the unworthiness of the ministers, as those errorists, the Donatists, alleged, who were thoroughly refuted by Augustine and were rejected by the whole church for valid reasons. For as the worthiness or piety of a minister does not add anything to the sacraments (since its power rests on God's Word and command), so also a minister's unworthiness or unbelief does not take anything away from it. As a seal, whether engraved in gold or lead, prints the same picture, so also the sacraments have one nature and power, whether they are administered by believing or unbelieving ministers.

"Therefore, a Christian should not easily be misled to remain away from the legitimate ministry, for in this way there soon will arise factions, sects, and schisms, or dissensions. As soon as you separate yourself from the called ministry, you also sever your connection with the church that acknowledges or tolerates such ministers in their office. . . . The state of a minister or pastor has been established and separated from that of the common Christian because there should be certain persons to preach the Gospel and in their office to administer the sacraments, since ordinary Christians must look after their work and support, just as people in general, and it is not given to everyone to teach others. So also [the ministry has been instituted] that the ministers might be well instructed in the pure and sound doctrine and live an upright life and that the Christians might not be tossed to and fro and be carried about with every wind of doctrine" (*Who Has the Power, Authority, and Right to Call Ministers?* pp. 32, 36).

Deyling: "The originator of the holy ministry is the Triune God, who in Christ has not only graciously provided salvation for the human race but also imparts it [salvation] by efficacious means and competent ministers. This He has not only promised to the church (Is. 62:6; Jer. 3:15; 23:4; Joel 2:23; cf. Luther's translation), but He also does what He has promised (1 Cor. 12:28; 2 Cor. 5:18), sending out companies of evangelists (Ps. 68:11; cf. Luther's translation, v. 12). . . . God also preserves the ministry of the Word, which He has instituted, to the end of the age (Eph. 4:11) and supplies His ministers with the needed gifts, granting them speech and wisdom (Luke 21:15; 1 Cor. 12:8–9). Such ministers of the Word therefore must finally give an account [of their ministry] as those whom the Lord has appointed and called and whom they serve. Therefore, they must perform their office diligently, reverently, and faithfully, and the hearers must ask God for faithful workers (Matt. 9:38). In this matter they must emulate the example of the apostolic church, of which we read that they ardently prayed whenever they chose pastors. Away, therefore, with all enemies of the Christian religion, the old as well as the new, who regard the ministry as a mere human and useless contrivance" (*Institutiones prudentiae pastoralis,* proth. gen., par. 4).

This same doctrine we find also in the writings of the teachers of the ancient church.

Ignatius: "I exhort you to seek to do all things in divine concord under the direction of the bishop, [who serves] in God's place, and of the elders, [who serve] in place of the apostolic council, and of the deacons, who are to me most precious as those to whom the ministry of Jesus Christ has been entrusted" (*Ep. ad Magnes* 6).

The same: "Which (the congregation at Philadelphia) is my everlasting and perpetual joy, especially if it agrees with the bishop, its elders, and its deacons, who have been appointed according to God's will" (*Ep. ad Philad.,* praef.).

Irenaeus: "God has established in the church first apostles, then prophets, and in the third place teachers. Wherever, therefore, the gifts of God have been placed, there we must learn the truth" (book 4, chap. 44).

Cyprian: "Our Lord, whose commandments we must reverence and keep, when ordering the dignity of a bishop and the constitution of His church, tells Peter: 'You are Peter, and on this rock I will build My church, and the gates of Hades shall not prevail against it. And I will give you the keys of the kingdom of heaven, and whatever you bind on earth will be bound in heaven, and whatever you loose on earth will be loosed in heaven' (Matt. 16:18–19)" (Ep. 28, par. 1).

Thesis III

The ministry is not an arbitrary office but one whose establishment has been commanded to the church and to which the church is ordinarily bound till the end of time.

1. Scripture Proof

Our Lord says: "Go therefore and make disciples of all the nations, baptizing them in the name of the Father and of the Son and of the Holy Spirit, teaching them to observe all things that I have commanded you; and lo, I am with you always, even to the end of the age" (Matt. 28:19–20). From these words it is evident that the ministry of the apostles by Christ's command is to continue till the end of time. But if this is to take place, then the church must constantly establish the true public ministry and in this establishment administer the means of grace till the end of the world.

2. Witnesses of the Church in Its Official Confessions

Apology: "But if they want to call the sacrament of ordination [so called by the papists] a sacrament in view of the ministry and the Gospel, we would not be opposed to calling it a sacrament. For the ministry has been established by God, and it has His glorious promise: 'The Gospel . . . is the power of God to salvation for everyone who believes,' etc. (Rom. 1:16). 'So shall My Word be that goes forth from My mouth; it shall not return to Me void, but it shall accomplish what I please' (Is. 55:11). If one therefore wants to understand ordination as a sacrament, one would also have to call the laying on of hands a sacrament. For the church has God's command to appoint ministers and deacons. Since then it is so very comforting to know that God desires to preach and work through men and those chosen

191

by men, it is proper highly to praise and honor this election [*Wahl*], especially against the devilish Anabaptists, who despise and blaspheme this election together with the ministry and the outward Word' [the written Word of Scripture]" (Art. XIII [VII], par. 11–13; German text, *Triglot,* p. 310).

Augsburg Confession: "This power of the keys and bishops is exercised and executed only by the teaching and preaching of God's Word and the administration of the sacraments either to many or to individuals as the call demands. By these [means] are given not bodily but eternal blessings [*Dinge*] and gifts [*Güter*] as everlasting righteousness, the Holy Spirit, and everlasting life. These gifts [*Güter*] can be obtained in no other way than by the ministry of preaching and the administration of the sacraments alone" (Art. XXVIII, par. 8–9; German text, *Triglot,* p. 84). Here the office of the keys, which the congregation possesses and by which it administers the means of grace, is identified with the power of the bishops, and to it the obtaining of the eternal gifts is bound. But this is not because the eternal gifts of Christ's kingdom could in no wise be obtained without the administration of the means of grace by official [*öffentlichen*] ministers [*Amtspersonen*], but because God desires ordinarily to impart these gifts to men only in this way.

3. Witnesses of the Church in the Private Writings of Its Teachers

Wittenberg Reformation: "Let this be said first for all men to know regarding the ministry, that we confess as the eternal, unchangeable truth that the ministry and the administration [*Dienst*] of the sacraments are necessary and that the church is bound to them, so that there are no people of God and no elect except in the assembly where the preaching of the Gospel and the sacraments are found. Again, this great benefaction is gratefully to be acknowledged: that God has commanded His church to choose men for the ministry and the administration of the sacraments, and that He desires to be efficacious through the persons chosen by the church. By these He purposes to awaken many and to illuminate them with special gifts for the church's edification. So Paul commanded Titus that he should ordain elders in every city (Titus 1:5)" ("Monograph of the Protestants on the Christian Reformation and Church Government, Composed for the Impending Diet and Signed by Luther, Pomeranus, Cruciger, Major, and Melanchthon," 1545, Luther's Works, St. Louis edition, 17:1150).

Luther: "Indeed, many blurt out and say: 'Why do we need more pastors and ministers, since we can read [the Bible] ourselves at home?' So they go their way in carnal security, and do not read it at home. Or even if they do read it at home, it is neither as fruitful nor as effective as the Word is efficacious when it is publicly proclaimed by the mouth of the pastor whom God has called and appointed to preach and teach it to you" (*House Postil,* "On the Eighth Sunday After Trinity," St. Louis edition, 13:2253).

The same: "Where this (the ministry) remains, there some are preserved among the many who accept and come to it. But even if it [the Gospel] resounds from the pulpit, it will little benefit those, few as they may be, who can read Scripture [at home] by themselves, thinking that they need no minister" (*Church Postil: Epistle Portion,* "On the Twentieth Sunday After Trinity," St. Louis edition, 12:927).

The same: "It is to be noted in particular that God, though speaking from heaven to Paul, did not purpose to abrogate the ministry and do something out of the ordinary, but He bade him go into the city to a minister or pastor. There he was to hear and learn what He wanted him to learn. God wants us to go and hear the Gospel from those who preach it; there we shall find Him and nowhere else. . . . Thus Paul had to come to the knowledge of Christ through Ananias. From that little match he had to get his light, though he was less than a finger compared with Paul and less than a little candle compared with the sun. This narrative teaches us above all to esteem the ministry very highly. For here we are told directly and clearly that Paul, the great doctor, received his instruction from the little doctor [*Doktorlein*] Ananias" (*House Postil,* "On the Conversion of St. Paul," St. Louis edition, 13:2654–55).

Chemnitz: "They loudly cry that those who disapprove of the papal priesthood abrogate all order in the church, cause dreadful confusion, grant to everyone of the common people the ministry (what Tertullian ascribed to the heretics), change the priests into laymen, and impose on laymen the priestly office, so that this no longer has any respect or dignity. In the first place, this slander must be refuted; for we rightly reject the Anabaptists and [other] enthusiasts who either abolish the use of the public ministry of the Word and sacraments in the church altogether, or who fabricate that it is useless and unnecessary. They teach that without the use of the public ministry of the Word and sacraments we must seek and expect new, special revelations and illuminations from God and that this way of calling, illuminating, and converting is much more excellent and glorious than that obtained by using the voice of the ministry.

"Now it is indeed God who by His power, operation, incitation, and inspiration begins, effects, increases, and preserves in men what belongs to their calling, illumination, conversion, repentance, faith, renewal; in short, to the [whole] matter of their salvation. But God has determined in His divine decree that He will impart these blessings not by granting new and special revelations, illuminations, and infusions into the souls of men without means but only by the public ministry of the Word. This office He did not entrust to angels so that we must ask and expect their appearances, but He has committed the word of reconciliation to men, and it is His will that the voice of the Gospel, revealed by God, should be proclaimed by them. Now indeed all Christians are priests (1 Peter 2:5; Rev. 1:6) inasmuch as they are to offer up to God spiritual sacrifices. Every Christian may and should teach the Word of God in his home (Deut. 6:6–7; 1 Cor. 14:35). But not every Christian dare appropriate or arrogate the public ministry to himself, for not all are apostles and teachers (1 Cor. 12:29) but only those who by a special and legitimate call have been separated for this office by God (Acts 13:2; Jer. 23:4; Rom. 10:15), which is done either immediately or mediately. And this is the legitimate way of calling by the voice of the church that Paul has prescribed in 1 Tim. 3:1–7 and Titus 1:6–9.

"Christ Himself called some immediately into the ministry to show that He recognizes the ministry of those who have been chosen and called by the voice of the church according to the rule laid down by the apostles. He also added the promise that He will be truly efficacious in the ministry of those who teach the Gospel, which the Son of God Himself will preserve in the church by constantly calling [ministers], as Paul declares: 'When He ascended on high, He led captivity captive, and gave gifts to men. . . . And He Himself gave some to be apostles, some prophets, some evangelists, and some pastors and teachers, for the equipping of the saints for the work of the ministry, for the edifying of the body of Christ' (Eph. 4:8, 11–12). All men therefore are to be referred to and taught the

194

use of this ministry, which God has instituted and which He pre-serves in the church in order that through it there may be granted to us eternal gifts and that by it God may receive us, save us from sin, the power of the devil, and everlasting death, and restore to us righteousness and eternal life. But this ministry has a certain power granted to it by God (2 Cor. 10:4–6; 13:3–4), though it is circum-scribed by definite duties and limits" (*Examen Concilii Tridentini,* "De s. ord.," 1).

Gerhard: "The necessity of the ministry depends on the divine institution, for 'it pleased God through the foolishness of the mes-sage preached to save those who believe' (1 Cor. 1:21). The result of this divine decree is the dependence of the highest and most precious effect, namely, the conversion and salvation of people, on the preaching of the Gospel and therefore also on the ministry in their inseparable cohesion. 'How then shall they call on Him in whom they have not believed? And how shall they believe in Him of whom they have not heard? And how shall they hear without a preacher?' (Rom. 10:14). Christ, exalted to the right hand of God, has given to His church 'some to be apostles,' etc. (Eph. 4:11–12). 'In doing this you will save both yourself and those who hear you' (1 Tim. 4:16). For this reason they [the ministers] are also called 'saviors' (Obadiah 21).

"The Son of God regarded His order and institution as so sacred and inviolate that He did not want to instruct even Cornelius in the way of salvation through the angel who spoke to him but directed him to the ministry, namely, to Peter, from whom he was to hear what he should do (Acts 10:6). And though He converted Paul in an extraordinary manner by a heavenly vision (so that the apostle denied that he had received his Gospel from man, Gal. 1:12), yet to honor the ministry He directed him to Ananias, from whom he was to learn what he should do (Act. 9:6). Augustine writes: 'Let us consider that even the apostle Paul, though cast to the ground and instructed, was sent to a man in order to receive the sacraments and be joined to the church.' This necessity of the ministry is con-firmed also by the very lamentable examples of the Israelites and the heathen. Of the Israelites, the prophet Azariah told King Asa: 'For a long time Israel has been without the true God, without a teaching priest, and without law' (2 Chron. 15:3). Of the heathen who had not yet been called into the kingdom of Christ by the

195

preaching of the Gospel, the apostle says: 'At that time you were without Christ, being aliens from the commonwealth of Israel and strangers from the covenants of promise, having no hope and without God in the world' (Eph. 2:12).

"Solomon teaches briefly but emphatically the sorry results that follow the abrogation of the ministry: 'When there is no revelation (that is, when the public ministry no longer prevails), the people cast off restraint' (Prov. 29:18). . . . Here we must also point out the climax that the apostle uses in Rom. 10:14 to show clearly that by the abolition of the ministry of the Word worship and salvation also cease, namely, when we keep in mind the ordinary way in which this [worship and salvation] is effected. Nevertheless, we must remember that this necessity is not absolute, for God can convert and save people also immediately and extraordinarily without the proclamation of the Word and the operation of the ministry. Therefore, it is conditional, depending on the divine decree of its institution and order" (*Loci theologici,* "De minist. eccl.," par. 3).

Ignatius: "For when you subject yourselves to the bishop as to Jesus Christ, you appear to me as such who live not according to human judgment but according to Jesus Christ, to Him who died for your sakes in order that, trusting in His death, you may escape death. It is therefore necessary, whatever you do, that you undertake nothing without the bishop, but that you subject yourselves to the elders just as to the apostles of Christ, who is our Hope and in whom we desire to be found living. Again, it is the duty of the deacons, who are the mystery of Jesus Christ, in every way to please all. For they are not servants of food and drink but ministers of the church of God. Therefore, they are in duty bound to guard themselves against every cause of accusation as against fire. Similarly, all should show due reverence to the deacons as commanded by Jesus Christ and to the bishop as to Jesus Christ, who is the Son of the Father; so also to the elders as to God's council and to the co-laborers of the apostles. Without these there is no church that deserves the name" (*Ep. ad Trall.* 2.3).

The same: "Follow the bishop as Jesus Christ [follows] the Father and the elders as the apostles, and to the deacons show due respect as commanded by God. Let no one do any of those things that the good of the church demands without the bishop. Holy Communion that is celebrated under the direction of the bishop or of him whom he allows should be regarded as valid. Wherever the bishop appears, there let also the congregation meet, just as wherever Jesus Christ is, there is also the church universal. It is not permitted to baptize without the bishop or to observe the agape [love feast], but whatever he regards as right, that also is pleasing to God. (To this direct yourselves) in order that all things that you undertake may be safe and valid. In short, it is well to become sober as long as we have time to be converted to God. It is laudable to acknowledge God and the bishop. Whoever honors the bishop will be honored by God. Whoever does anything behind the back of the bishop serves the devil" (*Ep. ad Smyrn.* 8.9).

The same: "So then, as children of the light and the truth, flee factions and false doctrines; wherever the shepherd is, there let the sheep follow. For many highly respected wolves in wicked self-seeking take captive those who are walking the way that God has ordained. But as long as you are united, they will find no room [to take you captive]. . . . For as many as are of God and of Jesus Christ will adhere to the bishop, and as many as penitently return to the unity of the church also belong to God and will henceforth lead a life in agreement with Christ Jesus. Be not deceived, my brethren; if anyone will follow him who causes dissensions, he will not inherit the kingdom of God, and if anyone will walk in another opinion [false doctrine], he renounces the holy Passion" (*Ep. ad Philad.* 2.3).

Thesis IV

The ministry is not a special or, in opposition to that of ordinary Christians, a more holy state, as was the Levitical priesthood, but it is a ministry of service.

1. Scripture Proof

According to the Word of God, all believing Christians, and they only, are priests (a priestly state). See 1 Peter 2:9; Rev. 1:6. There is among them no difference of rank; they are all together one in Christ Jesus (Gal. 3:26); they are all brothers (Matt. 23:8–12). But as in the Old Testament all sons of Aaron belonged to the priestly family and state, but only some performed the duty and service of a priest, so also in the New Testament those who perform the ministry of the Word are not for that reason priests or priests before others but merely those who minister among a priestly people. Therefore the holy apostle writes: "Who then is Paul, and who is Apollos, but ministers through whom you believed" (1 Cor. 3:5). Further: "We do not preach ourselves, but Christ Jesus the Lord, and ourselves your servants for Jesus' sake" (2 Cor. 4:5). " ... for the sake of His body, which is the church, of which I became a minister according to the stewardship from God which was given to me for you, to fulfill the Word of God" (Col. 1:24–25).

2. Witnesses of the Church in Its Official Confessions

Apology: "Among other reasons why the laymen should not receive both kinds [bread and wine in the Holy Supper] Gabriel [Biel] mentions also that there must be a distinction between priests and laymen. And I certainly believe that this is the greatest and most important reason why today they [the papists] so firmly adhere to

198

this, [namely,] in order that the state of the priests might appear holier than that of the laymen. Now this is a human figment, and its purpose can easily be judged" (Art. XXII [X], par. 9; German text, *Triglot,* pp. 358, 360).

The same: "In Greek, *liturgia* properly denotes an office by which the congregation is served. This agrees nicely with our doctrine that there [in Holy Communion] the priest is a common servant of those who wish to go to the Lord's Supper, administering to them the holy Sacrament" (Art. XXIV [XII], par. 88; German text, *Triglot,* p. 412).

3. Witnesses of the Church in the Private Writings of Its Teachers

Henry Barner: "The fact that they (the Christians) do not all publicly administer the office of teaching in *publico ministerio* (public office) is caused by *vocationis defectus* (lack of a call), for they were neither asked nor called [into it]. Here we must distinguish *inter statum et officium,* between status and office. To the office belongs *specialis vocatio,* a special call; that must be entrusted and commanded. But to the status [a call is] not [necessary]. All Christian indeed are priests, but they are not all pastors. For besides the fact that someone is a Christian and priest, [to be a pastor] he must also have an entrusted office and parish (Luther, vol. 5, fol. 157). It is the call that makes pastors and ministers (the same, vol. 1, fol. 290). All sons of the high priest were of high-priestly rank by their birth, but only one was high priest according to the office (the same, vol. 7, fol. 346). However, in cases of emergency all may administer the office.... That would not be possible if we would not all be priests (the same, vol. 1, fol. 290)" (*Summary of the New Man,* approved by the theological faculty at Wittenberg, 1659, 2:379).

Luther: "You might say: 'If it is true that we all are priests and should preach, how then will that turn out? Should there be no distinction among the people, and should even the women be priests?' Let me reply that in the New Testament no priest rightly should wear a tonsure, not because that would be evil in itself, for someone may [even] shave his head altogether, but because a distinction should not be made between them [the priests] and ordinary Christians, which the [Christian] faith cannot tolerate. Those who now are called priests should all be laymen as the others, and only some should be chosen by the congregation to be ministers and preach. Here indeed there is an outward distinction because of the office into which someone is called by the congregation. Before God, however, there is no distinction, but some are called out of the multitude to administer and execute the office in place of the congregation. All have this [office], and one has no more power than the other.

"Therefore, no one should of his own accord come forward and preach in the congregation. But the congregation should take one out of the assembly and ordain him, whom it may also force to resign if it so desires.[13] Now they [the papists] have established their own state as though that were of God, and they have gained so great a liberty that in the midst of Christendom [*Christenheit*] there is a greater distinction than between us [Christians] and the Turks. If you want to consider the Christians, you must not make any distinction. You must not say: That is a man or a woman; that is a servant or a master, old or young, as Paul teaches in Gal. 3:28. They all are one and an altogether spiritual people. They are all priests and may all preach God's Word, except the women, who are to keep silent in the churches and let the men preach, because they are commanded to be subject to their husbands, as St. Paul declares in 1 Cor. 14:34. God preserves this order, but He does not make any distinction as to authority. However, where there are no men but only women, as in the convents, there also a woman may arise among them and preach" ("Exposition of 1 Peter," second treatment, 1539, St. Louis edition, 9:1174).

The same: "Now it is sufficient to know that the Christian people is undivided, without any divisions and [distinctions of] persons. Therefore, no one should be a layman, cleric, monk, or nun. There should be no difference at all, whether people are married or chaste [in the papistic sense], as it pleases everyone. There is also in itself no distinction among bishops, elders, priests, and laymen. No one is distinguished from other Christians except that one has another office with which he has been entrusted to preach God's Word and administer the sacraments, just as a mayor or judge is not different from other citizens except that he is commanded to rule the city. Those who have invented and introduced such distinctions among Christians and have divided them into clerics and laymen have divided the unity of the Christian people so that some wear the tonsure and others do not; some wear the tonsure as monks and others as priests, and even the monks are distinguished from one another in many ways by their garments and food. Those are the ones who have destroyed the church and God's Word and with the craftiness of the old serpent have corrupted the minds and hearts of the Christians from the simplicity in Christ Jesus, as Paul says in 2 Cor. 11:3. So then the term 'bishop' or 'priest' is not the name of a rank but the term of an office. 'Priest' means the same as an elder, bishop the same as an overseer. Wicked people have changed these [terms] into ranks or dignities. Paul otherwise calls them dispensers, servants of Christ, servants of God, and priors" ("Monograph on the Abuse of the Mass," 1521, St. Louis edition, 19:1097–98).

The same: "From this arose the shameless tyranny of the priests over the laymen, so that on account of the bodily anointment by which their hands were anointed, then on account of their tonsure and garments, they not only prefer themselves and regard themselves as better than other Christian laymen who are anointed with the Holy Spirit, but they also look on them as unworthy curs who do not deserve to be numbered in the church. Therefore, they also do not hesitate to command them whatever they please, to demand it from them by force, to threaten, compel, and suppress them. In short the sacrament of ordination has proved itself an excellent strategy and a confirmation of all the perverse wonders that have occurred in the church and will yet occur. Here Christian brotherhood has come to an end. Here shepherds are turned into wolves, ministers into tyrants, and the spiritual state into one that is secular.

"What if we would compel them to confess that we all in like manner are also priests, whoever have been baptized (as indeed we are), and that the ministry has been entrusted to them alone with our consent? Then surely they would know that they have no authority or power to command us except in such things as we permit them of our own good will. It is written: 'You are . . . a royal priesthood, a holy nation' (1 Pet. 2:9). Therefore, as many of us as are Christians are priests. But those whom we call priests are ministers chosen by us to perform all functions [of the ministry] in our name. The ministry is nothing else than a service. So Paul writes: 'Let a man so consider us, as servants of Christ and stewards of the mysteries of God' (1 Cor. 4:1). From this it follows that whoever does not preach the Word of God for which he has been called by the Christian congregation is no priest and that the sacrament of ordination can be nothing else than a custom to choose ministers for the church" ("Of the Babylonian Captivity of the Church," 1520, St. Louis edition, 19:113–14).

The same: "But that is above all the greatest abomination against the precious and blessed Baptism, that they with their chrism and ordination make priests [*Pfaffen*] in the holy church, which is a far, far higher and holier state than what Baptism works. For an ordained priest who is anointed with chrism, compared with other baptized ordinary Christians, is like the morning star compared with a smoking flax. So Baptism, in which we are washed with Christ's own blood and are anointed with His Holy Spirit for everlasting life, compared with the filthy chrism or oil, which is without God's Word and command, shines like a dirty lamp compared with the sun. Yet with such chrism they are not anointed for life eternal but only for the private mass.

"Here also the tonsure and special garments are [accounted] of special value, as well as the term 'cleric,' as though they [the priests] were Christ's own. Likewise, they invent the 'character,' the spiritual token of the soul, which no ordinary Christian may have but only the ordained priests. So also is the pomp when a priest is to be degraded; that has to be attended by many bishops, sometimes even by as many as seven, though it takes only one to ordain him. Nevertheless, they cannot take from him the 'character' by such a splendid degradation. These are the truly wonderful words and works of the devil (2 Thess. 2:9), by which the glory and power of Baptism is weakened so that its spiritual divine chrism, which is the Holy Spirit Himself, should count as nothing at all compared with the bodily, temporal chrism of the papists, which was invented by human devotion.

"Baptism with the blood of Christ and the anointing of the Holy Spirit cannot ordain or make a priest, but a papistic bishop can ordain and make priests with his stinking, filthy chrism. You perverted, damnable fools and blind leaders, how atrociously you blaspheme our holy Baptism, the blood of Christ, and the anointing of the Holy Spirit and instead exalt before us your vain, injurious, dreadful private ordination for your private mass food with your bodily and temporal chrism, which is nothing else than mere tomfoolery and is without God's command and institution. The dear holy fathers I will excuse, and they should be excused, if they dedicated or ordained with chrism and called those who were so ordained priests [*Pfaffen*] or elders. They did not ordain any private mass priests nor anyone to celebrate private mass, but when they called anyone into the true Christian ministry and pastoral office, they wanted to adorn and exalt the call with such pomp before the congregation to distinguish them from the others who were not called, so also that everyone might be certain and know for sure which person should conduct the office and had command to baptize, preach, and perform the other functions [of the ministry].

"The apostles only laid their hands on the heads without chrism and prayed over those whom they called into the office or commissioned (Acts 13:3). Thus they did with Paul and Barnabas, and St. Paul taught Timothy not to lay on hands too soon. The dear fathers multiplied such ceremonies with chrism and other things with the best of intentions. But human devotion and opinion always turns out in such a way that afterward offense, error, and idolatry result from it if the spirit of the fathers does not follow and remain. That happened in many other matters. So also this good intention of the fathers and their ordination resulted in Baptism and Christ being weakened and obscured. It no longer remained an ordination for the call and pastoral office but a private ordination [*Winkelweihe*] to ordain private priests for the private mass. Then at last it created a real distinction and mark between true Christians and priests of the devil. For they do not serve the church but are an abomination that destroys and makes desolate everything in the holy place.

"Against that you must exalt and praise your Baptism as much as possible to weaken or destroy this atrocious abomination. For in the Christian church [*Christenheit*] there should be no making or ordaining of priests. The chrism, I say, and the bishop shall not make us priests, nor do we want or suffer it to become such through them. Let me again say that if we are not true priests prior to the bishop and his chrism, the bishop and his chrism will never make us priests. He may make us sham and carnival priests; in the same way he himself is a sham and carnival bishop, just as children in a play create kings, maidens, and other persons and actors. We do not want to be created priests; we want to be and be called priests by birth [through Baptism] and have our priesthood as an inheritance through our father and mother, for our Father is the true Priest and High Priest, as it is written: 'The Lord has sworn and will not relent, "You are a priest forever according to the order of Melchizedek" ' (Ps. 110:4). This He [Christ] also has proved by sacrificing Himself on the cross for us. This same priest or bishop now has a bride, a priestess or episcopal bride [*Bischöfin*], as it is written: 'He who has the bride is the bridegroom' (John 3:29). From this bridegroom and bride we are born through Holy Baptism, and so by heredity we are true priests in the Christian church [*Christenheit*], sanctified by His blood and ordained by His Holy Spirit. For so St. Peter called us: 'You . . . are . . . a holy priesthood, to offer up spiritual sacrifices' (1 Peter 2:5), and St. Paul praises us as priests when he commands us to present our bodies as a living sacrifice, holy, acceptable to God (Rom. 12:1).

"Now to sacrifice to God is the office of the priests alone, as everyone, even the pope, must confess. In addition, we are not only His children but also His brethren, as He says: 'I will declare your name to My brethren' (Ps. 22:22), and 'Whoever does the will of My Father in heaven is My brother and sister and mother' (Matt. 12:50). So then we have the right to be priests not only as children but also as brethren. We desire to retain our innate and inherited priesthood unhindered and unobscured, and we want to have it exalted, proclaimed, and praised with all honor so that it shines and gleams like the dear sun and hits the devil in the eyes with his shams and abominations, so that, in comparison with it, his private mass and chrism appear and stink worse than asafetida.

"For this reason the Holy Spirit in the New Testament also diligently prevented the name *sacerdos,* priest or parson [*Priester oder Pfaffe*], from being given to any apostle or any other office, but only the baptized or Christian name, that is, an innate, inherited name from Baptism. For none of us is born in Baptism as an apostle, preacher, teacher, or pastor, but we are all born simply as priests. Afterward they [the congregation] take some from such born priests and call and elect them for such offices so that they in the name of us all shall administer this office. That is our foundation in this matter, which no one can destroy. If the papistic ordination would be rightly conducted, it would be nothing else than the calling of such born priests into the pastoral office instead of making new, holier, and better priests than are the baptized Christians.

"Behold, that is the other way (as already said) in which they have desecrated, obscured, and weakened Baptism. In addition, they so atrociously and blasphemously suppressed and hid our glorious, eternal, innate, hereditary, priestly honor and in its place glorified their dead and nasty chrism so highly and gloriously that we did not fear and honor God Himself as much as they honored their farces and carnival shows. But we must make allowance to the fathers for calling their consecrated persons *sacerdotes* and thus establishing the custom, as well as for many other things. If their consecration and ordination would not have been changed, the *term* would not have done any harm, for they consecrated their pastors. But the abomination retained the name (because it was so very excellent) and forsook the consecration of the fathers; in its place they established ordination for the private mass and thereby destroyed our true priesthood and Baptism and made it unspeakably desolate" ("On the Private Mass and Holy Orders," 1533, St. Louis edition, 19:1256ff.).

The same: "It is a fabrication to call the pope, bishops, priests, and those in cloisters a spiritual state while princes, masters, laborers, and farmers are classified as a secular state. This indeed is a very subtle contrivance and hypocrisy, but let it not fill us with fear. For all Christians constitute a spiritual state, among whom there is no difference except only that of the office. St. Paul thus says that we all are one body (1 Cor. 12:12); nevertheless every member has his own special work with which to serve the other. This stems from the fact that we all have one Baptism, one Gospel, and one faith (Eph. 4:5) and are all equally Christians. For Baptism, the Gospel, and faith alone make a spiritual and Christian people. But the pope or a bishop by anointing, making a tonsure, ordaining, consecrating, and causing them to dress differently from laymen may make hypocrites or blockheads, but he never makes a Christian or a spiritual person.

"So then we all are consecrated by Baptism to be priests, as St. Peter says: 'You are . . . a royal priesthood, a holy nation' (1 Peter 2:9), and St. John: 'You have made us kings and priests to our God' (Rev. 5:10). If we would have no better consecration than that of the pope or bishop, then no one would be a priest by the consecration of the pope or bishop, nor could anyone conduct a service or preach or absolve. The bishop's consecration is nothing else than if he, in the name and stead of the whole assembly, would take one out of the many, who all have equal authority, and command him to exercise authority for the others, just as though ten brothers, all sons of a king and equal as heirs, would elect one to administer the inheritance. All of them would equally be kings endowed with equal power, and yet one is commanded to rule. Or to put it more clearly still, let us suppose that a little band of devout Christians were taken captive and placed in a wilderness. They would not have a bishop ordained by another bishop among them, so they would agree to choose one from among them, whether married or not, and entrust to him the office of the ministry, to baptize, conduct services, absolve, and preach. Such a one indeed would be as truly a priest as though all bishops and popes had ordained him. That is the reason why every Christian in an emergency may baptize and absolve, which he could not do if we were not all priests.

"But they [the papists] by their spiritual authority have almost abrogated such grace and power of Baptism and the Christian state and made it unknown to us. In this way formerly Christians chose from the assembly their bishops and priests, and these were then ratified by another bishop without the pomp that now prevails. Thus St. Augustine, Ambrose, and Cyprian were made bishops. Since the secular state is equally baptized with us and has the same faith and Gospel, we must admit that they are priests and bishops and regard their office as one that belongs to and profits the Christian congregation. For he who has received Baptism may glory that he is already ordained a priest, bishop, and pope, though it does not behoove everyone to administer the office. Though we all are priests, no one should come forward of his own accord and without our consent and election dare to do that for which we all have the same power. Whatever is common [to all] no one dare arrogate to himself without the will and command of the congregation. And if it would happen that anyone would be chosen for the office and would be deposed because of his abuse of it, he would be the same as he was before.

"Therefore, the state of a priest should be nothing else in the Christian church [*Christenheit*] than that of an official. Because he has an office, he is advanced; if he is deposed, he is a farmer or a citizen like all the rest. Hence, no priest is a priest if he is deposed. But now they have fabricated *characteres indelibiles* (indelible characters) and babble that a deposed priest nevertheless is something different than an ordinary layman; indeed, they dream that a priest may never become anything else than a priest or ever become a layman.

"All that is talk and law invented by men. Therefore, a layman, priest, prince, bishop, and, to use their terminology, the spiritual and secular [states] have truly no other essential difference except for the sake of their office or their work, not for the sake of their state. All are of the same state, true priests, bishops, and popes, but not all are of the same work, just as among the priests and monks not everyone has the same duties. That is, as stated before, just what St. Paul says Rom. 12:4ff. and 1 Cor. 12:12ff. and St. Peter in 1 Peter 2:9, [namely,] that we are all one body whose Head is Jesus Christ and of which we severally are members. Christ does not have two or three kinds of body, one secular and the other spiritual. He is the one Head and has but one body. Those who now are known as 'spiritual,' or priests, bishops, and popes, are not distinguished from other Christians by greater distance or dignity than that they should administer the divine Word and the sacraments. That is their work and office. Just so the secular government has the sword and rod to punish the wicked and protect the pious. A shoemaker, smith, and farmer all have their office and the work of their occupation, and yet all are equally priests and bishops. Each should benefit and serve the other by his office and work, so that all these manifold works in a community aim to benefit body and soul, just as the members of the body all serve one another" ("To the Christian Nobility of the German Nation," 1520, St. Louis edition, 10:270ff.).

The same: "They must confess that this figurative priesthood of the Old Testament no longer exists. So then we ask them who gave them the authority to say that they [the Roman priests] were prefigured by those priests and to make themselves of their own power priests of the New Testament. There is not a single letter in the whole New Testament that calls them priests. And what is their answer? The lepers were told to go to the priests, [but] where are the priests? St. Peter says in 1 Peter 2:9 that in the New Testament there are no special priests, but all Christians are priests, prefigured by those priests [of the Old Testament]" (*Church Postil: Gospel Portion,* "On the 14th Sunday After Trinity," 1521, St. Louis edition, 12:1454).

The same: "Whoever is in charge of this (office) is not a priest on account of the office (as are all the others), but he is a servant of all the others. And if he no longer can or will preach and serve, he again takes his place in the common assembly, entrusts his office to another, and is nothing more than any other ordinary Christian. Behold, in this way you must distinguish the ministry or the office of service [*Dienstamt*] from the common priesthood of all baptized Christians. For this office is no more than a public service that is entrusted to one by the whole congregation, who all are equally priests" ("Exposition of Ps. 110," 1539, St. Louis edition, 5:1037).

The same: "For a priest, especially in the New Testament, must not be made but must be born; he is not consecrated but created. And he is born not by his natural birth but by the birth of the Spirit, of water and the Spirit by the washing of regeneration. Therefore, all Christians are altogether and equally priests, and all priests are Christians. It is an accursed thing to say that a priest is something else than a Christian. For that is said without the Word of God merely on the basis of human doctrine or of ancient custom or because of the multitude that regards it in this way. If out of all these three, whichever you want, you make an article of faith, it is a blasphemy and an abomination" ("How One Should Choose and Install Pastors," 1523, St. Louis edition, 10:1570).

The same: "If now we pray thus, we ourselves are prophets or children and students of the prophets. Nor is it necessary that we receive revelations of future events. It suffices for the office of a prophet to understand the Scriptures, teach others, and help one another with our prayers. For whoever is no prophet can neither teach nor pray nor do any other good work. Therefore, the name 'prophet' belongs to all Christians, and whoever denies this must also deny that he was baptized and instructed in God's Word. There is only this difference: some have the Holy Spirit more fully and the others less fully. For though He is not as richly in me as He was in Elijah, yet according to His measure He is also in me" ("Exposition of Genesis," 20:17–18, St. Louis edition, 1:1366–67).

The same: "Now I judge from all this that it is certain that they who preside over the people with the sacraments and the Word neither may nor should be called priests. But the fact that they are called priests is done either according to pagan usage or has been left over from the laws of the Jewish people. Later it redounded to the great harm of the church. But according to the evangelical Scriptures, they should rather be called servants, deacons, overseers, and stewards; formerly, because of their advanced age, they were also called *presbyteri,* that is, elders. So Paul writes: 'Let a man so consider us, as servants of Christ and stewards of the mysteries of God' (1 Cor. 4:1). He did not say: 'Let a man so consider us, as priests of Christ.' He will know that the name 'priest' and his office belongs to all [Christians]. From this stems the common word of Paul, *dispensatio,* or in Greek *oikonomia,* in German *Haushalt* (managing the house), so also *ministerium* and *minister,* in German *Dienst* (service) or *Amt* (office) and *Diener* (servant). He calls himself *servum,* that is, a servant, and several times he says, 'Servio in evangelio,' that is, 'I serve the Gospel.' This he does in order that everywhere he may praise not the order or state but only the office and work and also that he may preserve the right and dignity of the priesthood in the congregation" ("How One Should Choose and Install Pastors," 1523, St. Louis edition, 10:1590–91).

Heshusius: "Since the Son of God, Jesus Christ, has performed His priestly sacrifice, which is valid forever, there is in the New Testament no more outward priesthood dealing with outward ceremonies and sacrifices. Since the truth has come, what need is there for figures and shadows? The pope desires an outward priesthood, but that is his own figment and is without God's Word, a real monkey business [*Affenwerk*], without sense and faith. The apostles and evangelists know nothing of such an outward priesthood. It is pure superstition, error, folly, and fraud, by which the pope devises that he is the high priest in place of Peter and that his bishops and prelates are the priests of the New Testament. All believing Christians, not only those who are in the holy ministry but also the secular rulers and artisans who are baptized and regenerated by the Holy Spirit, are priests and priestesses, having the prerogative and right to offer up spiritual sacrifices. The apostle Peter speaks not only of ministers, bishops, and pastors but of the whole congregation of God, of all who have received God's Word and believe in Christ, when he speaks of the royal priesthood. Therefore, the pope with his bishops does wrong in depriving the congregation of God of their title of honor and arrogates this glorious name alone to himself and his followers who wear the tonsure" (*Chief Articles of Christian Doctrine,* 1584, p. 785).

The same: "The error of the pope and his mass priests has been caused largely by the fact that they changed the holy ministry into a priesthood. But there is a difference in the New Testament between being a priest and serving in the holy ministry. Not all believers are pastors and ministers, only those who are called into this office and have been ratified with the laying on of hands. No one should take charge of the public ministry unless he has been called to do so. But all believers are priests and priestesses, consecrated by the Holy Spirit. It is not the ministry that makes anyone a priest but Holy Baptism, faith, and the Holy Spirit, who regenerates us and gives us the joy to come before God. It is He who makes us holy priests with the power to offer up spiritual sacrifices" (ibid., p. 786).

Gerhard: "In the New Testament the term 'priest' is nowhere given to the ministers of the church as a special title but to all true and pious Christians, who have been anointed with the Holy Ghost and so as spiritual priests offer up to God spiritual sacrifices: 'and has made us kings and priests' (Rev. 1:6; 5:10; 20:6). So also the apostle says: 'You also . . . are being built up a . . . holy priesthood, to offer spiritual sacrifices acceptable to God through Jesus Christ' (1 Peter 2:5). 'You are a chosen generation, a royal priesthood' (v. 9). Augustine writes: 'Now only the bishops and elders in the church are called priests, but so all Christians are called because of the mysterious anointing, they being members of the one Priest' (*City of God* 20.10). The first meaning is that of the church, the second that of Scripture. This is to be noted against the papists, who from the name 'priest,' which by the ecclesiastical writers is applied to the ministers in the New Testament church, desire to establish the sacrifice of the mass" (*Loci theologici,* "De min. eccles.," par. 14–15).

Sebastian Schmidt: "As in the Old Testament some were priests and the rest shepherds or farmers, so in the New Testament all believers are priests because they have the knowledge of salvation. The heathen are farmers, shepherds, and winegrowers outside the church because they do not have such knowledge" (Commentary on Is. 61:6).

Zacharias Grapius: "The laymen are priests and apt to perform all ecclesiastical functions of the ministry by virtue of an inward ability. So also they can administer the Lord's Supper. We must not think that a sacrament is a less valid sacrament when a layman administers it, moved perhaps by an emergency or an error" (*Syst. noviss. controv.* 4.89).

Justin Martyr: "We who through the name of Jesus (are what we are), full of holy fire by the Word of His calling, are the true high-priestly generation of God, as also God Himself attests when He says that in every place among the heathen there shall be offered to Him well-pleasing and pure sacrifices" (*Dialog.* d. 209).

Irenaeus: "All just [persons] have the priestly order" (*Adv. haer.* 4.20).

Tertullian: "Jesus, the Father's Chief and High Priest, has made us priests to God His Father, clothing us with His own high-priestly vesture, for those who have been baptized into Christ have put on Christ" (*De monog.* 7).

The same: "We certainly, called by Christ to be priests, are in duty bound to monogamy according to the pristine [Old Testament] law of God, which at that time He prefigured for us by His priests" (ibid.).

Clement of Alexandria: "Only those who lead a pure life are really priests" (*Strom.*, book 4, fol. 537).

Origen: "Do you not know that to you, that is, to the whole church of God and the communion of believers, there has been given the priesthood? Listen to what Peter says of the believers. He says that they are a chosen generation, a royal priesthood, a holy nation, a people of [His] possession. You, therefore, have the priesthood because you belong to a priestly people. . . . All, namely, who have been anointed with the oil of holy anointing (1 John 2:20) have been made priests, as Peter also says of the whole church: 'You are a chosen generation, a royal priesthood, a holy nation' (1 Peter 2:9). You, therefore, are of a priestly generation and may approach the sanctuary" (*Super Levitic.*, hom. 9., c. 1, 9. See *editio de la Rue,* 2:236, 243; in Lommatzach, 9:340, 361).

Chrysostom: "Take heed, therefore, how you sit in Moses' seat; for the seat (*cathedra*) does not make the priest, but the priest makes the seat. The place does not sanctify the man, but the man sanctifies the place. Not every priest is a saint, but every saint is a priest" (On Matt. 23; hom. 43).

Jerome: "This is the only difference between a householder and the servants: that he as a fellow servant has been placed over his fellow servants. Therefore, let the bishop and presbyter know that

the congregation consists of his fellow servants and not of his servants" (On Titus 1).

Augustine: "When John says in Revelation, 'Over such the second
death has no power,' and then adds, 'but they shall be priests of
God and of Christ, and shall reign with Him a thousand years' (Rev.
20:6), he by no means says this only of bishops and elders, who
now properly [according to their office] are called priests in the
church, but as we give to all [believers] the name 'Christians' because
of their mystic anointing, so also we give to all the name 'priests,'
because they are members of one Priest, just as the apostle Peter
calls them 'a holy nation, a royal priesthood' " (*De civit. Dei.* 20.10).

Thesis V

The public ministry [Predigtamt] *has the power to preach the Gospel and administer the holy sacraments as well as the power of spiritual judgment.*

1. Scripture Proof

Christ clearly and plainly shows the power of the ministry, which He instituted when sending out His apostles, by saying: "Go therefore and make disciples of all nations, baptizing them in the name of the Father and of the Son and of the Holy Spirit, teaching them to observe all things that I have commanded you" (Matt. 28:19–20). Further: "As the Father has sent Me, I also send you.... If you forgive the sins of any, they are forgiven them; if you retain the sins of any, they are retained" (John 20:21, 23). Further: "Feed My lambs.... Tend My sheep" (John 21:15–16). This is the power mentioned in the thesis above. Therefore the holy apostle writes: "Let a man so consider us, as servants of Christ and stewards of the mysteries of God" (1 Cor. 4:1).

2. Witnesses of the Church in Its Official Confessions

Augsburg Confession: "Now our adherents teach that the power of the keys or that of the bishops is, according to the Gospel, a power and command of God to preach the Gospel, forgive and retain sins, and administer and take care of the sacraments. For Christ sent His apostles with the command: 'As the Father has sent Me, I also send you.... Receive the Holy Spirit. If you forgive the sins of any, they are forgiven them; if you retain the sins of any, they are retained' (John 20:21–23). This power of the keys or of the bishops is exercised and administered only by teaching and preaching God's Word

213

and administering the sacraments, either to many or to individuals, according to the call. . . . Therefore, according to the divine right, it is the office of the bishops to preach the Gospel, forgive sins, judge doctrine, and reject teachings that are contrary to the Gospel as well as to exclude from the Christian congregation, not by any human power but only through God's Word, the wicked whose perversity is manifest. And in such cases the parishioners and congregations owe obedience to the bishops according to Christ's declaration: 'He who hears you, hears Me' (Luke 10:16)" (Art. XXVIII, par. 5–21; German text, *Triglot,* pp. 84, 86).

Apology: "But what kind of office or power the bishops have in the church we have stated in the [Augsburg] Confession. Those who are now called bishops in the church do not at all perform their episcopal office in the church, but let them nevertheless be bishops according to *canonica politia* (canonical polity), whose value we do not contest. But we speak of the true Christian bishops, and the old division or distinction pleases me very well, according to which it was said that the power of the bishops consists in *potestate ordinis* (the power of order) and *potestate iurisdictionis* (the power of jurisdiction), that is, in the administration of the sacraments and the exercise of spiritual jurisdiction [*geistlichem Gerichtszwang*]. Therefore, every bishop has *potestate ordinis,* that is, the power to preach the Gospel and administer the sacraments, as well as the power of spiritual jurisdiction in the church, that is, the authority and power in the church to exclude from the Christian congregation those who are found guilty of open crimes and again to receive and absolve them when they are converted" (Art. XXVIII [XIV], par. 12–14; German text, *Triglot,* p. 446).

Smalcald Articles: "In our [Augsburg] Confession and its Apology we have set forth in a general way what had to be said concerning the ecclesiastical power. For the Gospel commands those who should preside over the churches to preach the Gospel, forgive sins, and administer the sacraments. In addition, it confers on them the jurisdiction to excommunicate those whose vices are publicly known and to loose and absolve those who desire to make amends. Now everyone, even our adversaries, must confess that this command is given alike to all [believers] who preside over the churches, whether they are called pastors or elders or bishops" (Of the Power and Jurisdiction of Bishops, par. 60–61; German text, *Triglot,* p. 520).

3. Witnesses of the Church in the Private Writings of Its Teachers

Luther: "In the fifth place, the church is known by ordaining or calling ministers or taking care of the other offices. For there must be bishops, pastors, or preachers who administer and exercise the four duties [*Stücke*] or sacred things [*Heiligtum*] named above (preaching the Gospel, Baptism, the Lord's Supper, and the office of the keys) in the place and name of the church, but above all because of Christ's institution, as St. Paul says: 'He Himself gave some to be apostles, some prophets, some evangelists, and some pastors and teachers' (Eph. 4:11). For the whole assembly cannot do this, but they must entrust it to one, or let it be entrusted to him. What would happen if everyone wanted to preach or administer [the sacraments], and no one would yield to the other? It [the ministry] must be entrusted to one, and he alone must be permitted to preach, baptize, absolve, and administer the Sacrament. The others must be satisfied with this and agree. Where, therefore, you see these things, you may be sure that there is God's people and the Christian holy church [*Volk*]. . . . If there are no more apostles, evangelists, and prophets, then others must take their place till the end of the world. For the church must not cease until the end of the world. Therefore, apostles, evangelists, and prophets who attend to God's Word and work must remain, no matter how they may or should be called" ("Concerning the Councils and Churches," 1539, St. Louis edition, 16:2279).

Chemnitz: "This office [*ministerium*] has a power granted to it by God (2 Cor. 10:4ff.; 13:3–4) but one that is circumscribed by definite duties and limits, namely, to preach the Word of God, instruct the erring, rebuke the sinners, exhort the lax, console the anxious, strengthen the weak, resist the gainsayers, examine and condemn false doctrine, convict transgressions of morals, administer the divinely instituted sacraments, remit and retain sins, be examples to the flock, pray for the church, privately and publicly lead the congregation in prayer, care for the poor, excommunicate publicly the contumacious, receive those who repent and reconcile them with the church, install ministers according to Paul's prescription, and with the consent of the congregation introduce ceremonies that serve the ministry, are not at variance with God's Word, do not burden consciences, but promote order, dignity, propriety, peace, and edification. That belongs to the two chief parts, namely, to the power to preach the Gospel and administer the sacraments as well as to the power of jurisdiction" (*Examen Concilii Tridentini,* "De sacramento ordinis," sec. 1, p. 573).

Gerhard: "There are in general seven functions or duties of the ministers of the church to which others may easily be related: (1) Preaching the divine Word; (2) administration of the sacraments; (3) intercession for the flock entrusted to them; (4) an honorable, moral way of life; (5) administration of church discipline; (6) preservation of ceremonies in the church; (7) care of the poor and visiting the sick" (*Loci theologici,* "De min. eccl.," par. 265).

The same: "Some think that no power (of jurisdiction) either can or must be ascribed to the ministers of the church (1) since the term *ministerium* (service) excludes any authority of government [*obrigkeitliche Gewalt*]; (2) since Christ in the matter of authority places the secular and the ecclesiastical office into opposition to each other, as in Matt. 20:25; Mark 10:42; Luke 22:25–26: 'The kings of the Gentiles exercise lordship over them, and those who exercise authority over them are called "benefactors." But not so among you'; (3) since Paul denies that he and the other apostles wished to have dominion over the faith of the believers (2 Cor. 1:24); (4) since Peter forbade the elders to lord it over the Christian people (1 Peter 5:3). But all these and similar things by no means deny to the ministry of the church anything except (1) absolute power and (2) political power. The former belongs only to God, the latter to civil government. Therefore, the ministry dare not arrogate to itself either of the two.

"But the fact that besides absolute and political power there is another that belongs to the ministry is proved (1) by statements of Scripture: 'If [the trespassing brother] refuses to hear [the arbitrators], tell it to the church. But if he refuses even to hear the church, let him be to you like a heathen and a tax collector. Assuredly, I say to you, whatever you bind on earth,' etc. (Matt. 18:17–18). In John 20:23 the power of the keys is given to the apostles: 'If you forgive the sins of any, they are forgiven them,' etc. 'Even if I should boast somewhat more about our authority, which the Lord gave us for edification and not for your destruction, I shall not be ashamed' (2 Cor. 10:8). 'I write these things being absent, lest being present

216

I should use the sharpness, according to the authority which the Lord has given me for edification and not for destruction' (2 Cor. 13:10). (2) By the honorable titles of the ministers of the church, for they are called shepherds, fathers, teachers, superiors [*Vorgesetzte*], leaders [*Vorsteher*], which titles they could not have if a certain power were not given to them. (3) By examples, for Christ and His apostles in their office used the power of the keys, as Paul excommunicated the incestuous person at Corinth (1 Cor. 5:4), and others. (4) By [sound] reasons, for without power in the church the ministers could not perform the duties connected with their office nor could the organization of Christ's mystic body exist.

"From all this it is evident that Christ has granted to the office of the ministry such power. The first is clear from the fact that the office of the ministry consists in the preaching of the Word, the administration of the sacraments, the exercise of the binding and loosing keys, the administration of church discipline. But all this could not be done without such power given to the church. For the preservation of the unity and wholeness of the mystical body, those who maliciously continue in sin must be excluded from the communion of the church, and those who repent must again be received (1 Cor. 5:7; 2 Thess. 3:14). But this could not take place were the church without such power.

"Again, as a power is granted by God to the other states of the church, namely, the political and the domestic, so it is clear that authority is also given to the ecclesiastical [state]. For as neither the political nor the domestic state could serve the purpose for which these were appointed unless such power as is assigned to each of these states were given them, so also the church could not serve the purpose for which it was founded unless God has granted it authority in like measure. But what the power granted to the church is and what its nature is—on these points opinions vary greatly. . . . The Augsburg Confession, Art. VII, when dealing with the abuse of the power of the bishops, declares: 'Now our adherents teach that the power of the keys or that of the bishops is, according to the Gospel, a power and command of God to preach the Gospel, forgive and retain sins, and administer and take care of the sacraments.' (See above under 2.) From this it follows that the power granted to the church is twofold, namely, (1) the power to preach the Word of God and to administer the sacraments; (2) the power of the keys, by which sins are forgiven and retained. The former is called *potestas ordinis,* the latter *potestas iurisdictionis*" (ibid., par. 191–92).

Thesis VI

The ministry of the Word [Predigtamt] *is conferred by God through the congregation as the possessor of all ecclesiastical power, or the power of the keys, by means of its call, which God Himself has prescribed. The ordination of the called* [persons] *with the laying on of hands is not a divine institution but merely an ecclesiastical rite* [Ordnung] *established by the apostles; it is no more than a solemn public confirmation of the call.*

A. *The ministry of the Word is conferred by God through the congregation as the possessor of all ecclesiastical power, or the power of the keys, by means of its call, which God Himself has prescribed.*

1. Scripture Proof

Since the congregation or church of Christ, that is, the communion of believers, has the power of the keys and the priesthood immediately (Matt. 18:15–20; 1 Peter 2:5–10; cf. also what has been said under Part I, Thesis IV), it also and it alone can entrust the office of the ministry, which publicly administers the office of the keys and all ministerial [*priesterliche*] functions in the congregation, to certain competent persons by electing, calling, and commissioning. So we read that the apostle Matthias was chosen for his high office not merely by the eleven but by the whole multitude of believers gathered together, about 120 in number (Acts 1:15–26). Further we read that the deacons were chosen by the "whole multitude" (Acts 6:1–6).

If ministers who already administer the office belong to the calling congregation, they also of course belong to those calling; indeed, according to the office that they administer in the church, they above all [belong]. Hence, when their cooperation, which behooves them on account of their office, is denied, then there is no longer any call of the "multitude," for then the call is extended not by the [whole] congregation but by individuals in the congregation, which, when properly organized, consists of both preachers and hearers.

However, if no officiating ministers belong to the calling congregation, then indeed the call of the multitude even without them [the ministers] is valid. But in this case it is demanded (1) by the love and unity that according to Christ's will should exist and manifest itself among all members of His body, (2) by the honor that believers owe to the incumbents of the office, and (3) by the sacred character and importance of the matter itself, that a vacant congregation should not act alone and according to its own opinion [*Einsicht*] but seek the counsel of ministers in office whom it may consult. It should listen to their advice and instruction and concede to them especially the examination and the proper, public, solemn installation of the called [pastor]. As a pattern for this procedure, the action of the believers in Acts 6:1–6 is to serve the church as an example for all times.

2. Witnesses of the Church in Its Official Confessions

Apology: "The Sacrament [Lord's Supper], Baptism, etc., are not without efficacy or power because they are administered by unworthy or wicked [persons], for these are thereby the call of the church; so they do not represent their own person but that of Christ, as He Himself testifies (Luke 10:16)" (Art. VII. VIII. [IV.], par. 26; German text, *Triglot,* p. 236).

Smalcald Articles: "In addition it must be acknowledged that the keys belong and are given not merely to one man but to the whole church, as this can be proved sufficiently by clear and definite arguments [*Ursachen*]. For just as the promise of the Gospel belongs definitely and immediately to the entire church, so the keys also belong immediately to the entire church, since the keys are nothing else than the office by which this promise is imparted to everyone who desires it, just as it is actually manifest that the church has the power to ordain ministers of the church. Thus to His words 'Whatever you bind,' etc., indicating to whom the keys have been given, namely, to the church, Christ adds, 'Where two or three are gathered together in My name. . . .' Now the ministry is bound to no definite place or person, as was the office of the Levites by the Law, but it is dispersed throughout the whole world, and it is present wherever God grants His gifts of apostles, prophets, pastors, teachers, etc." (Of the Power and Primacy of the Pope, par. 24–26; German text, *Triglot,* p. 510).

The same: "Wherever the church is, there also is the command to preach the Gospel. Therefore, the churches must retain the authority to demand, choose, and ordain ministers, and such authority is a gift that is granted to it properly by God and that no human power can wrest from it, as St. Paul attests when he says: 'When He ascended on high, He . . . gave gifts to men' (Eph. 4:8). Among the gifts that belong to the church, he enumerates pastors and teachers and adds that they were given for the edification of the body of Christ. From this it follows that wherever there is a true church, there is also the power to choose and ordain ministers. In an emergency an ordinary layman may also absolve another and [so] become his pastor. Thus St. Augustine relates that there were two Christians in a boat; one baptized the other and was then himself absolved by the first.

"Here belong the statements of Christ testifying that the keys were given to the whole church and not to some special persons, as the text declares: 'Where two or three are gathered together in My name,' etc. (Matt. 18:20). Lastly also the statement of Peter confirms this: 'You are . . . a royal priesthood' (1 Peter 2:9). These words pertain properly to the true church, which, since it alone has the priesthood, must also have the power to choose and ordain ministers. This is attested also by the common custom of the churches, for formerly the people chose pastors and bishops. Then came the bishop residing at the same place or in the neighborhood who ratified the chosen bishop" (Of the Power and Jurisdiction of the Bishops, par. 67–70; German text, *Triglot,* pp. 522–24).

The same: "At the Council of Nicaea it was determined that every church should choose a bishop by itself in the presence of one or more bishops who were living in the neighborhood. This was observed for a long time not only in the Orient but also in other and Latin churches, as this is clearly attested by Cyprian and Augustine. For thus writes Cyprian in his fourth letter to Cornelius: 'Therefore, you must diligently observe the command of God and the custom of the apostles as it is observed among us and in many lands, [namely,] that to the congregation that is to choose a bishop there should come other bishops living near the place, and in the presence of the whole congregation, which knows the life and conduct of each, the bishop should be chosen. As we know, this was done also when our colleague Sabinus was chosen; for after the election by the whole congregation, on the advice of some bishops who were present, he was chosen to be bishop and hands were laid on him. This custom Cyprian calls a divine way [*Weise*] and an apostolic custom, and he testifies that it was observed at that time in almost all lands. . . . Finally, how can the pope by divine right be over the churches since the church has [the right of] election?" (Of the Power and Primacy of the Pope, par. 13–15, 20; German text, *Triglot*, pp. 506–08).

3. Witnesses of the Church in the Private Writings of Its Teachers

Luther: "They (the peasants in Swabia) have set forth 12 articles, among which some are just and right, so that they call for your forbearance [*das sie euch den Glimpf nehmen*] before God and the world. . . . The first article, in which they demand to hear the Gospel and to have the power to call pastors, you cannot deny by any right. Nevertheless, their own advantage is evident here also, for they pretend that they would sustain their pastors with the tithe, which does not belong to them. Yet this is the gist, that they should be permitted to hear the Gospel, and against that no government either could or should go. Indeed, the government should not hinder what everyone would teach or believe, be it either Gospel or falsehood. It is sufficient that it teaches to guard against rebellion and war" ("Admonition on Behalf of Peace," 1525, St. Louis edition, 16:49).

The same: "A whole congregation should have the power to choose and depose a pastor. This article is correct only if it is done in a Christian way (though the marginal notes do not add anything to suggest this). If then the goods of the pastor come from the government and not from the congregation, then the congregation may not give these same goods to the pastor whom it elects. For that would mean to rob and steal. But if it desires a pastor, then first of all it should humbly request him of the government. If the government refuses, let the congregation choose its own and let it support him from its own goods, leaving to the government its goods or acquiring them rightly from it. But if the government will not tolerate such a called and supported pastor, then let him flee into a different city, and let anyone who desires it flee with him, as Jesus teaches. That means to choose and have one's own pastor in a Christian and evangelical way. Whoever acts differently, acts in an unchristian way as a robber and blasphemer" ("Notes [Verlegung] on the Twelve Articles of the Peasants," 1525, St. Louis edition, 16:65).

The same: "But you say that since St. Paul commanded Timothy and Titus to ordain elders in every city, and since, according to Acts 14:23, Paul and Barnabas also ordained elders in every city, therefore, a congregation cannot call any pastor or undertake of its own accord to preach the Gospel among Christians, but it must wait until it obtains the permission of the bishops, abbots, or other prelates, who sit in the seat of the apostles. Let me reply: If our bishops, abbots, and others would be in the place of the apostles, as they extol themselves, it would make sense that we would let them do what Titus, Timothy, Paul, and Barnabas did when they ordained elders. But now since they sit in the devil's seat and are wolves and neither teach the Gospel nor tolerate it, they have as little right to ordain ministers and pastors among Christians as have the Turks and Jews. They should drive donkeys and lead dogs. In addition, even if they would appoint pious preachers, they neither could nor should do this without the consent, election, and call of the congregation, except in cases of emergency in order that no soul might perish because of the lack of the divine Word. For in such an emergency, as you have heard, not only may everyone secure a minister, whether by request or the power of the government, but he also should himself come forward, step up, and teach if he is able to do so. For an emergency is an emergency, and knows of no propriety; likewise, everyone should come and help if a city is on fire and not wait until he is asked to do so. Otherwise, where there is no such emergency and there are those who have the right, power, and grace to teach, a bishop should not appoint anyone without the congregation's choice, will, and call, but he should only confirm him whom the congregation has chosen and called.

"If he refuses to do that, then he [the called pastor] is nevertheless confirmed by the very call of the congregation. For neither

Titus nor Timothy nor Paul ever ordained an elder without his election and call by the congregation. This is clear from his statement: 'A bishop must be blameless' (Titus 1:7; 1 Tim. 3:2). Further: 'Let these [the deacons] also first be proved' (1 Tim. 3:10). Now Titus could not have known who was blameless, but a report to this effect had to come from the congregation; it had to give such a report. Again, in Acts 6:3, 6 we are told that the apostles themselves could not appoint deacons to a far inferior office without the knowledge and consent of the congregation. It was the congregation that chose and called the seven deacons, whom the apostles then confirmed. If then the apostles could not by their own authority institute an office that merely had to distribute earthly food, how could they have been so audacious as to impose the supreme office to preach on a congregation by their own authority without its knowledge, will, and call?

"But since now there is an emergency, and there is no bishop to appoint evangelical ministers, the examples of Titus and Timothy are not valid, but the congregation must call, whether, please God, he is confirmed by Titus or not. For thus also those whom Titus supplied would have done or should have done in the event that Titus would not have confirmed their minister or there would not have been anyone else who would have confirmed the preacher. Hence our own time is far different from that of Titus, when the apostles were in power and desired to provide true pastors; for now our tyrants seek only wolves and thieves. And why should these furious tyrants condemn us when we so choose and call? They themselves do the same thing; in fact, they must do it. No pope or bishop is appointed by his own authority, but he is chosen and called by the chapter; after that he is confirmed by others. The bishops are appointed by the pope as their head, but the pope is chosen by the cardinal at Ostia, who is his subject. And even if it should happen that anyone is not confirmed, he is nevertheless a pope or bishop.

"And now let me ask you, my dear tyrants: If the election and calling of your congregation creates bishops, and if a pope is a pope without the confirmation of any superior, why should not a Christian congregation create pastors merely by its call, especially since it regards the rank of bishops and popes higher than that of ministers? Who has given you the right to take it from us? Our calling has in its favor the Holy Scriptures, while your calling is mere human invention [*Menschentand*] without Scripture; but with that you deprive us of our right. You are tyrants and rascals, who deal with us as would the devil's own apostles. This is the reason why in some places even secular rulers, councilors, and princes appointed and paid their own pastors in their cities and castles, whomever they desired, without the permission or command of bishops and popes, and no one hindered them" ("That a Christian Assembly or Congregation Has the Right and Power to Judge All Doctrine and to Call, Appoint, and Depose Ministers: Reason and Cause from Scripture," 1523, St. Louis edition, 10:1545–48).

The same: "To Sebastian Steude, pastor at Joachimstal: Grace and peace in our Lord. From Master Calixtus you will hear everything I have told him. I advised him to leave of his own free will since your parishioners [*Thäler*] hate him so much. He can well be used in another place. But this should not be done without your consent, and he should not depart from them without a public notice in which he carefully states the reasons that aroused such enmity and why the congregation desires to get rid of him. After that, your office demands that your congregation or church does not force on you any pastor against your will. That would mean acting against the pastor just as tyrannically as if a minister would intrude into a congregation or church against its will. Therefore, both parties should submit their cases to the superiors; for if one party, either the congregation or the pastor, would maliciously and to the vexation of the other force in a pastor, then there would be no church or proper administration. Therefore, let them agree with you or be their own bishop. But if they appeal to another bishop against your will, let them realize that they are going against the rule of the Gospel and that God will not bless what they do" (Letter of 1541, St. Louis edition, 21:2639).

The same: "You (Hausmann) know that you are the rightly called minister and pastor at Zwickau, accepted by both the council and the congregation, so that on that day you must give an account of the church entrusted to you. And as long as you live, you are obligated to provide it with pure doctrine; earnestly to pray for, care for, and watch over it; to risk and lay down your life in all kinds of tribulation and danger such as pestilence and other sicknesses, no matter what they may be called; to preside over it against the gates of hell; and to do, suffer, and endure all things as behooves a pious, faithful minister and pastor because of his office. These certainly are all difficult, great, and, indeed, divine works, which, thank God, you have so far performed diligently and faithfully.

"But now since your council, moved by the evil spirit, has deposed Cordatus at St. Katherine, though he was never accused before any judge or convicted of any wrong, and since they undertook this of their own authority and malice as furious folk and real robbers of the church (not indeed robbing earthly goods but the office and honor of the Holy Spirit), and in the same matter have become both complainant and judge, it will never do for you to remain silent in this matter and consent to it; otherwise you may become a partaker of this strange robbery of the church and become guilty of this unjust and wicked tyranny perpetrated against the deposed brother.

"But had he been subject to punishment and had he by any wrong given cause that he should be deposed from his office, then this should have been done with your knowledge and on your advice as the pastor. But still worse, they appoint another in the place of the one deposed without your permission, indeed against your will, and so force him in by the same tyranny and injustice that is committed also against you.

"Here, my dear sir and friend, for Christ's sake let me warn you to be very careful (for this truly is not a small and minor matter) that you not become a partaker of the guilt of these robbers of the church and that not a part of the curse may fall on you. Now if you ask what to do in this matter, I indeed cannot give you much advice, but I regard it as well that you faithfully act in this case as I myself would act.

"In the first place, you should invite the uncalled minister who wormed his way in to see you in the presence of your assistants and kindly but earnestly show him the outrage and tyranny of the council. Again, you should point out to him that he was not called through you (to whom the church has been entrusted), for which reason he is a thief and a murderer, and yet he teaches and presides in the church for which you must give an account. He therefore should be made to see that he barged in by force and robbed you of your ministry without your knowledge and consent. After that you should admonish him to desist from such robbery or see to it how he can preside over his robbed office with a clear conscience.

"For the congregation has been entrusted and commanded to you, so that it behooves no one without your knowledge to administer the office of teaching and ruling. If he rejects this admonition administered especially in the presence of several persons, tell him that you intend to bring what you have told him privately to the attention of an honorable council. Do that in this way: Either ask them to see you or go to them. Then ask them, in the first place, whether they regard you as their minister and pastor of the congregation at *N*. If they agree, then show them by earnest words the duties and dangers of a faithful pastor: that you must give an account of this your church, and how much trouble, care, and labor it takes to provide for it, to endure in every kind of tribulation, such as times of pestilence and other epidemics that might occur, as it was shown above. But since you receive no better reward for this hard and difficult labor than that they forced on you, without your knowledge and even against your will, a preacher (of whom you know nothing as regards his doctrine and life), while at the same time they shamefully and maliciously deposed the former pastor behind your back and without any regard for what is right, you herewith testify before them that you have not consented to such malice and outrage, nor do you consent to it now, nor will you ever.

"In addition, you should admonish them to heed this carefully, because he was not called but crashed in by force so that he came as a thief and robber of the divine office. Tell them also that you want to be clean and clear of the blood of those who tyrannically robbed you of your office and of those who approved and confirmed it. This action is demanded by necessity, in order that you may not render yourself guilty of the sin of others. If that admonition between you and them in private does not move them, then tell them that you will announce all this publicly from the pulpit. Do this as you please by these or similar words: 'My dear people, you know that I am your pastor and that I must give an account of you. Every day I must risk my body and life for you against the devil and every peril of the soul, as I should and must provide you in this city with preaching. Now you have chased away your pastor before he was convicted before a court of justice and without my knowledge, though I should have acted first of all in this matter. In addition, you have placed another man into my office without my consent and so you deprived me of my ministry. Now, since I am your pastor

227

and must be, I will not flee or surrender my ministry to another until I am rightfully deposed.

" 'Meanwhile, since I cannot flee or surrender my ministry, I will do what the Lord says in Matt. 5:40 and Luke 6:29: "From him who takes away your cloak, do not withhold your tunic either." That I will now do, and I herewith declare that this parish is mine and that I have been commanded to attend to and administer the pastoral office; therefore, I cannot surrender it. But since it is taken from me tyrannically and forced from me, I must suffer this and let it be robbed and taken from me. For a while I will go away until God will reinstate me. Meanwhile, I will see who is so wicked as to place himself into the parish that has been taken from me by robbery, and how he can claim it with a clear conscience.'

"If you have blessed them thus, then depart from them for a while and either come to us or go somewhere else. For these wicked persons also want to praise themselves while they slander us before the ruler of the land as though we wanted to delve into the affairs of the state. They revile us as rebels in the most heinous way in which a person can be reviled, though they know that they do wrong and lie. They are *sacrilegi* (sacrilegious), not as those who are broken on the wheel for stealing church property, which indeed we might bear and let them go unpunished. But they are *sacrilegi* because they rob the Holy Spirit of His office and honor and make themselves the Holy Spirit, for they depose and appoint ministers according to their own will. They themselves want to be preachers and take charge of the ministry. In that way they have learned the Gospel.

"I have faithfully advised you. May God grant you courage to follow it; then, please God, it will not be without fruit. For in this matter I do nothing by way of disturbance or force, but I counsel that all things should be done kindly and humbly (though also earnestly) and be begun and carried out for conscience' sake. If thus you have bidden them farewell, then also Cordatus may protest, if he cares to, that he will not preach in a church that treacherously has been stolen and robbed and in which persons properly called have been tyrannically deposed from their office, in order that he may not be burdened with the sacrilege and sins of others. This might be one way to reintroduce the ban or interdict, for if anyone will force himself into your office, I will by my letter fill his conscience with such fear that I hope he will not readily stay there" ("That a Pastor Should Not Be Silent at the Unjust Deposition of a Minister," 1531, St. Louis edition, 10:1618ff.).

Fröschel writes in 1565: "Bugenhagen was called and accepted by the honorable university, the members of the council, and the whole congregation, as this is done still." (See Löscher, *Unschuldige Nachrichten* [1731], p. 695).

Wigand: "It is reported in Acts 14:23 that Paul and Barnabas chose elders in the various churches by vote" (*Centuriae Magdeburgenses* 1.5.4).

Chemnitz: "Here it may be asked who those are by whose voice and vote the election and calling should be carried out, so that it may be regarded as divine, that is, that God Himself by these means chooses, calls, and sends laborers into His harvest. And for this matter Scripture supplies definite and clear examples. In Acts 1:15–26 we are told that Peter, when another was to be substituted in the place of Judas, submitted the matter not only to the group of apostles but also to the other disciples, who at that time were known as believers and whose number, then assembled, amounted to about 120. To them Peter propounded from Scripture what kind of persons and how they were to elect, and to this prayers were joined. Here, indeed, lots were cast, because this election was not simply to be mediate but apostolic, but afterward lots were no longer used in calling. When deacons were to be chosen and called, according to Acts 6:2–6, the apostles did not wish to arrogate to themselves the right to call, but they convened the congregation. They did not entirely abdicate the care of calling or commit it to the desire of the blind and confused multitude, but they were, so to speak, governors and moderators of the election and call, for they set forth the doctrine and rule of electing and calling, what kind of persons and in what manner they were to elect. Those chosen were then placed before the apostles in order that they might by their verdict approve the election, whether it was done rightly. They then approved the election by their prayers and the laying on of hands.

"According to Acts 14:23, Paul and Barnabas ordained elders in the various congregations. They did not assume for themselves the right and authority to elect and call, but Luke here has the word *cheirotonēsantes,* which in 2 Cor. 8:19 is used of election by the voice and vote of the congregation. This term is taken from the

Greek custom according to which voting was done by raising the hands; it signifies creating, designating, or approving anyone's election [by raising the hands]. Paul and Barnabas therefore did not force elders on the congregations without their consent and against their will.

"When, according to Acts 15:22, men were to be sent to the congregation at Antioch with instructions, Luke writes: 'Then it pleased the apostles and elders, with the whole church, to send chosen men of their own company to Antioch with Paul and Barnabas.' It is well, however, to observe in the history of the apostles that sometimes the ministers and the rest of the congregation together proposed and chose at the same time those whom they regarded as suitable, as we read in Acts 1:23. Sometimes the congregation proposed and chose, and their choice was submitted to the apostles for approval (Acts 6:5–6). But often the apostles, who could judge much better in these matters, proposed to the congregations those whom they regarded as suitable for the ministry, and if the vote and consent of the congregation was added to this, then the call was valid. So Paul sent Timothy, Titus, Silvanus, and others to the congregations. According to Acts 14:23, the elders also were proposed and the church consented to them by *cheirotonia* (election by raising the hands).

"At times some also offered their services to the church, as we read in 1 Tim. 3:1: 'If a man desires the position of a bishop, he desires a good work.' But the consent of the congregation and the judgment and confirmation of the elders was always present and required at the time of the apostles at every legitimate call. So Titus was appointed to supervise and direct the election of the elders in order that this might be done rightly and that he might approve and confirm the election rightly performed by ordination. For Paul in Titus 1:5 uses for the appointment of elders the same word that is found in Acts 14:23, where at the same time mention is made of *cheirotonia* and the confirmation of the elders. And he commanded Titus to rebuke sharply those who neither were sound in doctrine nor taught what they should, speaking of this more clearly in 1 Tim. 5:22: 'Do not lay hands on anyone hastily, nor share in other people's sins,' that is to say, by approving an election and call not rightly performed.

"These examples of apostolic history clearly show that the elec-

230

tion or call in a definite way pertains to the whole church, so that both the elders and the people take part in it. And this apostolic form of electing and calling was also used later in the church. . . . When emperors and kings later adopted the Christian religion, their judgment and authority also began to be added and required for electing and calling, because they had to be nurses of the church. . . . This is the opinion of the apostolic, primitive, and ancient church regarding the legitimate election and calling of the ministers of the Word and sacraments. This opinion obtains also in those churches that have already been planted and established by the Word of God and where there are elders who hold the pure doctrine and a pious government and people that understand the doctrine and love piety. . . .

"From what we have said, it will be clear how we are to judge the decree of Trent regarding the legitimate calling and sending of ministers of the Word and sacraments. It was determined in the fourth chapter and the seventh canon that those are legitimate ministers of the Word and sacraments who have been called, ordained, and sent solely by the papistic bishops and their suffragans, and that the consent, call, or authority of either the faithful people or pious magistrates is not required. Indeed, an anathema has been pronounced on those who say that the consent of either the faithful people or pious magistrates is required for a legitimate call. But now we have clearly shown that this very form of the legitimate election and calling, which Trent has condemned with a curse, is of the apostolic, primitive, and ancient church" (*Examen Concilii Tridentini,* "De sacramento ordinis," fol. 586b–589a.b.).

Gerhard: "We say (1) that the highest and sovereign right to call ministers of the church belongs absolutely to the true God, the Father, Son, and Holy Spirit, at not only the immediate but also the mediate calling. Nor has He abdicated His right when He commanded and empowered the church to call ministers, but He has reserved it wholly and inviolately for Himself, though He desires to execute it mediately. (2) Nor does He desire ordinarily to execute His right and power of mediate vocation through angels or the appearance of the spirits of the departed, . . . but by men. . . . (3) He rather has given to the church, as to His bride, the keys of the kingdom of heaven (Matt. 16:19; 18:17) and promised that with regard to anything on which it would agree and ask, it would be given

231

the request by His Father (Matt. 18:19). He has entrusted to it the Word and the sacraments, just as the apostle says of the Israelite church: 'To them were committed the oracles of God' (Rom. 3:2), and 'Israelites to whom pertain the adoption, the glory, the covenants, the giving of the Law, the service of God, the promises' (Rom. 9:4). The church is the house of God (1 Tim. 3:15), in which the ministers of the church have been appointed stewards (1 Cor. 4:1). To it belongs also the office, as we read: 'All things are yours: whether Paul or Apollos or Cephas' (1 Cor. 3:21, 22). The church, therefore, has the delegated right (so to speak) to appoint competent ministers of the Word, and God desires to use its service to call pious teachers.

"(4) Since, furthermore, there are three different states in the church—the ecclesiastical, the civil, and the domestic, or the ministerium, the secular government, and the people, the church comprising all of these as its members—no state by any means is to be excluded from this work, but at the mediate calling everyone is to retain its part, performance, and authority. The fact that first the bishops and elders should be present when anyone is to be entrusted with the office is apparent from the apostolic command and normative examples of Scripture such as: 'They [Paul and Barnabas] appointed elders in every church' (Acts 14:23). 'Do not neglect the gift that is in you, which was given to you by prophecy with the laying on of the hands of the presbytery' (1 Tim. 4:14). 'Do not lay hands on anyone hastily' (1 Tim. 5:22). 'The things that you have heard from me among many witnesses, commit these to faithful men who will be able to teach others also' (2 Tim. 2:2). 'For this reason I left you in Crete, that you should . . . appoint elders in every city' (Titus 1:5).

"It goes without saying that those who are in the ministry and profess the pure doctrine can best judge the qualities of such as are to be called into the ministry; no one, therefore, dare say that they are to be excluded from the mediate calling. But since the ministry is not the entire church, but only a part of it (Eph. 4:11; 1 Cor. 12:29), the bishops and elders dare not arrogate the vocation entirely to themselves, excluding the other members of the church. But according to the example of the apostles (Acts 1:15; 6:2; 13:2; 14:23), they must also concede them their vote and participation, for they are not lords but servants and overseers of the congregation (1 Cor. 3:21; 2 Cor. 1:24; 1 Peter 5:3). The church, to which the mediate vocation belongs, is the mystical body of Christ that embraces all members (Eph. 4:12). The work of calling must therefore not be ascribed merely to one member, but all the several members must be permitted their participation.

"Finally, because the Christian government not only is a member of the church but has been appointed by God as its foster father (Is. 49:23) and its servant (Is. 60:10), in order that it might open the gates to the coming King of glory (Ps. 24:7), it therefore neither can nor must be excluded at the electing and calling of ministers, but it is to be allowed its part in this work. . . . We add that the calling of ministers must be performed by the whole church and all its three states in this way so that the proper order be observed and confusion be avoided, for God is not the author of confusion but peace (1 Cor. 14:33). This order is observed most properly if the matter of choosing and calling of ministers is handled by certain prominent members of the church in the name and with the consent of the whole congregation. But although, as it seems, no rule may be prescribed that covers every detail, . . . nevertheless if we judge by the general pattern, the examination, ordination, and induction belong to the ministerium; the nomination, presentation, and confirmation to the Christian government; and the consent, vote, and approbation, or under given circumstances also the demand, to the people.

"The general rule, therefore, that ministers should be elected with the consent of the congregation and that no one should be forced on it against its will is attested by clear passages of Scripture and has been tried out by the constant practice of the primitive church. But the form of the election according to its several parts differs; for at times the vote of the people is demanded for the nomination of the persons, while at other times only its confirming consent to the nomination already made is required. This is proved by the apostolic practice at the election of Matthias (Acts 1:15). At first Peter reminded the brethren of what kind of person was to be elected. After that the congregation proposed two men (v. 23) of whom the one, namely, Matthias, was elected by God through lots and was then chosen by the common vote of the disciples for the office (according to the Greek original, v. 26). Though the calling of Matthias was immediate, the vote of the believing people that was added is rightly cited as an example of [proper] mediate vocation.

"When, according to Acts 6:3, deacons were to be chosen, the apostles told the brethren, that is, the rest of the congregation: 'Brethren, seek out from among you seven men of good reputation, full of the Holy Spirit and wisdom, whom we may appoint over this business.' According to v. 5 they then chose Stephen with six others, presented them to the apostles, who laid their hands on them. These deacons, therefore, were placed into their office by the whole congregation. According to Acts 14:23 the apostles appointed elders in the newly established congregations by taking the votes of the church members according to the rule: 'Whomever you approve by your letters I will send' (1 Cor. 16:3). As 2 Cor. 8:19 says, Titus was chosen by the churches. According to the Greek original the congregation confirmed the election of Titus by their consent and voted for his person by their voice. In 1 Tim. 3:7 we read: A bishop 'must have a good testimony among those who are outside,' much more however of the congregation over which he is to preside. In 1 Tim. 5:22 it is said: 'Do not lay hands on anyone hastily,' namely, until he has the good report and consent of the congregation. According to 1 Tim. 4:14 the ministry was entrusted to Timothy by the laying on of hands by the elders. This means that he was chosen by the vote of the congregation, for here the term 'elders' does not designate merely those who preached the Word but also those to whom all matters pertaining to the congregation were entrusted in the name of the others; these attested the consent of the congregation by the laying on of their hands. From this apostolic practice it is clear which functions are to be conceded to the ministry and which to the Christian people. The fact that at this practice no mention is made of the civil government is due to the circumstance that the government at that time was not yet Christian and consecrated to the doctrine whose proclamation was commanded to the ministers" (*Loci theologici,* "De min. eccl.," par. 85–86).

The same: "To whom the keys of the kingdom of heaven have been entrusted by Christ, to him also belongs the right to call ministers. Now the keys of the kingdom of heaven have been entrusted to the entire congregation; therefore, the entire congregation has the right to call ministers. The protasis is proved from the definition of the keys of the kingdom of heaven; for by the keys we mean the church power, a part of which is the authority to call and appoint ministers. The apodosis is apparent from the words of Christ in Matt.

234

16:19, where Peter in the name of the congregation is told: 'I will give you the keys of the kingdom of heaven.' . . . This truth is proved also from Matt. 18:17–18, where the power to excommunicate impenitent sinners is given to the entire congregation. Now the power of excommunication is a part of the keys of the kingdom of heaven; therefore, the keys of the kingdom of heaven are given to the entire church. . . . How can Bellarmine prove that by 'congregation' [*Gemeinde*] in Christ's words 'Tell it to the church' [*Gemeinde*] only a church prelate or a council of church prelates is meant? A single prelate is not the church, which also Bellarmine admits, for he writes: 'A person cannot be called the church, since the church is the people and kingdom of God.' Therefore also, no council of prelates or bishops can constitute the church, for the hearers also belong to the church, and these must not be omitted when its nature is defined. Just as a city does not consist of a physician and of a physician but of a physician and of peasants, so also the church does not consist of a bishop and of a bishop but of a bishop and the church members [*Zuhörer*].

"But, it is objected, here the church is meant inasmuch as it is represented by individual persons and not as it consists of *all* its members, for the term 'church' in Christ's statement: 'Tell it to the church' (or congregation) cannot be interpreted to denote *all* church members. I reply: The bishops or teachers alone cannot represent the church, since to it, if correctly defined, the hearers also belong. Nevertheless, the ministerium may represent the church, and to this belong not only those who labor in the Word but also the elders who have been appointed to attend to the affairs of the church in its name. We admit, therefore, that by the term 'congregation' or 'church' may be understood the teachers, whom Bellarmine calls 'prelates,' but we deny that the hearers are to be excluded from it, for they are represented by the church elders, namely, the more eminent members of the rest of the church, who with the ministers constitute the ministerium or, as we are accustomed to call them in our churches, 'the consistory,' which carries out ecclesiastical business in the name of the church" (ibid., par. 87).

The same: "Whoever has the duty to discern between teachers and seducers, to examine sound doctrine, to distinguish between the voice of Christ, the Chief Shepherd, and that of false shepherds, not to follow a stranger, but to flee from him, to anathematize those who preach another gospel than that proclaimed by the apostles, to him also belongs the duty to call ministers according to his status and order. But all this is the duty of the flock of Christ or the hearers (Matt. 7:15; John 5:39; 10:27; Gal. 1:9; 1 Thess. 5:19–21; 1 John 4:1; 2 John 10–11). Therefore, this cannot be refused and denied them. The conclusion is clear: If the hearers are to beware of false prophets, they must therefore also in a proper order or way take heed that the consistory [*Kirchenamt*] does not place over them false teachers; and so they must let it be their concern that true and pious ministers are called into the office" (ibid., par. 88).

The same: "Those whose servants the pastors are and are called also have the right to call ministers. Now they are and are called ministers of the church; therefore, the church has the authority and power to call ministers. The apodosis is proved from such passages as: 'All things are yours: whether Paul or Apollos or Cephas, . . . all are yours' (1 Cor. 3:21–22). 'Not that we have dominion over your faith' (2 Cor. 1:24). 'Shepherd the flock of God which is among you . . . nor as being lords over those entrusted to you' (1 Peter 5:2–3). Bellarmine objects that the bishops are servants of the church because they work for it, not because they obey it, but because they rule and preside over it. I answer: The call of the hearers by their vote and their due respect for and obedience to the rightly called ministers must not be placed in opposition to each other. The people indeed should obey their rightly called ministers, but from this it must not be inferred that their vote should be excluded from the legitimate vocation. Whatever the rightly called ministers do when attending to their office, they do not in their own name but in that of God and the church. God is the Lord of the harvest and the Householder. The church is the glory, the house, and the matron. The ministers are the managers. Hence, they dare not in any way arrogate to themselves any political rule over their hearers nor arbitrarily demand for themselves any power to act or command" (ibid., par. 89).

The same: "Even the law of justice does not tolerate it that the right of the entire assembly be given to one state, while the others are excluded. Now the right to call ministers belongs to the entire church. Therefore justice does not tolerate it that this right be conferred on one state and the rest be excluded" (*Loci theologici,* "De min. eccl.," par. 90).

The same: "Bellarmine objects (1) that according to Chrysostom this (the election of Matthias by the believers) was granted not of necessity but by way of concession.... No mention is made here of any concession or papal indulgence, but Peter conceded this to the congregation, because he knew that it rightfully was theirs. Nor does Chrysostom mention any concession, but suggests that Peter did not wish to do anything in this matter arbitrarily or tyrannically. For so he writes in his third homily: 'See how he himself (Peter) does all things on unanimous resolution and nothing arbitrarily or tyrannically.' And afterward he adds that Peter let the others take part in the matter in order that it might not become controversial, but this danger is to be feared also when others are called. He finally states: 'He (Peter) lets the multitude judge and so fosters the respect of those who are called and frees himself from envy and dissension, which might arise among the others.' Nothing is here said of any concession, but much of very valid reasons for his action.

"Bellarmine objects (2) that this was not so much an election as rather a demand by which they asked God to have someone chosen in the place of Judas. I reply: They first chose two men; they then asked God by prayer that one of the two might be revealed and confirmed by Him through the lot. The prayer, therefore, should not be placed in opposition to the preceding election, nor does it exclude the election. Nevertheless, we admit that between this immediate election by lot and all other mediate vocations there is a difference, because at the immediate calling of Matthias a person was not finally to be chosen, but the election of one of the two was to be committed to the divine judgment. In a mediate vocation the final election and vocation belong to the church.

"Bellarmine objects (3) that from one example it cannot be proved that anything may be done by divine right, since there are contrary examples that at times bishops were chosen without the vote of the people. I reply: Such contrary examples will be considered later; here we merely suggest that we by no means draw our conclusions from a single example that is limited by certain circumstances but from the general practice of the apostolic church. We rather combine with the example of the vocation of Matthias also the other examples described in the Acts of the Apostles and the epistles of the apostles. Hence, we do not establish a general rule from one single example but from the adequate enumeration of all the examples recorded in Scripture. To this we add expressly that there is no divergent example showing that the apostles called ministers in congregations already established without the vote of such a congregation. From the entire apostolic practice, which is proved by all the examples recorded in Scripture, it is rightly inferred that the calling of ministers should not be carried out without the vote of the congregation" (ibid., par. 91).

The same: "Bellarmine objects that this passage (Acts 6:1–6) does not belong here since it treats of deacons who were to serve tables, not of the election of pastors. I reply that even if we would admit that the office of deacons was merely to serve tables, it would not in any way weaken our argument. For if the election of deacons, whose business it was above all to distribute food and provide for the body, did not exclude the vote of the people, how much less may the election by the people be excluded when pastors are called who must provide for the souls. This conclusion is confirmed by the fact that at the election of the elders (Acts 14:23) the same practice was followed by the apostles. But it is wrong to say that the deacons were merely to serve tables; for as we have shown above from the examples of Stephen and Philip, they also attended to the office of teaching" (ibid., par. 93).

Dedekennus: "The first place in the (calling) church belongs to the clergy or ministerium, or as we say today, the teachers or servants of the Gospel, if such are found in the congregation for which a pastor or minister of the Word is to be provided" (*Thesaurus consiliorum et decisionum* 1.2; fol. 376). This witness is not to be overlooked, for it explains that when our ancient teachers represent the cooperation of the incumbents of the public ministry as absolutely necessary for a valid vocation, they always proceed from the premise that in the calling congregation there already are ministers of the Word. They do not want to say that the authority to call is so distributed among the three states in the church that only by the cooperation of all three, at least of two, the ecclesiastical and the domestic, the divine order of the public ministry can be realized. They generally hold rather that the power of the church, even the parts of it that are administered by the pastors, rests with the communion of believers and so also the authority to elect and call ministers, but that according to the circumstances prevailing in a congregation, this power is to be exercised in proper order now by one state and then again by several. If several states are represented in the congregation, then its call is valid only if all the states have cooperated and none has been excluded. Indeed, if an affiliate church is joined by canonical right to a larger church group that is headed by a consistory or a bishop, then of course the ministerium is a part of the calling congregation even if the congregation has no pastor of its own. Therefore, the opinion quoted above declares quite rightly: "The pious patron of the congregation or its pious bishop above all, together with the others, is a part and citizen (member) of it, though he may not live near the place (of the congregation)" (ibid., fol. 378).

Veit Ludwig von Seckendorf: "It is therefore safest to adhere to the principle that Christ Himself has given when He said: 'Where two or three (not to speak of a larger congregation) are gathered together in My name, I am there in the midst of them' (Matt. 18:20). From this it follows that such an assembly or congregation in itself has the power to do and execute all things that are demanded for the exercise of divine worship and for which Christ has promised His gracious presence. Such an assembly, though it has an inward communion with other Christians and the same confession or religion, nevertheless is not of necessity or by obligation directed to anyone else, but it has Christ in its midst by His Word and sacraments, just as have the others. Hence, it must also have the proper and certain right to call persons for worship and ministry; for this belongs to the church or congregation, which has the authority to elect one or several competent persons to serve as presbyters or elders and leaders in doctrine. Now if the congregation already has pastors, they above all, together with the rest, belong to those who are to call and appoint pastors along with the magistrates, and no state should be excluded.

"Now if today a congregation of converted Christians would be organized, let us say, in India or on an unknown island by a Christian landing there, it follows from what has been said—and the theologians may expatiate on this matter—that such a congregation, according to God's Word, can establish the ministry and ministerium by its own power; and though thereby it essentially would become a member of the universal church, being united in doctrine, it would

239

not be absolutely bound to send its ministers for ordination or consecration to a bishop or a consistory or ministerium, especially if that would be difficult on account of great distance or peril; nor would it have to be governed in outward church matters by foreign authorities. Yet it would maintain communion with all other Christians by its same doctrine and faith without depending on any church government. However, it would be neither a sin nor a heresy if it would adhere to a certain church and its government, as some separatists in England think who greatly exaggerate the idea of liberty.

"We have examples of coreligionists living in distant lands, such as in Moscow, where for hundreds of miles there are no churches of our confession, who maintain congregations and public worship. Similarly, there are many congregations in Hungary under Turkish rule who have pastors and *exercitia religionis* (exercises of religion). These cannot be asked to become members of the external church in other countries and subject themselves to certain superintendents or consistories, but such congregations have the full right to appoint their own ministerium and ministers. The pastor whom they call does everything in such congregations that is the duty of a bishop or superintendent of a large diocese; for it is not the size or number in itself that determines the increase or decrease of the office. Thus, for example, the few disciples at Ephesus who were at first instructed by Apollos and then baptized by Paul, twelve in number (Acts 19:7), formed a church of Christ, and if its number had not increased, this little congregation would have had the same right that afterward the larger parishes had, of whose elders Paul says that the Holy Spirit had made them overseers to feed the church of God (Acts 20:28). He did not direct them to Jerusalem, Peter, or himself but only to the doctrine by which he declared to them all the counsel of God (v. 27).

"When we consider that the first church meetings were held, as time and place permitted, in humble private homes, perhaps also in the fields and woods or in caves and caverns, as well as that neither archbishops nor bishops administered the office of a minister or pastor in the way and with such authority as in later times, but very poor and simple persons who during the week, especially in poor congregations, had to support themselves by working on the farms, we can understand much better that the kind of church government that developed in the course of time and still prevails today is not a matter that stems immediately from any divine command or right, or that on this depends the truth of the doctrine or the very essence of the church" (*Christenstaat* 3, 11; par. 3, 5, 6).

Brochmand: "Our churches assign the right to elect ministers of the Word to the entire congregation and prove their claim from Acts 1:22–23. For when an apostle was to be elected in the place of Judas the traitor, Peter indeed, for the sake of good order, began and directed the election, but the entire congregation chose two, namely, Matthias and Barsabas, over whom they prayed and gave forth their lots. Now if the apostles, who had been called by Christ in an extraordinary way and were divinely supplied with special power, did not wish by themselves to establish the ministers of the church, why should the Roman bishops, who are not worthy to be compared to the apostles as regards their gifts, arrogate to themselves this power?" (*Universae theologiae systema,* "De min. ecclesiast.," fol. 349).

The same: "In the fourth place we urge the natural equity; for it is far more equitable and safe that the ministers of the Word be elected by all, though with proper propriety and order, than by a single bishop. It is certainly more equitable that those who serve the whole congregation and are supported by it should be chosen and confirmed by the whole congregation. Then also a single bishop may more readily be bribed than a whole congregation; but above all, because the administration of the sacred office will fare badly if men who are either odious or questionable or unknown to them are forced on the congregation" (ibid., fol. 350).

Quenstedt: "The principal efficient cause of the ministry of the church is God; the less principal cause of the ministry is the entire congregation. The power to elect and call the ministers of the Word rests by divine right not merely with the pastors or the 'spiritual state' nor merely with the secular government nor merely with the people but with the entire congregation. Without the consent and vote of the people the vocation cannot be performed legitimately" (*Theologia didactico-polemica,* part 4, chap. 12, "De min. eccl.," fol. 1509).

The same: "They [the papists] reply that it is not the business of the sheep to elect the shepherd, but the people and the government are the sheep while the bishops are the shepherds. I reply: (1) He

241

who is chosen is not the shepherd of him who chooses while he chooses; only after the election, calling, and installation are completed does the one elected deserve the name 'shepherd.' (2) The Holy Spirit describes the sheep of God as those who know the voice of the shepherd, can distinguish the shepherd from the hireling, and will not follow the voice of the hireling (John 10:3–21). These and similar titles of honor prove that the sheep should also take part in calling the shepherd. (3) The hearers are called sheep not in their relation to the ministers, who are called to pasture them, but only in their relation to Christ (John 10:12–21). This Shepherd the sheep neither can nor may elect and rule. (4) Even if they are called sheep in their relation to the ministers of the Word, the argument taken from this is not valid, because the spiritual and rational sheep may not be placed in the same category with the animal and irrational ones. (5) Arguments based on dissimilar things are incapable of proving anything" (ibid., p. 1513).

The same: "They object that the apostles ordained bishops here and there without the consent of the people. I reply: (1) We have proved the very opposite from Acts 1:6, 14. (2) What the apostles did by apostolic, that is, extraordinary, authority according to the circumstances of their times, during which the church was to be established among the heathen, has no validity as a perpetual rule and ordinary sanction. (3) When persons were to be sent to others, the vote of the congregation by which or from which they were sent was never omitted (2 Cor. 8:19)" (ibid.).

The same: "They object that there are certain embarrassing features (when the people elect ministers) as, for example: (1) The people are ignorant and unable to judge. (2) In a city there are always more who vote down those that are good and vote in men of their own kind. (3) The rule by the people is connected with the peril of great tumults and seditions. I reply: If the argument is to be taken from embarrassing features, then all the more the election may not be left to one bishop or merely to the clergy" (ibid., fol. 1614).

Hülsemann: "Since the appointment of the elders by the apostles did not exclude appointment by God, as Acts 20:28 shows, nor did God's appointment exclude that by the apostles, so also the appointment by the apostles did not exclude the election of the people by vote as Acts 1:23 and 6:3 prove. So far as the fathers are

242

concerned, both their principle and practice are clear; for they never excluded joint election by the laymen but always included it when bishops were to be elected. Nor did they regard an election as valid if the people objected or did not consent to it" (*Manuale Augustanae Confessionis,* disput. 12, "De ord. eccles.," pp. 469, 571).

Baier: "After the church has been established, it has the right and power to appoint ministers. For as the bride of Christ it has the keys of the kingdom of heaven given to it by the Bridegroom (Matt. 16:18; 18:17). Hence, as the church has the right to open and close the kingdom of heaven, so also it has the right to appoint ministers by whom it opens and closes. And when we remember that the church is, so to speak, a republic, and that the ministers of the Word are, as it were, the magistrates or the managers of its official affairs to whom the care of the entire republic has been commissioned and commended, it is easily understood that the power to appoint them, in itself and by its very nature, inheres in the entire congregation, and that it does not belong to one certain part, unless by common consent it has been conferred on that one certain part" (*Compendium theologiae positivae* 3.14; p. 1057. Preus edition [1864], p. 626).

Hartmann: "So today we must praise the excellent piety of our princes by which they provided for their subjects skilled and competent teachers, not in order that the congregations might be deprived of their right; but because the people either did not understand or use their prerogative, and its judgment was impeded by ancient errors, they became their patrons and represented the church in its functions" (*Pastoral.,* p. 76).

In addition let us now hear the ancient church:

Clement of Rome: "Also our apostles recognized through our Lord Jesus Christ that there might arise contention because of the name 'episcopacy.' Because of this, with perfect foresight of the future, they appointed those named before, and they ordered that after their departure other approved men should follow them in their ministry. Hence, those who were appointed by them or thereafter by other prominent men with the consent of the whole congregation, who served the flock of Christ blamelessly, humbly, quietly, and not after the manner of hirelings, and who for a long time enjoyed the good report of all, are now deposed unjustly, according to our opinion, from their office.

243

"Blessed are the elders who before them finished their course, for they enjoyed a blessed and in every way peaceful departure, and they need not worry that they may be deposed from the ministry that is now accorded them. I say this because it is obvious that you have driven some who attended to their office well away from the ministry in which they serve blamelessly" (*Ep. ad Cor.* 44–45).

Cyprian: "God does not hear the sinner, but if anyone fears God and does His will, him He hears. Therefore, you must with all diligence and careful examination elect those into the ministry of God whom God may be expected to hear. Let the congregation not flatter itself that it may remain free from the blemish of sin if it has communion with a vicious minister and gives its consent to the unjust and unlawful episcopacy of its pastor; for the divine rebuke by the prophet Hosea threatens them: 'Their sacrifices ... shall be like bread of mourners to them; all who eat it shall be defiled' (Hos. 9:4). This teaches and shows that all who became contaminated with the sacrifice of the profane and unjust priest were altogether besmirched with sin.

"The same is taught by the story of Korah, Dathan, and Abiram, who against Aaron the priest arrogated to themselves the right to sacrifice. Also in that case the Lord commanded the people through Moses to separate themselves from them in order that they might not become partakers of the same crime and perish with them in the same iniquity. Therefore, a congregation that obeys the commands of the Lord and fears God must separate itself from a vicious minister and may not participate in the sacrifices of a pastor who desecrates what is holy; for the congregation has the right to elect worthy ministers and to reject the unworthy. It is also supported by divine authority that a pastor is chosen in the presence of the people and in the sight of all, he being acknowledged as worthy and competent by public judgment and testimony, just as Moses received the divine command: 'Take Aaron and Eleazar his son, and bring them up to Mount Hor; and strip Aaron of his garments and put them on Eleazar his son; for Aaron shall be gathered to his people and die there' (Num. 20:25–26). In the sight of the whole congregation God wanted to have the priest chosen, teaching us thereby that ministerial appointments are to be performed with the knowledge of the assisting congregation. In the presence of the people the crimes of the wicked should be revealed and the merits of the good be praised. That is a just and legitimate ordination, which has been carefully proved by the vote and judgment of all. Later, as recorded in Acts, this was observed by Peter when, at the election of another apostle in place of Iscariot, he turned to the assembled disciples. The apostles observed this rule also when appointing deacons, not only bishops and pastors. The election of deacons was done carefully and cautiously by the whole assembled congregation in order that someone unworthy might not be consecrated to the ministry of the altar and the office of a pastor; for unworthy persons are ordained according to human presumption and not according to God's will. This displeases God, as He says through Hosea: 'They set up kings, but not by Me' (Hos. 8:4). Therefore, we must carefully preserve and maintain as a divine tradition and an apostolic practice what is also guarded by us and in almost all lands, that the appointment is rightly observed when the neighboring bishops of the province come to the congregation that best knows the life of each individual and can examine his way of living" (*De Martial. et Basilid.,* book 1, letter 4).

Origen: "Though the Lord had given rules regarding the appointment of a high priest, and He Himself had chosen one, nevertheless the assembly was convened. Hence, the presence of the people is required whenever a pastor is to be appointed in order that all may be sure that he be chosen who, in the opinion of the whole people, is the more excellent, learned, holy, and exceeding in every virtue, and that no other be elected into the ministry; this is done in presence of the people as witnesses in order that afterward no regret may occur to anyone nor may any have doubts. This is the very thing that the apostle inculcates when speaking of the election of a pastor by saying: 'He must have a good testimony among those who are outside' (1 Tim. 3:7)" (*Homil.* VI, 3, on Lev. 8; de la Rue edition, 2:216b; Lammatzsch edition, 9:277).

Ambrose: "I am very sorry that the Lord's congregation that is among you until now is without a pastor and that your attitude that has caused the impediment is ascribed to me. For when there are dissensions among you, how can we come to a conclusion and you to an election or acquiesce in anything? And how among you dissenters can anyone take on himself this office, which can hardly be sustained when people agree? Is that the fruit of your instruction by your confessing pastor? Is that the right conduct of children corresponding to the pattern of their just fathers, who recognized St. Eusebius, whom they had not known before, but whom they regarded as worthy as soon as they saw him, not minding the talk of their fellow citizens, so that they declared him worthy as soon as they copied him? He justly became so great a man because the whole congregation elected him, and rightly they believed that he in whose election the wish of all was expressed was chosen by God's own judgment.

"This pattern you should follow, especially as you were instructed by this holy confessor Eusebius, and you should do this far more than the fathers because you have been instructed and brought up by a far more excellent teacher. You should give proof of your modesty and concord by all of you uniting in the desire to have a pastor. For if the declaration of our Lord that where two should agree concerning what they will ask, this should be done to them by His heavenly Father (for He says: 'Where two or three are gathered together in My name, I am there in the midst of them'), how much more can you, when the whole congregation comes together and you fully agree, be sure beyond any doubt that the Lord Jesus will be the author of your desire, the arbiter of your petition, the director of your ministerial election, and the giver of your grace" (book 10, ep. 82).

Socrates [a Greek historian at Constantinople, ca. A.D. 440]: "When (in Milan on account of the election of a pastor) severe dissensions arose, a man called Ambrosius, in order to prevent any harm that might come to the city through sedition, hurried to the congregation to suppress the tumult. When he arrived there and had quieted the people by his admonition and instruction as to what would be beneficial to the congregation and so had curbed the foolish actions of the multitude, he was at once declared worthy of the ministry by the unanimous consent of all and was solemnly appointed for the office by everyone's vote. . . . To the present bishops this unanimous voice of the people appeared as God's voice from heaven. Therefore, they at once took Ambrosius, administered Holy Baptism to him (for he still was a catechumen), and chose him for the administration of the ministry. When he gladly accepted Holy Baptism but urgently refused the ministry, Emperor Valentinian was informed what had happened. Admiring the unanimity of the people and recognizing in the happening the work of God, he ordered the bishops to serve the will of Him who commanded that he should be chosen as pastor; for here the voice of God rather than that of men was obvious" (*Socratis Scholastici ecclesiast. hist.*, ed. Robertus Hussey [Oxford, 1853], vol. 2, book 4, chap. 30, pp. 553–54).

The Council of Nicaea: "Should the pastor of a congregation fall asleep, then those who shortly before were received into the ministerium should take the place of the departed, provided they are regarded as worthy and the people elect them" (*Concilium Nicenum* 1. in epistola ad Alexandrum apud Theodoretum l. 1. Hist. c. 9 circa finem).

The Third Council of Carthage: "No pastor is to be ordained who has not been approved by the examination of the ministers and the witness of the people" (*Council. Carthagin.* 3. Can. 22, in Mansi, 3:884).

Celestine: "No pastor should be forced on a congregation, for it [the election] requires the consent and desire of the clergy, of the congregation, and of the government" (*Epist.* 2; c. 5).

Leo: "He who is to preside over all should also be chosen by all" (*Ep.* 10 [al. 89]; par. 6).

The same: "When the election of a pastor is concerned, he should be presented to all, for this requires the unanimous consent of the clergy and the congregation. Should some vote for another, then the metropolitan should decide who is to be preferred, [namely,] he who has in his favor the overwhelming favor of the congregation and the overwhelming merits, but no one should be elected who is neither wanted nor demanded" (*Epist.* 12, par. 5).

Bede: "The believing people who through Baptism possess the area of the church must suggest pastors and teachers who ... preserve the words of the Law and the Holy Scriptures; for it is written: 'The lips of a priest should keep knowledge' (Mal. 2:7)" (On Deut. 27).

B. The ordination of the called [persons] with the laying on of hands is not a divine institution but merely an ecclesiastical rite [Ordnung] established by the apostles; it is no more than a solemn public confirmation of the call.

1. Scripture Proof

Whatever cannot be proved to be God's institution from His Word cannot be regarded and accepted as His own institution without committing idolatry. Scripture does not tell us of any divine institution of ordination; it merely attests that it was used by the apostles and that at that time the communication of precious gifts was connected with the laying on of hands. According to God's Word there is, of course, no doubt that even today ordination is not a meaningless ceremony if it is connected with the ardent prayer of the church, based on the glorious promises given in particular to the office of the ministry; it is accompanied with the outpouring of heavenly gifts on the person ordained.

2. Witnesses of the Church in Its Official Confessions

Smalcald Articles: "These words [Matt. 18:20; 1 Peter 2:9] properly refer to the true church, which, since it alone has the priesthood, must also have the power to elect and ordain ministers. This is attested also by the common custom of the church; for formerly the people chose the pastors and bishops. Then came the local bishop or one in the neighborhood and confirmed the chosen bishop by the laying on of hands; at that time ordination was nothing else (*nil nisi*) than such a ratification" (Of the Power and Jurisdiction of Bishops, par. 69–70; German text, *Triglot,* pp. 522, 524). Here our fathers testify that the divine institution of the public ministry is properly put into effect by the call and election of the congregation, and that ordination does not first create this divine work but merely acknowledges, attests, and confirms publicly where it already has taken place.

Apology: "If they wanted to call the sacrament of holy orders [*des Ordens*] a sacrament of the ministry and Gospel, we would not object to calling ordination a sacrament. For God has instituted and commanded the ministry, and it has His glorious promise (Rom. 1:16; Is. 55:11). If they wanted to understand the sacrament of holy orders in this way, we might also call the laying on of hands a sacrament. For the church has God's command to appoint ministers and deacons. Since then it is very comforting to know that God desires to preach and work through men and those elected by men, it is well for us to praise and honor this election very highly, especially against the satanic Anabaptists, who despise and revile it as well as the ministry and the outward [*leiblichen*] Word" (Art. XIII [VII], par. 9–13; German text, *Triglot,* p. 310).

Here our church confesses that ordination is to be regarded as divine only if by it is understood election into the ministry *per synecdochen* (by way of synecdoche) and not, as it is commonly understood, as a divine act that makes the call valid. Of this passage in the Apology Gerhard says: "Everyone understands that the Apology does not so much treat of the rite of ordination as rather of the office of the Word and the sacraments itself" (*Confessio catholica,* fol. 1328).

3. Witnesses of the Church in the Private Writings of Its Teachers

Luther: "Their own canon laws teach that a bishop who is consecrated [*geweihet*] by a simoniac (cf. Acts 8:9–24) or heretic is rightly consecrated; indeed, they regard it as right even if the most scandalous popes, such as Boniface VIII, Julian II, Clement VII, yea, even the devil, have done it officially. For it is important that the church and the bishop be one and that the church listen to the bishop and the bishop teach the church. So it was done. The laying on of hands, which blesses, ratifies, and attests this, just as a notary and the witnesses attest a secular matter and as a pastor blesses the bride and bridegroom, ratifying their marriage and witnessing that they were betrothed to each other before and that they publicly confess this. The bride is blessed even if the minister were an angel or a devil because it was done officially [*weil das Amt geschehen*]" ("An Example of How to Consecrate a True Christian Bishop," 1542, St. Louis edition, 17:114).

The same: "Though Paul commanded Titus to appoint presbyters (elders), it does not follow that Titus did this on his own authority; rather, following the example of the apostles, he appointed them with the consent and permission of the people. Otherwise the words of Paul would conflict with the example of the apostles. But the conclusion that he [King Henry VIII] draws from the laying on of hands regarding the ordination or consecration of priests is not pertinent, as even children can see, but in his papistic way he makes

Scripture say whatever comes to his mind. At that time the laying on of hands was the visible communication of the Holy Spirit" ("Against Henry, King of England," 1522, St. Louis edition, 19:347).

The same: "Therefore, it is not in vain that we use special ceremonies and customs [*Ordnungen*] in the church when we bless and join together persons entering into holy wedlock as well as when we ordain ministers. For we bless the bridegroom and bride, wish them Godspeed, read to them the Scriptures on the institution of this estate, and pray God that He would preserve, protect, and guard it. On the ministers of the Word we lay our hands, and at the same time offer our prayer to God, but only to witness thereby that it is a divine institution, as is not only this but also all other offices of the church, the secular government, and the home. In the papacy this doctrine had become altogether unknown and, as it were, buried and extinguished; then the people thought that the church is nothing else than a multitude of popes, cardinals, and bishops. They did not have the light of the divine Word nor the right prayer and invocation nor the proper humility and respect for this divine institution" ("Exposition of Genesis," chap. 41, 1544, St. Louis edition, 2:1344–45).

The same: " 'Whoever is called is consecrated and should preach to those who called him; that is our Lord God's consecration and true chrism.' Thus Luther wrote to Dorothea, widow of Jörger in Austria, when in 1534 she asked his advice about a minister whom the papists refused to consecrate" (See Seckendorf, *Commentarius historicus et apologeticus de Lutheranismo* 3.43, add. b).

The same: "The consecration of [papistic] priests is nothing else than human sham and monkeyshine [*Affenspiel*]. . . . The ministry of the Word and the church, that is, of the people, alone makes true priests" ("Brief Concluding Paragraphs on Vows," 1521, St. Louis edition, 19:1488 [quoted from the edition used by Dr. Walther]).

The same: "I will excuse the dear holy fathers, and they should be excused, if they consecrated or ordained with chrism and then called those thus consecrated priests [*Pfaffen*] or pastors; for thereby they did not consecrate private priests [*Winkelpfaffen*] nor did they consecrate anyone for the private mass. But if they called anyone into the true Christian ministry or pastoral office, they wanted to adorn and glorify this calling before the congregation with such pomp in order to distinguish them from others who were not called, in order that everyone might be sure and know which person should administer the office and was commanded to baptize, preach, and do other works. For really the consecration neither should nor can be anything else (if it is rightly done) than a call or induction [*Befehl*] into the pastoral office or the ministry" ("Tract on the Private Mass and the Consecration of Priests," 1533, St. Louis edition, 19:1257–58).

The same: "To conclude, just as the furious papistic abomination has destroyed Baptism, the Sacrament, and the preaching of the Gospel, so also it has destroyed by its shameful private chrism the ministry, its vocation, call, and the true consecration for the ministry or pastoral office. But nevertheless, here Christ remained with His power and miracle and has preserved the office and the call to the ministry in His holy place against their vile abomination. For the pastors or ministers always remained outside and above the chrism through princes, lords, and cities, as well as through bishops and even through abbots and abbesses and other states, and by their appointment the call and true consecration to the ministry or the pastoral office continued. In addition, such called pastors who received these investitures and offices were presented, that is, to the bishops of private masses [*Winkelbischöfe*] that they should invest and induct them, though this was not their call or investiture but only their confirmation of the call and not necessary. For the called pastors could have administered their office without their confirmation, as did the Maccabees, who were without priests by descent or call. But for the sake of peace they humbled themselves and permitted themselves to be ratified by the kings of Syria, who were nothing else than heathen and their enemies, as Antiochus and Demetrius.

"Such humility we likewise offered to our Antiochis and Demetriis so that they might have the authority to confirm our pastors, even though they were our enemies, in order that they might not have cause to complain that we were proud and would neither do nor suffer anything for the sake of peace and concord. But they despised our humility and wanted us to swear and subject ourselves to their chrism and other abominations; indeed, they wanted to kill and torment us. Therefore, we shall no longer treat them so graciously; let them keep their abomination and chrism. We shall see to it that we secure from Baptism and God's Word without their chrism pastors and ministers ordained and ratified by our election and call. And though we have tolerated this private chrism [*Winkelchresem*] until now, we in the future, to spite the papistic, pugnacious, impenitent, murderous, bloodthirsty abomination, will endeavor that a pastor, for the sake of distinction between their private consecration and our call, should rub his anointed fingers with lye, salt, and soap. So shall he wash off the mark or sign of the Antichrist and let his tonsure grow over with hair.

"If these private consecrators or bishops do not want to regard our called pastors as consecrated, let them do so, as the devil asks them to do, but let them not run their heads against the wall so that they might not hurt themselves. For even the pope himself has commanded in his canonical laws (though he took them from the ancient fathers) that the consecration or ordination of heretics should be regarded as a true consecration and that those who were consecrated by heretics should not be consecrated again. Now, since we Lutherans are no heretics, which the papists themselves must admit, they should regard our consecration and ordination as legitimate (even according to their own papistic canonical right and command), and they should have no thanks for it. For we have (praise God!) His Word pure and sure, as the pope does not have it. But where God's Word is pure and sure, there everything else must be: God's kingdom, Christ's kingdom, the Holy Spirit, Baptism, the Sacrament, the pastoral office, the ministry of the Word, faith, love, the cross, life and salvation, and everything that the church should have according to Christ's declaration: 'We will come to him and make Our home with him' (John 14:23), and 'I am with you always, even to the end of the age' (Matt. 28:20).

"But if the abomination of the papacy will not regard our Word as the right Word, we will not worry; in their conscience they know much better. If they pretend that the heretics who consecrated were bishops and for that reason the pope and the fathers regarded their consecration as valid, we admit that they were bishops, though not princes and lords, but as St. Jerome proves from St. Paul, a bishop and pastor then was one and the same person. And these heretics and other bishops did not have as large a parish or (as they are called now) diocese as a pastor at Torgau, Leipzig, or Grimme now has; for every city had a bishop, as all cities now have pastors. St. Augustine, who was consecrated or ordained by his pastor or bishop

Valerius and after his death became bishop in his place, never had a larger parish than our parish at Wittenberg, if indeed it was so large. Nevertheless, this little bishop or pastor at Hippo, St. Augustine, became greater in Christendom [*Christenheit*] than any pope, cardinal, or archbishop ever became or ever can become. This same little pastor or bishop, St. Augustine in his small parish, consecrated or ordained many pastors or bishops (since then there was no suffragan bishop or prince's bishop [*Fürstenbischof*], but only pastors) who were desired and called by other cities, just as we ordain and send from our parish at Wittenberg pastors to those cities that desire them, they having none themselves. For to ordain should mean and be to call into and commit the pastoral office, the power of which Christ's church has and must retain without any chrism and tonsures, wherever it is in the world, just as it must have the Word, Baptism, the Sacrament, the Spirit, and faith" (ibid., St. Louis edition, 19:1266ff.).

The same: "Hear now how simply St. Paul speaks of ordination: 'The things that you have heard of me among many witnesses, commit these to faithful men who will be able to teach others also' (2 Tim. 2:2). Here he speaks of neither chrism nor butter, but his only command is to teach God's Word. Whoever has such a person, him St. Paul regards as a pastor, bishop, and pope. For everything depends on the Word of God as the supreme ministry [*Amt*], which Christ Himself regarded as His own and as the highest; even the sacraments become what they are by the Word, which is the chief part in all sacraments, as the papists themselves call it, *formam sacramenti* [that which makes a thing a sacrament]. So also Christ most shamefully forgot the chrism when He said: 'Go therefore and make disciples of all the nations, ... teaching them to observe all things that I have commanded you' (Matt. 28:19–20). What then did He command them? Most certainly to preach the Gospel, to administer the sacraments, to forgive sins, etc. If, therefore, all heathen were to observe these things, they surely must have had the power and right to preach, baptize, administer the Sacrament, forgive sins, etc. So also St. Paul writes that he received it of the Lord and delivered it to the Corinthians (1 Cor. 11:23); he does not mention any chrism but only the office and command [to preach]" (ibid., St. Louis edition, 19:1284).

The same: "When Christ says: 'If you forgive the sins of any, they are forgiven them,' etc. (John 20:23), He does not establish the authority of Him who speaks but of those who believe" (*Church Postil: Gospel Portion,* "On the First Sunday After Easter," St. Louis edition, 11:733).

The same: "And here again we must note the difference between the abomination and the holy place, for the private priests [*Winkelherren*] haughtily extol their consecration and chrism. They pretend that they are the people that make the Sacrament or transubstantiate [*wandeln*] it, *quasi ex opere operato* (just by the mere act). That is, they boast of such power that by virtue of their chrism or consecration, the body and blood of Christ (though by the operation of God) must be present at once through their consecration of the bread and wine. So they also boast that neither any angel nor the mother of God nor any saint on earth can transubstantiate, and their argument is that these have not been consecrated and have no tonsure. But when we ask them to state their reason by which to prove that God has thus bound His power to their chrism (of which God knows nothing) and their *opus operatum,* they direct us to fairyland [*Schlauraffenland*] and say that this is the verdict of the church. That is enough; more than that is not needed.

"Therefore, note and know that it is an abominable doctrine that a priest, because of his chrism or consecration, can transubstantiate the bread into the body of Christ *ex opere operato* by his mere speaking or acting. The whole matter is as wickedly untrue and false [*erlogen und erstunken*] as is their chrism itself. The holy place or church teaches that neither a priest nor a Christian nor even the church itself makes a sacrament. Our ministry means and must be merely to administer or give, not to make or transubstantiate. A pastor or minister does not make the Gospel; his preaching or ministry does not change his word into the Gospel, for then everything he says must be Gospel, but he merely presents and communicates the Gospel by His preaching. For the Gospel exists before and must exist before. Our Lord Christ has made it, brought it down, and left it in this world. He first imprinted it on the hearts of the apostles and afterward on the hearts of Christians by the successors of the apostles. Then also He imprinted it in letters and pictures externally [in Scripture]. So then there remains nothing else for the pastoral office or the ministry to do than this one work:

to give and communicate the Gospel that Christ has commanded to preach.

"The pope and his abomination have indeed fabricated many doctrines out of their heads, but these are neither God's Word nor the Gospel. He who baptizes does not make Baptism, but Christ has made it before; he merely offers and imparts it. For that is Christ's rule, as Augustine expresses it: *Accedit verbum ad elementum et fit sacramentum* (if you take water and add to it the Word, then it becomes Baptism). Just so Christ commanded: 'Go therefore and make disciples of all the nations, baptizing them in the name of the Father and of the Son and of the Holy Spirit' (Matt. 28:19). It is this command and institution that does it; this causes water and the Word to become Baptism. Our work or action *ex opere operato* cannot do it. It is not called Baptism because I baptize or perform the work, even if I were more holy than St. John or an angel. But my baptizing is Baptism because Christ's Word, command, and institution have ordained that water and the Word should be Baptism. His institution [*Ordnung*], I say, makes Baptism, not our action or *opus operatum*. Our action merely communicates and imparts the Baptism that was ordained and created by Christ's command and institution.

"Therefore, He alone is and remains the one true, eternal Baptizer, who each day communicates His Baptism by our action or ministry until Judgment Day. Our baptizing should rightly be called a communication or imparting of the Baptism of Christ, just as our preaching is the presentation of God's Word. We may indeed call it our preaching and Baptism, yet with the understanding that nothing becomes Baptism or God's Word by our doing, but we give and impart to others what we have received of Christ. Similarly, a servant may call the bread that he distributes *his* bread, though he understands and declares that it is the bread of his master.

"So also the bread and wine become the body and blood of Christ not indeed by our doing, speaking, or work, much less because of our chrism or ordination, but because Christ has so ordered, commanded, and instituted it. So also St. Paul declares that when we come together and pronounce His words over the bread and wine, it becomes His body and blood [1 Cor. 10:16; Walther here has 1 Cor. 11:23, but Luther evidently quotes freely the passage we mentioned—Tr.]. Here again we do no more than impart and give the bread and wine with His words and according to His com-

255

mand and institution. His command and institution have the power and bring about that we do not impart and receive merely bread and wine but His body and blood, and His words declare: 'This is My body; this is My blood.' So it is not our doing or speaking but the command and institution [*Ordnung*] of Christ that make the bread His body and the wine His blood. And this continues from the first Lord's Supper until the end of the world as the Sacrament is administered daily by our ministry or office. For we hear the words 'This is My body' not as spoken by the person of the pastor or minister but as coming out of Christ's own mouth; He Himself is present and tells us: 'Take, eat; this is My body.'

"We do not understand these words in any other way, for we well know that the body of the pastor or minister is neither in the bread nor is imparted to us. In the same way we hear the command and institution of Him who says, 'This do in remembrance of Me,' not as spoken in the name of the pastor, but we hear Christ Himself speaking and commanding us by the mouth of the pastor to receive the bread and wine by His Word ('This is My body'), and in accordance with His command to eat and drink, we receive in them His body and blood. We must believe and be sure that Baptism is not ours but Christ's, that the ministry is not ours but Christ's, that the Sacrament is not ours but Christ's, that the keys for remitting or retaining sins are not ours but Christ's. In short, the offices and sacraments are not ours but Christ's, for He has instituted and left them to the church that they all might be administered and used till the end of the world. He does not lie or deceive us; therefore, we dare not change them into anything else but must obey His command and keep it.

"But if we change or emend it, then we void it. Then Christ is no longer present nor His institution. I will not join the papists in saying that neither an angel nor Mary can transubstantiate it, but I declare that even if the devil himself should come (if he were so pious that he could or would do this), and I would find out later that the devil had sneaked into the ministry or let himself be called to the pastoral office as a human being and had publicly preached the Gospel in the church and had baptized, conducted the divine service, absolved, and administered this office and Sacrament as a pastor according to the command and institution of Christ, we must certainly admit that the sacraments were legitimate, that we had received true Baptism and had taken the true sacrament of Christ's body and blood. For our faith must not rest on the person, no matter whether he is pious or impious, consecrated or not, called or sneaked in, the devil or his mother, but it must rest on Christ, on His Word, on His office, on His command and institution. Where these are rightly observed, there things must be and remain right, no matter who and how the person may or could be.

"If we regard the person, then the preaching, Baptism, and Sacrament that Judas and his followers have administered and imparted and still do according to Christ's command are the devil's preaching, Baptism, and Sacrament, for that means they are imparted and given to us by members of the devil. But since the ministry, the Word, Baptism, and the Sacrament are of Christ and not of Judas or the devil, we let Judas and the devil be Judas and the devil and nevertheless receive through them the gifts of Christ. When Judas went to the devil, he did not take along his apostolic office but left it behind, and it was given in his place to Matthias. The office and sacraments remain forever in the church, while the persons change continually. Just let us call and appoint men who can administer; then they will surely turn out rightly. If you place a young boy who can ride on a saddled and bridled horse, the horse will go just as well as though the emperor or the pope were riding it.

"In my youth I heard a story about a minister who suddenly became ill. When he was to preach, someone came and offered to preach for him. The stranger turned the pages of the Book and composed a sermon. Then he preached so impressively and earnestly that the whole congregation had to weep. Finally he told them, 'Do you want to know who I am? I am the devil and have preached to you so earnestly in order that I might all the more justly and vehemently accuse you on Judgment Day to your greater damnation if you do not keep it.' Whether this story is true or not, I leave to its own merits, but I know that it is not far from the truth. It is essentially true, for the devil may well administer and impart the Word, office, and Sacrament. He may well transform himself into an angel of light, indeed, into the very majesty of God (Matt. 4:9; 2 Cor. 11:14). I would not vouch for it that the devil never served as a pastor or minister, for so many atrocious things have happened through some ministers by way of sorcery, juggling, and similar works of the devil.

"Even in the area of creation nothing is accomplished by our doing or work but only by God's command and institution. When we plow, sow, and plant, we do the work that has been commanded us (Gen. 3:19). But our work never produces even one kernel; that is done only by the command and institution of God, who commanded the earth: 'Let the earth bring forth grass, the herb that yields seed, and the fruit tree that yields fruit according to its kind' (Gen. 1:11). Just so St. Paul says: 'So then neither he who plants is anything, nor he who waters, but God who gives the increase' (1 Cor. 3:7). Let this work be done by the devil or a man, by a rascal or a believer; whether he plants, sows, or waters, the institution and command of God is accomplished, and the earth brings forth fruit. In the same way, a husband and wife in a natural way become one flesh, just as God has commanded and created (Gen. 2:24). But it is not this act that bears fruit or a child but God's command and order: 'Be fruitful and multiply' (Gen. 1:28). If then even the devil would bring a man and a woman together, as happens in adultery and fornication, nevertheless God's institution holds, and from it comes fruit or a child. If a rascal, bastard, or thief inherits a strange heirloom, the heritage is regarded as his just as though the true heir had received it.

"Such is the case also with the sacraments. We add the water to the Word, but it is not our doing that brings about the Real Presence [*wandelt's nicht*] but Christ's institution. If then the devil or one of his members would observe and follow Christ's institution, it would nevertheless be a true Baptism and Sacrament. The devil and evil people cannot make Christ a liar or impostor in His church, but He baptizes and imparts His body and blood no matter how and whose the means may be by which He does it. Even the papists admit that Baptism performed by way of a joke or play is a true Baptism. It is recorded in church history that St. Athanasius at one time played with his mates and other children on the shore of the sea. So he baptized them as he had seen it done by the bishop, and Bishop Alexander regarded this as a true Baptism and did not baptize them over. Similarly, we are told in the legends that some jesters wanted to please the heathen and mock Baptism in a play as though to be saved by water were a foolish, ridiculous belief. But to one of them in the midst of the play appeared a writing with the words of St. Paul: 'One Lord, one faith, one baptism; one God and Father of all,' etc. (Eph. 4:5–6). This writing made him a believer. He accepted the Baptism performed in the play as true, became serious, and frankly confessed Christ. Then the heathen seized all the players, for they thought that the jesters had arranged the play to honor the Christians and spite the heathen. The other players then began to revile their mate and said that he had lost his mind. But he remained true to his baptism and faith, submitted to torture, and so ascended into heaven from the play. But the papists are blind and leaders of the blind. They regard only their own person and work, as though the Sacrament must become a sacrament because they are such persons and do such works. They do not care about Christ's order and institution, though our person and work can effect nothing; the institution of Christ alone effects it. Chrism, tonsure, chasuble, and similar pomp do not help. They themselves do not know what they do in their mass, nor can they know it.

"And now in answering the question that I put before, namely, what attitude to take (in one's mind) toward the priests in the papacy because all of them have been consecrated by private bishops [*Winkelbischöfe*] for the private mass [*Winkelmesse*], you should do this: Do not regard or consider their chrism or private consecration [*Winkelweihe*]. That certainly amounts to nothing, nor does it either profit or serve the church. But keep in mind that they are in charge of the ministry, which is not their office but Christ's. Nor let it faze you whether he has been rightly called, or whether he has entered the ministry by simony or force; no matter how he has entered it, whether by head or tail, whether he be Judas or St. Peter, regard all that as not essential. But separate the office from the person and the sanctuary from the abomination. He now is a pastor and Christ has thus preserved His holy, beloved ministry in the midst of abomination. So if he should preach the text of the Gospel in its purity then say: That is the sanctuary of Christ. If in addition he preaches another doctrine against the Gospel, then say: That is an abomination of the devil, who destroys the doctrine. If he baptizes and observes the institution of Christ (though he does not rightly understand what Baptism is), then say: That Baptism is right because of Christ's institution and not on account of the pastor or his work. When he publicly absolves you or forgives your sin, though no papist in the world can rightly understand what remission of sin is, for (as all their books show) they do not know whether they forgive the guilt or the punishment [*Pein*], let that not bother you. As long as he observes the Word and way [of Christ] and absolves you in the name of Christ, then say: Your holy, comforting absolution my Lord Christ gives me Himself through the keys, which He has given to the church.

"But if in addition he imposes on you a penance in order that thereby you should make satisfaction for your sins, then think: Behold, that is an abomination that for me would destroy the absolution of Christ, as though Christ were to sell me His grace for my merit. I will publicly make satisfaction to my neighbor if I have done him wrong. But before God there is satisfaction for me: Christ Himself with His precious blood. To that I will adhere; in that I will trust. If he reads mass, then note diligently this difference: If he observes the order and institution of Christ and in addition imparts and gives the Sacrament also to others, then know that there surely is Christ's body and blood on account of Christ's institution, not because of the work and sanctity of the pastor. However, inasmuch as he does not observe the institution and intention of Christ but changes and perverts it [into a private mass], you need not believe that it is Christ's body and blood. Indeed, you should not believe it, just as I have said before of other private masses; for whether it be a high mass or a low mass, or whatever they want to call them, they are private masses because nothing of the Sacrament is imparted or given to the congregation. Christ's order and institution are clear: 'This do in remembrance of Me.' What should we do? And what is meant by 'this'? Nothing else than what He indicated by action and Word when He took the bread, blessed and broke it, and gave it to His disciples, saying: Take, eat; this is My body, which is given for you. This do in remembrance of Me. After the same manner also He took the cup, gave thanks, and gave it to them, saying: Drink ye all of it; this is the cup of the new testament in My blood. This do ye, as oft as ye drink it, in remembrance of Me. [Luther here quotes the institution of the Holy Supper in a free way, stressing for his argument only the essential points.—Tr.] If then Christ's institution is to be observed (as He Himself says: 'This do'), we [pastors] must not only take the bread and wine with the words of Christ but also give and impart it to others" ("On the Private Mass and Holy Orders," St. Louis edition, 19:1268ff.).

Melanchthon: "From all this it is clear that the church has power to call competent persons into the pastoral [*bischöflichen*] office for the care of souls and to commit to them this ministry [*Amt*]. And it is usual and laudable that this is done in the presence of some Christian and learned pastors [*Seelsorger*], who listen to their teaching [*Lehre*] and by way of witnessing lay their hands on them. This election by the church is based on the following. Christ says: 'Tell it to the church' (Matt. 18:17). In this passage He establishes ecclesiastical jurisdiction [*Kirchengericht*] and assigns the supreme authority to the church" (See *Concerning the Calling and Dismissing* [Enturlaubung] *of Ministers* (Gießen, 1608), p. 19).

Chemnitz: "Although ordination does not make the call, nevertheless, when anyone has been rightly called, then this rite is a declaration and public confirmation that the call, which preceded it, is legitimate" (*Loci theologici,* "De eccl.," folio 126).

The same: "Moreover, this also is certain, that the call to the ministry of the Gospel ought to have the public testimony and the public attestation of the church, on account of those who run although they were not sent (Jer. 23:21). Therefore the apostles with some public testimony and public attestation of the church announced and as it were pointed out the call of those who had been legitimately chosen for the ministry of the Word and the sacraments. For the Holy Spirit willed that also Paul, who had been called immediately, should be declared and designated as the one who should be the apostle of the Gentiles. In that public approbation, attestation, or announcement, since it was a public action, the apostles employed the outward rite of the laying on of hands, which was customary at that time with those people, in part on account of the public designation of the one called, in part on account of the prayers and supplications which were made by the whole church in behalf of the person called. . . .

"Fasting was also added to the prayer (Acts 13:3). And this earnest prayer at the ordination of ministers is not without effect, because it rests on a divine command and promise. This is the meaning of Paul's words: 'The gift . . . that is within you through the laying on of . . . hands' [2 Tim. 1:6]. . . .

"Now the ministry of the Word and the sacraments has divine promises, and the prayer at ordination rests on these, but these promises are not to be tied to the rite of the imposition of hands, about which there is neither a command of Christ nor such a promise as there is about Baptism and the Lord's Supper" (*Examination of the Council of Trent,* "Concerning Holy Orders" [St. Louis: Concordia Publishing House, 1978], 2:693–95).

Balduin: "Ordination is nothing else than a public and solemn confirmation of the legitimate call so that it might be clear to all that the person did not arrogate to himself the ecclesiastical office, nor that he, like thieves and murderers, crept into it anywhere else, but that he came in by the true door.... Ordination is not simply and absolutely necessary, ... nor is it divinely commanded so that it might not be omitted. Nor is its effect as great as it is falsely made out to be in the papacy. Nor does the efficacy of the ministry depend on ordination as though without it the Gospel could not be taught profitably. But it is a church rite that commends the minister of the Word and reminds him of certain duties" (*Tractatus de casibus conscientiae,* pp. 1032–33).

The same: "May a person be admitted to ordination who as yet has not been called to a certain ecclesiastical office? I reply: By no means! For ordination is the confirmation of the call. If therefore there is no call, ordination can not yet take place. Therefore, the custom of the church at Geneva is rightly reprehended. There students of theology are sent to France to take charge of congregations, though they were not called by any congregation. No church has the right to send ministers to any other congregation to whose call it does not consent, in order that no one may be sent to it against its will" (ibid., pp. 1045–46).

Gerhard: "Wherever essential parts of any rite are observed, there may be no doubt concerning the integrity of the rite. But at an ordination performed by a ministerium that is not absolutely pure, the essential parts of the rite are observed, namely, the prayers and the laying on of hands. Hence under such circumstances there can be no doubt concerning the integrity of the rite" (*Loci theologici,* "De min. eccles.," par. 156). In order to maintain the absolute necessity of ordination people often point out that the laying on of hands is certainly an adiaphoron and merely an addition to ordination but that ordination itself is indeed necessary. But from the testimony of Gerhard it is clear that if the laying on of hands is omitted, then also the essence of ordination is destroyed. Hence, if the laying on of hands is admittedly an adiaphoron, then ordination itself is also an adiaphoron.

Gerhard: "Ordination is not a sacrament truly and properly so called, as is Baptism, but merely an ecclesiastical custom [*Gebrauch*]" (ibid.).

The same: "So far as the ordination is concerned, it is not necessary because of any divine command. Nor does the essence of the ministry depend on it. Nor does it imprint a certain character as the papists dream. Therefore, Rufinus writes in book 1, chapter 10, of his church history about the king of the Iberians, that he, while yet unconsecrated, became the apostle of his people. Nevertheless, the rite is useful because it is an ancient custom of the church and is connected with excellent admonitions. Therefore, it is not to be cast aside or omitted without valid reasons; for it is evident from the narratives and letters of the apostles as well as from the history of the church that the apostles themselves and their immediate successors observed the custom that one leader in the name of the presbyters ordained the ministers who were legitimately called by the congregation with the laying on of hands and prayer. But it is by no means absolutely and unconditionally necessary that three bishops should be present at an ordination" (*Loci theologici,* "De eccl.," par. 202).

The same: "We say that the custom of ordination should by no means be omitted, but it should always be observed when the ministry of the church is to be established, except in an emergency: partly on account of the ancient usage of the apostolic church and the times of the apostles after it, when the elders ordained the ministers chosen by the church with prayer and the laying on of hands, consecrating them, as it were, to God (Acts 6:6; 13:3; 1 Tim. 4:14; 5:22; 2 Tim. 1:6), and partly on account of the salutary purposes mentioned above. Although Paul was called immediately, he nevertheless was sent to Ananias in order that he might lay his hands on him and make known to the church his call (Acts 9:17). Later, when he was sent to the heathen, he was again appointed as the official [*ordinarius*] teacher of the Gentiles with the laying on of hands (Acts 13:3). This rite [*äusserliche Gebrauch*] was applied there in order that his call might be declared legitimate and that others might not boast of it in a similar manner [*consimiliter*]. Chemnitz writes: 'If this was done with him who was called immediately, how much more should it be done with those who are called mediately?' (*Loci theologici,* "De eccl.," chap. 4; p. 333).

"We deny however that ordination is necessary because of a special divine command, for this cannot be demonstrated, or because of a certain effect as this is ascribed to it by the papists, as though thereby there were imprinted a certain indelible character, or as though, if only it is performed, it by itself communicates the gifts that are necessary for the office, concerning which no promise can be adduced from the statements of Christ and the apostles, or because of an absolute necessity, as though at a time when ordination cannot be obtained, such as at the siege of a city or during a prevailing pestilence and similar difficulties, a person legitimately called could not administer the office until he were ordained or consecrated, for such an absolute necessity cannot be proved from Scripture.

"Chytraeus comments on Ex. 29: 'It should be known that those who have been called and chosen by the voice of the church and administer the office even without the laying on of hands are true ministers and may teach and administer the sacraments. For by this rite a special character is not imprinted on the ordained, nor does the power of the church or the right to teach the Gospel and administer the sacraments depend on this rite, nor does this rite render the ministry of the ordained efficacious, for the ministry is efficacious and a power for salvation to everyone who believes because of its divine institution. The custom of laying on the hands is added as a public declaration of the called persons; it also makes ordination more solemn and brings to remembrance certain duties'" (*Loci theologici,* "De minist.," par. 139).

The same: "In the apostolic and primitive church there were two kinds of presbyters who in Latin were called *seniores,* as we conclude from 1 Tim. 5:17. Some administered the office of teaching, or as the apostle there says, they labored in the Word and doctrine; these were called bishops, pastors, etc. Others, however, were appointed to be censors of morals and guardians of church discipline, since the pagan government did not support the teachers of the church in this manner; these were called governors and leaders (as we conclude from 1 Cor. 12:28 and Rom. 12:8). Ambrose comments on 1 Tim. 5 at the beginning: 'Also the synagogue and the church had seniors without whose advice nothing was undertaken. I do not know by what kind of carelessness this fell into disuse—perhaps by indolence or rather by the pride of the teachers who alone wanted to be esteemed as being something.'

"Both kinds were commonly called elders (Acts 15:22; 1 Tim. 5:17) and rulers (Heb. 13:7, 17, 24). Both formed the sacred college that Paul calls the presbytery, saying: 'Do not neglect the gift that is in you, which was given to you by prophecy with the laying on of the hands of the presbytery' (1 Tim. 4:14). From this passage we conclude that at the ordination of ministers, not only the pastors but also the elders chosen from the people laid their hands on the ordained person in the name of the entire congregation, just as not only Aaron but also the elders of Israel laid their hands on the Levites who were ordained (Num. 8:10). Some, however, think that here the term presbytery signifies in a special sense those elders who were pastors and bishops. Today the consistory or the church council [*senatus ecclesiasticus*], over which ecclesiastical and political officials preside and that concerns itself especially with church discipline, corresponds to the presbytery" (*Loci theologici,* "De minist. eccl.," par. 232).

Hülsemann: "As the (true) Catholics regard the laying on of hands as a sacred rite, applied by the apostles at the ordination of all ministers, so they retain it in their church and do not doubt that, moved by the prayers that according to apostolic custom are joined to the laying on of hands, God communicates grace to the person ordained. But they do not believe that on account of the pronouncement of certain words or because of certain ceremonies a certain grace is conferred on the ordained, nor has anyone until now proved this from the rite of the apostles" (*Manuale Augustanae Confessionis,* p. 450).

Dannhauer: "Ordination belongs to good order. We therefore do not read that the called apostles were ordained as soon as they were sent out" (*Hodosophia christiana,* p. 77, al. 149).

The same: "Is ordination necessary for conscience' sake? It certainly is necessary, but not because of any necessity of purpose or means (as though the purpose in view could only be accomplished by this means); for also without ordination Paul and Barnabas (Acts 9:24), as well as Aquila and Priscilla, Frumentius and Aedesius, could effectively administer the office of the ministry. It was therefore an unnecessary and purposeless anxiety that caused the Bohemian Brethren to deal with the question whether an ordination is legitimate if an elder chose an elder but not a bishop; therefore, they cast lots to decide the question, as the Moravian Comenius relates. Nevertheless, it (ordination) is necessary according to the necessity of an apostolic and positive (not moral) command: 'Separate to Me Barnabas and Saul' (Acts 13:2) and the ancient apostolic custom (1 Tim. 5:21). There is also a necessity that accrues from the benefit that the examined and unexamined teachers of the church may be distinguished and no one may raise the accusation that the Lutherans often use certain scholars who are not yet ordained with the laying on of hands as vicars, permitting them to hear confession, feed the sick, and administer Holy Communion.[14] Nor should anyone think that the case of a pastor and a reporter were one and the same. . . . Thus the solemnization of a marriage by a pastor is not absolutely necessary. Nor is a bridal wreath necessary, though it is beneficial to use this ornament. Nor is the crowning at Frankfurt something without which the Roman emperor could not exist; yet it serves to enhance the glory of the emperor. (Cf. Ph. Melanchthon's exposition of 1 Tim. 3; Nikolas Hunnius, *Ministerii Lutherani divini adeoque legitimi demonstratio,* p. 285; Dr. Hülsemann's excerpt, chap. 19, p. 368).

"Who then is the opponent of good order who superciliously despises this custom? He is neither peaceful, because he goes counter to the church, nor conscientious, because he regards the means that serve to calm consciences as worthless; but he is an obstinate ass" (*Liber conscientiae,* p. 1005–06).

Kromayer: "Ordination is used in a wider and in a narrower sense. In its wider sense it denotes the call itself; in its narrower sense it designates the solemn attestation before the congregation. The call is necessary, but ordination (in its narrow sense) is an adiaphoron. Nevertheless, though it is not commanded, it has examples (serving as patterns), and thus more than other matters it receives the nature of necessary things" (*Theologia positivo-polemica,* p. 1060 [Dr. Walther's translation]).

Calov: "Although we readily admit that ordination is not unconditionally and absolutely necessary and that it is not founded on a divine command, nor does it exist by divine right, but that it is an ecclesiastical and indifferent custom, and though we do not hold that by it *ex opere operato* (that is, by itself, if it is merely administered, no matter whether he who administers it or he who receives it believes or not) the gifts are communicated that are necessary for the ministry, we nevertheless believe that this ecclesiastical order has been established for important reasons, that it rightly should be highly esteemed and observed by the church, and that it should not be omitted except in an emergency. Much less should it be abolished, though superstition attaches to it in the papacy.... Though today by the laying on of hands extraordinary miraculous gifts are not communicated, we do not doubt that at ordination the gifts of the Holy Spirit necessary for the sacred ministry are increased by the public and private prayers of the church and the ordaining ministers. Of this the laying on of hands is a certain token, since this used to be applied when the gifts of the Holy Spirit were communicated (Acts 8:15; 19:6)" (*Socin. proflig.*, p. 921–22).

In place of dogmatic statements from the writings of the ancient church teachers we here repeat what Dannhauer reports of the ancient church: "Origen was not ordained, but when persecution set in, he went to Jerusalem, where he was permitted to preach and administer the sacraments. But Demetrius, the bishop of Alexandria, disliked this, because thereby the canons of the church were not observed. However, Alexander, bishop of Jerusalem, answered him very aptly that nothing is done against custom if anyone teaches and administers the sacraments without ordination, as long as he has been called" (*Th. casual.*, p. 230).

The Ecumenical Council of Chalcedon in 451 resolved: "No one should be absolutely ordained as a presbyter or a deacon or in general as an incumbent of any ecclesiastical office if the person to be ordained has not specially been designated for a congregation in a city or village or for the chapel of a martyr or for a monastery. The holy synod has decreed regarding such absolutely ordained persons to declare the laying on of hands as invalid and, to the shame of the ordained person, as absolutely ineffective" (Mansi, *Nov. et ampl. coll. sacr. conc.*, 7:361 [Dr. Walther's translation]).

Thesis VII

The holy ministry [Predigtamt] *is the power, conferred by God through the congregation as the possessor of the priesthood and all church power, to exercise the rights of the spiritual priesthood in public office in the name of the congregation.*

1. Scripture Proof

Since we have shown in Theses I–IV that the spiritual priesthood, which all believing Christians possess, and the ministry of the Word or the pastoral office are not one and the same thing according to God's Word; that an ordinary Christian is not yet a pastor because of his spiritual priesthood and that a pastor is not a priest because he is in charge of the public ministry; and that the spiritual priesthood is not the public ministry in the church, nor is the public ministry a special state [*Stand*] different from that of all Christians but merely a ministry of service (nevertheless established by Christ Himself when He instituted the apostolic ministry); again, since, as we have shown in Thesis V, pastors in the name of the congregation publicly administer their office, which originally the church, and therefore also every believing Christian, possesses as the true royal priesthood; and finally, since in Thesis VI we have shown that pastors receive their office and power from God through the congregation as their original possessor, therefore the office of the holy ministry cannot essentially be anything else than the power conferred by God through the congregation, as the possessor of the priesthood and all church power, to exercise in public office the rights of the spiritual priesthood in the name of the congregation. The proof from God's Word has already been given under Theses IV and VII of the first part and under Theses I, IV, V, and VI of the second part.

Here I may only remind the reader that Holy Scripture represents the church, that is, the believers, as the bride of the Lord and as the mistress of the household to whom the keys have been entrusted and with them the right of and access to all rooms, sacred things, and treasures of the house of God as well as the authority to appoint stewards over these. Every true Christian according to Holy Scripture is a spiritual priest and therefore empowered and called not only to use the means of grace for himself but also to impart them to those who as yet do not have them and therefore also do not yet possess with him the rights of the priesthood. However, since all possess these rights, no one may exalt himself over the others or exercise them over against the others, but in all places where Christians live together the rights of the priesthood are to be administered publicly in the name of the congregation by those who have been called by the church in the manner prescribed by God.

Therefore, the incumbents of the public ministry in the church are called in God's Word not only ministers and stewards of God but also ministers and stewards of the church or congregation. They are represented as those who administer not merely their own rights, powers, goods, treasures, and offices but those of the church. Hence, they act not only in the name of Christ but also in the name and place of His bride, the church of believers. Christ indeed has Himself instituted the order of the public ministry in His church and has designated the rights and powers that it should have. But these are not rights and powers that the incumbents of the office possess apart from and exclusive of the church; they are the rights and powers that Christ has given to His church with these keys for its possession. However, according to His express command and will (cf. above Theses II and III of the second part), these should not be publicly exercised in the church by all in common and without distinction [*promiscue*] but by certain called men, who are competent, supplied with the necessary gifts, and through these gifts granted and assigned to the church by the Lord Himself, and so are to be called.

Although therefore the general spiritual priesthood and the public ministry in the church are not one and the same thing, the latter is the fruit of the former, or as our fathers used to say, the latter is "rooted" in the former. He who becomes an incumbent of the ministerial office does not thereby become a priest (since he is

269

rather to be taken out of the number of Christian priests), but he administers the sacred office of the Christian priests. Hence, the holy apostle writes of himself: "I might be a minister of Jesus Christ to the Gentiles, ministering the gospel of God" (Rom. 15:16).

2. Witnesses of the Church in Its Official Confessions

Smalcald Articles: "Lastly this is confirmed also by the statement of Peter when he says: 'You are . . . a royal priesthood' (1 Peter 2:9). These words properly pertain to the true church, which, because it has the priesthood, must also have the power to elect and ordain ministers" (Of the Power and Jurisdiction of Bishops, par. 69; German text, *Triglot,* p. 523). Here the theologians convened at Smalcald, in the name of our church, confess that the church, because it possesses the rights of the priesthood, must also have the power to confer the office of the ministry, which exercises and administers these priestly rights. Here our Confessions therefore declare that the public ministry is a power by which the priestly rights of all believers are exercised in public office in the name of the congregation and by virtue of the extended call.

Therefore, the *Apology* among other things also declares the preaching of the Gospel to be a sacrifice of the Christian priesthood: "In addition to this one atoning sacrifice, namely, the death of Christ, there are other sacrifices, all of which are merely sacrifices of thanksgiving, such as all suffering, preaching, and good works of the saints. These are not sacrifices by which we are reconciled or that we may perform for others" (to acquire some gain for others) "or that earn *ex opere operato* forgiveness of sins or reconciliation. For they are offered up by those who already are reconciled. Such sacrifices are ours in the New Testament as the apostle Peter declares: 'You . . . are . . . a holy priesthood, to offer up spiritual sacrifices' (1 Peter 2:5)" (Art. XXIV [XII], par. 25; German text, *Triglot,* p. 390).

"As we call the sermon a sacrifice of praise, so the rite [*Ceremonia*] of the Lord's Supper in itself may be called a sacrifice of praise but not a sacrifice that justifies before God *ex opere operato* or that can be performed for others to obtain for them remission of sins" (ibid., par. 33; German text, *Triglot,* p. 394).

"The sacrifice of the sons of Levi, that is, of those who preach in the New Testament, is the preaching of the Gospel and the good fruit of the preaching, as Paul says: ' . . . that I might be a minister of Jesus Christ to the Gentiles, ministering the Gospel of God, that the offering of the Gentiles might be acceptable, sanctified by the Holy Spirit' (Rom. 15:16). For in the Law the slaying of oxen and sheep prefigured both the death of Christ and the ministry of the Gospel, by which the Old Adam is daily put to death and the new and eternal life is begun" (ibid., par. 34; German text, *Triglot,* pp. 394–95).

Smalcald Articles: "In addition it must be admitted that the keys do not belong merely to one person but to the whole church, as this can be proved sufficiently by clear and convincing arguments. For just as the promise of the Gospel belongs surely and without means to the whole church, so also the keys belong to the whole church without means (in the Latin original: *principaliter et immediate,* i.e., originally and immediately). For the keys are nothing else than the ministry [*Amt*], by which the promise is communicated to everyone who desires it, as indeed it is obvious that the church has the power to ordain ministers. When Christ said: 'Whatever you bind,' etc. [Matt. 18:18], He indicated at once to whom the keys were given, namely, to the church, by adding: 'Where two or three are gathered together in My name' [v. 20]" (Of the Power and Primacy of the Pope, par. 24; German text, *Triglot,* p. 510).

By these words our church confesses that the whole church, not merely the large and well-ordered organization but also its smallest parts, has the keys and so also the ministry [*Amt*] of the Gospel, just as a whole face reflected in a mirror appears in every single part of it, though it may be smashed into a thousand pieces. Therefore, the church has the power to elect and ordain ministers. Hence, the power of the public ministry rests in the church and is conferred by the church according to Christ's express direction on certain persons specifically called to the ministry of the Word. This power the church does not have mediately by the incumbents of the office entrusted with it for the benefit of the church, but the church possesses it immediately, while on the contrary the incumbents of the office have it mediately, for they received it from the church, to which it originally belongs.

The same: "Where the church is, there also is the command to preach the Gospel. Therefore, the churches must retain the power to demand, elect, and ordain ministers. This power is a gift that has

271

been given properly to the church by God and cannot be taken from the church by any human force, as St. Paul attests: 'When He ascended on high, He . . . gave gifts to men' (Eph. 4:8). And among such gifts that properly belong to the church he enumerates pastors and teachers and adds that these are given for the 'edifying of the body of Christ.' From this it follows that wherever there is a true church, there is also the power to elect and ordain ministers. In an emergency, of course, any layman can absolve another, as St. Augustine tells the story of two Christians in a ship; one baptized the other and then was absolved by him. Here belong also the statements of Christ that testify that the keys were given to the whole church and not to some special persons, as the text says: 'Where two or three are gathered together in My name, I am there in the midst of them' [Matt. 18:20]" (ibid., par. 67–69; German text, *Triglot,* p. 522).

Our church thus attests, in the first place, that the church must have the right to appoint ministers because to it has been given the command to preach the Gospel. Therefore, our church confesses that the incumbents of the public ministry do nothing else than what has been commanded to the church, that is, to the believers in common, but as incumbents of the public ministry, they do it in the place of the congregation and in its name. In the second place, when our church declares that in an emergency a layman also may baptize, absolve, etc., and in such special cases may act for a pastor and so shows that the whole church has the power to elect ministers, even if there were only two or three, it thereby evidently confesses that the ministry is nothing else than what Thesis VII says. No matter how hard and often this proof from an emergency baptism or an emergency absolution, which our Confessions use so frequently, is contested today, it is nevertheless clear and unanswerable; for if the whole church, that is, every believing Christian, does not possess the right to administer the means of grace, the emergency alone could not give him this right, just as little as a Christian in an emergency has the right to steal.

But since every Christian of himself has that right, although the practice of the right, as long as the church exists on earth, has been limited by the Lord Himself when He instituted the public ministry— though only for the sake of good order—therefore, a Christian in an emergency can make use of this right without arrogating to himself something not belonging to him. In that case he sets aside an order for the sake of Christian love, just as a little child who usually expects its bread from the hand of its father or its appointed guardian or housekeeper may in an emergency help itself to the food in the pantry. The very right of the ordinary Christian in an emergency to execute the ministry of the Word shows where the right exists essentially [*wesentlich*]; therefore, the ministry of the Word is not the special power of a preferred state [*Stand*] but merely an order by which common rights are to be administered, though this order is neither human nor ecclesiastical, but divine.

To avoid tedious repetition, the reader at this point may be directed to the development of the preceding theses, in particular, of those of Theses IV and VII of the first part and Theses IV and VI of the second part, as well as to the following witnesses of our venerable church teachers.

3. Witnesses of the Church in the Private Writings of Its Teachers

Luther: "Therefore, we all are priests, as many of us as are Christian. But those whom we call priests are ministers [*Diener*], elected by us to administer all things in our name; and so the ministry [*Priestertum*]" (the incumbents of the office of the congregation) "is nothing else than a service. So Paul says: 'Let a man so consider us, as servants of Christ and stewards of the mysteries of God' (1 Cor. 4:1)" ("On the Babylonian Captivity of the Church," 1520, St. Louis edition, 19:114).

The same: "Therefore, everyone who wishes to be a Christian should be sure and diligently consider it well by himself that we all at the same time are priests, that is, that we all have the same power over the Word and every sacrament. Nevertheless, it does not behoove everyone to use this power unless by the permission of the congregation or by the call of the superiors. For whatever belongs to all in common, no one should arrogate to himself in particular until he is called to do this. Hence, if the rite [*Sakrament*] of ordination is anything at all, it dare not be anything else than a common custom to call someone into the ministry of the church. From this it is obvious that the ministry [*Priesterschaft*] is nothing else than a service of the Word—of the Word, I say, not of the Law but of the Gospel" (ibid., p. 117).

The same: "The priesthood and power must be there before, obtained through Baptism, and it is common to all Christians by faith that rests on Christ, the true High Priest, as St. Peter here says. But to exercise this power and to put it into practice does not behoove everyone, only those who are called out of the assembly or who have the command and consent of the assembly. These do the work in place of the persons of the assembly and by its common authority" or in place of the congregation ("Tract Against His Error, Forced by the Most Learned Priest of God, Mr. Jerome Emser," 1521, St. Louis edition, 18:1361).

The same: "If not all could preach and merely one had authority to speak, why should it be necessary to maintain and command order? But for this very reason, because all have power and authority to preach, it is necessary to observe order" ("On the Abuse of the Mass," 1522, St. Louis edition, 19:1086).

The same: "But we are taught something else: 'One is your Teacher, the Christ, and you are all brethren' (Matt. 23:8). Therefore, we all are regarded as equal, and we all have only one right. For He will not tolerate it that those who are called brethren and who all have one communion should let one be above the other, receive a greater inheritance, and have a greater right than another, especially in spiritual matters of which we now treat. But all this we have said only concerning the common right and power of all Christians; for since all things that we have enumerated so far and that we also have supported and proved are common to all Christians, it does not behoove anyone of his own will to exalt himself and arrogate to himself what belongs to all.

"Take this right on yourself and put it into practice if no other has received the same right. But it is demanded by the right of the congregation that one, or as many as the congregation may be pleased to elect and receive, should publicly administer these offices in the place and name of all those who have the same rights, in order that dreadful disorder might not arise among the people of God and the church be turned into a Babylon; for in it all things should be done decently and in order, as the apostle has taught us (1 Cor. 14:40). These two things are entirely different: if someone exercises the common right by command of the congregation, or if anyone uses the same right in an emergency. In a congregation in which everyone possesses the right, no one should arrogate it to himself without the consent [*Willen*] and election of the whole congregation; but in an emergency everyone may use it as he desires.

"Let us now address ourselves to the papistic priests and ask them whether their priestly office [*Priestertum*] embraces any other offices than these. If it embraces any others than these, then their priesthood is not a Christian priesthood. But if it embraces what we have enumerated, then it cannot be a special priesthood. Therefore, we conclude that no matter what they may reply, they either do not have a priesthood that is different from what is common to all Christians, or if they say they have another priesthood, then it must be of Satan. Christ has taught us in Matt. 7:20 that by their fruits we shall know all trees. We have so far learned to know the fruits of our common priesthood. Let them therefore either show us other fruits than these, or let them confess that they are not priests. That these fruits are borne privately [*sonderlich*] or publicly does not prove a different priesthood but only another and a different use of the priesthood. But if to prove to us their priesthood, they will show us merely their tonsure and chrism, as well as their long gown, we will admit that they glory in what is worthless [*des Drecks*]; for we know that people may easily shear or smear a sow or a ram [*Bloch*] and put on it a long gown.

"We insist that there is no other Word of God except what Christ has commanded all Christians to preach; that there is no other Baptism except the one that all Christians may administer; that there is no other remembrance of the Lord's Supper than the one every Christian may receive, as Christ has instituted it to be kept; that there is no other sin except what every Christian may bind or loose. Likewise we hold that there is no other sacrifice than the body of every Christian [Rom. 12:1]; that no one may or can pray except a Christian; and that no one should judge doctrine except a Christian. But all these are priestly and kingly offices. Therefore, let the papists either show us other offices of the priesthood or surrender their priesthood and give it up [*verzeihen sich des*]" ("How One Should Choose and Ordain Pastors," Letter to the council and congregation of the city of Prague, 1523, St. Louis edition, 10:1588ff.).

The same: "As you formerly adhered to the simple meaning, so

275

also do now. The keys are given to him who stands on this rock by faith, to whomever the Father has given it. Now you cannot tell whether any person remains on the rock, for one falls today and the other tomorrow just as Peter fell. Therefore, no one is certain to possess the keys except the church, that is, those who stand on this rock. Only the Christian church has the keys; otherwise no one, not even a pope or bishop, may use them as having been entrusted with them by the congregation. A pastor performs the office of the keys, baptizes, preaches, administers the Sacrament, and performs all other functions [*Aemter*] by which he serves the congregation not in his own name but in the place of the congregation.

"For he is a minister of the whole congregation, to which the keys have been given, though he himself may be a rascal. What he does, the church does, and what the church does, God does, but there must be a minister [*Diener*]. If the whole congregation wanted to gather and baptize, the child might be drowned, for then a thousand hands might grab it. But that does not profit, so there must be a minister who does this in place of the congregation. The keys to bind and loose are the power to teach, not merely to absolve; for the keys pertain to everything by which I may help my neighbor: to the comfort that one can give to another; to public and private confession, absolution, and whatever else there may be. But above all they pertain to preaching. To preach 'He who believes will be saved' means to open heaven, and to preach 'He who does not believe will be condemned' means to close heaven. The binding rests on this: When I preach, 'You belong to the devil wherever you may stand or go,' heaven is closed to such a one. But if he should fall down and confess his sin and I say, 'Believe in Christ; then your sins are forgiven,' that means to open heaven. Thus Peter used the keys when, as reported in Acts, he converted three thousand persons in his sermon (Acts 2:41). So all of us Christians have the power to bind and to loose" (*Church Postil: Gospel Portion,* "On the Day of Saints Peter and Paul, Apostles," 1525, St. Louis edition, 11:2305).

The same: "You yourselves [you papists] declare with one accord that a priest reads mass and blesses the bread not in his own name but in the name of the whole congregation. To this declaration you are compelled by the truth, your conscience, your need, and the unanimous confession [*Rede*] and faith of the whole world in order that the Christian church [*Christenheit*] might exist and be worthy

276

even if the priest would not be pious, believing, and worthy (and no saint is sufficiently worthy). Who then is the true priest? He who does it as a servant or he in whose name he does it? Who is the priest, he who does and performs the work or the servant who bears and brings it? The priest is a messenger and servant in this work; therefore, another must be the true priest. I hold that it has been proved clearly enough that we all are priests, and that these priests are not another kind of priest, but they are the servants and officials [*Amtsleute*], as said above, of the common priesthood; there are not two kinds of priesthood in the Christian church [*Christenheit*] as you have been dreaming" ("Reply to the Superchristian . . . Book of the Goat Emser," 1521, St. Louis edition, 18:1286–87).

The same: "This is said of the priesthood, which is the common possession [*Gut*] of all Christians. But it is a different matter when this is said of those who have an office in the Christian church [*Christenheit*] as deacons [*Kirchendiener*], preachers, ministers, and pastors. These are not priests (in the sense in which Scripture speaks of priests) because of the call or office which they have. They already were priests before their office, from their Baptism. Scripture calls them servants, bishops, or overseers; the apostles call them *presbyteros, seniores,* that is, elders (1 Cor. 4:1; 1 Tim. 3:2; Tit. 1:5). The term *presbyter* means nothing else than an elderly man, because for such an office the best persons were chosen, who were advanced in age, well tested, learned, and rich in practice and experience. This is fitting in all forms of government, and Scripture commands that such people should be elected.

"These people then are elected in the church solely on account of the office and are separated from the ordinary assembly of Christians, just as in the secular government some officials are elected and appointed out of the entire group of citizens [*Bürgerschaft*] or community [*Gemeine*]. There someone does not become a citizen because he has been chosen to be a mayor or judge. But because he has the right of citizenship and is a member of the whole group of citizens, he is elected to the office of mayor. The same is true of a woman or mistress of a house. She does not become a woman because she marries a man. If she were not a woman before, she would never become the mistress of a house by marriage. She rather brings her womanhood [*weiblich Wesen*] into wedlock, and then she obtains the keys to the house. The same is true of all other

277

offices and states, such as father, mother, teacher, and government official. The office does not create the essence or right that anyone has, but the office and right must be there from a person's birth and render him competent to administer the office. God has so ordained and created things that first of all we are born as human beings, men or women. Then He distributes to everyone his office and state as He wills, and He knows how to distribute them in many ways.

"So too it happens in the church. There everyone must first be a Christian and a born priest before he becomes a pastor or bishop, and neither a pope nor any other man can make him a priest. . . . But if you ask in what the priesthood of Christians consists or what their works are as priests, let me reply: The very ones that have been mentioned above, namely, to teach, sacrifice, and pray. . . . After we have become Christians by this Priest and His Priesthood and have been incorporated into Him in Baptism by faith, then we also receive the right and authority to teach and confess publicly [*vor jedermann*] the Word that we received from Him, everyone according to his calling and state. Though we are not all called into the public ministry, yet every Christian may and should teach, instruct, admonish, comfort, and reprove his neighbor from God's Word whenever and wherever he is in need of it, just as parents must teach their children and servants or anyone his brother, neighbor, fellow citizen, and the like. For a Christian may teach and exhort from the Ten Commandments, the Creed, the Lord's Prayer, etc., anyone who is ignorant or weak, and he who is so instructed should receive it of him as God's Word and confess it publicly.

"In this way Christians possess and offer up their priestly sacrifice not in order thereby to obtain remission of sins for themselves or others, for that they have solely by the sacrifice of Christ, which alone avails as an atonement for all people, but by their sacrifice they laud and praise God. . . . To such sacrifice prayer is also added, to which they are urged by manifold suffering and tribulation. Behold, in such a way every Christian has and exercises his priestly works. But in addition to this there is the pastoral ministry that teaches and inculcates doctrine publicly, and for that we need ministers and pastors. In a congregation not all can administer this office, nor is it proper for all to baptize and celebrate Holy Communion in their homes. Therefore, the congregation must elect and appoint

278

some who can preach and study the Scriptures so that they can administer this office and defend the doctrine. Likewise, they must administer the sacraments so that all may know who is baptized and all things may be done decently and in order. Otherwise, a congregation would be slow in growth and spiritual care if everyone would preach to the other and all things would be done without order. This is not the priesthood but the common public office administered in place of those who are all priests, that is, Christians" ("Second Exposition of Ps. 110," 1539, St. Louis edition, 5:1036).

The same: "None of us is born in Baptism as an apostle, minister, teacher, or pastor, but there we are born merely as priests. Then the congregation takes some out of such born priests and calls and elects them to those offices in which they perform their ministry in the name of all of us" ("On the Private Mass and Holy Orders," 1533, St. Louis edition, 19:1260).

The same: "Thank God, in our churches we can show a Christian the true Christian Mass according to the order and institution of Christ as well as according to the right and true intention of Christ and the church. There our pastor, bishop or minister [*Diener*] steps before the altar rightly, duly, and publicly called. But before that, he was consecrated, anointed, and born as a priest of Christ regardless of private chrism. He publicly and clearly chants the formula [*Ordnung*] instituted at the Lord's Supper. Then he takes the bread and wine, gives thanks, and distributes them, giving them by virtue of Christ's words, 'This is My body; this is My blood; this do,' etc., to us and the others who are present and desire to receive Holy Communion. And we, especially those who desire to receive the Sacrament, kneel down beside, behind, or around him—man and wife, young and old, master and servant, mistress and maid, parents and children—just as God has brought us together. And we all are true and holy fellow priests, sanctified by the blood of Christ and anointed and consecrated by the Holy Spirit in Baptism. And in our priestly honor and adornment, which we received by birth and inheritance, we are there assembled, bearing on our heads our golden crowns (as this is pictured in Rev. 4:4) and having our harps in our hands and our golden censers. We do not let our pastor speak the service merely for himself as for his own person. But he is the mouth of all of us, and we all speak the words with him from the hearts and with our faith directed to the Lamb of God, who is for and with us according to His institution [*Ordnung*] to nurture us with His body and blood. That is our Mass, indeed the true Mass, which we surely possess" (ibid., p. 1279).

Johann Brenz: "But what about it? Has the office to forgive and retain sins been entrusted only to the apostles? These happened to be present with a few others when Christ spoke the words (John 20:30). But this office has not been bound to their persons; it belongs to the whole church. Christ says: 'If he refuses even to hear the church, let him be to you like a heathen and a tax collector. Assuredly, I say to you, whatever you bind on earth,' etc. (Matt. 18:17–18). ... Although every believer may privately forgive another his sins when he explains to him the Gospel, ... nevertheless for the public assembly of the church the Holy Spirit has established His order so that nothing may be done improperly and dishonorably.

"Therefore, it is not permitted that a woman should speak in the church, or even a man, unless he has been called. But the church has its ministers [*Diener*], to whom the public preaching of the Gospel, that is, the forgiving and retaining of sins, has been entrusted. According to Acts, Paul told the elders of the congregation at Ephesus: 'Take heed to yourselves and to all the flock, among which the Holy Spirit has made you overseers, to shepherd the church of God' (Acts 20:28). From this and other passages of Holy Scripture it is obvious that the office to forgive and retain sins, which is the office to preach the Gospel, has indeed been given to the whole church, but it has been so regulated that the church should be edified and not be confused" (Commentary on John 20).

Johann Gallus answers the question of whether in an emergency Holy Communion may be administered by a layman and whether such a dispensation would be efficacious as follows: "It is the judgment [*Meinung*] of the Holy Spirit that in a congregation, according to Paul's direction in 1 Cor. 14:40, all things should be done decently and in order. Therefore, God has also instituted and established the ministry of the Word, and it is His will that no one should administer it unless he has been duly called. However, Christ did not give the power to remit and retain sins merely to the apostles; He commanded all pious believers in common to announce the Gospel to their penitent fellow members. Therefore, not only ministers but, in a most urgent and extreme emergency (that is, when no pastor can be obtained and a Christian is asked by a fellow believer), laymen also are permitted to administer Holy Communion, to baptize, and to pronounce absolution" (*Bidembachii consil.,* p. 390).

Heshusius answers the question of whether a layman [*Privatperson*], who has not been called into the public ministry, may in an emergency absolve penitent sinners, baptize, and administer Holy Communion as follows: "There can be no doubt that in an emergency, when no duly called pastor can be obtained, every Christian has the power and is permitted, according to God's Word and out of Christian love, to attend to the ministry of the Word by preaching the divine Word and administering the sacraments. . . . But here we speak of what a Christian may do in an emergency when no godly and sincere minister of the church may be obtained, for example, when some Christians are in a place where no appointed pastor is to be had; or when some Christians, for the sake of the truth, are held captive or are in peril on the sea; or when some Christians are among the Turks or in the papacy, where there is no true pastor; or when some Christians are among Calvinists, Schwenckfelders, Adiaphorists, or Majorists, whom they must avoid as false teachers; or when some Christians have pastors or ministers who publicly exercise tyranny and cruelly persecute the sincere confessors of the truth and thus clearly show that they are not members of the true church, for which reason conscientious [*gottselige*] Christians must refrain from fellowshiping with them so as not to strengthen their tyranny and help condemn innocent Christians.

"In such and similar emergencies, which indeed have often occurred, when sincere pastors whose teaching and confession are sound and in agreement with God's Word cannot be secured, individual laymen and believing Christians may absolve penitent sinners, comfort the weak with God's Word, baptize infants, and administer Holy Communion. In such emergencies a Christian should not be troubled about being a busybody in another's business, but he should know that he is performing a true and due call of God and that his ministry is just as efficacious as if it were ratified by the laying on of hands for the office of the ministry in the whole church." (See further under Thesis IV, Part I).

"This does not mean that two or three Christians should separate themselves from the true church, avoid the regular called ministers, and cause factions, but I say this of emergency cases when either there are no pastors or those who exist spread false doctrine and so must be avoided. In addition there is also the emergency that the use of the sacraments cannot be found in other places. In such cases, every Christian, with the consent of two or three, is authorized and justified to administer the sacraments and strengthen the weak in the peril of death. . . .

"Ministers and pastors have been appointed and separated from ordinary Christians in order that there might be certain persons who preach the Gospel, serve the congregation, and administer the sacraments. Christians, like all other people, must attend to their work and the earning of their daily bread. It is also not given to everyone to teach others. Finally, pastors must also be well instructed in pure and sound doctrine and be examples in their way of life, so that the Christians might not be carried about with every wind of doctrine. Otherwise, there is no difference between ministers and ordinary Christians. In the kingdom of Christ the one has no more authority than the other. From this it also follows that ordinary Christians, in such cases when no upright minister of the Word is to be had, may preach the Gospel, remit sins, baptize, and administer the Lord's Supper" (Dr. Felix Bidembach, *Consil. theol.,* decade 3, cons. 5; p. 383ff.).

Polycarp Leyser writes in the continuation of the gospel harmony of Martin Chemnitz: "It may happen that a pious, penitent Christian in time of need, when he cannot obtain a regular minister of the Word or a pastor, may confess his sins to a brother Christian and request absolution of him. In such an emergency every Christian may absolve a truly penitent sinner, and what he looses on earth is also loosed in heaven. This is the case because Christ Jesus has made us believers of His Father kings and priests to His glory and for His everlasting kingdom (Rev. 1:6). . . .

"Although the public ministry ordinarily belongs only to those who have been duly called by the church and who in the name of God and the church exercise the power to loose and bind, nevertheless, in an emergency this power reverts to the next best Christian. For as the power to loose and bind was promised to Peter (Matt. 16:19) and was conferred on all apostles (John 20:23), so this power was given by Christ to the congregation (Matt. 18:18), which ordinarily can confer it on persons legitimately called for this purpose. But by way of exception and in an emergency every true member of the church has the same right and may use it to God's glory and in the service of his neighbor" (*Harmonia quatuor evangelistarum* 92; fol. 1748).

The same: "Christ has left to the church the keys of the kingdom of heaven (Matt. 18:18). We do not worry about the mockery and derision of the Jesuits, who blurt out: 'So among you all shoemakers and tailors, all cooks and laborers, have the power of the keys, and so you build a Babel and cause utter confusion.' I reply: We do not deny that in an emergency every believer may baptize, teach, and absolve another and so may open to him the gates of the heavenly city, so to speak, by means of the keys. And this emergency the church has always acknowledged, as Jerome writes and attests against the Luciferians and Augustine in his letter to Fortunatus. But except in an emergency, no one is permitted to do this unless he is a rightly called and appointed minister of the Word. For that would go counter to the divine rule: 'How shall they preach unless they are sent?' (Rom. 10:15). Again: 'I have not sent these prophets, yet they ran' (Jer. 23:21).

"Nevertheless, every single Christian, even the most humble, retains his right inviolate, which he has because of Christ's bestowal of the keys. For as all citizens of a free city, as many as live in it, have a common right and equal liberty so far as the republic is concerned, and as they nevertheless, for the sake of order, elect senators and place a mayor at their head, handing over to him the keys and statutes of the city in order that he might use them in the common name of all and rule the republic according to them, so also do the citizens of the city of God. They indeed have a share in all holy things, and all things are theirs, whether it be Paul or Peter, life or death, things present or things to come (1 Cor. 3:21). They possess all things under their one Head, Christ, who has given to His church all things necessary for salvation, which he procured by His sacrificial merit, and in it to every single member in particular, even to the most humble. But for the sake of order, they elect certain persons to whom they entrust the administration of the keys of the kingdom of heaven. So there are among us deacons, pastors, doctors, bishops, or superintendents so that all things, according to Paul's direction, are done decently and in order (1 Cor. 14:40).

"Here the Jesuits will cry out: 'Very well! This example also confirms the supremacy of the pope, who in the church of Christ, together with the college of cardinals, is exalted above all, as are

283

the mayor and the senators in a city.' But this example does not at all support the pope; it rather subverts his whole tyranny. A mayor is lord neither of the senators nor of the citizens, but he is a fellow citizen. He has been placed at the head of all merely for the sake of order. He does not dare undertake anything arbitrarily, much less anything against the liberty of the citizens. But he is held to do all things according to the law and the counsel of the senate.

"Of the pope the teachers of canon law, his adulators, once boasted (and the Jesuits have not recanted it to this very day), 'The power of the pope is of such a nature and so great that no person dare ask him: Why do you do that?' (See section 40 of the canon law, the chapter, 'If the Pope.') It is certain that if a free republic would get such a mayor, they would chase him out of the city before sunset. This troublemaker has grieved and oppressed the church now already for 800 years, since the days of Phocas. In addition, a mayor with his senate may preside over only one city, under one prince or king. But the Jesuits declare that their Roman sovereign has been placed over all cities, principalities, provinces, and kingdoms, indeed over the whole world. This St. Peter never did, nor is it possible for any man to do so. The several local churches [*Particularkirchen*] have their pastors and ministers [*Lehrer*] under one Head, Jesus Christ, as Paul teaches in Eph. 4:11. These things had to be said to explain to whom the keys of the kingdom of heaven have been promised and given" (ibid., 85; fol. 1627).

Balduin: "As all the apostles received the keys under the name of Peter, so under the name of the apostles the whole church has received them. It now exercises them through the ministers of the Word. Otherwise our ministers would not have any power to bind or loose sins" (*Commentar. in omnes epp. Pauli,* Prolegomena, p. 3).

Gerhard: "Augustine writes: 'These keys He has given to His church in order that what they loose on earth might be loosed in heaven, and what they might bind on earth might be bound in heaven.' This verdict of Augustine is confirmed by all the passages of Scripture in which the church is called Christ's bride and mistress of the house (Ps. 45:10; John 3:29; Ps. 68:13 [cf. Luther's translation of these passages—Tr.]). Now as the keys are given by the master of the house to the mistress, so Christ, the Lord of the house of God, which is the church (Heb. 3:6; 1 Tim. 3:15), has given them

284

to the church as to His bride. The ministers of the Word use them merely as stewards (1 Cor. 4:1) and servants in the name of the church" (*Loci theologici,* "De min. eccl.," par. 87).

The same: "Here I quote an excellent passage from a certain anonymous writing, whose author was a papist and whose work was published at Frankfort in 1612 under the title: *Various Smaller Works of the Theological Faculty at Paris as Well as of Other Theologians and Canonists,* etc. In the first chapter, 'On Ecclesiastical and Political Power,' we read: 'It is a general and indubitable principle that God in nature first and immediately has in mind the whole rather than a part of the whole, even though that part is most important. For this reason, the ability to see has been given to the total man in order that it might be exercised by the eye as by the instrument and servant of the person; for the eye exists by and for the sake of man. Supported by this infallible axiom, the school at Paris, in agreement with all the ancient church teachers, has always and constantly taught that Christ, when founding the church, gave the keys primarily, immediately, and essentially to the whole church rather than to Peter or, what amounts to the same thing, that He conferred the keys on the whole church, in order that they might be put to use by one as its minister. Thus the whole ecclesiastical jurisdiction belongs primarily, properly, and essentially to the church. The Roman supreme bishop possesses it, together with other bishops, merely as an instrument and servant and only ministers so far as its exercise is concerned, just as the ability to see belongs to the eye' " (ibid.).

The same: "Assuming that there is no regular minister of the Word, the administration of Baptism should still not be omitted, since for the essence of Baptism it is not at all required that he who administers this sacrament should be a minister of the church; therefore, in this case the order yields to the need. . . . Circumcision was commanded to Abraham (Gen. 17:11), who was a prophet of the Lord (Gen. 20:7), and from this we conclude that very probably the administration of this sacrament, together with other functions of the ecclesiastical office, was later transferred to the Levitical priesthood. There can be no doubt that this sacrament ordinarily was administered by men. But since in an emergency more consideration was given there to the sacrament than to the order, the same must be observed regarding Baptism, especially since in the New

Testament, after the abrogation of the Levitical distinction of persons, all Christians are a royal priesthood (1 Peter 2:9; Rev. 1:6), and also since in Christ there is neither male nor female (Gal. 3:28)....

"Wherever the same relation exists, the same right also exists. But absolution, which any layman [*Privatperson*] may announce to a dying person from the Gospel, and Baptism, which a layman may administer in an emergency, namely, when no regular minister of the Word can be obtained, stand in the same relation. Hence, there exists here also the same right. Laymen act properly when they instruct or comfort a congregation that is without a regular shepherd or sick people or those who in any way are afflicted, as in times of a siege, pestilence, persecution, etc. Here belong in a certain way also the examples of the prophetesses in the Old Testament, such as Deborah (Judg. 4), Huldah (2 Kings 22:14), Anna (Luke 2:36), as well as Priscilla, whom Paul calls his helper (Rom. 16:3), and who expounded to Apollos the way of God more perfectly (Acts 18:26), and Lois and Eunice, who taught their grandson and son Timothy from a child the Holy Scriptures (2 Tim. 1:5; 3:15). Why then should laymen not in an emergency administer Baptism, since they are a royal priesthood (1 Peter 2:9) and have been made kings and priests to God (Rev. 1:6; 5:10)?" (*Loci theologici,* "De baptismo," par. 34, 36).

The same: "As the right of calling belongs to the whole congregation, so also ordination, which is the declaration and attestation of the call, is performed in the name of the whole congregation. The elders [*Presbyterium*] lay on hands, but the church adds to this its prayers. Though for the sake of propriety and good order it is proper that the bishop, together with the elders, should lay his hands on the person who is being ordained, he here does not act according to his private will or by his own power but in the name and by the right, vote, authority, and consent, indeed with the prayers, of the whole congregation. Hence, the execution is done by the bishop, but the act itself is that of the whole church, as is obvious from Acts 6:3; 14:23" (*Loci theologici,* "De min. eccles.," par. 154). If, according to this statement, everything that an incumbent of the office does, even ordination, which otherwise more than others is a special function of the ministers, is an action that the church performs through its ministers, then the public ministry can be nothing else than the exercise of the rights of the universal priesthood, which the church possesses and which is publicly performed in its name.

The same: "We distinguish between the power itself and the exercise of the power. The power itself is and remains that of the church, but the exercise of the power is that of the bishop and elders, that is, of the ministers and those who represent the whole congregation. The power is and remains properly that of those in whose name and by whose authority it is executed. Now the exercise of church power in calling and electing ministers and in loosing and binding sins is carried out in the name and by the authority of the whole church. The power therefore is and remains that of the church" (ibid., par. 87).

Hülsemann: "In an emergency not only the elder [*Presbyter*] but also the seniors (lay elders) of any particular congregation [*Particularkirche*] may ordain, because the power to ordain does not inhere in one member, such as, for example, in a bishop as a permanent habit or character but rather as a power that is conferred and transitory, such as an authorized agent or business manager receives from his employer" (*Praelect. Form. Conc.,* art. 15, s. 15, p. 838).

Balthasar Meisner: "Wherever there is an emergency, there the general order is no longer in force. The order does not domineer the sacrament but serves it. The order exists for the sake of the sacraments; the sacraments do not exist for the sake of the order" (Disp. IX, "De sacr.," par. 18).

Jacob Martini: "In an emergency ordinary laymen, even women, may also teach. We must remember that official ministers are also spiritual priests along with the laymen. Hence, they have in common with their hearers and people that they should pray for themselves, for others, and the whole congregation, praise God, teach the divine Word, comfort, and the like. But in an emergency an ordinary layman who is well grounded in Christian truth may come forward, teach publicly, preach, pray, and admonish the brethren to repent in order that they may receive from God forgiveness of sins. For all this he has an inner call; therefore, he can do this in an emergency" (*Append. consil. Dedekenni,* pp. 436–37). It is clear that when Martini here ascribes to laymen an inner call for the ministry, he does not intend to support the enthusiasts, who, claiming such an inner call, interfered with duly called ministers even when no emergency existed. He only wishes to show why laymen in an emergency can efficaciously perform ministerial functions. For by Baptism a layman has been called inwardly to do those works for whose public exercise the incumbent of the pastoral office has been officially called or, vice versa, because the functions of the incumbents of the ministerial office are those that all Christians possess. Their exercise of these functions is limited only by the order of the public ministry, as long as they live here on earth.

Dannhauer: "If in an emergency the order (of the public ministry) ceases, the church can through any competent member of its communion teach, baptize, and absolve, since in Christ they have all been made kings and priests (Rev. 1:6)" (*Hodosophia christiana* 2, p. 111).

Johann Müller: "If only 10, 50, or 100 or more captive Christians are assembled in Turkey, should they not have power to do all things that a Christian congregation may do even if none of them has been ordained as a pastor? It is indeed a Christian church. If it now unanimously commands one person to preach, administer the Sacrament, and absolve, what reason is there for him not to have the power?" (*Luth. def.,* p. 154).

Let us now hear some ancient teachers.

In the so-called *Apostolic Constitutions* we read among other things: "Even if a teacher is a layman, as long as he knows the Word and is of a worthy character, he shall teach; for they all shall be taught of God" (8.33).

Tertullian: "The right to baptize is certainly that of the chief priest, who is the bishop; after him the presbyters or deacons possess it, but not without the consent of the bishop. This is for the honor of the church; if that remains inviolate, then also peace remains inviolate. In addition, laymen also possess this right (for what we receive in the same measure, we can also give in the same measure), even if they cannot yet be called learning (beginning) bishops, elders, or deacons. The Word of the Lord may not be wrested from anyone. Therefore, Baptism, which everywhere is God's same gift, can be administered by all."

Thesis VIII

The pastoral ministry [Predigtamt] *is the highest office in the church, and from it stem all other offices in the church.*

1. Scripture Proof

Since the incumbents of the public ministry [*des öffentlichen Predigtamtes*] have been entrusted with the keys of the kingdom of heaven, which the church possesses originally and immediately (Matt. 16:19; 18:18), in order that they may administer them officially [*in öffentlichem Amte*] in the name of the congregation [*von Gemeinschafts wegen*] (John 20:21–23), their office must of necessity be the highest in the church, and all other offices stem from it; for the keys embrace the whole power of the church. Therefore, in Scripture the incumbents of the ministerial office are called elders, bishops, rulers [*Vorsteher*], stewards, and the like, and the incumbents of subordinate offices are called deacons, that is, servants, not only of God but also of the congregation and the bishop. Of the ministers in particular it is said that they should feed the flock of God and watch over souls as those who must give account (1 Tim. 3:1, 5, 7; 5:17; 1 Cor. 4:1; Tit. 1:7; Heb. 13:17).

Hence at Jerusalem the holy apostles in the beginning administered not only the pastoral office but also that of the deacons until the growth of the congregation made it necessary that this office should be entrusted to others in order to relieve the apostles (Acts 6:1–6). When the Lord instituted the apostolate, He instituted only one office in the church, which embraces all others and by which the church of God should be provided for in every respect. Hence the highest office is that of the ministry of the Word, with which all other offices are also conferred at the same time. Every other public office in the church is part of the ministry of the Word or an auxiliary office that supports the ministry, whether it be the elders who do not labor in the Word and doctrine (1 Tim. 5:17) or the rulers (Rom. 12:8) or the deacons (the office of service in a narrow sense) or whatever other offices the church may entrust to particular persons for special administration. Therefore, the offices of Christian day school teachers, almoners, sextons, precentors at public worship, and others are all to be regarded as ecclesiastical and sacred, for they take over a part of the one ministry of the Word and support the pastoral office.

2. Witnesses of the Church in Its Official Confessions

Apology: "The ministry is the highest office in the church" (Art. XV [VIII], par. 43; German text, *Triglot,* p. 326).

Smalcald Articles: "Therefore, the church can never be better ruled and preserved than if we all live under one Head, Christ, and all the bishops, equal in office (though unequal in gifts) will diligently stand together in unity of doctrine, faith, sacraments, prayers, and works of love. St. Jerome writes that the priests at Alexandria, together and in common, ruled the church, as the apostles did also and afterward all bishops throughout all Christendom until the pope raised his head over all" (Part II [Art. IV], par. 9; German text, *Triglot,* pp. 473–74).

The same: "So we have a certain teaching that the ministry stems from the common call of the apostles, and it is not necessary that all should have the call and confirmation of this one person, Peter. In 1 Cor. 3:6 Paul makes all ministers equal" (Of the Power and Primacy of the Pope, par. 10; German text, *Triglot,* p. 506).

The same: "The Gospel commands those who preside over the churches that they should preach the Gospel, forgive sins, and administer the sacraments. In addition, it gives them the jurisdiction to excommunicate those who publicly wallow in vices and to loose and absolve those who desire to amend their lives. Now all must confess, even our adversaries, that this command is given to all who preside over the churches, whether they are called pastors, elders, or bishops. So Jerome also declares in clear words that there is no difference between bishops and elders, but that all pastors at the same time are bishops and priests, and he quotes the passage of Paul: 'For this reason I left you in Crete, that you should . . . appoint elders in every city' (Tit. 1:5). Afterward he calls them bishops: 'A bishop must be the husband of one wife.' Peter and John also call themselves elders or priests.

"Then Jerome says further: 'That only one is elected, who has others under him, was done in order to hinder division, so that one here and another there would not attract a congregation to himself and the church thus be torn to pieces.' He says: 'At Alexandria, from Mark the evangelist to the bishops Heracles and Dionysius, the elders always elected one from among themselves and esteemed him more highly, calling him a bishop, just as soldiers elect one as their captain. The deacons also elect one from among themselves who is qualified and call him archdeacon. So tell me, what more does a bishop do than every elder, except that he ordains others to the ministry?'

"Here Jerome teaches that the distinction between bishops and pastors stems merely from a human arrangement, just as we may see also from the work. For the office and command are the same; and afterward only ordination determined the distinction between bishops and pastors. Then it was so arranged that a bishop could also ordain persons for the ministry in other churches. But because, according to divine right, there is no difference between bishops and pastors or ministers, there is no doubt that if a pastor in his church ordains competent persons for offices in the church, such an ordination, according to divine right, is efficacious and right" (Of the Power and Jurisdiction of Bishops, par. 60–65; German text, *Triglot,* pp. 502–03).

Formula of Concord: "We believe, teach, and confess that . . . the whole church of God, indeed every Christian, but especially the ministers of the Word as those who preside over the church of God" etc. The Latin text reads: "Praecipue ministri verbi Dei, tamquam ii, quos Dominus ecclesiae suae regendae praefecit," that is, "especially the ministers of the Word of God, as those whom the Lord has placed at the head of His church to rule it" (Thorough Declaration, Art. X, par. 10; German text, *Triglot,* p. 1054).

3. Witnesses of the Church in the Private Writings of Its Teachers

Luther: "If the office of the Word is entrusted to anyone, then all other offices that are performed by the Word in the church are also entrusted to him, such as to baptize, to bless, to bind and loose, to pray, and to judge or decide matters. The office to preach the Gospel is the highest of all, for it is the apostolic office that lays the foundation for all others that belong to all, first of all, to edify, for which there are the offices of teachers, prophets, and rulers as well as the gifts of healing, as Paul lists them one after the other in 1 Cor. 12:8–10, 28. Even Christ above all only preached the Gospel as He who was to administer the highest office and not to baptize. So also Paul boasts that he was sent not to baptize, which is a minor and subsequent office, but to preach the Gospel, which is the foremost office (1 Cor. 1:17)" ("How One Should Choose and Ordain Pastors," Letter to the council and congregation of the city of Prague, 1534, St. Louis edition, 10:1592).

The same: "Therefore, the custom also remained that in some places the secular government, such as councilors and princes, appointed and salaried their own ministers in their cities and castles, whomever they desired, without any permission or command of bishops or popes, and no one interfered. Although (I fear) they did this without knowing the Christian right, but because these spiritual tyrants despised the ministry and regarded it as of little value, separating it widely from the spiritual rule, nevertheless it [the ministry] is the highest office, on which all others depend and follow. Again, wherever the ministry does not exist, no other office follows. John 4:2 tells us that Christ did not baptize but that He only preached, and Paul boasts that he was not sent to baptize but to preach the Gospel (1 Cor. 1:17).

"Therefore, the one to whom the ministry is entrusted is entrusted with the highest office in Christendom. After that he may also baptize, administer the Sacrament [*Meß halten*], and minister to souls. Or if he does not desire these duties, he may adhere merely to preaching, letting others baptize and administer the minor offices, as did Christ and all apostles (Acts 6)" ("That a Christian Assembly or Congregation Has the Right and Authority to Judge All Doctrine and to Call, Appoint, and Depose Ministers [*Lehrer*]," 1523, St. Louis edition, 10:1547–48).

The same: "From this story (Acts 6) we learn in the first place how a Christian congregation should be constituted. In addition, we have a true pattern of spiritual government that the apostles here provide. They care for souls, occupy themselves with preaching and prayer, and yet also see to it that the body is cared for; for they suggest several men who are to distribute the goods [*Güter*], as you have heard. Thus the Christian rule supplies the people in both body and soul so that no one suffers want, as Luke tells us, that all were richly fed and well cared for in both body and soul.

"This is a very fine pattern, and it would be well for us to do likewise, if only the people were so minded. A city could be divided, as here, into four or five parts, and every part would receive a minister and several deacons to supply the people with preaching, distribute the goods, visit the sick, and see to it that no one suffers want. But we do not have the persons for that. Therefore, I do not have the courage to start it until our Lord God Christ will do it. . . . When you desire to introduce a common treasury, you must know what kind of officials [*Aemter*] preside over a congregation. A 'bishop' means a steward of God who is to distribute the divine and spiritual gifts, preach the Gospel, and supply the people with the Word of God. He must have servants, and these are the deacons who serve the congregation in such a way that they have a list of all the poor people and care for them in all their needs with the money of the congregation, visit the sick, and in every way handle the supplies with great care" (*Church Postil: Gospel Portion,* "On the Day of St. Stephen, Holy Martyr," 1525, St. Louis edition, 11:2065).

The same: "This ruling (Rom. 12:8) or presiding is to be understood only of the common offices of the Christian church [*Christenheit*], and not of secular rulers, such as the masters of houses and the princes. They refer to those who preside over the Christian church, of whom the apostle says: 'If a man does not know how to rule his own house, how will he take care of the church of God?' (1 Tim. 3:5). They are the ones who are placed over every office to see to it that the teachers are not negligent and that the deacons rightly distribute the provisions [*Gut*] and are not to be lax in reproving sinners and excommunicating the impenitent, so that all offices are rightly performed. That should be the business of the bishops; for this reason they are also called overseers or *antistites* (as St. Paul here designates them), that is, presiders and rulers.

"It behooves these in particular to exercise care not for themselves (which Christ forbids in Matt. 6:25) but for others, so that it may be a care of love and not one for selfishness. For since it behooves him to keep his mind on all, to do and perform all things, and everything depends on him, just as a driver must see to it that horse and wagon move along, he must not be negligent, sleepy, or lax but brave and careful, though all the others might be negligent and careless. If he wants to be lax and careless, no other offices will succeed, and it will be as though a driver were asleep on his wagon and letting the horse and wagon go as they please. In such a case nothing good may be expected or hoped for, especially on the dangerous roads and ways that Christians [*Christenheit*] must go in the midst of devils, which eagerly desire to overthrow and destroy them at all times.

"But how is it that St. Paul reverses the order by not placing ruling first of all and at the head but first mentions prophecy, then serving, teaching, admonishing, and giving and then places ruling in the last, or sixth, place among the common offices? The Holy Spirit did this no doubt because of the impending abomination, namely, that the devil would start nothing but tyranny and secular control in the Christian church [*Christenheit*], and everyone in the Christian church must submit to their tyranny and malice. Every prophecy, service, doctrine, admonition, and giving must pass away before this tyranny will be abolished, and they will be guided by prophecy, doctrine, and the other offices. But we must know that nothing is higher than God's Word and that this ministry [*Amt*] is above all others. Ruling is its servant, which should incite and wake it up, just as a servant wakes his master from sleep or otherwise reminds him of his duty [*Amt*], so that what Christ says remains true: 'He who is greatest among you, let him be your servant' (Luke 22:26; Luther's translation), and 'The first shall be last' (Matt. 20:16).

"Again, teachers and prophets should obey and follow the ruler and humble themselves so that every Christian work and office might be servants of one another. Thus what St. Paul writes in this epistle must remain true [Rom. 12:7–16; namely,] that no one should regard himself as the best, exalt himself over the other, or think of himself more highly than he ought to think. But all should let one office or gift be more precious than the others, yet in such a way that one should serve the other with his office or gift and be subject to him. Thus the office of ruling is the most inferior, and yet all others are subject to it, while it again services all others by caring and providing for them. So also prophecy is the highest and yet it follows him who rules" (*Church Postil: Epistle Portion,* "On the Second Sunday

294

After the Epiphany," 1525, St. Louis edition, 12:338–39).

The same: "The office of deacon is not the service of reading the Gospel and Epistle, as is the custom today, but of dispensing provisions of the congregation to the poor in order that the pastors [*Priester*], freed from the burden of temporal provisions [*Güter*], may more diligently and freely attend to prayer and the Word of God. For, as we read in Acts 6:3, the deacons were appointed for that purpose" ("On the Babylonian Captivity of the Church," St. Louis edition, 19:117–18).

The same: "We know that it is held in the Christian church [*Christenheit*] that all congregations are equal, and that there is no more than one holy church of Christ in the world, as we confess: 'I believe one holy Christian church.' A church may be wherever it will in the whole world, yet it has no other Gospel or Holy Scripture, no other Baptism and Sacrament, no other faith and Spirit, no other Christ and God, no other 'Our Father' and prayer, no other hope and everlasting life than we have here at Wittenberg, and their bishops are equal to our bishops, pastors, and ministers. No one is the master or servant of the other. All have the same mind and heart, and everything that belongs to the church is equal. But as is stated in 1 Cor. 12:8ff. and Rom. 12:6ff., one minister or Christian [layman] may be of stronger faith and have other and greater gifts than another. For example, one may expound Scripture better, rule better, preach better, judge the spirits better, comfort better, know more languages, and the like.

"But such gifts do not create inequality or rule in the church; indeed, they make no one a Christian (Matt. 7:22–23), but all must be Christian first. . . . Listen to Peter himself, who truly was an apostle, not the Peter of the pope, who writes in his epistles to his bishops in Pontus, Galatia, Cappadocia, Asia, and Bithynia: 'The elders who are among you I exhort, I who am a fellow elder and a witness of the sufferings of Christ, and also a partaker of the glory that will be revealed: Shepherd the flock of God which is among you, serving as overseers,' etc. (1 Peter 5:1–2). Notice that St. Peter calls himself a fellow elder, that is, a fellow pastor or fellow minister. He does not want to soar above them but to be like them, though he well knows that he is an apostle. The office of the ministry of the Word [*Predigtamt*] or of a pastor [*Bishofsamt*] is the highest; the Son of God Himself administered it, as did also all the apostles, prophets, and patriarchs. God's Word and faith indeed are exalted over all other matters, over all gifts and persons. The term 'elder,' in Greek *presbuteros,* sometimes denotes 'age' as we speak of an 'elderly man.' But here it stands for an office, because elderly and experienced persons were appointed to the office. Today we call them pastors, ministers, or spiritual advisers [*Seelsorger*]" ("Against the Papacy at Rome, Instituted by the Devil," 1545, St. Louis edition, 17:1115–16).

The same: "All those who serve in the pastoral ministry [*Pfarramt*] or the ministry of the Word are in a holy, true, and good order and state and are pleasing to God, such as those who preach, administer the Sacrament, preside over the common treasury, as well as the stewards, messengers, and servants who assist such persons, etc." ("Confession Concerning the Lord's Supper of Christ," 1528, St. Louis edition, 20:1098).

Seckendorf: "It is the opinion of our churches that the difference between bishops and pastors [*Priester*] stems from order and custom in the church and not from Christ's clear command or the apostles' express institution [*Anstalt*]. For this opinion we adduce adequate Scripture proof from the New Testament, namely, that according to the divine institution and because of their special office, bishops and pastors are one and the same thing. From this it follows that where no ecclesiastical government and no episcopal inspection has been established, a pastor has to perform and execute all functions of his office without regard for any presiding superintendents or bishops. This refers not only to the teaching of the divine Word and the administration of the Sacrament but also to other matters of church discipline and ceremony as well as to church collections [*das geistliche Einkommen*] and alms" (*The Christian State,* III, par. 2; p. 534).

Chemnitz: "Because many offices pertain to the ministry in the church that in a large assembly of believers cannot well be attended to in whole and in part by one person or a few, the church, as it began to increase, began to distribute these ministerial offices among certain grades of servants in order that all things might be done orderly, decently, and in an edifying way. Later these were called *taxeis* or *tagmata* in order that everyone might have his definite place where he could serve the church by performing certain ministerial functions. Thus in the beginning the apostles administered the office of the Word and the sacraments as well as that of distributing and managing alms. Later, when the number of disciples increased, they entrusted the part of their ministry dealing with alms to others, whom they called deacons or servants. They did this in order that they might give themselves "continually to prayer and to the ministry of the Word" (Acts 6:4). This origin of ministerial grades and orders in the apostolic church shows the cause, reason, purpose, and use of these grades and orders. According to the circumstances of a congregation, the various ministerial functions thereby were to be performed more readily, more rightly, more diligently, and with greater order and becoming dignity to the edification of the church.

"Since the apostles appointed some of the deacons who had proved themselves, such as Stephen and Philip, to the ministry of the Word [*Lehramt*], we conclude that these grades or orders were also to serve the purpose of preparing and testing some in the minor offices in order that later they might be entrusted with more important functions of the ministry with greater security and profit. That is just what Paul says: 'Let these also first be proved; then let them serve as deacons' (1 Tim. 3:10); likewise: 'Those who have served well as deacons obtain for themselves a good standing' (v. 13). According to Acts 13:1, there were both prophets and teachers in the ministry of the church at Antioch. Of these, the former either predicted future events or expounded more difficult Bible passages (1 Cor. 14:3ff.), while the latter instructed the people in the elements of the Christian faith (Heb. 5:12–14). Paul and Barnabas took Mark with them as their assistant (Acts 13:5). But he was not merely to render them bodily service; he was to be entrusted with some functions of the ministry of the Word, as Paul states (Acts 15:38). In the church at Corinth there were apostles, prophets, and teachers; some spoke with tongues, others expounded the Scriptures, others spoke psalms, others prayers, praise, and thanksgiving not merely in private devotions [*Privatgottesdiensten*] but in the public assemblies of the congregation (1 Cor. 12:8ff.; 14:2ff.).

"In Eph. 4:11 the following grades of ministers are enumerated:

"1. *Apostles.* These were not called to any particular church, nor were they called by men, but they were called immediately by Christ, who commanded them to preach everywhere. They were also supplied with the witness of the Spirit and of miracles so that they could not err in their teaching; their doctrine was divine and heavenly, and to it all other teachers are bound.

"2. *Prophets*. These either received revelations concerning future events or expounded the 'tongues' and Scriptures to the more mature; this is ascribed to the prophets of the New Testament in 1 Cor. 14:27ff.

"3. *Evangelists*. These were not apostles, nor were they appointed for any definite congregation; they were sent to various churches to preach the Gospel but especially first to lay the foundation. Such evangelists were Philip (Acts 21:8), Timothy (2 Tim. 4:5), Tychicus, Silvanus, and others. Eusebius attests that there were also such evangelists after the times of the apostles.

"4. *Shepherds* (pastors). These were placed at the head of a certain church, as Peter declares in 1 Peter 5:1–2. They not only taught but also administered the sacraments and watched over the hearers, as the pastoral office is described in Ezek. 34:11ff.

"5. *Teachers*. These were not commanded to rule or watch over the congregation, but they only instructed the people in doctrine, as the catechists did later. So Paul in Rom. 2:20 speaks of a 'teacher of babes,' and the term 'teaching' is used in precisely the same sense in Heb. 5:12.

"The apostles included all these grades in the terms 'elder' and 'bishop.' At times they also called them by the general term 'deacon,' to whom the ministry of the Word and the sacraments was entrusted (Col. 1:7; 1 Thess. 3:2; 1 Cor. 3:5; 11:23; Eph. 3:7). Paul himself sometimes attended to the ministry of the Word in such a way that he entrusted the administering of the sacraments to others: 'For Christ did not send me to baptize, but to preach the Gospel' (1 Cor. 1:17). In 1 Tim. 5:17 he mentions two kinds of elders, some of whom labored in Word and doctrine, while others presided over church discipline. This latter type Tertullian mentions in his *Apologetics* (ch. 39). These are in general the grades into which the ministry of the Word was divided at the times of the apostles.

"But it must be kept in mind (1) that God did not command which and how many grades or orders there should be; (2) that at the times of the apostles there were not always and in all congregations the same number of grades or orders, which we conclude from the letters that Paul addressed to the various congregations; and (3) that at the times of the apostles these grades were not so divided that one and the same person did not often take over and administer all these ministerial functions, as we know from the history of the apostles.

"Such orders, therefore, were free in the days of the apostles, and they were arranged in the interest of order, decorum, and edification. At that time certain other gifts, such as tongues, prophecy, and miracles, which properly belonged to the apostles, were given to certain persons in particular. But those grades of which we have spoken above were not above and outside the ministry of the Word and sacraments; the very functions of the ministry itself were divided into these grades" (*Examen Concilii Tridentini,* part 2, locus 13, "De sacramento ordinis," pp. 574ff.).

Gerhard: "The question is whether the authority to ordain according to divine right belongs only to the bishops. Bellarmine proves this from the custom of the church. But the proof was to be supplied that this prerogative stems from Christ's institution. Even if Bellarmine had proved that the apostles themselves had established such a distinction between bishops and elders, and that the former and not the latter had been entrusted with the right to ordain as well as with the supervision of the other elders—which some think they can prove in all probability from Tit. 1:5, where Titus, as bishop of Crete, was commanded to appoint elders in every city— he would not have proved that according to divine right the bishops are more than elders.

"That arrangement was only a part of good ecclesiastical order, not a command establishing a divine right. It was merely a regulation to execute this ecclesiastical function in a becoming way. But it was by no means to prescribe for an extraordinary emergency.... If Jerome could acknowledge that the distinction between bishops and elders stems from the apostles without acknowledging that it existed by divine right, then there certainly is no necessary and immediate connection between the two statements, 'It was introduced by the apostles,' and 'It exists by divine right.' Above we have shown from 1 Tim. 4:14 that in the apostolic church the elders were by no means excluded from the laying on of hands. But for the sake of good order the chief elder, who in a special sense was called 'bishop,' performed the ordination in the name of the church and of all the elders. As the election by the congregation is not to be excluded from the calling of the elders whom Titus was to appoint in every city, so also the laying on of hands by the elders is not to be excluded at the ordination of these elders" (*Loci theologici,* "De minist. eccl.," par. 238).

Hülsemann: "It must certainly be acknowledged (1) that the term 'church' is ascribed to the assembly that in one home or in one family of one home professes one and the same faith in Christ. It must also be acknowledged (2) that the division into patriarchal, episcopal, city, and temple dioceses in one city existed by human right, provided that temples corresponded to pastors in such a way that all the people there, joined into one congregation, could hear in one church the voice of the pastor, and all belonging to the various dioceses could readily be served by the pastor. Concerning the division into four chief patriarchates, the first council of Nicaea passed a resolution (ch. 6). Even the apostles themselves divided the dioceses and provinces in the whole world among themselves (Gal. 2). . . .

"But when the Puritans infer from this that even the smallest assembly is independent of any other particular congregation in the neighborhood so far as agreement in church ceremonies is concerned, and that it is free from the obligation to preserve unity in doctrine and faith, then they are wrong in both these conclusions. There is indeed a difference between independence of any other congregation so far as jurisdiction (government) is concerned and the obligation to preserve the unity of faith and doctrine with other particular churches of Christ. For the latter exists by divine right (1 Cor. 12:24ff.) while the former is of human right (that is, the relation of one congregation to another but not that of the congregations to their pastors). Every one of the Independents [Congregationalists] regards himself as free not only in regard to its doctrinal obligation toward another congregation but also in regard to the obligation of the hearers to their pastors. This is obvious from what Henry Bourton in *Timothy No Bishop* replies to the writing of Joseph Hall, namely, 'that Timothy was a bishop and that he administered this office by divine right,' though the latter joined personal faith too closely to the faith and doctrine of the bishops. Therefore, the opponents went to the other extreme and recognized no other agreement for the preservation of the truth in the church than that in the chief (though not in all) articles of the Apostles' Creed" (*Prae-lectt. ad Breviar.* chap. 17, par. 2; pp. 1216ff.).

The same: "Above all, a distinction must be made between the possibility of independence at a certain time and the perpetual right and continued practice of independence. This regards both independence from the jurisdiction of other churches and independence from other churches in regard to harmony. Independence from doctrinal agreement that prevailed in the past with other churches is possible not only when it is found that they have fallen into error regarding the faith, ... but this possibility became real at the time of Elijah (1 Kings 19), as well as at the time of our fathers under the papacy and is yet to be expected under Antichrist. In these cases independence became necessary and will remain necessary not only as regards doctrinal agreement with the other churches, at least in those points in which they err, but also with regard to the jurisdiction of the regular pastors" (ibid., p. 1218).

Irenaeus: "It is necessary to obey those elders who preside over the congregation, for their office stems from the apostles, who with the succession of the episcopacy have received a certain charisma of the truth according to the good pleasure of the Father" (*Adversus haereses* 4.26.2).

Basilius: "Christ imparted to all pastors and teachers the same power, which is proved by the fact that they all bind in an equal manner" (*Asc.* 22?).

The *Fourth Council of Carthage:* "When an elder is ordained and the bishop blesses him and lays his hands on him, then all elders present shall lay their hands on him next to those of the bishop" (Canon 3).

Jerome: "An elder is the same as a bishop, and before the devil had incited factions in the church so that the people said, 'I am of Paul,' or 'I am of Apollos,' or 'I am of Cephas' (1 Cor. 1:12), the congregations were governed by the common council of the elders. But when everyone regarded those whom he had baptized as belonging to him and not to Christ, it was resolved in the whole world that one should be elected from the elders and placed at the head of the others. ... Let the bishops then know that they have preeminence over the elders rather by custom than by the truth of a divine institution and that they are to rule the church in common [with the elders]" (Commentary on Tit. 1:7).

The same: "The apostle teaches most clearly that elders are the same as bishops. But that afterward one was elected and placed at the head of the others was done to secure a remedy against factions. For also at Alexandria, from the evangelist Mark to the bishops Heracles and Dionysius, the elders always called the one who was elected from their midst and placed on a higher level a 'bishop,' just as an army chooses a captain, or deacons elect one whom they know to be industrious and call him archdeacon. For what does a bishop do that an elder does not do, except that he ordains [elders]?" (*Epist. 146* [al. 101] *ad Evagr.*).

The same: "Wherever there may be a bishop, whether at Rome or in Eugubium or in Constantinople or in Rhegium or in Alexandria or in Tanis, they all have the same dignity [*meritum*] and the same ministry [*sacerdotium*]" (*Ad Evagr.*).

Ambrosiaster: "The first elders were called bishops" (Commentary on Eph. 4:11).

Thesis IX

To the ministry there is due respect as well as unconditional obe-dience when the pastor uses God's Word. But the minister must not tyrannize the church. He has no authority to introduce new laws or arbitrarily to establish adiaphora or ceremonies. He has no right to inflict and carry out excommunication without his having first informed the whole congregation.

A. To the ministry there is due respect as well as unconditional obedience when the pastor uses God's Word.

1. Scripture Proof

Though the incumbents of the public office of the ministry do not form a more sacred state, different from that of ordinary believers, but only administer the rights of all Christians entrusted to them for official and orderly execution, nevertheless, on that account they are not servants of men. The principal efficient cause of the ministry of the Word is God, the sovereign Lord Himself. The ministry is not an establishment of men for the sake of propriety and well-being [*Heilsamkeit*] but the institution of the Triune God: Father, Son, and Holy Spirit. Therefore, if a congregation has entrusted the official authority to a person by means of a regular and rightful call, that person has been placed at the head of the congregation by God Himself, though through the congregation (1 Cor. 12:28; Eph. 4:11; Acts 20:28). Hence, the installed pastor is not only a servant of the congregation but also at the same time a servant of God and an ambassador of Christ, by whom God admonished the congregation (1 Cor. 4:1; 2 Cor. 5:18–20).

"Therefore, when a pastor uses God's Word in his congregation, whether by teaching, admonishing, reproving, or comforting, either

303

publicly or privately, then the congregation hears Jesus Christ Himself out of his mouth. In that case it owes him unconditional obedience as the one by whom God desires to make known to it His will and lead it to eternal life, and the more faithfully a pastor administers his office, the more highly it should esteem him. A congregation has no right to depose such a faithful servant of Jesus Christ; if it does this, it rejects Jesus Christ Himself, in whose name he ministers to it. A congregation can depose an incumbent of the holy ministry only if it is clear from the divine Word that God Himself has deposed him as a wolf or hireling. Of this we read in the Holy Scriptures:

"He who hears you hears Me, he who rejects you rejects Me, and he who rejects Me rejects Him who sent Me" (Luke 10:16).

"Obey those who rule over you, and be submissive, for they watch out for your souls, as those who must give account. Let them do so with joy and not with grief, for that would be unprofitable for you" (Heb. 13:17).

"We urge you, brethren, to recognize those who labor among you, and are over you in the Lord and admonish you, and to esteem them very highly in love for their work's sake. Be at peace among yourselves" (1 Thess. 5:12–13).

"Let the elders who rule well be counted worthy of double honor, especially those who labor in the Word and doctrine. For the Scripture says, 'You shall not muzzle an ox while it treads out the grain,' and, 'The laborer is worthy of his wages' " (1 Tim. 5:17–18; cf. Gal. 6:6–10).

"When you go into a household, greet it. If the household is worthy, let your peace come upon it. But if it is not worthy, let your peace return to you. And whoever will not receive you nor hear your words, when you depart from that house or city, shake off the dust from your feet. Assuredly, I say to you, it will be more tolerable for the land of Sodom and Gomorrah in the day of judgment than for that city!" (Matt. 10:12–15).

2. Witnesses of the Church in Its Official Confessions

Augsburg Confession: "Therefore, it is the office of a bishop according to divine right to preach the Gospel, forgive sin, judge doctrine, reject all doctrine that is contrary to the Gospel, and exclude the wicked whose ungodliness is manifest from the Christian church without human power but alone through God's Word. And in this matter the ministers and congregations owe the bishops obedience according to Christ's Word: 'He who hears you hears Me' (Luke 10:16)" (Art. XXVIII, par. 20–22; German text, *Triglot,* p. 86).

The same: "Therefore, for the comfort of their consciences our adherents were compelled to clarify the distinction between the spiritual and the secular power, sword, and rule. They taught that for the sake of God's command both rules and powers should be honored and highly esteemed with all reverence as two very great gifts of God on earth" (ibid., par. 4; German text, *Triglot,* p. 84).

Apology: "Also factions easily may arise when the people most quickly censure and criticize everything regarding the walk and life of their bishops or pastors or, becoming tired of their minister, even some small fault of his; great harm results from that. Then in their bitterness they will soon seek other teachers and ministers. On the other hand, perfection and unity are preserved; that is, the church remains united and complete when the strong suffer and bear with the weak, when the people exercise patience with their pastors, and again when the bishops and pastors know how to overlook all sorts of weaknesses of the people, as the case may be" (Art. III, par. 112–13; German text, *Triglot,* p. 184).

Large Catechism (Fourth Commandment): "To this commandment belongs also an explanation concerning all manner of obedience toward superiors who must command and rule, for from the authority of parents stems and extends all other [authority]" (par. 141; German text, *Triglot,* p. 620).

"Therefore, we have two kinds of fathers presented to us in this commandment: fathers of blood and fathers of office, or those who care in the home and in the land. In addition to these, there are also spiritual fathers, not such as were those in the papacy, who indeed had themselves called so but who did not function as fathers. Only those are called spiritual fathers who rule and direct us by the Word of God, as St. Paul boasts of being a father in 1 Cor. 4:15, where he says: 'In Christ Jesus I have begotten you through the Gospel.' Since these are fathers, they are entitled to honor, even perhaps before all others. But here honor is shown least, for the world is accustomed to honor them in such a way that it chases them out of the land and begrudges them even a piece of bread.

In short, they must be (as St. Paul says [1 Cor. 4:13]) the filth of the world and everyone's refuse and foot rag.

"But it is necessary to urge this on the people, since those who desire to be called Christians are in duty bound before God to esteem those who care for their souls worthy of double honor, treat them well, and provide for them. God will give you enough and not let you suffer want. But here all refuse and resist for fear that their belly might languish. Now they cannot support one righteous pastor, whereas before they filled 10 fat bellies. For this we deserve that God should take from us His Word and blessing and again let false preachers arise who lead us to the devil and, in addition, suck out our sweat and blood.

"But those who keep God's will and command before their eyes have the promise that they shall be richly rewarded for everything they spend on their bodily and spiritual fathers and do to their honor—not that they should have bread, clothes, and money merely for a year or two, but a long life, food, peace, everlasting riches, and blessedness. Therefore, by all means do what is your duty and let God take care how He will feed and provide for you abundantly. He has promised this, and since He has never lied, He will not lie to you.

"This should always move us and give us a heart that melts for pleasure and love toward those to whom we owe honor, so that we lift up our hands and joyously thank God for having given us such promises, for which we should run to the ends of the earth. For although all the world would cooperate, it could not add one little hour to our life or give us a single kernel out of the earth. But God can and will give you all things exceeding abundantly according to your heart's desire. However, he who despises this and casts it to the winds does not deserve to hear even one Word of God. Of this more than enough has been said to all who come under this commandment" (ibid., par 158–66; German text, *Triglot,* pp. 626–27).

3. Witnesses of the Church in the Private Writings of Its Teachers

Luther: "In short, whoever we may be, they must receive the Gospel, absolution, and the Sacrament from their pastors and called ministers and not despise this divine institution if they desire their salvation. For if God had wanted to establish it otherwise, He would have preferred them and commanded them to speak before others and ordered us to be silent and listen to them. God also selected such poor sinners, as St. Paul and we have been, to check the arrogance and pride of these smart alecks [*Klügler*]. He does not want to have such secure and impertinent Christians for this office, but those who have been chastened, tried, and broken down. They should know and confess that they were great sinners [*böse Buben*] and heavily laden with sins, indeed, most grievous transgressors before God and enemies of God and Christ. Thus they will remain humble and not become presumptuous or boast of themselves (as do these fresh Christians) that they were so pious, holy, and learned that God chose them for this office.

"A pious Christian does not act that way. If he hears someone preaching something that is not right, he remains humble and admonishes the preacher in a friendly and brotherly way and does not scrap and scrape as they do. . . . In short, whatever pertains to our person we must and will bear gladly, but what pertains to grace, especially to this office, which has and bestows nothing but grace, we want everybody to honor. . . . Yet we must also boast against the papacy and all enthusiasts [*Rotten*] that God has given us His Word and true ministers of it. Though they may despise us and condemn us as heretics, we nevertheless are true ministers and servants of Christ. In addition, we were called and appointed as teachers by the pope himself, and this honor and boast we do not despise, not because thereby we are better before God, but in order that our doctrine may be all the more firmly impressed on the people and there be no doubt or vacillation. For if we ourselves would vacillate and doubt, then also our whole following will vacillate and become uncertain in this matter" ("Sermon on 1 Cor. 15:8–10," 1534, St. Louis edition, 8:1121ff.).

The same: "Therefore, this admonition of the prophets is most necessary: Wherever the holy Gospel is being preached, everybody should receive and keep it with due reverence. We see that it was not God's will that the Gospel should be preached by angels, for He entrusted the ministry to men. However, as God has earnestly forbidden them to misuse their ministry, thereby to acquire external, secular [*rechtliche*] power and rule or to amass money and wealth, so also He has commanded the Christian church to honor the ministers of the divine Word in every way, support them abundantly, and reverence them in a Christian way.

"For this reason Holy Scripture praises and lauds the ministry of the Word in such grand words as: 'How beautiful upon the mountains are the feet of him who brings good news, who proclaims peace, who brings glad tidings of good things, who proclaims salvation, who says to Zion, "Your God reigns!" ' (Is. 52:7). The prophet Micah compares our Gospel ministers in a beautiful, fitting figure of speech to the dew from heaven and the fertile rain. In another passage they are called angels (Mal. 2:7). It is not without purpose that the Holy Spirit praises the ministers of the divine Word so highly, for He desires to awaken in us the same respect toward the servants of the Word.

"There are also many examples showing that God the Lord earnestly punished those who despised His ministers. I will not speak of the deluge or the destruction of Sodom and Gomorrah or how Korah and his companions were devoured by the earth or how, when Elisha was ridiculed by the children, bears appeared and tore 42 of them to pieces. But these children mocked him merely because of his baldness and might have been excused on account of their youth. How much more then will God the Lord not punish older persons who despise the ministry and think they might extenuate and cover their rascality and wickedness by bringing it into contempt through their false, fictitious accusation [*Auflage*]" ("Exposition of the Prophet Micah," 5:9–10, 1542, St. Louis edition, 14:1103–04).

The same: "In the third place, it is true that we owe obedience to all persons who have been called into the ministry of the Word and sacraments and who truly do this great, divine work, rightly preach the Gospel, and administer the sacraments according to the divine command, whether they are called bishops, ministers, or pastors. We owe them this by God's command in all matters that the Gospel prescribes or forbids at the peril of eternal damnation, according to the passage: 'He who hears you hears Me, and he who rejects you rejects Me, and he who rejects Me rejects Him who sent Me' (Luke 10:16). Furthermore, we owe pastors obedience in all matters of church discipline [*Kirchengerichten*], which the church is to exercise so that the accused shall appear, be convicted [of his sin], and accept discipline [*Strafe*]. . . .

"In short, we owe to the ministry or *ministerio evangelii,* through which God works and is present with us, true cordial respect with becoming humility, and it is the highest service of God to help preserve this ministry with food, protection, and good will [*Gutwilligkeit*]. Therefore, God has also promised a rich reward to the pious who show kindness to the ministers, as Christ said: 'Whoever gives one of these little ones only a cup of cold water in the name of a disciple, assuredly, I say to you, he shall by no means lose his reward' (Matt. 10:42)" ("Wittenberg Reformation," etc., signed by Luther, Pomeranus, Cruciger, Major, and Melanchthon, 1545, St. Louis edition, 17:1150).

The same: "Because pastors have the office, name, and honor to be co-workers of God, let no one be so learned or holy as to neglect or despise the least sermon, for no one knows when the hour will come in which God will accomplish His work through the minister" (*Church Postil: Epistle Portion,* "On the First Sunday in Lent," 1525, St. Louis edition, 12:436–37).

The same: "What is here meant by 'all the world' and by 'reprove'? If we here search the text [*örtert*] rightly, we shall find what is said. The phrase 'all the world' does not mean merely Annas, Caiaphas, the high priest, the Pharisees, lawyers, elders, princes, and the king of Jerusalem. It signifies all who are in the world, at Jerusalem and in all other places in the world—all the wise, the prudent, the learned, the holy, the powerful, emperors, kings, noblemen and commoners, peasants and citizens, high and low, young and old. To 'rebuke' means to allow no good in anyone but by the Word to attack all they do and are, telling them all, whoever they may be, that they are culpable and unrighteous before God and that they all must obey this Gospel concerning Christ or else be eternally condemned and lost. Thus all people on earth are subject to the ministry, which the apostles and their successors administer by divine right; they have to submit themselves and follow it if they really want to receive God's grace and be saved" (*House Postil,* "On the Fourth Sunday After Easter," 1536, St. Louis edition, 13:1989).

The same: "It is true that whoever despises the ministry will not esteem the Gospel very highly" (Exposition of Matt. 7:6, 1532, St. Louis edition, 7:598).

The same: "We know that contempt for the ministry of the Word

[*Kirchenamt*] does the very greatest harm" (Exposition of Gen. 12:4, St. Louis edition, 1:766).

The same: "The minister is not a servant of the court or of the peasant. He is God's minister and servant, and his command goes beyond the master and servant, as here the psalm says: 'He judges among the gods' " (Exposition of Ps. 82:1, 1530, St. Louis edition, 5:707).

The same: "This you may yourself consider: a co-owner of a farm [*Gutgeselle*], who has studied all his life, consumed his father's goods, and suffered all manner of tribulation, should be pastor at Zwickau. As rumor has it, they want to be lords, and the pastor should be the servant who every day should be kept in doubt [*auf der Schuckel säße*]: If Mühlpfort desires it, he might stay; if not, he must leave. No, dear sir, do not let it come to that, or you shall not keep a pastor. We neither will do nor suffer it unless they admit that they are not Christians. We might suffer it from heathen, but of Christians even Christ will not suffer it" (Letter to Valentin Hausmann, 1531, St. Louis edition, 21:1645–46).

Chemnitz: "Just as there is a legitimate way to call anyone into the ministry, so also there is a legitimate way to depose anyone or to transfer him from one congregation to another. Also in our congregations many do not rightly understand this matter. For as he who hires a servant also has the right to dismiss him when he desires it, so many think they have the right to dismiss a pastor even without a just cause. There are also some who think that no minister may with a good conscience leave one parish for another. But as the only God reserves for Himself the right to call, even when the call is mediate, so it properly behooves Him to depose or remove anyone from office.

"As long, therefore, as God permits His servant who teaches rightly and lives blamelessly to remain in office, the church has no right to dismiss someone else's servant. But when he no longer edifies the congregation in doctrine or life but destroys it, then God Himself deposes him (Hos. 4:6; 1 Sam 2:30). So there are two reasons why God removes unfaithful servants from their office: first, because they teach false doctrine (Mal. 2:7: 'The lips of a priest should keep knowledge, and people should seek the law from his mouth')—if he casts this (pure doctrine) aside, he will himself be cast aside by God; second, because of their life, namely, when they so live that the name of God is blasphemed. In that case the church not only has the power to remove such a one from office, but it must do so. For as God calls by means, so also He removes by means. However, as the call should be according to the instruction of the Lord of the harvest, so also the congregation that intends to depose someone from his office must be able to prove beyond all doubt that this is the verdict and the will of God. And as the call, so also the removal pertains to the whole congregation in a certain order" (*Loci theologici,* "De eccl.," III, p. 331).

Gerhard: "For the hearers there lies in this term (ministers) the admonition (1) that they should duly honor and respect their pastors as legates and ministers of God. When, therefore, the apostle had said that the household of Stephanas had devoted themselves to the ministry of the saints (1 Cor. 16:15), he added at once 'that you also submit to such, and to everyone who works and labors' (v. 16). Pastors are indeed servants of God and of the church; however, they must not be regarded as the lowest slaves but as servants to whom, according to God's own prescription, we owe honor, reverence, and obedience (1 Tim. 5:17; Tit. 2:15; Heb. 13:17; etc.). (2) They should receive them with filial love and sincere kindness since they hear that they are not forced under the yoke of civil servitude but are called to the fellowship of spiritual freedom by those who desire not to rule over them despotically, much less tyrannically, but to embrace and treat them in a fatherly way with paternal benevolence" (*Loci theologici,* "De minist. eccl.," par. 7).

Kromayer: "The minister may not be engaged by those who call him through a contract for certain years or with the reservation to dismiss the freely called person. God nowhere has granted or permitted those who call the right to make such a contract. Hence, neither the one calling nor the one who is called may regard such a call or dismissal as divine" (*Theologia positivo-polemica,* part II, p. 530):

B. The minister must not tyrannize the church. He has no authority to introduce new laws or arbitrarily to establish adiaphora or ceremonies.

311

1. Scripture Proof

Our Lord said to His disciples: "You know that the rulers of the Gentiles lord it over them, and those who are great exercise authority over them. Yet it shall not be so among you" (Matt. 20:25–26). "Do not be called 'Rabbi'; for One is your Teacher, the Christ, and you are all brethren" (Matt. 23:8). In addition, Christ testified before Pilate: "My kingdom is not of this world. If My kingdom were of the world, My servants would fight, so that I should not be delivered to the Jews" (John 18:36).

From these passages we learn that the church of Jesus Christ is not a kingdom of rulers and subjects but one large, holy brotherhood, in which no one may rule and exercise authority. This required equality among Christians is not abrogated by the obedience that the hearers render to their ministers who teach them the Word of Jesus Christ; for in that case they obey not the ministers but Christ Himself. However, this equality of believers is abrogated and the church is changed into a secular organization if a minister demands obedience not only to the Word of Christ, his own Lord and Head and that of all Christians, but also to what his own insight and experience regards as good and suitable. As soon, therefore, as adiaphora or things indifferent, that is, things that are neither commanded nor forbidden in God's Word, come in question in the church, a minister may never demand absolute obedience to what merely appears to him to be best.

On the contrary, it is rather the concern of the whole congregation, of the minister as well as the hearers, to decide on what should be accepted or rejected. It of course behooves the minister, according to his office as teacher, supervisor, and watchman, to direct the deliberations that are held on the matter. He must instruct the congregation and see to it that also in the determination of adiaphora and the establishment of ecclesiastical regulations and ceremonies the congregation does not act frivolously or establish something that is hurtful. Therefore, the holy apostle writes: "The elders who are among you I exhort, I who am a fellow elder: . . . Shepherd the flock of God which is among you, serving as overseers, not by constraint but willingly, not for dishonest gain but eagerly; nor as being lords over those entrusted to you, but being examples to the flock" (1 Peter 5:1–3). And Paul, who before had asked the

Corinthians for alms on behalf of the poor at Jerusalem: "I speak not by commandment, but I am testing the sincerity of your love by the diligence of others" (2 Cor. 8:8). Again, when he had recommended celibacy for the time of persecution: "This I say for your own profit, not that I may put a leash on you, but for what is proper, and that you may serve the Lord without distraction" (1 Cor. 7:35).

If then the holy apostles write such things as: "The rest I will set in order when I come" (1 Cor. 11:34), it is clear from what has been said that they established such indifferent regulations not by way of command but by way of advice and with the consent of the whole congregation.

2. Witnesses of the Church in Its Official Confessions

Augsburg Confession: "This power of the keys or of the bishops is administered and exercised only by teaching and preaching God's Word and administering the sacraments, either to many or to individuals, as the call may be" (Art XXVIII, par 8; German text, *Triglot,* p. 84).

Apology: "It is also certain that this statement of the Lord Christ, 'He who hears you hears Me' (Luke 10:16), does not speak of traditions but is altogether contrary to them; for here the apostles do not receive a *mandatum cum libera,* that is, an altogether free and unlimited command and authority, but a limited command, namely, to preach not their own word but that of God and the Gospel. By these words ('He who hears you hears Me') the Lord Christ desires to strengthen the whole world, which indeed was necessary so that we may be absolutely sure that the preached [*leibliche*] Word is God's power and that no one may look to heaven and seek a different word. Therefore, this statement ('He who hears you,' etc.) cannot be understood of traditions.

"Christ here desires that they should so teach that by their mouth people hear Christ Himself. Hence they must not preach their own words but His Word, His voice and Gospel, so that Christ is heard. This comforting statement, which supports our teaching most strongly and contains much needed doctrine and consolation for Christian consciences, these foolish asses refer to their silly traditions, such as food, drink, clothing, and other kid stuff [*Kinderwerk*].

"They also quote the passage: 'Obey those who rule over you'

313

(Heb. 13:17). This passage demands that we should obey the Gospel. It does not give the bishops any rule of their own or any lordship outside the Gospel. Hence, the bishops should not introduce traditions against the Gospel, nor should they interpret their traditions against the Gospel. If they do this, then the Gospel forbids us to obey them, as Paul writes to the Galatians: 'If anyone preaches any other gospel to you . . . let him be accursed' (Gal. 1:9).

"We reply the same thing to the passage: 'The scribes and the Pharisees sit in Moses' seat. Therefore whatever they tell you to observe, that observe and do' (Matt. 23:2–3). It is certain that this passage does not command us *universaliter,* generally, that we should observe all things that they command, even things against God's Word and command; for in another passage Scripture teaches: 'We ought to obey God rather than men' (Acts 5:29). If they teach anything unchristian and unscriptural, we should not obey them. Hence, this passage does not establish any rule outside the Gospel. Therefore, they cannot prove their authority, which they have established outside the Gospel, from the Gospel; for the Gospel does not speak of traditions but of teaching God's Word" (Art. XXVIII [XIV], par. 18–21; German text, *Triglot,* p. 448).

Smalcald Articles: "In 1 Cor. 3:6, 21 Paul makes all ministers equal and teaches that the church is greater than the ministers. Therefore, it cannot truly be said that Peter had any superiority or power over the church before the other apostles and all other ministers. For he writes: 'All things are yours: whether Paul or Apollos or Cephas' (1 Cor. 3:21–22). That is to say: Neither Peter nor any other minister may arrogate to himself any power or superiority over the church. No one should burden the church with his traditions, but it remains true that no one's power or respect has greater validity than God's Word.[15] We dare not regard the power of Cephas higher than that of the other apostles, following those who said: 'Since Cephas, who is the most eminent apostle, favors this or that, therefore also Paul and the others should favor it.' 'No,' says Paul, pulling off Peter's little hat, that is, the claim that his respect and power should be greater than that of the other apostles or of the church" (Of the Power and Primacy of the Pope, par. 11; German text, *Triglot,* p. 506).

The same: "And with the words, 'Whatever you bind,' etc. (Matt. 18:18), Christ adds, 'Where two or three are gathered together in

My name,' etc. (v. 20) in order to indicate to whom the keys were given. Likewise, Christ gives the highest and final jurisdiction [*Gericht*] to the church when he says, 'Tell it to the church' (v. 17)" (ibid., par 24; German text, *Triglot,* p. 510).

3. Witnesses of the Church in the Private Writings of Its Teachers

Luther: "The spiritual rule has to do only with sin. Wherever there is sin, there this rule should also be, but nowhere else. . . . But here we speak of sins that are real and true sins, that no one has fabricated, but in which we were born: sins that transgress God's commandments and against which the divine commandment testifies" (*House Postil,* "On the First Sunday After Easter," St. Louis edition, 13:541ff.).

The same: "Therefore, I say that neither the pope nor a bishop nor any other person has the authority to prescribe to a Christian even the least command [*eine Silbe zu setzen*] unless he consents to it. Whatever else is done stems from a tyrannical spirit" ("On the Babylonian Captivity of the Church," 1520, St. Louis edition, 19:68).

The same: "But how, if they were compelled to admit that we all, as many of us as are baptized, are also priests? Such indeed we are, and we have entrusted to them alone the ministry, but with our consent. Therefore, they must also acknowledge that they have neither the right nor the power to command us, except as we ourselves permit them of our own free will" (ibid., pp. 113–14).

The same: " ' . . . nor as being lords over those entrusted to you' (1 Peter 5:3). These like to rule for the sake of honor, ride high, and act as mighty tyrants. Therefore, he admonishes them not to conduct themselves as though the people were subject to them and they could be the lords and do as they please. We indeed have one Lord, who is Christ, and He rules our souls. The pastors [*Bischöfe*] should do nothing but feed the flock. In this way St. Peter overthrows and condemns with one word the whole rule of the pope. He clearly concludes that they do not have the power to issue a single command. They should rather be servants and say: 'Your Lord Christ says this, and therefore you should do it.' Christ says that very thing: 'The kings of the Gentiles exercise lordship over them, and those who exercise authority over them are called "benefactors." But not so among you' (Luke 22:25–26). Against this the pope now says: 'You

315

shall exercise lordship and have authority' " (Exposition of 1 Peter 5:3, 1523, St. Louis edition, 9:1102–03).

The same: "But you might say: 'Since then among Christians there should be no secular sword, how are they to be ruled outwardly [*äußerlich*]? There must be government even among Christians.' I reply: Among Christians there neither shall nor can be government, but everyone should be subject to the other, as Paul writes: 'In honor giving preference to one another,' and 'Associate with the humble' (Rom. 12:10, 16). And Peter says: 'Yes, all of you be submissive to one another' (1 Peter 5:5). Christ also demands that: 'When you are invited by anyone to a wedding feast, do not sit down in the best place. . . . Go and sit down in the lowest place' (Luke 14:8, 10).

"There is among Christians no master [*Oberster*] except Christ Himself. How then can there be a government if all are equal and have one and the same right, power, possession, and honor? In addition, no Christian desires to be the master of the other, but everyone wants to be only the servant of the other. Among such persons it is impossible to establish a government, even if some would like to have it, since neither their disposition nor their nature allows them to have masters; here no one would or could be a master. But where there are not such persons, there also are no true Christians.

"What then are priests and bishops? I reply: Their rule is neither a government nor a power but a service and office, for they are neither higher nor better than are other Christians. Hence, they also should not put any law or command on others unless these consent and permit. Their office is nothing else than to teach God's Word. By that they direct Christians and overcome heretics. For, as said before, Christians can be ruled by no other means than by God's Word alone. Christians must be ruled by faith and not by outward works. But faith cannot come by any word of man, only by God's Word, as St. Paul says: 'Faith comes by hearing, and hearing by the Word of God' (Rom. 10:17).

"Those who do not believe are not Christians. They do not belong to the kingdom of Christ but to the secular kingdom, and they must be forced and ruled by the sword and outward government. Christians of their own will do everything that is good without coercion. Only God's Word satisfies them" ("On Secular Government," 1523, St. Louis edition, 10:405–06).

The same: "A bishop as bishop has no right to impose on his church any law or ceremony unless the church consents either expressly or silently. Because the church is free and the ruler, the bishops must not rule over the faith of the church or burden and trouble it against its will. They are only servants and stewards, not lords of the church. But if the church, as one body with the bishop, agrees, they may impose on each other whatever they will if only godliness does not suffer from it; they also may abolish such things as they please. But this kind of power the bishops do not seek; they want to rule and have all things their own way [*alles frei haben*]. This we will not grant them, nor in any way will we become partakers of their injustice and oppression of the church and the truth. . . .

"Therefore, we will not allow the bishops by either ecclesiastical or secular right to issue to the church any command, even if this would be ever so just and pious. For they must not do any evil in order that something good may result from it. But if they want to use tyranny and coercion, we must not obey or yield to them but rather die to preserve the distinction between these two rules, that is, for the will and command of God and against such wickedness and sacrilege [*Kirchenräubereien*]" ("Luther's Reply to Questions Concerning Human Laws Submitted by Melanchthon," 1530, St. Louis edition, 16:1014).

The same: "We must have that Man of whom it is written: 'Who committed no sin, nor was guile found in His mouth' (1 Peter 2:22). We will hear whatever He does and says according to the command of His Father (Matt. 17:5); by that we will judge both the apostles and the church, together with the angels. We indeed obey the apostles and also the church but only inasmuch as they bring with them the mark of that Man who said to them, *'Ego mitto vos, ite et praedicate Evangelium'* (I send you; go and preach the Gospel), and again, *'Docete eos, quae mandavi vobis'* (Teach them all that I have commanded you). If they do not bring that mark, we shall hear them no more than St. Paul listened to Peter (Gal. 2:11ff.). Let them cry as loud as they want to; we will do nothing else" ("On the Private Mass and Holy Orders," 1533, St. Louis edition, 19:1234–35).

Melanchthon: "The laws of priests in civil affairs are contrary to

317

love and have been issued by sheer tyranny" (*Loci theologii,* cf. "Decad.," 704).

Chemnitz: "If anyone would have ascribed to the apostles during their lifetime divine authority to issue laws for which they had no command or testimony in the divine Word or said that they could reestablish what Christ had abrogated or again establish what He had abolished, they doubtless would have cried out aloud, while rending their garments, that they could neither acknowledge nor approve such authority" (*Examen Concilii Tridentini,* "De bon. opp.," p. 179).

Gerhard: "Some divide the *potestas ordinis* (the power of the ministry) into two special parts, namely, (1) the dogmatical part, which is the power of the church regarding doctrine and the articles of faith or the power to preserve the Scriptures as a notary, read them diligently, judge articles of faith according to Scripture, distinguish as a judge between the genuine or true Scriptures and the spurious or false, prove the doctrine from Scripture, and reject all false doctrine; and (2) the constitutive part, which is the authority to establish in outward or indifferent things directions and rules or definite ceremonies for order and propriety as well as to foster agreement among the members of the congregation for public worship or also to abolish them, as this is demanded by the need or benefit of the church. But these powers belong to the whole church and not especially to the clergy [*dem geistlichen Stand*]. However, we readily admit that the first and chief parts of this power pertain to the ministry of the church [*dem Kirchenamt*]" (*Loci theologici,* "De minist. eccl.," par. 193).

The same: "(The papists object:) 'Paul writes: "The rest I will set in order when I come" (1 Cor. 11:34), that is, because of the power given to him by God (2 Cor. 10:8). Hence, the apostle claimed for himself unlimited power arbitrarily to reestablish ordinances [*Einrichtungen*] in the church.' To this I reply: The apostle did not order these things by any unlimited power of his but with the added consent of the congregation. 2 Cor. 8:8: 'I speak not by commandment' " (ibid., par. 201).

Balduin: "It is useful and almost necessary that when customs are to be changed, it should not be done merely by the ministers or by the government, but the matter should be considered in an assembly of the congregation. The apostle himself and pious emperors—Constantine the Great, the two named Theodosius, Martian, Charlemagne, and others like them—convened synods in matters of religion. By no means did they commandingly cast a snare on their consciences by these innovators" (*Tractatus de casibus conscientiae,* 1139).

Dannhauer: "The ministers are servants of the congregation, and to the latter the final decision must be left" (*Hodosophia christiana,* p. 179).

Carpzov remarks on the statement of the Augsburg Confession: "Bishops or pastors may make ordinances," etc. (Art. XXVIII, par. 53; German text, *Triglot,* p. 90) as follows: "All this however does not exclude the consent of the church but rather includes it. The bishops must always have the consent of the church and can never make ordinances without the consent or against the will of the church" (*Isagoge in libros ecclesiarum luth. symbolicos,* p. 745).

We must keep in mind that our confessors indeed concede to the bishops the right to make ordinances, but they do not number this power among those that they have by divine right. Regarding such ordinances, therefore, our Confession says that the pastors may [*liceat*] make them, and that it behooves [*conveniat*] the Christian congregation to accept them "for the sake of love and peace" in order that in the church no disorder and confusion [*wüstes Wesen*] may arise. A Christian, therefore, is not compelled to observe such ordinances. Further down, Carpzov writes: "It must not be overlooked that when the Augsburg Confession here permits the bishops to establish ceremonies, this is done (1) according to the circumstances of that time when this authority was accorded them by human right, as the words, 'But that the bishops otherwise have power,' etc., remind us; (2) that thereby nothing was to be taken away from the right of the whole church, which also the Augsburg Confession indicates very clearly" (ibid., p. 750).

Calov: "In the holy ministry there are indeed grades regarding order but not regarding jurisdiction. With regard to this, however, there is a distinction between the Old and the New Testament. For in the Old there was a certain ecclesiastical jurisdiction as, for example, that of Aaron over the priests, Levites, and doorkeepers. But in the New Testament we do not acknowledge any ecclesiastical jurisdiction by divine right except the general rule that in the church all things should be done decently and in order. However, according to human and positive right, the lord of a territory exercises jurisdiction either by consistories or superintendents, as perhaps was the position that Titus had in Crete, or in whatever other way it may please him. But the proper order should not be violated, nor should the incumbents of the ministry be summoned before the village judges, or as they are called, the village mayors [*Schultheißen*] or also before the burgomasters and be forced by them to be put on trial.

"The late Dr. Myslenta has definitely proved how indecorous and unbecoming this is. Therefore, in well-ordered churches consistories have been established that will decide matters pertaining to the ministry, church, marriage, the investigation of transgressions by ministers, the visitation of congregations, matters of supervision, and the like" (*Systema locorum theologicorum,* 8:288).

Walch: "If a church is in a natural condition consisting of such persons as reside outside the civil community, then the whole congregation exercises the rule [*Regiment*]. It can administer this itself by collecting the votes or refer the supervision to a few persons or to one who shall govern the church" (*Lexikon,* "Kirchenregiment," p. 1556).

The same: "From what has been said, it may easily be judged how the apostolic church was ruled. There was nothing else than the power to establish in outward ecclesiastical matters whatever belonged to the maintenance of good order and to an easier way of realizing the purpose of the church. This power was common to ministers and hearers, and it excluded all sovereign authority. The fact that not only the apostles and ministers, though their authority prevailed above that of the others, but also the hearers had this power we learn from the books of the New Testament. From these we know that if there was something to consider and decide, the people also cast their vote" (*Compendium historiae ecclesiasticae recentissimae,* p. 431).

Chrysostom: "And how, you ask, does he (the minister) say to me what he himself does not do? . . . It is not he who tells you this. If you obey him [for his sake], then you already have your reward. It is Christ who admonishes you. I will say yet more: You may not even obey Paul if he should say something of his own, something human. But you must obey the apostle who has Christ speaking in him" (Sermon 2 on 2 Tim. 1; Montfaucon edition, 11:669).

Tertullian: "It is the Lord's right and free decision (to remit sins), not that of the minister; it is God's, not the priest's" (*De pudic. 21 fin.*).

Origen: "Whoever is called to be a bishop is not called to sovereign authority but to the service of the whole church" (*In Es. hom.* 6—Lommatzsch, 13:273; de la Rue 3:116).

Optatus: "The state is not in the church, but the church is in the state" (Quoted by Dannhauer, *Liber conscientiae* 1:901).

Bernard: "Let those prelates hear this who always want to terrify those entrusted to them but seldom profit them. Be instructed, you judges of the earth. Learn that you must be mother to your subjects and not lords. Strive to be loved rather than feared, and if at times severity is necessary, let it be paternal and not tyrannical. Prove yourselves mothers by loving care and fathers by earnest discipline. Why do you make the yoke of those heavier, while it behooves you to bear their burden?" (*Serm. 23 super Cant.*).

The same: "This is the apostolic way: Tyranny is forbidden but serving is commanded. This is recommended to you also by the example of the Lawgiver, who, while giving the Law, said: 'I am among you as a servant.' Who should be dishonored by this title, which the Lord of glory gave to Himself as an example for us?" (*L. I de consideratione*).

C. The minister has no right to inflict and carry out excommunication without his having first informed the whole congregation.

1. Scripture Proof

It is certain that the office of the keys in a more narrow sense, namely, the power publicly to loose and bind, is also entrusted to the incumbents of the ministry of the Word. Nevertheless, it does not lie within the power of the minister to excommunicate a sinner without his having first informed the congregation. Otherwise the congregation would have to obey the minister blindly, even in matters pertaining to salvation. Here he deals not merely with a clear doctrine of the divine Word but with a judgment of a person's spiritual condition [*Seelenzustand*]. And this judgment is of such a nature that it closes heaven to the person in question and forbids him brotherly fellowship with Christians, and vice versa. Therefore, although the public enforcement of excommunication belongs to and must remain with the incumbents of the ministry of the Word, according to the Lord's command and sacred institution, nevertheless, it must be carried out according to the Lord's express command and order only after the whole congregation (that is, the minister and hearer) has considered and made the final judicial decision on the matter.

For so it is written: "If your brother sins against you, go and tell him his fault between you and him alone. If he hears you, you have gained your brother. But if he will not hear you, take with you one or two more, that 'by the mouth of two or three witnesses every word may be established.' And if he refuses to hear them, tell it to the church. But if he refuses even to hear the church, let him be to you like a heathen and a tax collector. Assuredly, I say to you, whatever you bind on earth will be bound in heaven, and whatever you loose on earth will be loosed in heaven. Again I say to you that if two of you agree on earth concerning anything that they ask, it will be done for them by My Father in heaven. For where two or three are gathered together in My name, I am there in the midst of them" (Matt. 18:15–18).

Here Christ clearly gives the supreme jurisdiction to the church or congregation, as our Confessions say, and He desires that a sinner in a congregation be regarded as a heathen and a tax collector and that the dreadful judgment of excommunication be pronounced on him only after manifold private admonitions and the public admonition before and by the congregation have proved themselves fruitless, so that the congregation has unanimously decided to excommunicate him through its pastor.

For this reason even Paul did not desire to excommunicate the incestuous person at Corinth without the congregation, but he wrote them that, though he himself regarded the sinner as deserving excommunication, the congregation itself ("when you are gathered together") should put away from among themselves that wicked person (1 Cor. 5:4, 13). So also St. John severely rebuked Bishop Diotrephes because he loved to have the preeminence (*philoprō-teuōn*) and arbitrarily cast out of the church pious Christians who perhaps opposed his tyranny (3 John 9–10).

322

However, it is hardly necessary to mention that what the congregation did man for man at the time of the apostles (2 Cor. 2:6; 1 Tim. 5:20) also may be done by the presbytery or consistory alone, wherever a ruling congregation is represented by a presbytery or consistory made up of ecclesiastical and secular states, so that the excommunication is valid and legitimate if only it is accomplished with the knowledge and consent of the church members.

2. Witnesses of the Church in Its Official Confessions

Smalcald Articles: "It is certain that all pastors should have the common jurisdiction to excommunicate those who wallow in manifest vices, and that the bishops have tyrannically arrogated this power to themselves and have shamefully abused it to their own benefit. For the officials have intolerably perverted it and have dreadfully tormented people of avarice or some other wicked cause, excommunicating them without any preceding process of law. What kind of tyranny is it that an official in a city should have the power merely because of his arbitrary judgment and without due process of law to plague and coerce the people in such a way by excommunication? And they indeed have used coercion in all kinds of things, not merely thereby to punish real vices for which excommunication is due but also for other minor matters, such as when the people did not rightly fast or observe the festivals. At times they did punish adultery, but they often slandered and defamed innocent persons.

"Since such an accusation is very grievous and weighty, no one should be condemned in such a case without due process of law and after proper admonition. But since the bishops tyrannically arrogated this jurisdiction to themselves and shamefully abused it, and there is also otherwise good reason not to obey them, it is right that this robbed jurisdiction should again be taken from them and restored to the pastors, to whom it belongs according to Christ's command, and that efforts should be made to use it in a right manner to better people's lives and increase God's glory" (Of the Power and Jurisdiction of Bishops, par. 74–75; German text, *Triglot,* p. 524).

The same: "And Christ adds to the words: 'Whatever you bind,' etc., in order to indicate to whom He has given the keys, the statement: 'Where two or three are gathered in My name,' etc. Likewise, Christ gives the highest and final jurisdiction to the church when

He says: 'Tell it to the church' " (ibid., par. 24; German text, *Triglot*, p. 510).

3. Witnesses of the Church in the Private Writings of Its Teachers

Luther: "In this passage you hear that there must be certain public sins of certain persons, as when a brother sees another sin; in addition, it must be such a sin as has been reproved before and has finally been proved publicly before the congregation. We read in the bulls and letters of excommunication: *'Excommunicamus ipso facto, data sententia, trina tamen monitione praemissa. Item de plenitudine potestatis'* (We excommunicate by this very fact, judgment having been given after a preceding threefold admonition. Therefore by the fulness of the power ...). Such an excommunication we call in German an excrement excommunication. I call it the devil's excommunication and not that of God when people are wickedly excommunicated against Christ's command before they have been convicted publicly.

"Just so are all excommunications with which officials and spiritual courts deceive and by which people are excommunicated merely by a notice attached to a church more than 10, 20, or 30 miles away, though in that congregation and before the pastor the persons have not been reproved, accused, or convicted. Instead, a bat flew there out of some official corner without any witnesses or God's command. Do not be afraid of such excrement excommunications. If a bishop or some other official desires to excommunicate a person, let him go or write to the congregation and its pastor that such and such a person should be excommunicated, and let him do what is right according to Christ's command. All this I say in order that the congregation that must excommunicate should know and be sure why the person deserves excommunication and how it has come to this, as the words of Christ here say. Otherwise it might be deceived, accept the excommunication, and do the neighbor an injustice.

"That would mean to blaspheme the keys, disgrace God, and violate love for the neighbor, and this a Christian congregation must not tolerate. For it also must take part if anyone is to be excommunicated, as Christ here says, and it need not believe the official's notice or the bishop's letter; indeed, it must not believe it, for in God's matters men must not be believed. A Christian congregation is not the servant of an official, nor is it the taskmaster of a bishop, so that he might say: 'Listen, Greta; listen, Johnny; excommunicate this or that person.' Oh, indeed, we do welcome you, dear official! In the secular government this certainly might make sense, but here where souls are concerned the congregation should also be judge and mistress. St. Paul was an apostle, yet he did not desire to excommunicate the incestuous person. He wanted the congregation to act also (1 Cor. 5:1, 5, 13)" ("Concerning the Keys," 1530, St. Louis edition, 19:950–51).

Flacius comments on the words, "In the name of our Lord Jesus Christ, when you are gathered together" (1 Cor. 5:4), as follows: "He (Paul) prescribes the way and manner of excommunication. They should gather together according to the command of Christ, and with prayer and equipped with the power of the keys and excommunication, which Christ has given them, they should excommunicate him" (*Clavis scripturae*).

In the ancient *Cynosura* of the church of Württemberg we read: "Ministers may counsel against, forbid, or by way of suggestion [*bittweis*] suspend from Holy Communion, but no minister shall administer public excommunication by his own authority" (Cf. Eckard, *Pastor conscient.*, p. 177).

Heshusius: "The final and highest church discipline, excommunication or exclusion from the church, must be administered by the congregation as Christ attests: 'If he refuses even to hear the church, let him be to you like a heathen and a tax collector.' . . . A small congregation of 10 or 20 persons that knows Christ rightly has just as much power in Christ's kingdom as a church consisting of many thousand persons" (Bidembach, *Cons. th.,* dec. 10, p. 226).

The same: "The highest power that the church has on earth is to retain the sins of impenitent, obstinate sinners and by excommunication to exclude them from the congregation. This jurisdiction properly belongs to the church, and if it is exercised by ministers, this is done only in the name and by the command of the congregation" (ibid., dec. 3, cons. 5, p. 387).

Chemnitz: "What Christ tells Peter in Matt. 16:19 He expressly tells the congregation in precisely the same words: 'Whatever you loose; whatever you bind,' etc. . . . In Matt. 18:15–16 Christ has established the procedure that sinners should be reproved either privately or before witnesses or publicly before the congregation (1 Tim. 5:20). If they accept the admonition and promise to make amends, Christ does not want to have anything inflicted on them but says: 'You have gained your brother' (Matt. 18:15). Similarly, Paul writes: 'A servant of the Lord must not quarrel but be gentle to all, able to teach, patient, in humility correcting those who are in opposition, if God perhaps will grant them repentance, so that they may know the truth, and that they may come to their senses and escape the snare of the devil, having been taken captive by him to do his will' (2 Tim. 2:24–26).

"But if the sinner will not listen to such admonitions, then tell it, as the Lord says, to the church, which (in apostolic times) publicly and in the name of all earnestly and sharply took such sinners to task, reproved, rebuked, reprimanded, and excommunicated them. This is what Paul means by the rebuke 'in the presence of all' (1 Tim. 5:20). But when afterward they noticed from the very fact that such excommunicated persons were sorry in a godly manner (2 Cor. 7:9), acknowledged the greatness of their sins, and earnestly requested forgiveness and reconciliation with God and the congregation so that they might again be received into the congregation— when the congregation saw that the discipline had its desired effect—it applied due moderation that the sinner, who already was sorry in a godly manner, might not by too rigid severity be driven to despair, hardening, or stubbornness or, as Paul says, be swallowed up with overmuch sorrow and Satan get the advantage of him (2 Cor. 2:7–11). . . .

"The church at Corinth had administered church discipline in its full severity to the incestuous person because he had been secure and impenitent. But when it noticed that by the work of the Holy Spirit the desired end of the discipline had been attained, namely, that he recognized the greatness of his sin and was made sorry by knowing and feeling God's wrath and that he humbly and earnestly sought divine grace, asking with ardent prayer that he might be absolved from his sin by the ministry of the Word, then the congregation resolved that the sinner should again be received, assured of forgiveness from the Gospel, and granted remission of sins by the keys of the kingdom of heaven.

"But because the committed crime was very great and they had

326

been sharply rebuked by the apostle because of their extreme levity toward the sinner, they reported the matter to him, asking what they were to do now. And since the circumstances were such as we depicted them above, Paul, approving the opinion and decision of the Corinthians, replied: 'This punishment which was inflicted by the majority is sufficient for such a man' (2 Cor. 2:6), that is, inflicted by the whole congregation. Therefore, as before when he was secure and impenitent, you accused, rebuked and bound him by retaining his sins, so now when he has been led to repentance, 'on the contrary, you ought to forgive and comfort him, lest perhaps such a one be swallowed up with too much sorrow' (2 Cor. 2:7). Afterward he adds another reason: 'Lest Satan should take advantage of us; for we are not ignorant of his devices' (v. 11).

"To confirm the verdict of the Corinthians Paul adds the words: 'Whom you forgive anything, I also forgive' (v. 10). Then showing his own example regarding the reinstatement of the sinner, he writes: 'For if indeed I have forgiven anything, I have forgiven that one for your sakes in the presence of Christ' (v. 10), who namely in Matt. 18:20 has promised: 'Where two or three are gathered together in My name, I am there in the midst of them.' Paul therefore admonishes them that as the incestuous person before had been excommunicated by the official [*öffentliches*] verdict of the congregation and delivered to Satan, that is, by the unanimous vote of the congregation had been declared to be no longer a member of Christ but of Satan, so now they were to confirm his reinstatement and readmission by the official authority of the congregation and its unanimous vote.

"For that is what the words of Paul express: 'Reaffirm your love to him' (v. 8); that is, prove and ratify your love, with which you will receive the repentant sinner, toward him, namely, by your official vote. For the Greek verb *kuroun* means to approve something by unanimous vote and with official authority and so to ratify it, render it valid, and keep it so. The fact that this is the sense of the Pauline passage (2 Cor. 2:6–11) is proved by the circumstances of the case, the context, and the very narrative itself, which I here wanted to treat at somewhat greater length. For this is, as we commonly say, the proper seat of the doctrine of church discipline, namely, of excommunication, public repentance, public absolution, and reinstatement of sinners, showing how it was constituted in apostolic times and with what aim, for what reason and purpose, and with what moderation it was instituted, observed, and applied. The Council of Trent should have considered how this apostolic discipline, which would be useful and salutary and in these times by all means necessary, might be restored" (*Examen Concilii Tridentini,* "De indulgentiis," pp. 75–78).

Gerhard: "Neither major nor minor excommunication may be administered by the ministers of the Word without the decision of the ecclesiastical senate [church council] or the consistory, because the power of excommunication does not belong to the bishop but to the elders who represent the whole congregation. In Matt. 18:17 we are told: 'Tell it to the church. But if he refuses even to hear the church,' that is, the elders and the council of seniors, 'let him be to you like a heathen and a tax collector,' who are outside the communion of the church. Indeed, major excommunication may be administered only with the knowledge and confirmation of the whole congregation. 'I indeed ... have already judged. ... In the name of our Lord Jesus Christ, when you are gathered together, along with my spirit ... deliver such a one to Satan' (1 Cor. 5:3–5). 'This punishment which was inflicted by the majority is sufficient for such a man' (2 Cor. 2:6).

"The most important acts of the church may not be undertaken without the consent of the whole church body, as Pope Leo writes: 'What concerns all should be done with the consent of all." But what could be more important and concern Christ's body more than to cut off a member from the body? And if the congregation is to abstain from all familiar and intimate fellowship with the excommunicated person, the excommunication should be administered in the assembly of the whole congregation and with its tacit approval" (*Loci theologici,* "De min. eccl.," par. 286).

Calov: "Concerning those who here (at the excommunication) participate, this may be administered neither alone by the ministers of the Word nor alone by the congregation but by the ministers and the assembly of the congregation together. Thus Paul calls himself absent in body but present in spirit, and the congregation is gathered together with his spirit in the name of Jesus Christ (1 Cor. 5:3–4). Grotius falsely interprets this to mean not all Christians but the best of them, but it would have been uncertain whom then to gather and declare to be the best. ... Though the apostle in this passage

328

joins the congregation, he here comes into consideration not as an apostle but as a minister of the church (1 Cor. 4:1). . . . The congregation however not only wafts prayers to God but also pronounces a judicial verdict that is valid in heaven" (*Biblia illustrata,* on 1 Cor. 5:5).

The same: "It is known that the church has the right to call, just as the keys and the authority of church discipline have also been entrusted to it (Matt. 18:18; 1 Cor. 3:21; 4:1; Rom. 3:2; 9:4; 1 Cor. 3:1ff.). The church, however, has not only entrusted this to the sacred ministry but administers it by itself and in consultation with all states" (*Systema locorum theologicorum* 8:334).

Dannhauer: "The third degree is that the matter be brought before the congregation (hence not before one single judge, as in ancient times at the Jewish judgment the final decision terminated with Moses [Ex. 18:21], but as divinely inspired and the mouth of God [v. 19]). Such a congregation consists of more than 'two or three,' that is, of an entire assembly, of 'the majority' (2 Cor. 2:6) or 'all' (1 Tim. 5:20). It may be representative and in this case either particular or general, consisting of classes of individuals, or it may be collective, consisting not of individuals of all classes, though none is to be excluded by any means. And excommunication may either be representative before the elders of the seniors according to ancient custom or before the consistory, or if the gravity of the case demands it, it may be collective before the whole congregation, or in case of an epidemic it may be at the general gathering of several congregations" (*Liber conscientiae apertus,* pp. 1153–54).

Theological Faculty at Wittenberg, 1638: "Just as the ecclesiastical government alone may not represent the church senate, so also the secular alone may not represent it. For when Christ commands that dissensions that cannot be resolved by private persons should be judged by the congregation (Matt. 18:17), He does not mean merely the apostles and the ministers of the Word much less merely the secular government but the whole congregation and those who represent the congregation. Therefore, among our adherents the consistories are made up not merely of secular states or merely of ecclesiastical states but of both the ecclesiastical and the secular, by whom church discipline is to be administered" (*Consilia Wittenb.* 2:136).

Brochmand: "Although the administration of the binding keys belongs especially to the duly called ministers of the divine Word, God has prevented pastors in so difficult a case from undertaking anything without the counsel of the elders and the whole congregation. Christ's instruction in Matt. 18:17 reads: 'If he refuses to hear them' (namely, the brethren that admonish privately), 'tell it to the church. But if he refuses even to hear the church, let him be to you like a heathen and a tax collector.' The fact that Paul followed this admonition of Christ at the excommunication of the incestuous person at Corinth is clear from his words: 'In the name of our Lord Jesus Christ, when you are gathered together, along with my spirit . . . ' (1 Cor. 5:4–5).

"That this should be done so today is demanded by the necessity of the matter itself. For since major excommunication means exclusion of a person from the house of God and the voluntary separation of the whole congregation from such a person, it is obvious that for the desired execution of so important a matter the agreement of the whole congregation is necessary. . . . Stapleton, in order to weaken our statement, raises these objections: (1) the authority and example of Paul, who alone excommunicated the incestuous Corinthian (1 Cor. 5:3: 'I . . . have already judged, as though I were present'); (2) the constant practice of the apostolic church, in which the decision, judgment, and power of excommunication belonged alone to one prelate, pastor, or bishop but never to the congregation; for only to Peter was it said: 'Feed My sheep' (John 21:6), and he alone excommunicated Simon Magus (Acts 8:21). So also Paul alone delivered Hymeneus and Alexander to Satan (1 Tim. 1:20), not to speak of the statements and procedure of Gregory of Nyssa, Chrysostom, Ambrose, and Jerome in various cases.

"It is not difficult to refute these objections. (1) Although the apostle took the lead at the excommunication of the incestuous Corinthian with his verdict, showing the church at Corinth as its pastor the way it should go, he did not at all deny the congregation its part in this difficult matter of excommunication. He rather, following the command of Christ, 'Tell it to the church,' addressed the church with these or similar words: 'When you are gathered together, along with my spirit, . . . deliver such a one to Satan. . . . Therefore purge out the old leaven' (1 Cor. 5:2–7).

"(2) What Peter did according to Acts 8:21 does not prove anything in his favor; for there is a difference between the two acts of announcing to an impenitent sinner that he would have neither part nor portion in the kingdom of God and excluding an impenitent sinner altogether from a congregation so that access to the sanctuary shall be closed to him and no pious church member may henceforth have any intimate fellowship with him. The former every minister of the Word may do according to Christ's command (Matt. 18:18), but the latter belongs to the congregation, as Christ declares in Matt. 18:17 and Paul in 1 Cor. 5:1ff.

"(3) Concerning Paul, who according to 1 Tim. 1:20 is said to have excommunicated Hymeneus and Alexander, there is not even the least word showing that the apostle excommunicated these persons alone and without the consent of the congregation. But even if he did, nothing may be proved from this case to favor the opinion of the opponents, for the apostle's authority and that of our bishops today is not at all the same. The latter may err in their judgment, but the apostles were led by the Spirit into all truth, and there was no danger of error (John 16:13)" (*Universae theologiae systema,* 2:379–80).

When Philumen and Fortunatus were to be excommunicated, *Cyprian* wrote: "I could not declare myself to be the judge alone, since many of the clergy were absent, and the matter had to be treated and investigated by every one of them at greater length, and that not only together with the colleagues but also with the whole people" (*Ep.* 28).

Augustine: "It behooves the bishop, as watchman over all, diligently to note sins. If he hears of one and carefully considers it, he should correct the matter by act. If he cannot do this, then according to the rule of the Gospel he should avoid the slaves of vice. For 'if (as the Lord says in the Gospel) your brother sins against you, go and tell him his fault between you and him alone. . . . If he refuses even to hear the church, let him be to you like a heathen and a tax collector' (Matt. 18:15–17). According to this order, whoever refuses to obey a minister or bishop is to be expelled, and he who is expelled according to this order must not be received by any other minister or bishop" (*De duodecim abus. gradibus*).

331

Thesis X

To the ministry of the Word, according to divine right, belongs also the duty [Amt] *to judge doctrine, but laymen also possess this right. Therefore, in the ecclesiastical courts (consistories) and councils they are accorded both a seat and vote together with the clergy.*

1. Scripture Proof

The fact that it is the duty of the ministers to judge doctrine requires no proof, for the ministerial office could not be administered without judging doctrine. However, according to God's Word, the right to judge doctrine has not been taken away from the laymen by the establishment of the ministry. On the contrary, this is their most sacred duty, as in the first place all those passages of Holy Scripture that command laymen to judge doctrine incontestably declare. The holy apostle Paul thus writes: "I speak as to wise men; judge for yourselves what I say. The cup of blessing which we bless, is it not the communion of the blood of Christ? The bread which we break, is it not the communion of the body of Christ?" (1 Cor. 10:15–16). Further: "Test the spirits, whether they are of God" (1 John 4:1; cf. 2 John 10–11; 1 Thess. 5:12).

Further proof may be found in all those passages in which Christians are asked to beware of false prophets (Matt. 7:15–16; John 10:5), as well as from those in which their zeal in testing doctrine is praised. Of the Christians at Berea we are told: "These were more fair-minded than those in Thessalonica, in that they received the Word with all readiness, and searched the Scriptures daily to find out whether these things were so' (Acts 17:11). Finally, the Book of Acts tells us that at the first council of the apostles laymen not only were present but also spoke. The resolutions were prepared by them as well as by the apostles and elders and were drawn up also in their name. Hence, there can be no doubt that in ecclesiastical courts and at synods laymen should have both seat and voice together with the ministers of the Word.

2. Witnesses of the Church in Its Official Confessions

Smalcald Articles: "Thus the pope acts on both sides as a tyrant, for he defends such errors with tyranny and fury and will not suffer any [lay] judges. And this second part does more harm than all his fury, for when the church has been robbed of its right judgment and knowledge, it is impossible to hinder adulterated doctrine and false services, and so many souls must be lost. . . . But since the judgments of the councils are those of the church, not of the pope, it behooves princes and kings not to yield to such papistic wicked-ness [*Mutwillen*]. The churches should not be robbed of their power to judge doctrine, and all things should be judged according to Holy Scripture as the Word of God. Just as Christians should rebuke all other errors of the pope, so they are in duty bound to reprove the pope himself if he wants to avoid or hinder the right judgment and true knowledge of the church" (Of the Power and Primacy of the Pope, par. 51; German text, *Triglot,* p. 518).

3. Witnesses of the Church in the Private Writings of Its Teachers

Luther: "It belongs to each and every Christian to know and judge doctrine, indeed so much so that anyone who weakens this right even in the least is condemned. For Christ Himself has commanded this right in many irrefutable passages, as, for example, Matt. 7:15: 'Beware of false prophets, who come to you in sheep's clothing.' This admonition he certainly addresses to the people against the teachers, commanding them to avoid their false doctrine. But how can they avoid it if they do not recognize it? And what good does it do to recognize it if they do not have the right to judge it? He not only gives them the right to judge but also commands them to judge.

"This one passage suffices against all popes, fathers, councils, and all the declarations of the schools that ascribe the right to judge and to decree [*schließen*] to the bishops and clergy alone while they

333

wickedly and sacrilegiously have taken it away from the people, that is, the church, the queen. For here Christ comes [*stehet*] and says: 'Beware of false prophets.' And almost all words [*Silben*] of the prophets agree with that. For what else would the prophets do than warn the people not to believe false prophets? What else does this warning mean than to show that the people have the right to judge and recognize? What else does this mean than to announce and certify that the people must take care of all it does and always carefully beware of what their priests and doctors teach? Hence, we conclude that as often as Moses, Joshua, David, and all other prophets in the Old Testament [*im alten Gesetz*] call the people away from and warn them against false prophets, so often they cry, command, announce, and confirm the people's right to judge and recognize all teachings of all men. And this they do in ever so many passages.

"Can our Hank [*Heinz*—King Henry VIII of England] or any infamous Thomist say anything against this? Have we not here stopped the mouth of all those who at this point teach error? But let us return to the New Testament. When Christ says: 'My sheep hear My voice' (John 10:27); 'they will by no means follow a stranger, but will flee from him' (v. 5), does He not appoint the sheep as judges and give the hearers the right to recognize? ... Whatever Christ says by way of command in Matt. 24:23–24 and elsewhere [*allenthalben*] of false teachers, Peter and Paul of false apostles and masters, and John of proving the spirits all serves to declare that the people have the right to judge, prove, and condemn, and this with absolute authority. For as everyone believes rightly or wrongly at his own peril, so everyone should justly see to it that he believes rightly. Hence even common sense and the need to be saved suggest that the hearer must of necessity judge doctrine.

"Otherwise Scripture says in vain: 'Test all things; hold fast what is good' (1 Thess. 5:21). Again: 'He who is spiritual judges all things, yet he himself is rightly judged by no one' (1 Cor. 2:15). But every Christian is spiritual by the Spirit of Christ. 'All things are yours: whether Paul or Apollos or Cephas' (1 Cor. 3:21–22), that is, you have the right to judge all words and deeds. So you see what spirit moved the infamous, atrocious councils that dared ascribe to the popes the right to judge and recognize against such important passages and thunder blasts and against such clear declarations [*Sprüche*], and to award to them absolutely and in all things the right to command and enact laws. Without doubt this was the devil's strategy [*Gedanken*], by which he flooded the world with all actions of unrighteousness and placed the abomination of desolation in the holy place. In addition, the people were robbed of the power to judge by this greatest tyranny, which otherwise all false prophets were apt to avoid. Finally, by the foolish and superstitious obedience and endurance of the people the way was paved for all kinds of errors and abominations, which then could gain ground everywhere.

"And as I here think of my Hank and the sophists whose faith is built on the length of the times and the multitude of the people, it is undeniable that this tyranny, by which the people's right was robbed, lasted perhaps more than a thousand years. For already at the council of Nicaea, which after all was the best, they began to enact laws and to arrogate to themselves this right. And gradually it spread so far that nothing is more common or more firm than this right, because it can be proved by the multitude of persons and the duration of the custom. So today it is not easy for anyone who does not regard it as salutary, right, and divine. But here you see that it is nothing but sacrilege [*Kirchenraub*] and wickedness against the clearest and most convincing divine Scriptures. Hence, since so great an error and sacrilege has prevailed against the divine truth for so long a time and with so many people who either approved it or were misled by it or became accustomed to it [*beigefallen*], I herewith want to grind to powder, for the benefit of all sophists and papists, their primary foundation and stop their mouth in order that they might see that God does not want us to believe any creature, whether it is long, great, big, or broad, but only the Word of God, which alone is infallible.

"Accordingly we believe as an incontrovertible truth that the right to recognize, judge, or test doctrine is ours and not that of the councils, popes, fathers, and teachers. But from this it does not follow that we have the power to make laws. That authority belongs only to God, but to us belongs the right to recognize, prove, and judge His Law and Word and to separate that from all other enactments. But we have no right to enact laws or to command anything. From the words of Christ, 'Beware of false prophets,' it does not follow that we have the power to prophesy. Indeed, as Peter says: 'Prophecy never came by the will of man, but holy men of God spoke as they were moved by the Holy Spirit' (2 Pet. 1:21). So also, from the words, 'My sheep hear My voice,' it does not follow that My sheep will make [*geben*] or create My voice. On the contrary, the very opposite follows: I will cause My voice to be heard, but My sheep will recognize, test, and follow it when I have made it known. . . .

"But now they will say: 'If everybody has the authority to judge and test, how shall we deal with the situation when the judges do not agree and everyone judges according to his own opinion? There must of necessity be someone with whom all judges agree and are satisfied in order that the unity of the church might be preserved.' Answer: Such silly talk [*Schwätzerei*] becomes no one better than the Thomists. Let me in return ask: How shall we today assert our right, since we all are subject to the judgment of the pope? How is the unity preserved under these circumstances? Does it preserve the unity inviolate if people nominally join the pope? What becomes of the unity of the heart? Who is assured in his conscience that the pope judges rightly? Where there is no assurance, there also is no unity. So then there is in the papacy an outward appearance and show of unity, but inwardly there is nothing but the most atrocious Babylon, where no stone is left on the other and no one [*Herz*] agrees with the other.

"So you see how wonderfully human arrogance can counsel with its decrees in spiritual matters. Therefore, we must find another way for the unity of the church, and that is none other than what Christ mentions: 'They shall be all taught by God. Therefore everyone who has heard and learned from the Father comes to Me' (John 6:45). The inward Spirit alone causes us to dwell together in a house with one accord. He teaches us to believe the same thing, to judge the same thing, to recognize the same thing, to prove the same thing, to teach the same thing, to confess the same thing, and to follow the same thing. Where He is lacking, unity cannot exist. Where there is any other kind of unity, it is only outward and whitewashed.

"Therefore, God also does not care whether wicked people agree or not, for they are without the unity of the Spirit. It suffices His children for outward unity that they have one Baptism and one Bread as their common tokens and symbols (or watchwords). Thereby they confess and practice their faith and the unity of the Spirit. The papistic church seeks its unity in accord with its outward idol, the pope, though inwardly it is torn to pieces by the most horrible errors to the great joy of Satan" ("Against Henry, King of England," 1522, St. Louis edition, 19:341ff.).

The same: "Human words and teaching have established and decreed that we should leave it to bishops, scholars, and councils alone to judge doctrine. What they decide the whole world should regard as right and as an article of faith. That is sufficiently proved by their continuous [*täglich*] boasting of the pope's spiritual authority. For we hear almost nothing else of them than this boast that the power and authority is theirs to judge what is Christian or heretical, and that the common layman [*der gemeine Christenmann*] should wait for their judgment and adhere to it. Behold how arrogant and foolish is this boast that they have forced on the whole world and that is their greatest defense and armor, and how fiercely it opposes God's law and Word! For Christ teaches the very opposite, taking from the bishops, scholars, and councils both the right and the authority to judge doctrine and giving it to everyone, to all Christians in common. He says: 'The sheep . . . know his voice' (John 10:4). Again: 'They will by no means follow a stranger, but will flee from him, for they do not know the voice of strangers' (v. 5). Again: 'All who ever came before Me are thieves and robbers, but the sheep did not hear them' (v. 8).

"Here you clearly see whose right it is to judge doctrine. Bishops, popes, scholars, and everyone else have the power to teach, but the sheep should judge whether they teach Christ's voice or whether it is the voice of a stranger. My dear friend, what are these soap bubbles [*Wasserblasen*] going to say against these words? They scrape and scratch [*scharren*], crying: 'Councils, councils! Oh, you must listen to the scholars, the bishops, the big crowd [*die Menge*]! You must observe the ancient usage and custom!' Do you think I will allow the Word of God to yield to your ancient usage, custom, and bishops? Never! We will let bishops and councils decree and establish whatever they desire. But where we have God's Word before us, it should be ours and not theirs to say whether a thing is right or wrong, and they must yield to us and obey our Word. Here I think you see clearly enough how those who deal with souls by the word of man may be trusted. Who does not see that all bishops, religious establishments, cloisters, learned schools, and everything that belongs to them rage against this clear Word of Christ, arrogantly taking from

337

the sheep the right to judge doctrine and by their own law and wickedness usurp it to themselves? Therefore, it is certain that they must be regarded as murderers, thieves, wolves, and renegade Christians who here have been convicted publicly as not only denying God's Word but also opposing and acting against it, according to the prophecy of St. Paul in 2 Thess. 2:3–4.

"Again, Christ says: 'Beware of false prophets, who come to you in sheep's clothing, but inwardly they are ravenous wolves' (Matt. 7:15). See, here Christ gives the authority to judge not to prophets and teachers but to pupils and sheep. For how can they beware of false prophets if they should not consider, judge, and test doctrine? Hence, there can be no false prophet among the hearers, only among the teachers. For this reason, all teachers with their doctrine must be subject to the judgment of the hearers.

"A third passage is from St. Paul: 'Test all things; hold fast what is good' (1 Thess. 5:21). Here the apostle does not want any teaching or law to be observed unless the congregation that has heard it has first tested and approved it. This proving does not belong to the teachers, but the teachers are first to declare what is to be tested. So also here the right to judge is taken from the teachers and given to the pupils among the Christians. Hence, among Christians it is by far a different matter than with the world. In the world lords command whatever they desire, and the subjects submit to it. However, as Christ says, among you it shall not be so, but among Christians everyone is the judge of the other and again is also subject to the other. But the ecclesiastical [*geistlichen*] tyrants have turned Christendom into a secular government.

"A fourth passage is again from Christ: 'Take heed that no one deceives you. For many will come in My name, saying, "I am the Christ," and will deceive many' (Matt. 24:4–5). In short: What need is there to adduce more passages? All warnings of St. Paul such as Rom. 16:17–18; 1 Cor. 10:14; Gal. 3:4–5; Col. 2:8; and others, as well as all declarations of the prophets that teach that the doctrines of man should be avoided, do nothing else than take the right and authority to judge doctrine from the teachers and with earnest prayer place it on the hearers at the peril of their souls as those who not only have the right and power to judge everything that is preached but also are in duty bound to judge in order that they might not incur the displeasure of the divine Majesty.

"For we see in what unchristian way the tyrants have dealt with us by taking this right and command from us, usurping it to themselves. By that they have richly deserved that they should be driven and chased out of Christendom as wolves, thieves, and murderers who tyrannize and teach us against God's Word and will. So we conclude that wherever there are Christian congregations with the Gospel, they not only have the right and authority, which they assumed toward Christ in their Baptism, but also the duty, at the peril of their souls, to avoid, flee, reject, and renounce the tyranny that bishops, abbots, cloisters, religious establishments, and their ilk now exercise; for it is obvious to all that they teach and tyrannize us contrary to God and His Word. Therefore, for the present this is grounded surely and firmly enough, so that we may rely on the fact that it is divinely right and necessary for our salvation that bishops, abbots, cloisters, and whatever other similar rulers there may be must be abrogated or avoided" ("That a Christian Assembly or Congregation Has the Right and Authority to Judge All Doctrine," 1523, St. Louis edition, 10:1540ff.).

The same: "The seventh and last office [of a congregation] is to judge and recognize all doctrine. There is indeed no small reason why these hypocritical priests [*Priesterlarven*] and painted Christians have usurped this office for themselves. They well knew that if this office would be held by the congregation, none of those mentioned before would remain theirs. For if the right to judge doctrine is taken from the hearers, what might or could not a doctor or teacher dare [to teach]; if it were possible, it would be even worse than the devil. On the other hand, if the right to judge doctrine were granted or commanded to the hearers, what might or could a teacher venture even though he were more than an angel? For if that were permitted, then Paul would not only reprove Peter but would condemn even an angel from heaven.

"No doubt the popes and councils would have spoken and decreed about the priesthood, the ministry, and such other offices as to baptize, bless, bind, pray, and judge doctrine with much greater fear and trembling [*Schrecken*] if they would have had to fear the judgment and condemnation of the hearers; in fact, the papacy would never at all have developed if this rule would have prevailed. Hence, they did themselves a good turn by usurping this office solely to themselves. They were able to do and preserve this until the

339

wrath of God will be fulfilled, as the prophet says in Dan. 11:36. But now since Christ comes and enlightens us with His glory [*Zukunft*], this rascal [*Schalk*; the pope] is beginning to be destroyed. The breath of His mouth kills this Antichrist, 'who opposes and exalts himself above all that is called God' and His glory (2 Thess. 2:4–8).

"Here stand the words of Christ: My sheep 'do not know the voice of strangers' (John 10:5). 'Beware of false prophets' (Matt. 7:15). 'Beware of the leaven of the Pharisees and of the Sadducees' (Matt. 16:6). 'The scribes and the Pharisees sit in Moses' seat. Therefore whatever they tell you to observe, that observe and do, but do not do according to their works' (Matt. 23:2–3). By these and other similar passages of the Gospel and of all Scripture (which admonish us not to believe false teachers) what else does Jesus teach us than that everyone should take heed to his eternal welfare and salvation so that he may know and be sure what he should believe and whom he should follow? So also that he should be a free, authoritative judge of all those who wish to teach him, since inwardly he is taught of God (John 6:45)? God will not condemn or save you by the doctrine of someone else but only by *your* faith. Anyone may teach or preach whatever he desires, but you must see to what you believe, to either your great harm or benefit" ("How One Should Choose and Install Pastors," Letter to the council and congregation of the city of Prague, 1523, St. Louis edition, 10:1585ff.).

The same: "Behold, therefore, what kind of doctors of Holy Scripture St. Paul creates, namely, all who believe and no one else. These should decide and judge all doctrine, and their judgment should stand, even if it concerns the pope, the councils, and the whole world. For faith is and must be the lord and god of all doctrine. From this you see how the clergy [*geistliche Stand*] act who do not leave this judgment to faith but have usurped it to themselves as they have arrogated to themselves all the power of the people [*Menge*] and of the secular government [*der weltlichen Höhe*]. But you should know that popes, councils, and all the world with all they teach are subject to even the humblest Christian, though he be a child of seven years, if he has faith, and you should accept his judgment regarding their doctrines and laws. Christ says: 'Take heed that you do not despise one of these little ones' (Matt. 18:10). Again: 'They shall be all taught by God' (John 6:45). It is certainly not right to despise those whom God has taught, but all should hear them"

340

(*Church Postil: Epistle Portion,* "On the Second Sunday After the Epiphany," 1524, St. Louis edition, 12:335–36).

The same: "Perhaps they will rebuke you before the common people and those who otherwise are unwise, since they are not yet recognized by the church as wolves and false teachers, but are regarded as true Christians. Yes, it is wisely and well said that if the sheep should not flee from the wolves before the wolves by their Christian councils and public condemnation have commanded the sheep to flee, then the sheepfold will soon be empty, and the shepherd someday will find neither milk, cheese, butter, wool, meat, nor claw. That certainly would be some shepherding of the sheep! What then did Christ, our Lord, have in mind when He ordered and commanded us to beware of the wolves without waiting for the council of the wolves? He not only commanded the whole flock of sheep to flee from the wolves, but each sheep for itself has the right and authority to flee from the wolves wherever it may be. This He says: 'My sheep will flee from the stranger' (John 10:5).

"How? Have they [the papists] no attorneys or have they all become mad and foolish? Our attorneys as well as our reason say that no one should be his own judge, just as our Book, Holy Scripture, also forbids this. Now it is clear that we have become opponents of the papacy and they again oppose us. Who then may or should be the judge here? There is no one above the pope and the papacy except God alone, as he himself admits (but oh, how reluctantly!). Now God acts as Judge through His holy Word, which they themselves are forced to confess. But why do they want to be judges when they are opponents [*Part*] and admit that God's Word condemns and opposes them? Or do they think that we should be afraid of those who have convicted and condemned themselves through God's Word? We might mock such fools or pray for such erring people, but we cannot be afraid of such devil's masks [*Teufelslarven*]. Yet our body, property, and honor may be at stake! Indeed, they [the papists] are secure and grown old [*sie sitzen in der Gewähr und Verjährung*], that is, [having] *possessorium, praescriptio* (possession, judicial exception).

"Now all laws declare that no one is to be removed from his possession. But this is going to get too high and hard for me. Where then can I secure a good attorney and procurator? I answer simply: God is God, and no creature has any possession or judicial exception against Him and His Word, for He is eternal, and eternity exceeds possession and judicial exception. Otherwise the serpent would justly have gained the victory over God, because from the beginning of the world it has strengthened its seed against that of the woman and has bruised His heel, as it still does until the end of the world. If it would concern the possession of a cow, that is, if it would concern temporal and worldly goods, then possession might count. But in spiritual and eternal matters, of which we speak here, possession, judicial exception, right, justice, holiness, and religion, indeed, all angels from heaven mean nothing. But God alone means all in all—all hours, all times, in all places, and all persons. For He will and must not be limited, possessed, or judicially excepted. Otherwise He will possess and judicially except all things in hell, as He will do on Judgment Day.

"Therefore, be silent in this matter and do not speak for your possession, acquired right, or whatever you want to mention. God and spiritual matters do not trouble themselves about such things. Be guided by that, for nothing else will come from it. He has the power at all times to cast out the devil. Do not hinder Him in that. So also He has the power to change the world essentially. About this He will not consult you. Who can prescribe to Him the goal, time, right, place, and person, since He must create, make, and do all this?

"Let this suffice for the first part. Whoever has no ears cannot hear, and whoever has no eyes cannot see. But whoever has ears has herewith heard enough. God's judgment has decreed that no wolf should be a bishop in the Christian church. Even if emperors, kings, popes, and all the devils would command and decree anything else, they cannot prevent Christ's sheep from listening to the voice of their Shepherd. Nor can they command the sheep to obey the voice of a wolf. And even if they should undertake this, they (the sheep) should and must flee from the wolves, following their command [from the Lord] as the wolves follow theirs. That is what God desires against all emperors, indeed against all devils, who are nothing and vanity as the prophet says in Is. 40:17" ("Example of How to Ordain a True Christian Bishop," 1542, St. Louis edition, 17:102–04).

The same: "Nevertheless, in every way the matters should be heard soon and rightly judged. To such a trial not only the priests are to be invited but also pious, learned persons from the secular states and eminent members of the church. For when our Savior Christ says, 'Tell it to the church,' He by these words commands the church to be the supreme judge. From this it follows that not only one state [*Stand*], namely, that of the bishops, but also other pious and learned persons from all states are to be appointed as judges and have decisive votes" ("The Wittenberg Reformation," 1545, St. Louis edition, 17:1159).

Heshusius: "In Matt. 18:17–18 the Lord Christ entrusts the supreme jurisdiction and power in matters of the church not to the secular government but to His congregation. Among these matters the most important are the election and calling of ministers and the right to judge doctrine and to depose unfaithful pastors. He says expressly that whoever does not want to hear the church shall be regarded as an excommunicated heathen and a tax collector. This is to be understood in the sense not only that the church has the power to excommunicate impenitent sinners but also that the congregation has the supreme authority in all church matters such as reproof, church discipline, divisions, judging doctrine, and appointing pastors, to mention only these things" (*Concerning Calling and Deposing Ministers* [Gießen, 1608], pp. 50–51).

For the doctrine set forth in this thesis *Chemnitz* supplies the best testimony by his own example. For when a certain school principal in Brunswick held an erroneous doctrine and among other things also rejected the Formula of Concord, Chemnitz presented the matter to the whole congregation as to the final and supreme judge. This matter is described at great length in Val. Löscher, *Unschuldige Nachrichten* (1728), pp. 223ff., which the reader may consult.

Gerhard: "Bellarmine objects that since the people are ignorant they cannot judge the doctrine of the pastor in any other way than by comparing it with that of his predecessors or the regular pastors. I reply: That this is false is obvious from the example of the Christians at Berea, who daily searched the Scriptures to find out whether things were as Paul and Barnabas presented them (Acts 17:11). They did not regard the teaching of the regular pastors as the norm by which to judge, but the Scriptures, which were entrusted to them for this purpose by the Holy Spirit. The [spiritual] illiteracy of the people of which Bellarmine speaks stems from the command of the pope not to read the Holy Scriptures. For this sacrilege the per-petrators will in due time be severely called to account.

"But we reverse the argument of Bellarmine: If the illiteracy of the people does not prevent them from comparing the doctrine of their ministers with that of their predecessors or the regular pastors, then it will also not prevent them from comparing their doctrine with that of Christ, the prophets, and the apostles set forth in Scrip-ture. By this norm they will be able to distinguish a true prophet from one that is false. If the first is true, then the second must also be true. The connection between the two conclusions is obvious from the fact that Christ and the prophets and apostles were able to speak as clearly as do the regular pastors and actually have done so.

"When Christ and the prophets and apostles administered the office of teaching here on earth, they preached not only to the learned but also to the unlearned and indeed in such a way that the latter could understand their doctrine. Why then should the Scriptures of the prophets and apostles be so obscure and per-plexing that ignorant people should not be able to judge doctrine from them? Without doubt the prophets and apostles wrote nothing else than what they proclaimed with their living voice.

" 'But,' Bellarmine might say, 'if the people themselves could judge the doctrine of their pastor, then no ministers would be nec-essary.' I reply: What logic [*Zusammenhang*] is there in this infer-ence? God has commanded both, namely, that the people should judge the teaching of the pastor, and that there should nevertheless be appointed and regular ministers in the church, for not all are teachers (1 Cor. 12:29; Eph. 4:11). It is something else to judge doctrine and distinguish between heresies and true doctrine and between false prophets and true teachers, which is a general calling pertaining to all Christians, than publicly to teach in the church, which is a special calling. We do not change the sheep into shep-herds but command them to be and remain sheep. But we do not want them to be irrational sheep who neither can nor should dis-tinguish between shepherds and wolves.

"The reason that Bellarmine adds is altogether unchristian. He says: 'If the regular minister and someone who is not called teach something contradictory, then the people must follow their own pastor rather than the other, even if it should happen that the pastor would err.' But it is wrong to say that the people must follow their regular pastor even if he should err, for this means nothing else than that the sheep should follow their shepherd even to a noxious pasture, or that Christians should prefer darkness to light or error to the truth or human institutions to divine authority. Bellarmine indeed adds that it is not probable that God would let the regular pastor err in such a way as to deceive the people. But it is in vain to dispute whether that may happen, when it is manifest that this has actually taken place. Regular pastors have often erred and deceived the people, and this cannot be denied without the greatest impudence.

"Here then we press Bellarmine, asking him if the people should follow their pastor even if he should err. If he should reply in the affirmative, then he would make it clear that he has sold himself to him (the pope) who in the canonical law roars thus: 'If the pope, forgetting his own salvation and that of his brethren, should be found negligent, unprofitable, and remiss of his works and in addition would draw uncountable persons unawares from the good (which would in fact harm himself more, but nevertheless also all), indeed whole crowds with himself as the first son of hell, who would for all eternity suffer with him the greatest agony, nevertheless no one among mortals might dare reprove his sins, because he who himself is to judge may be judged by no one.' . . .

"Bellarmine adds the finer stipulation that the people may indeed judge between a true prophet and one that is false, but they may not for this reason depose a false shepherd, if he is a bishop, and substitute another for him, since both the Lord and the apostle only command that false prophets should not be heard by the people, not that the people should depose them. In addition it has been the custom, which the church has always maintained, that heretical bishops should be deposed by councils of bishops or by popes. I reply that we also do not approve Anabaptist disorder when false prophets are to be deposed. But we maintain that the right to elect competent ministers of the Word and to depose those who are false pertains to the whole church.

"All false prophets should be avoided in every case; indeed, they must be expelled, but nothing should be done against the order that God has established. Therefore, if wolves take the place of the shepherds in the vineyard of the Lord, they must be resisted in the lawful way and not allowed at their will to destroy the vineyard and defraud Christ's sheep of the nurture of pure doctrine. The other church members must mutually help the congregation, according to its right to elect competent ministers and to depose those who are false, in the proper order to find countermeasures against this evil" (*Loci theologici,* "De min. eccl.," par. 88).

The same: "The fact that the right to make church laws belongs not merely to the prelates or pastors, much less merely to the Roman pope, we prove in the first place from the granting of the keys. He to whom Christ has entrusted the keys also has the right to make laws, since he who has received the keys also has everything that belongs to the administration of the power of the keys. But the keys have been granted to the whole church.

"In the second place, we prove this right from the administration of church polity at the time of the apostles. The practice then was such that other believers besides the apostles were also admitted to the common deliberations concerning matters of church polity (Acts 1:16; 6:2). Therefore, the right to make church laws belongs not only to the bishops, the successors of the apostles in the ministry, but also to other believers.

"In the third place, we prove this right also from the circumstances of the apostolic council. The right to make church laws belongs to those by whom ceremonial laws were prescribed at the apostolic council (Acts 15). But these ceremonial laws were prescribed not only by the apostles but also by the whole congregation. For at Jerusalem not only the apostles but also the elders came together (Acts 15:6), and by these are to be understood not only pastors but also other officials of the church. Both came together for the same purpose, namely, 'to consider this matter' (v. 6), whether circumcision and other Mosaic rites should still be valid in the New Testament. Indeed, 'all the multitude' of believers (v. 12) were together and on the basis of a common vote the resolution was adopted: 'Then it pleased the apostles and elders, with the whole church . . . ' (v. 22). And the heading of the synodical resolution was formulated as follows: 'The apostles, the elders, and the brethren' (v. 23), and this is repeated in vv. 25 and 28.

"In the fourth place, we prove this right from the practice of the primitive church" (*Confessio catholica,* fol. 627a).

"The true church does not command the observance or omis-

346

sion of adiaphora because of its command but only to preserve propriety and decorum so that order may be preserved and offense avoided. As long as these are not violated, it leaves consciences free and does not impose any scruple or demand" (ibid., fol. 627b).

Brochmand: "It is the judgment of our churches that the power to investigate, prove, and judge the questions that are being considered may and should be conceded to all who know Holy Scripture and regard it as the only norm of truth and do not seek anything else than to spread the divine truth revealed in the Word. But this should be done in such a way that good order will be preserved when the opinions are asked for or gathered in. This is accomplished first of all when the opinions of those who are called to the office of teaching and governing the church are requested; second, when they are requested of laymen [*Privatpersonen*], provided that they know the Scriptures and love the divine glory and truth; third, when the highest magistrates are asked for their opinions, provided they are of the kind as described in Deut. 17:18–19. Then at last with unanimous consent, faithfully based on the Word of God, the resolutions should be drawn up and published in the name of the whole synod" (*Universae theologiae systema* 2:332).

Quenstedt: "Besides the presidents there are in the councils assistants and judges, men of every state [*Stande*], who are apt and competent to judge, namely, not only bishops and elders or pastors and teachers to whom the regular supervision of the congregation and religion has been entrusted, but also government officials [*politische Personen*] and laymen, as we call them, who are distinguished by their knowledge of doctrine and experience in divine and ecclesiastical matters as well as by piety, holiness of life, zeal for the truth, and acumen of judgment. These should be elected by the congregations and sent to the synodical convention so that they may vote on the matters submitted to them. This is manifest from the first apostolic council, at which not only the apostles inspired by God but also elders and other pious men investigated, decided, and judged the problems of the church at Antioch" (*Theologia didactico-polemica* 2:1627).

Calov: "It is said that at Antioch a dispute and controversy arose not only among the apostles but also among the elders, indeed, in the whole congregation or the gathered assembly, until Peter spoke and Paul and Barnabas related the miracles of God that were done among the heathen. Then all the multitude kept silent (Acts 15:13). After James, who voiced his opinion supported by Scripture, also had been heard, it pleased not only the apostles but also the elders, and not merely these but also the whole church (Acts 15:22), to send certain men to Antioch with a synodical letter drafted by all who attended the council. This was written in the name and with the knowledge, consent, and agreement of all (vv. 22–23). So then at this synod the apostles did not conceive of the resolutions alone but with the elders and the whole congregation. Whatever concerning the matter in question or the election of those to be sent or the synodical letter pleased not only the apostles but also the elders and the whole congregation was regarded as the resolution of the synod.

"Luke not only tells us that it pleased them all or that it was decided and resolved by all who were present, but the very letter itself attests this, since it begins: 'The apostles, the elders, and the brethren ... ' (v. 23). Then in the body it is said: 'It seemed good to us, being assembled with one accord ... ' (v. 25) or according to the Syrian translation: 'We all who came together decided. ...' And in v. 28 we read: 'It seemed good to the Holy Spirit, and to us,' that is, to all mentioned before (v. 22). Hence, contrary to the judgment of the papists, neither the elders nor the laymen were excluded from the synod or the inscription.

"Bellarmine asserts that only the apostles and elders were called together; and this is proved by the words: 'The apostles and elders come together to consider this matter' (v. 6). No mention is made here of the people. Then he infers from the words, 'When there had been much dispute' (v. 7), that the apostles and elders spoke until the dispute was ended. Hence, after this inquiry into the controversial question only the apostles adopted the resolution. This he seeks to prove from the fact that Luke mentions only Peter, Paul, Barnabas, and James as having spoken. But these opinions drawn from reason are easily disproved by the context. If indeed the words, 'The apostles and elders came together' (v. 6), are to be taken in an exclusive sense so that the people would be excluded because they are not mentioned, then we would have to say that the people did not at all come together, not merely that they were not 'called together.' But that the people were present Luke's narrative attests most clearly and definitely, as Bellarmine himself must admit.

"Therefore, these words do not exclude the multitude of the people but merely mention the more respected and important persons, while the others are indicated at the same time. This great controversy at the council is limited by Bellarmine to the apostles and elders without just cause; for it is altogether absurd to conclude from the words, 'There had been much dispute,' that this was caused by the apostles and elders. But by whom then? It is called a 'great dispute' (*magna disceptatio*) perhaps because it was conducted by men who enjoyed great esteem! But Luke tells us that it was much discussed, many-sided, and widely spread. If conclusions are to be drawn, it may be said that it was started by the multitude of the people. This truly is more certain, since later it is said that 'all the multitude kept silent' (v. 12) after they had listened attentively to Paul and Barnabas. So no doubt the multitude had spoken before and consequently had expressed their opinion.

"There is no doubt that the controversy had been started by converted Pharisees and Jews as an opposing party, for we are told: 'Some of the sect of the Pharisees who believed rose up' (v. 5), that is, some who were converted to Christ. These said: 'It is necessary to circumcise them, and to command them to keep the law of Moses' (v. 5). If the congregation came together to consider this statement and to discuss the matter, there can be no doubt that those who were present at Jerusalem and had caused the controversy were admitted to the investigation so that they might be heard. For the apostles and elders this painful investigation certainly was not necessary, but since the controversy was many-sided and great, it may be held that the Pharisees contended with them and tried to defend their case.

"Even equity approves this, and the historical custom of the synods confirms it, for as is well known, they always permitted the opponents to speak also. Therefore, Peter refuted them after he had listened to them and contradicted them face to face: 'Now therefore, why do you test God?' (v. 10).

"Finally, the fact that the apostles and they alone, who after the disputation are introduced as speaking, pronounced the final judgment, for which reason Luke introduces only them as speaking, is nothing else than an anacoluthon. Neither did their judgment constitute the final decision, namely, according as the opposing party made deciding resolutions, nor were the elders or the people then present excluded from the decisive resolution of the synod. In fact, they are included according to unmistakable words. Here 'to speak' and 'to give a deciding opinion' are not the same thing. We are told that Paul and Barnabas spoke. But does this mean that their judgment was decisive? That is what Bellarmine avers. But Luke declares the very opposite when he says that they spoke only of the miracles that had been accomplished among the heathen. So also the address of Peter was not so much a definite decision as rather a reminder of the calling of the Gentiles and a refutation of the opposing party, for he pointed out the impossibility of their keeping the Law. James finally uses the term 'judge,' and the resolution is ascribed to him, not to Peter or the others. But are the papists ready to deny the other apostles a decisive judgment? It will therefore be more correct to conclude from the resolution of the synod, as Luke records it, the context suggests, and the letter written by the council shows, that the resolution of the council came not merely from the apostles or from the elders with the apostles, but from the apostles, the elders, the whole congregation, and all the rest of the multitude" (*Biblia illustrata,* on Acts 15).

Tertullian: "Do you then not think that every believer is permitted to conceive and to establish whatever is pleasing to God, conducive to discipline, and profitable for salvation?" (*De cor. mil.* 4).

The same speaks of the public assemblies of Christians and the subjects discussed in them at that time as follows: "We are a body conscious of the truth of religion, discipline, and the covenant of hope. We come together as an assembly and congregation that we may together beseech God by our prayers as one man. This power is pleasing to God. We pray also for the emperors, for their servants and powers, for the state, for public peace, and for the delay of the end. We come together for the study of the sacred Scriptures, if perhaps the condition of the present times forces us to warn in advance or to examine ourselves afterward. We certainly nurture the faith with holy words, restore hope, confirm confidence, and nonetheless strengthen the discipline of (divine) precept by earnest admonitions. There also are exhortations, corrections, and divine censure. For judgment is also held with great gravity as with those who are certain of the presence of God and of this being the greatest prejudgment before the future Judgment. If anyone sins in such a way that he must be cast out of the communion of prayer, the assembly, and all sacred fellowship, then there preside certain approved elders (laymen) who have attained that dignity not by bribe but by good reputation, for nothing divine can be secured by bribery" (*Apologeticus* 39).

Appendix A

Additional Quotations from Ancient Church Teachers

Regarding the Question of Church and Ministry
Newly Compiled by E. A. W. Krauss,
Professor of Church History at Concordia Seminary, 1905–24
Presented as a Supplement to the Third Edition

Additions to Part I

Thesis I

Clement of Alexandria: "I do not call the place a church but the congregation of the elect" (*Strom.* 7).

Lactantius: "The church is the true temple of God, which consists not of walls but of the hearts of believing persons who trust in Him and are called believers" (*De ver. sap.* 4.13).

Cassiodorus (Christian historian at Rome; d. 575): "The church is the bride of Christ, consisting of the individual souls of believers." And: "The church is the Christian people adhering to the faith and extending throughout the whole world."

The same: "The church is the assembly of all believers and saints, one heart and one soul, the bride of Christ, the Jerusalem of the future world, of which Jesus says in the Song of Solomon: 'Let her kiss me with the kiss of her mouth' " (Source: *Centuriae Magde-burgenses* [Basel, 1562], 6:234).

Smaragdus (Abbot of the Benedictine cloister of St. Michael at Lothringen; lived at the beginning of the ninth century): "The church is a spiritual house made up of the living stones of the righteous and the souls of the saints" (on 1 Peter 2).

Thesis IV

Flacius: "The fact that Christ has given His church the keys of the kingdom of heaven is clearly taught by His words: 'I will give you the keys of the kingdom of heaven,' etc. (Matt. 16:19). . . . This conferring of the keys does not pertain only to the disciples, who do not constitute the church by themselves, but to the entire church or all believers" (*Centuriae Magdeburgenses* [Basel, 1559]).

The same: "The fact that the keys constitute a power given to the church is taught by Paul in 2 Cor. 2:6–10. . . . The fact that the authority to excommunicate belongs to the church and its ministers is taught in 2 John 10–11. . . . Finally, the apostles teach by both word and example that the power to forgive the sins of individual sinners belongs to the church, though in an emergency forgiveness may be pronounced by the ministers" (ibid., 1b:357).

Augustine: "As the church has the keys to [eternal] life, so it also has those to hell; for it is said to the church: 'If you forgive the sins of any,' etc. (*Hom. 2 in Apocal.*).

Beda Venerabilis (a learned English priest of the Benedictine Order; d. 735 or 738): "Though it may appear that the power to bind and loose has been given by the Lord to Peter alone, it can nevertheless be known without any doubt that it was also given to the other apostles. . . . And now the same office is given to the whole church in [the person of] the bishop and elders" (Book 4, on Luke 14).

Rabanus Maurus (Archbishop of Mainz; d. 859): "In the person of St. Peter, God has given the church the power to bind and to loose, for He said: 'Whatever you bind on earth,' etc. Peter here stands in the place of the church, which has the power to forgive sins" (*De serm. propriet.* 4.1).

Thesis V

Flacius: "We must now see which are the true and proper marks that Christ ascribes to the church. The first and most important is the pure Word as it has been revealed by Christ. . . . The second is the true and right use of the sacraments and the keys according to Christ's institution. . . . The third is the church's confession, constancy, and perseverance. A fourth is obedience to the ministry in those things that He Himself has taught and sanctioned" (*Centuriae Magdeburgenses* 1a:173).

Thesis VI

Origen: "In the church are vessels of wrath and vessels of mercy" (Sermon 7 on Ezekiel and sermon 3 on Jeremiah).

Cassiodorus: "If you will here seek the congregation of the just, it seems to be really hard to find all the elect in this life, since the church is filled with a mixture of good and evil" (*Centuriae Magdeburgenses* 6:236).

Gilbert (a Benedictine from Normandy; d. 1114 or 1117): "As clean and unclean things entered the ark, so in the church the good and the evil are mingled" (*In libr. alterc.,* 6).

Additions to Part II

Thesis II

Flacius: "From Christ's words and history it is manifest that both offices [namely, the present ministry no less than that of the apostles] have their origin in God, who moves the agencies that bear fruit and desires that they should administer the office of the public ministry, for which God will also graciously grant them the gifts and powers" (*Centuriae Magdeburgenses* 1a:186).

The same: "The office of the public ministry did not arise without purpose and by chance, but God Himself has instituted and established it. To this very day He has given pious teachers and will preserve His order till the end of the world" (ibid., p. 187).

Thesis V

Flacius: "The evangelical or ecclesiastical ministry, as it is called, consists in nothing else than the public office, resting on a legitimate call, to teach the doctrine that God has revealed and handed down in His inerrant Word—above all, the article concerning the remission of sins by faith in Christ alone—and then to administer the sacraments according to His institution" (*Centuriae Magdeburgenses* 1a:186).

Thesis VI

Flacius: "In the fourth place, the church has the power to elect, call, and ordain suitable ministers and to depose and avoid false prophets. This is clear from the institution of the office of the keys (Matt. 18:17–18) and from Christ's command: 'Therefore pray the Lord of the harvest,' etc. (Matt. 9:38). . . . This is taught also by the examples of Christ and John, who elected and called disciples, and that of the apostles (Acts 1:15–26), who elected and appointed Matthias in place of Judas by prayer and casting lots" (*Centuriae Magdeburgenses* 1a:180).

Beda Venerabilis: "The faithful people, who by Baptism possess the church in its whole area, must appoint ministers and teachers . . . who are to preserve the words of the Law and of Holy Scripture; for 'the lips of a priest should keep knowledge' (Mal. 2:7)" (On Deut. 27).

Theses VII and IX

Haymo (Bishop of Halberstadt): "The bishop excommunicates as the mouth of the church; with him the whole church agrees and says Amen" (On Ps. 150 [?]).

Thesis X

Flacius: "Christ has given to the church the power to judge every doctrine. He has commanded all members of the true church without exception to judge all doctrines that they hear, to accept as His own teaching those agreeing with what Christ clearly revealed, and to avoid and anathematize those that do not agree [with it]. . . . Christ teaches that the church also has the gift to interpret Scripture when He says: 'It has been given to you to know the mysteries of the kingdom of heaven, but to them it has not been given' (Matt. 13:11)" (*Centuriae Magdeburgenses* 5:411).

Appendix B

Index of Christian Authors Quoted in This Book

Ambrosiaster, author of a commentary on the epistles of St. Paul, formerly found in the works of Ambrosius; perhaps the somewhat older contemporary of Ambrosius, the deacon Hilary of Rome.

Ambrosius (Ambrose), bishop of Milan, Italy; b. ca. 340; d. 397.

Augustine, bishop of Hippo Rhegius, North Africa; b. 353; d. 430.

Baier, John William, professor of theology at Jena; shortly before his death general superintendent at Weimar; b. 1647 at Nuremberg; d. 1695.

Balduin, Frederick, professor of theology at Wittenberg; b. at Dresden 1575; d. 1627.

Barner, Henry, pastor at Dreßheim; b. there 1594; d. 1664.

Basilius (Magnus), bishop at Caesarea in Cappadocia; b. ca. 330; d. 379.

Bernard, abbot of the Cistercian monastery at Clairvaux; b. at Fontaine in Burgundy 1091; d. 1153.

Brenz, John, provost at Stuttgart; b. at Weil, Württemberg, 1499; d. 1570.

Brochmand, Caspar Erasmus, bishop of Zeeland; b. at Kögen on the island of Zeeland (Denmark) 1585; d. 1652.

Calov, Abraham, professor and general superintendent at Wittenberg; b. at Mohrungen, East Prussia, 1612; d. 1688.

Carpzov, John Benedict, professor of theology at Leipzig; b. at Rochlitz, Saxony, 1607; d. 1682.

Chemnitz, Martin, superintendent at Brunswick; b. at Treuen-Briezen, Province of Brandenburg, 1522; d. 1586.

Chrysostom (John), bishop of Constantinople; b. in Antioch ca. 347; d. (in exile) not far from the city of Comanum [Ankara] in Pontus 407.

Clement (Titus Flavius), catechist and presbyter at Alexandria; d. between 212 and 220.

Clement of Rome, bishop of the congregation there; the third of the so-called apostolic fathers, perhaps the one mentioned in Phil. 4:3; d. as a martyr at the beginning of the second century.

Coelestinus (I), bishop of Rome; d. 432.

Cruciger, Caspar, professor of theology and pastor of the Wittenberg castle church; b. at Leipzig 1504; d. 1548.

Cyprian (Thascius Caecilius), bishop of Carthage, North Africa; formerly pagan teacher of rhetoric; converted 245; d. as martyr in exile 258.

Dannhauer, John Conrad, professor of theology at Straßburg; b. at Kundringen in Breisgau (Grand Duchy of Baden) 1603; d. 1666.

Dedekennus, George, pastor at Hamburg; b. at Lübeck 1564; d. 1628.

Deyling, Salomon, superintendent and pastor at Leipzig; b. in Weyda, Saxony, 1677; d. 1755.

Eckard, Melchior Sylvester, pastor in Biberach; later in Stetten, Württemberg; b. at Kirchheim 1600; d. 1650.

Firmilianus, bishop of Caesarea, Cappadocia; d. after 265.

Flacius, Matthias (Illyricus), from 1544 professor of Hebrew at Wittenberg; later professor of theology at Jena; b. at Albona, Illyria, 1520; d. at Frankfurt am Main 1575.

Fröschel, Sebastian, deacon at Wittenberg; b. at Amberg, Bavaria, 1497; d. 1570.

Fulgentius, bishop of Ruspe, Numidia; b. in North Africa ca. 478; d. 533.

Gallus, John, professor of the Augsburg Confession and pastor at Erfurt, where he was born and where he died in 1587.

Gerhard, John, professor of theology at Jena; born in Quedlinburg, Province of Saxony, 1582; d. 1637.

Göbel, John Conrad, pastor at Stuttgart; later in Augsburg; b. at Bertlingen near Göppingen, Württemberg, 1585; after repeated banishments d. in his homeland 1643.

Grapius, Zachary, professor of theology at Rostock; b. there 1671; d. 1713.

Gregorius (Magnus or Gregory I), bishop of Rome; b. at Rome ca. 540; d. 604.

Hartmann, John Louis, superintendent at Rothenburg on the Tauber in Bavaria; b. there 1640; d. 1684.

Heilbrunner, James, court preacher at Pfalz-Neuburg; later general superintendent in Bebenhausen, Württemberg; b. in Ebertingen (Württemberg) 1548; d. 1619.

Heshusius, Tilemann, superintendent at Gesslar; professor of theology at Rostock and Heidelberg; superintendent at Magdeburg; court preacher at Pfalz-Neuburg; professor of theology at Jena; bishop of Samland; professor of theology at Helmstädt; b. at Wesel, Duchy of Cleve, 1527; d. 1588.

Hilary, bishop of Poitiers (the "Athanasius of the West"); d. 368.

Hollaz, David, provost at Jacobshagen; b. at Wulckar (or Wulckow) not far from Stargard, East Pomerania, 1648; d. 1713.

Hülsemann, John, professor and superintendent in Leipzig; b. at Essens, East Frisia, 1602; d. 1661.

Hunnius, Aegidius, professor of theology at Marburg; later professor and superintendent at Wittenberg; b. in Winnenden, Württemberg, 1550; d. 1603.

Hunnius, Nikolas, son of Aegidius; professor of theology at Wittenberg; later superintendent at Lübeck; b. at Marburg 1585; d. 1643.

Ignatius, bishop of Antioch, the fourth of the so-called apostolic fathers; d. 107 or 108 at Rome, devoured by lions in the Colosseum.

Irenaeus, bishop of Lugdunum and Vienna, Gaul, where he had settled with immigrants from Asia Minor; b. ca. 140; d. as a martyr ca. 202.

Isidorus, abbot at Pelusium, Egypt; b. before 370; d. ca. 440.

Jerome (Sophronius Eusebius), presbyter at Antioch; later abbot of a monastery at Bethlehem; b. at Stridon on the border of Dalmatia and Pannonia 331 or 332; d. 420.

Justin (the Martyr), the oldest church teacher after the apostolic fathers; the "evangelist robed in the gown of a philosopher"; apologist; b. at the beginning of the second century at Shechem, Samaria, ca. 110; d. as martyr ca. 166.

Kromayer, Jerome, professor of theology at Leipzig; b. at Zeitz, Province of Saxony, 1610; d. 1670.

Lactantius (Lucius Coelius), called Firmianus; teacher of rhetoric in Nicomedia; later teacher of Crispus, the son of Constantius; the "Christian Cicero"; d. ca. 330.

Leo (Magnus or Leo I), bishop of Rome; b. ca. 395; d. 461.

Leyser, Polycarp, professor of theology at Wittenberg; superintendent of Brunswick; later chief court preacher at Dresden; b. at Winnenden 1552; d. 1610.

Luther, Martin, professor at Wittenberg; the "great Reformer"; b. at Eisleben 1483; d. there 1546.

Major, George, superintendent at Eisleben; later professor of theology at Wittenberg; b. at Nuremberg 1502; d. 1574.

Martini, James, professor of theology and provost of the castle church at Wittenberg; b. at Langenstein not far from Halberstadt 1570; d. 1649.

Meisner, Balthasar, professor of theology at Wittenberg; b. at Dresden 1587; d. 1626.

Meisner, John, professor of theology and provost of the castle church at Wittenberg; b. at Torgau 1615; d. 1681.

Melanchthon, Philip, Luther's prominent co-worker in the Reformation; b. at Bretten, Grand Duchy of Baden, 1497; d. at Wittenberg 1560.

Menzer, Balthasar, the elder; professor of theology at Marburg, then at Gießen, then again at Marburg; b. in Allendorf, Hesse, 1565; d. 1627.

Müller (also written Möller), **John,** senior of the ministerium at Hamburg; b. in Breslau 1598; d. 1672.

Nicholas de Lyra of Normandy; professor of theology at Paris (a Franciscan); d. 1340.

Optatus, bishop of Mileve, Numidia, d. ca. 380.

Origen (also called Adamantius), catechist in his home town Alexandria; d. at Tyre 254.

Pomeranus (his proper name: John Bugenhagen), pastor and rector at Treptow; from 1523 professor and pastor at Wittenberg; from 1536 superintendent of Electoral Saxony; b. in Wellin, Pomerania, 1485; d. 1558.

Quenstedt, John Andrew, nephew of John Gerhard; professor of theology at Wittenberg; b. at Quedlinburg, Province of Saxony, 1617; d. 1688.

Seckendorf, Veit Ludwig, Baron von; attorney who held many positions of honor in Saxony; later privy councilor of Elector Frederick III of

Brandenburg and chancellor of the University of Halle; b. in Herzogenaurach near Erlangen 1626; d. 1692.

Schmidt, Sebastian, professor of theology at Strassburg; b. in Lampertheim, Alsace, 1617; d. 1696.

Selnecker, Nikolas, court preacher at Dresden; professor of theology at Jena; general superintendent and court preacher at Wolfenbüttel (1568–70); after 1577 superintendent at Leipzig; b. at Hersbruck near Nuremberg 1530; d. 1592.

Socrates, called Scholasticus; author of a church history covering 306–439; attorney in Constantinople in the fifth century; d. ca. 480.

Tertullian (Quintus Septimius Florens), presbyter at Carthage, North Africa; b. there ca. 160; d. 217 or 218.

Walch, John George (son-in-law of Buddeus), professor of theology at Jena; b. in Meiningen, Saxony, 1693; d. 1775.

Wigand, John, professor of theology at Jena; bishop of Königsberg; b. at Mansfeld 1523; d. at Liebmühl 1587.

Zeämann, George, professor of theology at Lauingen; chief pastor in Kempten, Bavaria; later superintendent at Stralsund; b. at Hornbach, Bavaria, 1580; d. 1638.

Notes

1. For the sake of agreement, all quotations from the Confessions of the Evangelical Lutheran Church are taken (often in an amended translation of the German text) from *Triglot Concordia* (St. Louis: Concordia Publishing House, 1921), which best agrees with Dr. Walther's quotations.—Tr.

2. So those were called who deprecated the use of the Law among Christians and wanted to have only the Gospel of the forgiveness of sins preached to them, thus abrogating the doctrine of sanctification.

3. In the Latin text we read: "Christ speaks of the appearance of the church when He says: 'The kingdom of heaven is like a dragnet' or 'ten virgins.' That is to say, Christ speaks of the outward appearance, the outward manifestation, or the outward aspect of the church when He says: 'The kingdom of heaven is like a dragnet,' etc."

4. A synecdoche is that figure of speech in which something is said of the whole that is to be understood only of a part of the whole, and vice versa.

5. Persons who hold religious opinions contrary to the orthodox doctrine.—Tr.

6. The Latin text reads: "And it does not deprive the sacraments of their efficacy that they are administered by unworthy [persons] because they do not represent their own persons by virtue of the call of the church, but that of Christ."

7. I would not please the pope.

8. Inasmuch as the pope knows that they are wrong, and also inasmuch as they deprive the Christians under the pope of what still makes them Christians despite the opposition of the pope.

9. What Luther says here of the gifts, rights, and powers, etc., that the papacy still has is true, of course, of all other sects that do not altogether deny God's Word, as do, for example, the so-called "free congregations" [rationalistic communions], in which there are no longer any Christians or Christian rights.

10. This quotation lacks clarity in both the original and Walther's translation.—Tr.

11. This, of course, does not refer to the denomination that now bears the name "Reformed" and is commonly known by that term but to the Evangelical Lutheran Church, which, true to God's Word, is the truly reformed church.

12. The fact that Luther here describes false Christians and hypocrites as also being outside the Christian church shows that he is speaking of the invisible church, for they certainly are in the visible church.

13. Luther does not mean to say here that a congregation may depose a minister arbitrarily; he merely wants to declare that a minister does not have an indelible character [as the papists teach: once a priest, always a priest].

14. But here we cannot deny what Kromayer writes: "Students of theology in certain places, as in the congregations at Wittenberg (Württemberg?), sometimes also here in Sweden, administer the sacraments" (*Theologia positivo-polemica,* p. 1059).

15. Namely, if anyone has more power than the other, then although all have the Word of God, the word of the one who has greater authority must be above God's Word.